D1328520

America's Last Great Newspaper War

AMERICA'S LAST GREAT NEWSPAPER WAR

The Death of Print in a Two-Tabloid Town

Mike Jaccarino

EMPIRE
STATE
EDITIONS

AN IMPRINT OF FORDHAM UNIVERSITY PRESS

NEW YORK   2020

Funding for this book was provided by:
Furthermore: a program of the J. M. Kaplan Fund.

Visit us online at www.fordhampress.com/empire-state-editions.

Library of Congress Control Number:2019956126

Printed in the United States of America

22 21 20   5 4 3 2 1

First edition

For all the runners and shooters who fought the war—
and believed with abandon in the holiness of the get

CONTENTS

Photographs follow page 152

"Shell Shock for News Nuts"

New York Post headline, March 24, 2005

ON MARCH 23, 2005, a *New York Post* delivery truck stopped in front of the New York *Daily News'* midtown Manhattan headquarters at 33rd Street and Tenth Avenue. Its driver exited the banana-yellow-colored vehicle and opened its rear doors to behold five 100-pound sacks filled with—if you believe the following day's account in the *Post*—a total of 1 million peanuts. The sacks came addressed to their intended recipients: Mort "Zero for Readers" Zuckerman, the *News'* owner; Les "For Them, More for Us" Goodstein, its president; Martin "The Dunce" Dunn, the paper's editorial director; and Michael "Our Goose Is Cooked" Cooke, its editor-in-chief. The deliveryman then hefted some portion of his cargo toward the *News'* front doors, although he was intercepted at the curb.

"There's no deliveries in this building for something as ridiculous as this!" cried a security guard who stopped him there. "I'm responsible for the safety of this building."[1]

Here, a *Post* reporter who had accompanied the deliveryman asked the guard what he thought so suspicious about the sacks. "You think peanuts are unsafe?" the scribe asked, to which the guard, or *"News* shill," as he was so branded in the *Post's* next-day account, cried, "That's right!"

Temporarily deterred, the deliveryman lugged the bags back to the truck and motored around the corner to yet another entrance. Here, two days earlier, an angry mob had laid siege to the *News'* building, chanting, "Show us the money!" and "Buy the *Post!*" Now, the area along Tenth Avenue had returned to something more like its default quiescence, but while the crowds had mostly dispersed, the deliveryman and reporter discovered more "goons" dispatched by "nervous *News* execs"—there to resist their "good-natured gift" of "tasty legumes," as the *Post* later put it. "This is viewed as a threat to me," one "factotum" informed the driver. "There could be a bomb in there. No peanuts!"

And so continued the peculiar events surrounding the Great Scratch 'N' Match Scandal of 2005.

The scandal had begun five days earlier, on a Saturday, when scores of *Daily News* readers had been misinformed that they'd won prizes ranging from $1,000 to $100,000 as contestants in the paper's weekly lottery-like game, Scratch 'N' Match. The game worked like this: Every Sunday, the *News* came with a Scratch 'N' Match game card consisting of eight scratch-off areas containing fifteen numbered spaces apiece. Each "area" corresponded to one of the seven days of the week, with two allotted for Sunday. The *News* then published a number each day indicating which space contestants should scratch off on the game card "area" corresponding to that day of the week. If the *News* published a "5" on Monday, contestants scratched off the space marked "5" on Monday's game card area. If it published a "12" on Tuesday, they scratched off the space for "12" in that area. Once the spaces were scratched, the numbers revealed a sum. If by Saturday the game card revealed three like-amounts of money, the contestant won the indicated sum.

But it didn't work correctly on March 19. The outfit that managed Scratch 'N' Match on behalf of the *News*—a D. L. Blair out of Long Island—transmitted an incorrect number to the paper on Friday night. The *News* published this wrong number in Saturday's paper, leading thousands of its readers to mistakenly believe they had won prizes when they had not. Some held numerous "winning" game cards. Alfred Lenquan had five for $100,000 each.

The *News* responded with an apology, fiery rhetoric about D. L. Blair, and the promise of another, special drawing to be held among the would-be winners to conclude with five $100,000 winners, five $10,000 winners, and 12,790 winners of an undisclosed amount. The reaction to this make-good offer, as one might expect, was outrage among the "winners."

"It's peanuts!" Lenquan told the *Post* as he protested outside the *News* on March 21, lending the paper's editors the quote they would use to underpin this headline the following day: "UN'MATCHED' INEPTNESS—'WINNERS': NEWS OFFER PEANUTS." But Lenquan unwittingly gave the *Post* more than just headline fodder. From the scandal's start, the tabloid had been searching for novel ways to shame its arch-rival, although until that point its efforts had been confined to print. Now, Lenquan's quote inspired the *Post*'s editors to do something truly creative—the delivery of *real* peanuts to the *News*.

"SHELL SHOCK FOR NEWS NUTS," screamed the next-day headline over this first paragraph, or "lede": "The desperate *Daily News* wants to pay peanuts to the thousands of readers bamboozled out of big bucks in its botched Scratch 'N' Match game—so the *Post* yesterday kindly offered the paper a million real peanuts to help out in their currency crunch."

Other "winners," as the *Post* observed, included a Mineola guy who had hoped to use his winnings to buy a new truck, "to get his life together"; Herb Shostack, a sixty-five-year-old Upper East Side salesman, who told the *Post* he planned to use his $10,000 to buy a headstone for his sister's grave; Claudette Muir, a Brooklynite, who told the *Post* she had planned on using her $10,000 to help her "money-strapped uncle bury her twenty-nine-year-old cousin, who had just died in a car crash in New Jersey"; and a Brooklyn limo driver who had promised his seven-year-old kid a trip to Walt Disney World. Beneath stories the *Post* ran on the topic were a question and call to action: "Have your dreams been stiffed by the *Daily News*? Call the *Post* at (212) 930-8626." America's last, great tabloid war was off and running.

1

"Serb Thug to New York...
Kiss My Ash"

New York Post headline, June 27, 2008

WE CALLED IT "RUNNING." Generally, the word was used as a figure of speech to describe all field reporting, but especially one's getting to the scene of a story, or the people concerned, as quickly as possible, ideally before the rest of the media world and—if you worked for the New York *Daily News*—definitely before the *New York Post*. Sometimes we substituted "chasing," but more often than not it was called "running," even though we rarely, if ever, used our legs for locomotion. Most drove, and a few took the subway or car service. But true to the idea of "running," we did whatever we were doing quickly and with a single-mindedness about the competition, which was also doing its best to get to the location before you. The "running," as I said, didn't so much concern the actual act as the way you hustled and the consequences of arriving late.

A reporter who "ran" was called a "runner," while a photographer was called a "shooter," although when a shooter was engaged in pursuing a story—and especially breaking news—his pursuit of that story, and hustle to the scene of it, was called "running" as well. You might, therefore, have asked a shooter about his day and received the reply, "I ran on two MVAs [motor vehicle accidents] in Borough Park and Brownsville, then on an EDP [emotionally disturbed person] in East New York."

Some shooters carried scanners to eavesdrop on the NYPD's and FDNY's dispatch frequencies and thus know when and where news was breaking. By doing so, they might achieve a head start on their running versus the opposition. One *News* shooter even jury-rigged a scanner into the console of his car amid a shrine-like arrangement of photos portraying NYPD and FDNY officers. These were prayer cards from the funerals he'd covered after 9/11, although they acted, for him, as more than just dashboard ornaments. One day, he confided to me that "those dead heroes watch over me" from beyond their graves and that he needed such protection because he often drove recklessly, going the wrong way on one-way streets, to reach breaking-news scenes before the *Post* or, worse, the NYPD shut them down to the media.*

This was *Daily News* shooter Todd Maisel, and Todd had a practiced method for running, or rather being in good position once the scanner crackled to life and the running began. Todd told me that when he wasn't otherwise engaged in a scheduled assignment, or covering breaking news, he spent summer days at Coney Island, near the pier, so as to be close enough to document any swimmers caught up by rip tides. In the winter, he parked near Prospect Park's skating pond in an equally grim vigil for anyone who might fall through the ice. If you called Todd on his cell phone and got voicemail, his recorded message was "Hi, this is Todd Maisel. I'm at a homicide or a fire. Leave a message."

While some shooters like Todd used police scanners, others invested in a BNN, or Breaking News Network pager, which outsourced the monitoring of the NYPD and FDNY frequencies to a third party. This contractor then culled newsworthy events from the chaff of mundane chatter and forwarded the specifics along to a pager in the form of text notifications. Some photographers harbored phony police lights that could be affixed to a roof mount on their vehicles to aid in the navigation of traffic while running to a scene. Todd, in particular, was renowned for driving on the Brooklyn–Queens Expressway's shoulder while employing such a yellow light, dodging mountains of traffic citations only by virtue of a hoarded treasure in PBA cards. Regardless, had he been cited, the fine could then have been expensed to and reimbursed by the *News*, or argued in court with the aid of a form letter curated by the photo desk. This form letter had spaces allocated for media affiliation, the description of the circumstances that had led to the citation, and an explanation of how the demands of serving the public good as a journalist offset the danger one had posed to society by breaking the law. In some cases, I knew journalists to fill out

---

* The NYPD, as a matter of course, sequestered crime scenes with the use of yellow police tape and, if a story merited, sentries. Beating the cops to the location thus allowed for more intimate viewing or photography of newsworthy mayhem.

this last area with rhetoric far more befitting a civil rights attorney's closing argument than any pleading for leniency from a traffic violation. Regardless, runners and shooters did not slow for fear of additional citations. The reality of competition and the incredibly short half-life of breaking news ensured that, if anything, they ran even harder.

Back then, the *News* and the *Post* assigned shooters geographic areas in which they would wait, often in their vehicles, monitoring NYPD and FDNY dispatch. Then and once they heard broadcast of an incident constituting breaking news, the race, or running, began. At the time of this narrative, Todd had South Brooklyn for the *News* and Gary Miller had it for the *Post*; Debbie Egan-Chin had North Brooklyn for the *News* and Paul Martinka had it for the *Post*; Michael Schwartz and Sam Costanza had northern Manhattan and the South Bronx for the *News* and Robert Kalfus had it for the *Post*; Anthony DelMundo had much of Queens for the *News* and Ellis Kaplan covered it for the *Post*. Each tabloid could thus better reach breaking-news scenes—or just "scenes"—before the other. Runners, on the other hand, were typically dispatched from the newsroom or permitted to linger near their homes until the demands of breaking news required otherwise. It should be noted that the aforementioned shooters were in addition to the armies fielded to surveil certain locations of import, or just float from place to place as a supplement to those already listed.

The *Daily News* runner Kerry Burke once said the first thing he considers after receiving an assignment is "How in Christ am I going to get there first? You need to get there before everything shuts down, before the police version is rehearsed, while the actual witnesses are still around. You need to get a participant, a principal to the story. If that means commandeering a cab, it's commandeering a cab!"[1]

Newsday, the Long Island tabloid, employed a runner named Matt Nestel who often arrived late to scenes, or later than the *News* and the *Post*, not through any fault of his own but because *Newsday* took only an occasional interest in city affairs and typically got tips long after its more plugged-in rivals. Nestel often had to timidly ask victims, and loved ones, to repeat what they'd already said, and what he got was rarely as good as what the *News* and the *Post* had gotten. Nobody wanted to discuss a loved one's murder a single time, never mind twice, for late-arriving reporters who'd missed the first act. And even if they did, what they said was rarely as good as that first, almost sublime, go 'round, when all their anguish and anger came right out of their hearts and into your notebook. After that, they often became numb. But, as I said, Matt's tardiness was through no fault of his own.

Those who ran worked "the street," as opposed to "rewrite" reporters who cobbled the quotes, color, and facts that runners obtained in the street—then phoned to the newsroom—into polished, published accounts. Some runners were deemed "monsters" and others soft. It was hard to come back once a runner was branded one or the other, but not impossible. A few good "gets" could redeem anyone and especially if a *News* or *Post* runner had gotten them and their rival had not. In this way, runners developed reputations, which were hard-won and preceded them. They meant the world to us. Sometimes, after ten days on stakeout in front of the same address, they felt like all we had.

Most runners smoked, the routine necessity of loitering in a single place for long periods demanding some method of reliable distraction. It was during my time on the street I became first a casual smoker, then a committed one. Most, too, lived on bodega diets, pizza, anything obtained quickly and scarfed en route back to the stakeout, or scene, you had dangerously abandoned to obtain food. Often, you agreed with the *Post* to go simultaneously (the same applied to bathroom breaks), but if you went, and they didn't and then scored, you likely would not get another chance to apply the lesson you had learned.

Concerning dress, most runners wore some variation of jeans and a button-down, casually dressed as one might be on a Saturday afternoon for a street fair or football game. Some took this casualness too far—*News* runner Matt Lysiak comes to mind—and wore shorts and a T-shirt, although even Matt donned jeans and a sweater or button-down when temperature, or circumstances, demanded. Most, if not all, runners wore sneakers. And I would say the corps, as a whole, mistrusted any runner who wore dress shoes to a scene. One, I recall, consistently wore penny loafers and became an object of scorn behind his back and derision not behind his back, although in the latter case the derision was tempered in the form of teasing. Whoever was teasing him might have believed they were doing him a favor—but in that way, he never comprehended the seriousness of his offense and so persisted in the wearing of penny loafers.

There was a specific reason for dressing casually, apart from the obvious demand for comfort in a job requiring you to spend considerable time outdoors, or loitering for long periods—that is, we didn't want to stand out too much from the crowds in the poor neighborhoods where violent crime most often occurred and to which we, as runners, were most often dispatched. Also, we dressed casually so the inhabitants of these neighborhoods might feel some solidarity when solicited for a quote. The thinking went that if you looked too well-to-do, you were more likely to inspire contempt than sympathy, no matter what might be the realities of your paycheck and its similarities to that of the source to whom you were speaking. Also, we didn't want anyone mistaking us for a cop. In many such neighborhoods, no one would talk to you if they thought you were one, whereas they might if you were only a reporter, and especially a slovenly dressed one. There were, of course, situational-specific departures from this general rule of dressing casually. If one were, say, sneaking into a wedding or a funeral—and in the latter case, especially to eavesdrop on the eulogy—you would likely dress in the mode of those in attendance, or perhaps even leverage a pair of penny loafers to your advantage. But, as I said, you wouldn't want to wear such shoes unless there was a good reason.

A few runners and shooters achieved such respect among their colleagues that they were permitted certain eccentricities concerning dress. Kerry Burke, for one, wore the same outfit every day—a white collared shirt, black jeans, black tie, and black shoes that came as close to being sneakers without crossing the line. When temperature demanded, he added a hoodie and an overcoat—an outfit, in sum, theoretically underpinned with notions contradicting the aforementioned prevailing wisdom among runners. As Kerry once said:

> We're walking into their lives, very often on the worst day of their lives. They don't owe us anything [and] this might seem like an old Catholic-school boy, but I . . . show up with a shirt and tie. Basically, they don't know me from jack, and I'm going into their homes, their places of worship, their hospital rooms. A shirt and a tie convey respect. It's very basic stuff. It also conveys authority: I'm someone you *should* talk to. I mean, it's not something I grew up doing. Hell, I was a rock critic for a number of years with a ripped T-shirt and a leather jacket. But this is a remarkably different game. And dress shoes. Always wear dress shoes. People look at your shoes. Dress shoes say you're important. They say you're official. They say you're employed. People respond to that. I'm nobody special; I just happened to be the dude in the shirt and tie. I'm always looking at these cats that show up looking like second-string Hunter S. Thompsons. People don't respect them. Detectives don't want to talk to them.[2]

But Kerry's outfit wasn't the most interesting part of his attire. That would be the book bag that he wore perpetually slung over his shoulder and whose contents the *New York Times* once described as "tools for survival and infiltration, including a heavy-duty flashlight and enough trail mix for a 24-hour stakeout."[3] And maybe because this account left room for speculation, but more likely because we loved all things Kerry, runners from both the *News* and the *Post* filled our long stakeout hours concocting outlandish inventories for the bag. Grappling hooks! Granola! Pens! Wigs! Mustaches! Spare notebooks! In that same *Times* story, Kerry was quoted as telling tabloid rookies, "You have not adequately covered a homicide if your shoes are not wet with the victim's blood."

Daily News shooter Marc Hermann preferred a vintage approach to daily attire, dressing as an actor would in, say, a 1920s period drama. (Marc did audition for and appear as an extra in several such shows, including Cinemax's "The Knick.") Every day, he wore outfits from that era—big, wide ties; suit vests; and fedoras with his NYPD-issued press credential stuck under the hat band as they did in the days of Winchell—appropriate in some sense because, for newspapers, at least, their trajectory was mostly downhill from there.

And then there was Todd, who didn't dress unusually unless the stakes of a given story, as it concerned the *News'* battle with the *Post*, had reached sufficient levels of hysteria. Then he would retrieve from the trunk of his Chevy Malibu what looked like a bulletproof vest but was, in fact, the flak jacket he'd worn while embedded with U.S. troops during the second Iraq war. He'd drape this over his photographer's/fly fisherman's vest and work in that fashion. I once asked him about the jacket and he replied, "Because when you go to war, you have to bring the right equipment." The war, of course, no longer concerned America's battle with Saddam Hussein but the *News'* struggle with the *Post*.

Most of the time, a runner's day concerned the carrying out of what were called "door knocks." Someone had been shot. Someone had been named in a legal action. The tabloid's "library," or research department, would trace that person's address—and those of their relatives, associates, or anyone in a position to lend context, color, quotes, and "studio"*

---

* In running parlance, a "studio" photograph referred to any image taken of an existing photo for purposes of reproduction in the paper, as well as the original image from which the reproduction was made. It usually worked like this: A runner would attempt to convince a family member to speak about a newsworthy individual—let's say a murdered man—and then would inquire whether that source had any relevant photos of the victim. A shooter—runners and shooters routinely worked in pairs—would then photograph the existing photo. The result was a "studio." This method provided a workaround to borrowing the original photo and then going to the trouble of returning it once the image had run.

photographs. It was the runner's job to get to these locations, knock on the door, and convince whoever answered in that ten-or-so seconds before they slammed it shut to discuss something immensely personal. Some runners made an art of the door knock and routinely delivered. Others had spottier records. In the aggregate, I imagine, the art involved was the same as, or similar to, that of making a cold call to hawk a parcel of stock.

Some door knocks were impossible, and no matter what the runner said, the person simply would not talk. Maybe they had money and felt above having their name in the paper. Or they lived in some big, fancy house in a fancy ZIP code and felt entitled to politely tell the runner to fuck off. Then there were door knocks where negligence was involved—and the person who answered, or their kin, was a plaintiff in a civil action naming the city, their landlord, building super, the mayor, and/or even the commissioner of police; and in those instances they'd present you with a business card embossed with their lawyer's name, the one who had directed them not to—under no circumstances—talk.

Conversely, there were door knocks in which the person's willingness to speak, even zest for the opportunity, made it impossible to fail. They opened the door and reacted as if they'd been awaiting your arrival. Maybe they were angry society—the city or the NYPD had somehow failed them and they had an axe to grind in print. Or maybe they felt so long neglected by the same institutions that now, here, was that rare, if not singular, instance when people actually cared about their thoughts and what they had to say—and they felt honored that their private pain was finally deserving of public attention.

But most of the time the person who answered the door was surprised by your interest. Sure, they felt put off, or at least initially, by questions concerning what was naturally a private matter. But you could win them over. You could win them over with sincerity, concern, empathy—real or faked—for their pain, and solidarity with their gripes. *Believe me, I agree with you. You can't raise a family in a neighborhood like this. You try and you try—and there's nothing you can do in the end. Yes, I can hug you. I'm so . . . so sorry for your loss. And would you please tell me all about your murdered husband—and kindly provide a photo of him, too?* In such instances, you could also win them over by telling them their daughter or son was now dead and their words might be the last time anyone would hear anything about them. *This is your chance, perhaps your last one, to give voice to their dreams, struggles, ambitions, and what they would have done had such a tragedy not occurred. Tell me. Tell me and I will make sure they live on and people remember!* You were like an undertaker selling the notion of a public memorial, even though the eulogy wouldn't be delivered in forty-five minutes but expressed in two quotes.

And sometimes—and especially in the ghettos of the Bronx—you could fall back on the old saw that the more press an incident generated, the more public outrage would ensue, and that outrage would pressure an otherwise uncaring bureaucracy to pursue justice on their loved one's behalf. *Don't let those bastards get away it! The D.A.? He's snowed under. You think he cares? Help me help you!* Jerry Maguire, New York tabloid style.

And sometimes, in working-class neighborhoods you could express your mission in terms of blue-collar solidarity and thus create sympathy for your aims of attaining a quote. *Look, I hate being here. I really do. And I didn't want to knock on your door and certainly not in your hour of pain. But it's my job. And I got bosses just like you. And they're yelling at me to get my job done. Can't you give me something? Something to satisfy them? Get them off my back? Just a few good words. I know you don't much want to and you're damn right in feeling that way. But one working guy to another . . . just a few good words.*

And then—one time out on Long Island—a *Daily News* runner did a door knock on a guy who was involved in some scandal and the person came to the door with a gun.

Some went right and most went wrong, the latter followed by that long walk back to the car so much shorter than it felt, the notebook pages blank, the cold feeling of questions unasked, the ones that occurred to you only now, icy in your gut—and could I have asked the ones I did ask any differently? There must have been some way—*some fucking way!*—to phrase them differently, so that they would have been answered and not just answered, but truthfully and emotionally and powerfully so the copy would sing!

But I didn't ask them, did I? And so now the runner is returning to the car and sitting and playing with the interview as it had regrettably happened, twisting it like a Rubik's Cube, inserting the questions he should have asked—but was too stupid to have asked—into the gaps where the source had said nothing, or even had rebuked him. Damn it! And then came the uncertainty: Did I ask everything? Was some angle of the story neglected?

And then, finally, the call to the city desk and the explaining how the person had been ready to the shut the door from the moment it had been opened, and I really did get everything that could have been gotten. *No, she didn't say more. No, she didn't want to talk about that. No. No. No.*

I asked about it. I did. Twice . . . in different ways. Yes, I tried. I did. Yes, on that one, too. I'm really lucky to have gotten anything at all. And the unspoken reproach hanging in the air, the whole time, that someone— Kerry Burke?—could have done it better, could have gotten the "get" had he been sent and not you.

It was common for runners to fray emotionally, or grow calloused—and even indifferent to the suffering of others—after years of performing door knocks and pushing the envelope for gets, knowing if you didn't, the *Post* would—and the story might be lost. In one case, I recall a *News* runner embracing a father outside a Bronx hospital after the father had learned his young son had died in traffic on the Grand Concourse. The father burrowed his head into the runner's shoulder and was wailing to God and Jesus Christ, or both. The runner held him and prompted him to continue while also motioning with his free hand to a *Post* runner in that way often intended to demonstrate to your waiter you are ready for the check but in this case was meant to ask the *Post* runner to take the notes he otherwise could not with his arms occupied. The father could not see him do this because, as I said, his head was buried in the runner's shoulder—and he was weeping and crying out. Not once did the *News* runner betray any more emotion than was necessary to keep the man wailing for dramatic effect. It was just a story, or it became that way over time.

Only a few runners never frayed, Kerry Burke being one, although Kerry had an origin story, and a rationale rooted in that origin story, with which he warded off any disillusionment or cynicism he may have developed over time. He once told an interviewer about this, after the interviewer asked, "Do you ever feel that you're intruding on people's lives and exploiting their misery?" Kerry responded:

> Well, I am intruding on their lives. Absolutely. That's one of the reasons I'm so polite. It's not always going to work out for the people involved, but I try to do justice to the story, and thereby justice to everybody involved. I deal in other people's agony. I do. You can't candy-coat that. But if you can't live with that, you shouldn't be in this game. I'm not some nice person from a nice place. I'm not. I do my damnedest to be a decent man and an honest reporter.[4]

The interviewer asked, "But besides the paycheck, you must see some value in what you do?" Again, Kerry:

> If these stories aren't told, then these people don't count and these places don't exist. They don't. I'm from the old neighborhood, as it

were, of Dorchester in the Boston area, and I know a little bit about being outside of society. Frankly, the awful things that happened in our neighborhood were the things that really impacted our lives. A homicide in Bed-Stuy* says volumes to the people who actually live there. It tells them about the gang problems, the gun problems. I was talking to some professor who said, "If it bleeds it leads"—implying that these stories aren't important stories. I was like, "Where are you from, Princeton?" In East New York, people want an explanation for the madness outside their door. I remember growing up and occasionally some horrific shit would go down in my neighborhood. And it would be ignored by the media. It told us we didn't count. It made plain that we were outside society. These stories count, just like the people who live in these neighborhoods. People say, "You're a part of this 'it bleeds it leads' culture," and I'm like, you bet your ass. I have no apologies for that.

Finally, Kerry:

Like I said, I'm not a very nice person. I'm not from a nice place. At the same time, I love these people. These are my people . . . I know the fields in which I labor . . . And I'm always moved by their generosity. You find decency in the most staggeringly bad places.

The *News–Post* war took runners around the world. In 2008, a State University of New York athlete named Miladin Kovacevic fled to his native Serbia after pummeling a fellow student into a coma during a bar brawl. The *News* dispatched runner Rich Schapiro to his hometown of Kula, ninety minutes north of Belgrade, to find him. But by the time Rich arrived, the *Post* had interviewed his family and extracted a promise not to grant any seconds to late-arriving *News* runners. "SERB THUG TO NEW YORK . . . KISS MY ASH," roared the *Post*'s front page over a menacing family photo of Kovacevic holding a shotgun while smoking an equally long Churchill cigar. (Kovacevic had not participated in the *Post*'s interview— but had, in fact, gone into hiding in the Serbian countryside.)

Back then, the *News* and the *Post* ran on anything and everything. Level Three 10-10 at Monroe Street and Throop Avenue? Go! 10-37, Code Two, one yellow tag, possible entrapment at Hillside Avenue and 164th Street? Go! It made no sense, but little did when the calculus of action was dictated based on fear of what the other tabloid would get if they went and

---

* Bedford-Stuyvesant is a neighborhood in Brooklyn that has lately gentrified but historically been one of the toughest in New York City.

you didn't. I recall doing 70 mph through Queens with one eye on the road and the other on an atlas. It was reckless and fun—and it'll never, ever happen again. Today, the *Post* and the *News* might deploy one runner per shift, whereas both fielded fifteen to twenty per side as late as 2008. But today is a different age—and one that has brought a new reality to both institutions—and America's last tabloid war is decidedly over.

There is an analogy from evolution to describe the circumstances from mid-2006 to the stock market crash of 2008, or that twenty-six-month span from when the *Post* surpassed the *News* in average daily circulation over a six-month period for the first time in the history of both papers to when the print ad money spigot dried up for good. It holds that when two organisms—or competing papers in the same city—occupy a single evolutionary niche, they can both survive until an environmental pressure is applied. Then they must battle until one goes extinct. This story took place when both New York City tabloids, under pressure from the digital revolution, waged just such a Darwinian fight and duked it out, one story at a time, with the conflict's foot soldiers the runners who met each day in journalistic hand-to-hand combat. It gives me pride to say I was part of it. It saddens me to know I got there right before the whole thing crashed down on all of us.

2

"All Play, No Pay for Page Fix"

Daily News headline, April 10, 2006

AT THE TIME OF THIS NARRATIVE, the *Daily News* was owned by real estate mogul Mort Zuckerman and the *Post* nominally by News Corp., but tangibly by that company's founder and CEO, Rupert Murdoch. Unlike Murdoch, Zuckerman wasn't much involved in his paper's day-to-day editorial operations other than to, say, phone in dispatches from Donald Trump's third wedding. The *News* was unable to secure an invite whereas the *Post* had, and so it fell to "Uncle Mort," as *News* employees branded him, to fill that void.

Both papers, over the years, habitually attacked the other tabloid's owner in print. As reporter Choire Sicha wrote in 2010, "Over the last ten years, the *New York Post* has called *Daily News* owner Mort Zuckerman a cheapskate, a tyrant, an illegal maid-payer, a friend to unsavory characters, a bad businessman, a racist, a friend of terrorism, a firer of pregnant women, a publisher who uses his editorial page for his own real estate interests, a constructor of dangerous buildings, the provoker of staff suicides, as well as wild-eyed, mercurial, panicky, a cheater of readers, a scoffer at laws, a 'horrible, nickel-and-diming boss,' and the publisher of boring publications."[1] The *News*, meanwhile, portrayed Murdoch as a manipulator of politicians, the "Prince of Darkness," and a tax cheat.[2]

At some point, however, the moguls engineered a *détente* through the brokerage of P.R. man Howard Rubenstein, who'd done work for both men. It was a tenuous peace ex–*News* columnist Lloyd Grove described in *The New Yorker* as "a gentleman's agreement that nothing personally critical could be written" about either man or their families.[3] But this gloves-on deal extended to neither their tabloids nor the staffs those papers employed. On July 6, 2004, the *Post* reported that Democratic presidential nominee John Kerry had selected Missouri congressman Dick Gephardt as his running mate. "KERRY'S CHOICE," blared the *Post*'s front page, which hit newsstands hours before Kerry announced his actual choice, North Carolina Senator John Edwards. On July 7, the *News* published a jeering commentary, disguised as a laughably unbiased news report, headlined: "ANOTHER POST 'EXCLUSIVE' KERRY PICKS GEPHARDT? WRONG!" "Not since the *Chicago Tribune* proclaimed 'DEWEY DEFEATS TRUMAN' in the 1948 presidential election has there been such a colossal flub," wrote the *News*. "Leave it to the *New York Post* to further tarnish its shoddy reputation with yesterday's front page." That same article also reported that comedian Will Ferrell had appeared on the *Today* show as his comical "Anchorman" creation Ron Burgundy, brandished a copy of the *Post*, and deadpanned, "This is an excellent journalism periodical."

But the *News* didn't stop there, reporting as well that *Post* editor-in-chief Col Allan had "personally approved the Gephardt front page" and attributing the absence of a byline on the corresponding story to "no reporter want[ing] to be connected to Allan's Hail Mary headline." Then came the *News' pièce de résistance*: the delivery of twelve bottles of Cold Duck champagne to the *Post*'s offices accompanied by the wry note, "Congratulations on your 'exclusive'!!"

Months later, the *News* and the *Post* leveraged another scandal—this one centered upon unrelated publications—to trade even more poisonous attacks. These weren't Ha-Ha reports, like the "Scratch 'N' Match" salvos, but articles undermining the profitability of the papers themselves through attacks on the circulation figures used to sell advertising. The scandal concerned *Newsday*, its sister Tribune Co. paper *Hoy*, and others, like the *Dallas Morning News*. But the *Post* on October 26, 2004, published a 2,982-word exposé claiming the *News* had inflated its circulation, too, by encouraging retailers to give the product away by reimbursing them after the fact. The story cited interviews with nine New York City grocers and *Daily News* invoices for the copies it had sold to them.

The *News* responded with an official denial, and Martin Dunn, its editorial director, told the *New York Times*, "It baffled me that the *Post* had someone there who could write anything as long as three pages, and spell a word as long as 'circulation.'" Finally, the *News* published a counterpunch—"FEDS SEEK *POST* RECORDS"—about how the U.S. Department of Justice had expanded its inquiry into the nationwide scandal with a subpoena for the *Post's* circulation and advertising files, as well. The *News* conveniently buried toward the end of the article the fact that it had received the same subpoena.

In retrospect, the attacks proved to be, according to the *Times*, the Sarajevo shot to kick off the *News* and *Post's* final showdown. In a November 4 story on the war of words, headlined, "SLAM COMES TO SLAP AS THE *POST* AND THE *NEWS* FIGHT IT OUT," the *Times* observed, "Forget the imperishable [Dick] Gephardt flub. Ixnay the 'Scratch 'N' Match' snafu* [of 1999]. The traditional, garden-variety sniping, hammering, and *kvetching* between the *New York Post* and the *Daily News* has now evolved into an outright tabloid war. At last, an issue that eclipses even the cut-and-slash over Paris's breakup and the results of Britney's pregnancy test: circulation padding."

It would get funny—then worse. On December 16, the New York Mets officially introduced their newest free agent at Shea Stadium, pitching sensation Pedro Martinez. Just two months earlier, Martinez had helped propel Boston to a World Series victory with a 2–1 playoff record and his adoption of a lookalike dwarf named Nelson De La Rosa as his personal good luck charm and *de facto* team mascot. Repeatedly, during the curse-of-the-Bambino–breaking run, the twenty-eight-inch De La Rosa posed for pictures in the laps of the team's coaches and players and allowed Martinez to scoop him up into the air after victories. The *Post*, of course, sensed opportunity. The scheming paper obtained reporter's credentials for the Martinez press conference in the name of Upper East Side–bred dwarf Tim Loomis, who, once in attendance at Shea Stadium, stood on a chair and offered to become Pedro's new "personal mini-mascot," thus replacing De La Rosa. "How about you make me your good luck charm here in New York?" Loomis asked. Pedro played along and "scooped" up Loomis as he once had De La Rosa. The *Post's* next-day headline: "SIZING UP NEW MET; *POST'S* LITTLE PEDRO MAKES HIS PITCH."

That night, *News* reporter Jose Martinez was putting the paper to bed with city editor Dean Chang. Inevitably, the conversation trended toward the *Post's* story—and how De La Rosa likely felt about having been so casually dismissed. "Why don't we find out?" Jose asked, never thinking

---

* The "Scratch 'N' Match Scandal" of 2005 wasn't the first time the *News* printed the wrong numbers—and the *Post* shamed its rival with snarky stories about its error. The first mistake came in 1999, although the *Post* ran only a single story that time. Likely as a function of the tabloid war in which they were embroiled by 2005, the *Post* wrote exponentially more stories about the second Scratch 'N' Match flap.

that Chang would approve the expense. De La Rosa was a Dominican citizen, and locating him would likely require a costly trip. Nevertheless, the following morning, Jose boarded a pre-dawn flight aboard American Airlines, departing from JFK, to the Dominican Republic. For the next two days, he scoured Santo Domingo until Nelson's brother informed him that his sibling was, in fact, in Providence, Rhode Island. Jose flew there directly and tracked his pint-sized prey to his workplace, a gas station mini-mart. But De La Rosa was in no mood to talk. Initially confronted, the dwarf fled toward the mini-mart's door but found he wasn't tall enough to reach the knob that would have permitted him definitive escape inside. At this point, the cornered little person conceded to Jose that Pedro—and thus the *Post*—"broke my heart." The *News*' next-day story was headlined: "WHO'S YOUR DWARF?" and included a quote from De La Rosa saying, "I'm the one and only. I'm still Nelson, and that's from the heart."

And yet the matter was still not concluded. By branding Loomis a "midget" in the story's text, Jose unwittingly opened the door to a *Post* counter-attack. On the 21st, the tabloid published a brief item in its "Page Six" gossip column quoting an aggrieved Loomis as equating Jose's semantic misstep to "calling someone a 'k**e' or a 'n****r.'" "It's a very offensive term," he lectured. "They should be polite and correct, and use either 'dwarf' or 'little person.'" He also took a shot at De la Rosa, noting, "I'm also a lot taller than him." Some months later, Jose again contacted the Rhode Island gas station at which De La Rosa worked. The Mets were due to play in Boston, and the *News* wanted both to attend the game and heckle Pedro. But Jose was told that De La Rosa was occupied in China—being shot out of a cannon for pay.

That March, the *News* suffered its second Scratch 'N' Match scandal in six years, a peculiar mishap that some at the paper astoundingly attributed to the *Post*'s having had "a man on the inside"[4] of D. L. Blair. The Long Island contractor had bungled the contest by transmitting "unlucky 13," as the *Post* put it, rather than "12." Had someone been paid off? Had a *Post* runner gotten to some Mineola family man with something to hide? Regardless, the *Post* capitalized and through far more than the slapstick delivery of peanuts.

From the start—and improbably as 2005 wore on—the drumbeat of *Post* stories about Scratch 'N' Match continued as if pounded out by the stroke master on a Roman galley: twenty-two, in all, from March 21 to August 3, not counting a Keith J. Kelly column linking undefined "Scratch 'N' Match apathy" to "high-profile [*News*] departures" like those of business editor David Andelman and reporter Robert Port. In the former case, Kelly wrote, Andelman had quit after a newsroom shouting match that was "quite the spectacle."

On March 22, alone, the *Post* published four Scratch 'N' Match stories, including a particularly vicious Andrea Peyser column about a Brooklyn grandmother named Lillian Diamond. Diamond, she wrote, had erroneously "won" $1,500 during the *News'* first Scratch 'N' Match scandal in 1999—only to be victimized, again, in 2005, to the tune of $100,000. "She didn't think it possible," Peyser wrote, "but the sweet Brooklyn grandma has been screwed over by New York's 'Hometown Newspaper' not once but twice." "GRANNY GETS PLAYED AGAIN IN DAILY DOUBLE WHAMMY," roared the *Post* over Peyser's column, quoting Diamond as having said, "Saturday night, I was using the money to pay off bills. I guess I'm just a stupid, old, 76-year-old lady to have trusted them."

March 23 brought three more *Post* stories on "Scratch 'N' Stiff," as the paper began referring to the scandal. One quoted Debra Cherif, a forty-year-old Manhattan woman who told the *Post* she'd become homeless after losing her job and sending her kids to live with her disabled husband's family in Africa. According to the *Post*, after she'd "won" $100,000 in Scratch 'N' Match, she phoned her children and joyously told them, "We're coming [to Tunisia] and we're building a house, and we're never leaving you again!" "Now," she added in the next mournful breath, "I don't know when I'll see my kids." Meanwhile, another March 23 hatchet job quoted Queens lawyer Steven Gildin as promising a class action lawsuit against the *News*, "as soon as the dust settles and . . . we round up all these victims." Finally, a second Peyser column bludgeoned the paper with the woeful tale of Lucy Tirado, whose one-room Bushwick, Brooklyn, leasehold was being sold out from under her at month's end. As she complained to Peyser, she'd planned to "pay the back rent and have a deposit for a new apartment" with her phantom Scratch 'N' Match haul, but now—as she stood outside the *News'* building among other jilted, would-be winners chanting, "Boycott the *Daily News*!" and "No pay, no readers!"—she realized, "I'm a joke."

"Look at the people who played this game," moralized Peyser, "and you see the kinds of folks on whom the *Daily News* has long preyed. You saw hourly wage slaves. A handful of students. Immigrants. The elderly and infirm." All of them believed "that New York's self-described 'Hometown Newspaper' would make good on a promise. This is a paper that makes a pretense on its pages of caring for the weakest, the poorest, the hardest-working of this city. . . . Better luck next time. Maybe."

On the 25th, Kelly violated the Rubenstein-brokered accord, reporting that while the scandal raged back in New York, Zuckerman was off yachting in the Galapagos Islands: "As Nero fiddled, Rome burned," he wrote. "And as the Scratch 'N' Stiff scandal continues to rattle loyal readers of the *Daily News*, the paper's billionaire Chairman and CEO, Mort Zuckerman, remains adrift, literally aboard a yacht in the Pacific." Meanwhile, back at the *Post's* Sixth Avenue headquarters, the paper's gloating management toasted their arch-rival's misfortune to *The New Yorker's* Ben McGrath. "They're still shoving fifty papers a day in bulk into the prisons of the mentally insane on Wards Island!" quipped Col Allan, while Lachlan Murdoch, the *Post's* publisher and Rupert's son, added, "I might even read the *Daily News* if I were stuck in a white padded cell!"[5] Outside, a newsroom hotline dedicated to Scratch 'N' Match victims harvested complaints.

Improbably, the *Post* headlines continued into August: "NEWS OUT OF SCRATCH; PAPER'S PRESIDENT PLEADS POVERTY WHILE CONTEST WINNERS FIGHT BACK" . . . "HUGE HOTEL SITDOWN FOR THE '$TIFFED'" . . . "BAD NEW$ BARED—PAPER MAY OWE WINNERS $444 MILLION." One story crowed how the *Post* had bought a Walt Disney World vacation for a Harlem woman who'd promised to take her grandson there with her $100,000 Scratch 'N' Match chimera. The story's lede: "Fairy tales can come true, it can happen to you—if you believe in the *New York Post*."

But there would be a reckoning, and one so vicious once it occurred that the *Times* would have cause to write of it, "In New York's tabloid newspaper war, revenge is a dish best served boldface." Indeed, almost a year to the date after the Scratch 'N' Match hysteria reached a crescendo, the *News* received a tip that the city was being "flooded with free *Posts*." Unopened, waist- and knee-high plastic-wrapped bundles dropped off at corners, delis, transit hubs, and other "storefronts across the city." *Daily News* staffers fanned out and soon uncovered what appeared to be a "bizarre" and complex "circulation-pumping operation." They watched as vans arrived at the locations provisioned with unattended *Posts*, loaded them up, and pulled away. From several sites in Queens, *News* field personnel pursued the vans "to the home of a newspaper distributor in Jamaica, where the *Posts* were dumped in the man's backyard." When a *News* shooter arrived "on the scene," the fellow hastily pulled a tarpaulin over the "still-bundled *Posts*." In Brooklyn, *News* runners and shooters followed the vans to two recycling centers in Gowanus and Greenpoint. There, they watched—shocked!—as the bundles were "unceremoniously" tossed on to the floor, scooped up with a payloader, transported to a baler, and loaded onto tractor trailers that ferried them to ships bound for China. "NEW YORK POST GETS DOWN IN THE DUMPS," roared the March 31, 2006, *News* headline: "Thousands of papers go from presses to the trash."

But improbable as it might seem, an even more ferocious tabloid takedown was just then looming. This concerned Jared Paul Stern, a "Page Six" gossip reporter caught shaking down California billionaire Ron Burkle for $220,000 in exchange for a promise to stop printing fabrications about him in the *Post*. The story broke in the *News* on April 7 and began thusly: "A *New York Post* Page Six writer solicited $220,000 from a high-profile billionaire in return for a year's 'protection' against inaccurate and unflattering items about him in the gossip page." That same day, the *News* dispatched a shooter to News Corp.'s midtown offices, where the shutterbug obtained "gotcha" photos of Murdoch getting into—and out of—his limousine. A day later, *News* runner Angela Mosconi intercepted "Page Six" editor Richard Johnson at a Palm Beach, Florida, yacht club while he was walking to—of all things—his wedding reception. "I'm not giving interviews right now, not a word," he said while boarding the 120-foot *Mariner II* clad in a white tuxedo and abreast of his new wife. Then, on April 10, the *News* coined the *bon mot* that would enduringly serve as the sobriquet for the scandal: "ALL PLAY, NO PAY FOR PAGE FIX. GOSSIP-PAGE FAVORITE THREW EDITOR 50G BACHELOR PARTY IN MEXICO." Below this ran a story documenting Johnson's having accepted gifts from people who had received positive "Page Six" coverage, including "Girls Gone Wild" mogul Joe Francis, who'd hosted Johnson's bachelor party days before "Page Six" published a glowing item about his plan to become the next Hugh Hefner. For years, afterward, the *News* would refer to "Page Six," even casually, as "Page Fix."

More *Daily News* headlines followed: "POST CANS FOUR GOSSIP SCRIBES" . . . "HOW HE MADE HIS MOVE: SHAKING DOWN A BILLIONAIRE" . . . "DATE WITH THE DEVIL. *POST* WRITER'S TRIP INTO SKULLDUGGERY" . . . "NEXT *POST* DISH: GRILLED GOSSIPS" . . . "HE QUITS *PAGE SIX* MESS—*POST* HASTE." On June 3, the *News* notched a new low even for its rancorous war with the *Post*, publishing an out-and-out hit piece documenting Johnson's "shameful drunken-driving arrest" the night prior, complete with lurid details about how the scandal-scarred gossip editor had "reeked of alcohol, had bloodshot eyes and slightly slurred speech."

All of this was enough for observers even accustomed to *News–Post* sniping to take notice. On April 10, the *Times* published a story on the tabloids' growing war of words, improvising on the *Daily News'* famous 1975 Gerald Ford headline to create one of its own: "POST TO *DAILY NEWS*:

DROP DEAD."* In it, Col Allan, the *Post*'s editor-in-chief, described the *News*' coverage of his paper as something less than unbiased: "The *Daily News* has lost tens of thousands in circulation to the *Post* in recent years," he said, "and the *Post* is poised to overtake the *Daily News*' circulation. Of course, it's driving their agenda." Meanwhile, Michael Cooke, by then the *News*' ex-editor-in-chief, countered that the Stern scandal was a good story on the merits, although he did confess, "There is a wonderful added bonus of delight that it happened to the evil *New York Post*." In that same *Times* story, a voluble Cooke—whom the *Post* had repeatedly branded "The Cookie Monster"—further conceded that the *News* was preoccupied with trumping its rival "every minute of every day, from the highest levels of the newsroom to the interns. And that's not because they're scared of them. It's because it's a war, and in a war it's 24-7."

The *Times* story, though, predictably tempered all this tabloid bombast with sober scrutiny, as well—analysis that, it turns out, still proves instructive insofar as it places the *News–Post* war into the context of the newspaper industry's general decline. "It is indicative of the changes in the media landscape over the last few decades," wrote *Times*man Richard Siklos, "that America's bloodiest tabloid newspaper war is also a rarity." The story also quoted an industry analyst named John Morton, who said, "There are very few places where this occurs any longer because there are very few places that have competitive newspapers."

I caught up with Morton in 2015. By then, the newspaper watcher was firmly ensconced in retirement in a suburb equidistant between Baltimore and Washington, D.C. His thirty-one-year career as co-author of the *Morton-Groves Newspaper Newsletter* and oft-quoted industry oracle was well behind him, after he had published a final offering eight years earlier. In fact, he was initially resentful of being bothered further about newspapers and newspaper wars—and why they ended, grumbling, "I don't do this kind of thing anymore unless some sumbitch reporter calls up and bothers me." But I pleaded and ultimately prevailed upon the maven for one final encore that would explain exactly why the *News–Post* dynamic was unique and how in the world matters had gotten so out of hand.

"You have to look at the market," Morton finally said. "In New York, you have the *Times* and the top 15 percent of households. For the great, broad middle class of New York City, the Archie Bunkers, if you will, that was the *News*' [bread-and-butter] audience. The *Post* appealed to the lower rung.

---

* This *Daily News* headline characterized, rather than quoted, President Gerald Ford's response to New York City officials' request for federal aid during the 1970s fiscal crisis.

As late as the '80s, the *News* would have been content with the middle class and the *Post* with the people who read with their lips moving. But the readers disappeared, and both tabloids were left fighting tooth and nail for what was left."

Morton then digressively offered a bit of tabloid lore to illustrate his point. He said Rupert Murdoch once grew so frustrated with failing to place luxury retail advertising in the *Post* that he called up Bloomingdale's CEO, Marvin Traub, to complain. Traub, it's alleged, patiently heard Murdoch out, then replied, "But Rupert! Your readers are our shoplifters!"

Interestingly, Morton told me that American newspaper wars—or as he less dramatically put it, two or more commercially competitive newspapers in the same city—were actually once quite common. In fact, in 1911, he said, 689 U.S. cities claimed at least two such rivals, while some large cities, like New York, possessed a dozen. But the Great Depression knocked out many of the weaker dailies such that by World War II's start, the tally of cities with competing newspapers had dwindled to 140. By 1970, the rolls had further eroded to 43 with the growth of local radio and TV. And in 2015, by Morton's reckoning, fewer than a dozen American cities still claimed commercially competitive dailies, if one didn't count papers like the *Philadelphia Daily News* and *Philadelphia Inquirer*, which belonged to a cooperative, where circulation and/or advertising and printing capabilities were pooled independent of newsroom staffs.* In New York, Morton said, these vast macro trends didn't eradicate the *News* or the *Post* but put them on a collision course, forcing them to compete for the same audience.

At this point, Morton wheezed through an apology about not wanting to talk further. I asked if he was a reformed smoker. He said he hadn't touched a cigarette in decades but still enjoyed a pipe now and then, adding, "But I don't do that as much I used to. Come to think of it, I don't do anything as much as I used to . . . and that includes talking to reporters."

Over the six-month period that ended on March 31, 2006, the *News* and the *Post* were ranked as the sixth and seventh most widely circulated

---

* In a March 18, 2009, story, "Table for Two?", the *Columbia Journalism Review*'s Jane Kim put the number of major American metro areas still claiming at least two competitive newspapers at ten.

American daily newspapers, following—from first to fifth—*USA Today*, the *Wall Street Journal*, the *New York Times*, the *Los Angeles Times*, and the *Washington Post*. The *News* had a weekday circulation of 708,477 and a Sunday tally of 795,153. The *Post* had a weekday count of 673,379 and Sunday sales of 413,763.[6] Those were averages, meaning that on any given day, the *Post* might sell more than the *News*, or vice versa, depending on a host of variables, not the least of which was the quality of the scoops their runners and shooters had obtained in the field.

It hadn't always been that close. The *News* had a grizzled editor named Bob Kappstatter, whom no one called Bob or Kappstatter. Everyone knew him as "Kappy." He was as old as the antique typewriter the *News* kept as a lobby showpiece and as ageless in disposition as Phil Rizzuto. I rarely, if ever, saw Kappy frown—one of those people whom time and travails never beat down. He was about 5′8″ with a lithe frame most men would kill for at his age: no paunch, few wrinkles, and mirthful eyes that twinkled with unheard laughter. He was in his mid- to late sixties by the mid-2000s but looked more like fifty-five. He'd been an assistant city editor and even run an afternoon edition, when the *News* still had the chops to put one out. By 2006, he was the Bronx bureau chief, head of one of the *News'* three borough offices. The others were in Brooklyn and Queens.

Kappy lived in Bay Ridge—on Brooklyn's far side, near the Verrazzano-Narrows Bridge—but commuted to and covered the Bronx. If he attended one of the cop socials or political galas at which he harvested fodder for his weekly seen-and-heard column the night before, he would sleep on a futon in his office. More than once, I arrived at the Bronx bureau earlier than my stated hours to find him manicuring his silver-colored beard in his boxers. Because of this, he was the only boss I ever had who resented my arriving too early.

He liked to drink, but not too much, and he had exhausted, I believe, two marriages. For one, he held the reception in their garage. Why waste cash, he'd said. He maintained a Marine's buzz cut at the hands of an Italian barber two blocks from the Bronx bureau who spoke just enough English to give him an approximation of what you'd requested. I patronized him, too. It wasn't a stylistic decision but one born from economics and expediency. He charged $12 and rarely—if ever—had someone ahead of you. And if something broke while you were in the chair, you could always run back to the office.

Kappy loved Elaine's, the Upper East Side watering hole patronized by writers, editors, and actors. He also loved Facebook, and when an interesting obituary or arrest crossed the Associated Press wire, Kappy would paste the obit's first line as a status update and then add a mock headline.

Then his Facebook friends, some in journalism and some not, would try to top his offering, the winner judged informally by the greatest number of "likes." Some threads would number thirty-five posts. "William Ronan, the first chairman of the Metropolitan Transportation Authority, whom many credit with dethroning Robert Moses as New York's most influential transportation planner in the late 1960s, died Wednesday." "EX SUBWAY BOSS SIX FEET UNDER." "TOKEN BEFORE HIS TIME." "THIS TRAIN IS OUT OF SERVICE." "END OF THE LINE," etc. Still another: "A Florida man with an extensive history of domestic battery was arrested after he allegedly flew into a jealous rage and broke his ex-wife's sex toy." "SEX TOY ATTACKER CHARGED WITH ASSAULT AND BATTERIES! FACES UP TO TWO YEARS OF HARD LABIA." "FLORIDA MAN RUBS EX-WIFE THE WRONG WAY. ADDED CHARGE: DISTURBING THE PIECE."

I remember sitting in the Bronx bureau one day when I heard a slam and off-kilter ringing from Kappy's office. A gush of invective followed, concluded by an explanation for his having slammed his phone: a flack— or public information official—had given the *Post* an exclusive. The story concerned the gorilla exhibit at the Bronx Zoo. A new gorilla was in town. Or maybe one had given birth. But the point was Kappy said this "shit would never have flown back in the day," which probably meant the early to mid-'70s. He said—appropriately but I don't think with an intentional attempt at a pun—the *News* had always been "the 500-pound gorilla in New York, and the *Post* nothing more than a fly embedded in its shit." And he was right, of course, at least in describing the abiding chasm between the two papers. The *Daily News* first published on June 26, 1919, as America's first tabloid newspaper. It proved a roaring success, enchanting the city's commuters with its ease of use. (A tabloid, it's worth noting, only incidentally concerns its editorial style, but strictly speaking, its format is what makes it different. Tabloids open like books while "broadsheets," like the *New York Times*, fold in half.)

By 1925's end, the *News* was America's largest newspaper, claiming a daily circulation of 1 million. And things only grew. By 1947, the *News'* circulation reached 2.4 million on weekdays and 4.7 million on Sundays,[7] astronomical figures that will never again be reached by an American metro. Throughout the 1950s, the numbers remained marginally the same, and the *News* remained the nation's largest daily newspaper. The *Post*, meanwhile, wasn't durably published as a tabloid until 1942. When Dorothy Schiff sold it in November 1976 to Rupert Murdoch, it claimed a circulation of 489,067.[8] The *News*, meanwhile, sold 1,925,643, on average, for the six months ending September 30, 1976.[9]

Probably no one is more responsible for the modern *News–Post* rivalry than Rupert Murdoch. When he arrived, the *News* and the *Post* didn't directly compete. Schiff's *Post* was an afternoon paper that published Monday through Saturday, and the *News* a morning offering with a massive Sunday audience. The *News* did publish a Night Owl edition that came out around 8 P.M., but it claimed a modest circulation of about 75,000.[10] But from the moment Murdoch bought the *Post*, he seemed to understand that New York, as large as it was, was not big enough for both papers. Long before digital proved him right, he would act as if obsessively intent on eradicating the *News*.

First, Murdoch transformed the *Post* itself, turning it into the pirate ship that still menaces society today. In fact, by the time he hoisted his Jolly Roger over the *tabloid*—his eighty-fourth paper—he'd already gained a reputation as a publisher who favored sex, crime, celebrity, and sleaze.[11] The *Post*, under Schiff, had a flavor of those elements, but as *The New Yorker's* John Cassidy wrote, "[I]ts layout was restrained and its coverage sober, with long articles about education, foreign affairs and other serious subjects."[12] And Schiff's *Post* was liberal. As Murdoch told Cassidy, "It was totally tribal [when I arrived]. The blue-collar workers, the Irish and Italians, they all took the *Daily News*. The middle classes, the Jewish in particular, the schoolteachers, the *Post* was their paper. When we went door-to-door with the *Post*, the *News* readers would say, 'We don't want that commie rag here.'"

But under Murdoch's direction, the *Post's* opinion pages veered hard right, story lengths were cut, photos and headlines enlarged. On January 3, 1977, the *Post* instituted "Page Six,"[13] the gossip column that continues today as a source of salaciousness and sleaze. Writing in the *Harvard Crimson* on January 8, 1982, a precocious Jeffrey Toobin described Murdoch's overhaul of the post-Schiff *Post*: "[It] went heavily into crime ("Gutsy Hell Camp Victim Foils Thugs"—a story about a mugging of a concentration camp survivor . . .), sentiment ("Medal for New York's bravest little girl . . .") and gossip (at least two pages' worth every day). Then he packaged it in the most attention-grabbing manner, [and] hired the most garish cartoonist in the United States, Paul (Rorschach Test) Rigby . . . And he added one more thing: sports. Sports now takes up a solid half of the *Post*."[14]

Again, *The New Yorker*: "This type of journalism was hardly unheard of in New York—Pulitzer and Hearst had pioneered it almost a century before . . . [but] some people were outraged. *Time* showed Murdoch as King Kong atop the World Trade Center."

Through Murdoch's first years in ownership of the *Post*, press accounts show the paper and the *News* repeatedly trading threats to invade each other's turf. Then on August 9, 1978, a pressmans' strike brought matters to a head, shuttering all three of the city's mass-market dailies, along with the *Times*. A news blackout across New York City! Initially, Murdoch vowed solidarity with his competitors, even acting as the publishers' association president and the triumvirate's spokesman.[15] But on the strike's eleventh day came news that a morning strike paper called the *Daily Metro* would begin publication a day later on August 21. "MURDOCH BELIEVED TO BACK NEW YORK STRIKE PAPER," declared the *Washington Post* above a story quoting the *Daily Metro*'s unlikely publisher, Frederick Iseman—a twenty-five-year-old temporary summer assistant on the *Times*' op-ed page—as confirming he'd gone to the *Post* for financing. "I told them I have a paper," Iseman said, "I need cash up front for distribution. Are you interested? They said, 'Yes.'"[16]

Over the ensuing months, Murdoch insisted he hadn't financed the *Daily Metro*—and had committed only to purchasing 150,000 daily copies for distribution to the *Post*'s news-starved readership.[17] But on September 6, Iseman confessed to what the *Washington Post* said had "been rumored"—he'd secretly borrowed hundreds of thousands of dollars from the Aussie press baron and had even given him an option to buy the *Daily Metro*. His newsroom walked out the same day. All were Newspaper Guild members from the striking *News*, *Times*, and *Post* and feared Murdoch intended to shutter the unionized *Post* and replace it with the non-union *Daily Metro*. To coax them back to their desks, Iseman was forced to cancel Murdoch's option to buy his paper—and Murdoch was forced to find another means of directly challenging the morning *Daily News*.[18] It would take him about a month.

During October's first week, Murdoch announced a separate peace with the pressmen that cleverly "left the basic strike issue of manpower and hours worked in the pressroom pending whatever agreement the other publishers eventually reached."[19] "RUPERT THE RUTHLESS," crowed *The Economist*. But the declaration that the *Post* was returning came with two, likely more alarming, developments for *Daily News* execs: Murdoch would publish the *Post* on Sundays as a generous "public service to readers and advertisers" and push up his weekday press runs in a blatant swiping of the *News*' morning audience.

On the day the *Post* reappeared, October 5, it published a front-page love note . . . to itself. "WELCOME BACK!" On that same day, the *Daily Metro*, not mysteriously, announced that October 5's would be its final edition. As the *Washington Post* observed, "Its lead story was on the return of the *Post*, and an accompanying story was headlined: 'Goodbye.'"

Murdoch's assault on the crippled *News* continued. On October 19, he announced plans to publish a new morning tabloid, the *New York Daily Sun*, in just a week's time. It would publish six days a week, focus on "sports, crimes and sex," and sell for 10 cents, or half the price of the *News*. "It will be a bright, entertaining, street-smart paper, not unlike what The *Daily News* was like [sic] years ago," said Neal Travis, a Murdoch adjutant tapped to be the *Daily Sun*'s editor.[20] But it never happened. On November 2, Murdoch conceded he couldn't convince the drivers' union to deliver the *Sun*. He also slapped the *News* with a $75 million anti-trust lawsuit alleging its executives had "threatened to eliminate drivers' jobs at the *News* if the *Sun* were allowed to appear." "CHARGING A CONSPIRACY, MURDOCH SUES RIVAL NEWSPAPER," roared a November 3 *Washington Post* headline.

On November 1, the striking pressmen announced an agreement with both the *Times* and the *News*. On Monday, November 6, both papers resumed publication after eighty-eight days. The *News'* welcome-back edition featured the banner headline, "HELLO THERE! REMEMBER US?" and a photo of pressman Phil Gillick pushing a button to re-start the *News'* press run. Inside was less joy—and a harbinger of turbulence to come. In one of its retrospective stories on the strike, the *News* cheekily said New York was a "two newspaper town again," purposefully ignoring its rival and instead referring to it as a strike paper. Murdoch, for his part, suspended the *Post*'s Sunday edition after eight weeks, and both tabloids, for the moment, returned to their respective pre-strike corners. The calm wouldn't last.

By March 31, 1980, the *News* had plummeted to an average of 1.55 million in daily circulation over the prior six months,[21] shedding 450,000 from its pre-strike levels. Working-class New Yorkers—and especially white, outer borough "ethnics" who had so long formed its readership core— were fleeing Snake Plisskin's New York City. The *Washington Post*'s Lee Lescaze addressed this trend—and its ramifications for the tabloid—in a May 11, 1980, story entitled "NEW YORK NEWSPAPERS IN A NEW SURVIVAL CONTEST":

New York City has lost about 600,000 blue-collar jobs over the past decade, and most of the people holding those jobs were *News* readers. In the Bronx and sections of Brooklyn there are only empty lots where there used to be apartment buildings full of *News* readers.

New arrivals over the decade generally have been people who don't read newspapers, but even if the *News* could sell them subscriptions these generally poor people are not the readers advertisers want to reach.

Meanwhile, the *Post* had the opposite problem. It had grown circulation to 654,314[22]—but couldn't sell ads. "It is not an editorial environment that we would be comfortable with," one advertiser told Lescaze, who noted the *Post's* "puny" 7.8 percent share of 1979 advertising lineage, versus the *News'* 38 percent and the *Times'* 55.7 percent. Left unsaid was the *Post's* practice of publishing lurid photo spreads such as its city-wide search for the "perfect 10" woman.[23]

Through the spring, *News* execs held a "flurry of top-level meetings" in Chicago with their Tribune Co. overlords to convince them that a direct assault on the *Post's* afternoon market was the answer to the tabloid's woes.[24] Over June's first days, Henry Wurzer, the *News'* executive vice president, conceded "research is under way to test the water for an afternoon paper." The *Post*, meanwhile, said it, too, was studying a morning incursion.[25]

Then a match was thrown into the tabloid tinder. Michael Goldstein— former publisher of the *SoHo Weekly*—announced plans to publish, that June, a sixteen-page afternoon "information sheet" at 5 P.M. on weekdays called the *Wall Street Final*. It would offer closing stock prices and short news items, and it would claim a modest staff of 15.[26] The *News'* response was swift. On June 21, the paper announced it would pour $15–$20 million over two years into its own, new afternoon edition. "Our objective is to reverse a seven-year slide," publisher Robert M. Hunt told union leaders. "We really believe the solution for the A.M. side of the *Daily News* is to get this newspaper out with late news and sports."[27]

Five days later, Murdoch responded—announcing plans to publish a morning *Post* and extend its afternoon runs to include closing stock prices. But while the new, morning *Post* would be "expanded but basically the same" as its regular afternoon edition,[28] the *News* said it intended to hire a new staff of 300 for its afternoon edition. "The *Daily News'* efforts are intended to put us off the streets!" decried Murdoch, while Goldstein called it "highly suspect" that both tabloids had announced new editions within two weeks of *Wall Street Final's* inaugural edition.[29]

On July 22, 1980, the *New York Post* officially invaded the morning field.[30] Nearly a month later, on August 19, 1980, The *Daily News* published its inaugural P.M. edition, *Daily News Tonight*.[31] Finally, the two tabloids were competing head-to-head—and the feeling on the street was palpable.

Longtime, now-former *News* shooter John Roca: "It wasn't the same audience until Murdoch started the morning edition. We had the strap-hangers in the morning and they had them in the afternoon. [Before that], we competed on big stories, like any newspapers in the same town, but I don't remember feeling it until the Aussie came along. Plus, it wasn't until Murdoch that the *Post* got venomous."

The era did have its humorous asides. To bolster flagging circulation and soften the blow of a 25-cent Sunday price hike, the *News* introduced in November 1980 a Scratch 'N' Match forerunner called "Zingo," which doled out cash prizes of $75,000 a week. But even this proved a point of challenge. The *News* ran the game until August 1981, shuttered it with no apparent intention of an immediate return, then quickly revived it after learning that Murdoch was hustling his own version, called "Wingo," to market. In the end, Zingo returned to the streets one full week before the *Post* debuted Wingo on September 13 with a front-page headline declaring, "WINGO FEVER!" Six days later, the *Washington Post* observed, "Wingoism and Zingoism are rampant in the Big Apple. This city's tabloid arch rivals . . . are locked in a circulation war being fought with bingo-like weapons."

Weapons, indeed! Some years later, in August 1984, the *Post* used Wingo to poke fun at the *Daily News*' new publisher James F. Hoge. Hoge had gotten the job that March after a decorated run at the *Chicago Sun-Times*. *Post* shooter David Handschuh, who went on to a distinguished career with the *News*, was a young staffer at the *Post*. He described how he and *Post* reporter Paul Tharp managed to pose an unwitting Hoge at a gala holding a blown-up Wingo game card, as if to endorse his rival's game offering.

We jumped on this like a full frontal assault [Handschuh said]. The *Post* was up on Hoge's movements. We were *actually* stalking him! So, finally, we tracked him to some kind of an event at a midtown skyscraper. Suits but still less than a formal affair. This was the days before airport-like security going into office buildings, so we just sort of walked in. Tharp hands him this card and Hoge is looking at it and it says, "Welcome to New York" on the side that's facing him, and on the other—the one facing me—is this blown-up Wingo card they'd made specifically for this reason. So, Hoge's looking down at

"Welcome to New York" and I'm photographing the Wingo side. At some point he turns it over, realizes what's going on and throws it to the floor and I was like, "I'm out of there!" and Tharp was left to explain who he was and what he was doing.

A few days later, the *News* ran an item in which Hoge was quoted as describing the photo as "doctored." The *Post* quickly responded by publishing a trio of Handschuh's shots, or what the paper was calling by then its "now famous Wingo photo."
Again, Handschuh:

This was James Hoge! Publisher of the *News*! I was terrified. I was a kid doing this. It was like, "Oh my God! how can we do this?" I had come from journalism school and we were violating every tenet of ethical journalism and even a few that hadn't been invented yet. Eight years of college down the drain! I heard the voice of every journalism professor I had had telling me don't do this and then the voice of my editor in a British accent saying, "Hey, mate, go for it!" But that's what the *Post* was back then. It was like a high school newspaper being run by adults. People came into the office hung over, they slept in the darkroom, reeking of liquor, kick-me signs hanging on the backs of chairs. It was the greatest experience a twenty-one-year-old entering journalism could ask for.

Within a year of first publishing, *Daily News Tonight* had proven a big loser, selling, by one estimate, fewer than the 75,000-strong Night Owl edition it had replaced.[32] On August 28, 1981, the *News* shuttered the afternoon offering, although the morning *Post* remained entrenched, with the paper claiming an average, all-day circulation of 764,387.[33] The *News*, in all, had fallen to 1.491 million[34] and Murdoch sensed his rival was on the ropes. Through 1983 and 1984, Murdoch, according to *Times*man Alex S. Jones,

continued to push for more circulation, paying the delivery cost to sell papers sometimes hundreds of miles from New York City and spending millions in promotion costs. His sales force aggressively sought advertising, undercutting the *News'* rates with heavy discounting. The strategy, according to associates who asked not to be named, was to bleed the *News* in hopes the Tribune Company would close it or sell it to Mr. Murdoch. Mr. Murdoch also sought to interest the *News* in joining the *Post* in a joint operating agreement in which they would merge all but editorial functions and share profits. . . . But the *News* did not fold and the *Post*'s share of the city's advertising revenue did not increase.[35]

In 1985, Murdoch pivoted to TV with the purchase of WNYW (formerly WNEW), the city's channel 5. Three years later, regulators forced him to sell the *Post*. In May 1988, under new ownership, the *Post* folded its afternoon edition.[36] But Murdoch would be back, re-buying the *Post* in March 1993. It was almost as if the tycoon couldn't abide the unfinished business he'd left when he first sold it. The *News* was, after all, still alive and kicking.

⣿

The year 2000 proved a watershed moment in the history of the *News–Post* conflict. On January 24, Modern Times Group, a Swedish company, began distribution of a free tabloid called *Metro* to Philadelphia commuters in conjunction with the city's transit authority, SEPTA. It then held ultimately aborted talks with the *Post* about launching such an offering in New York.[37] Spooked—or perhaps inspired—the *News* announced in mid-August plans to launch its own giveaway, *Daily News Express*, to be distributed in the afternoon at eighty-five city commuter hubs.[38] On September 4, the *Post* retaliated, halving its newsstand price within the city limits to 25 cents, undercutting the *News*, which sold its regular morning edition for 50 cents.[39] At that point, the *News* claimed a daily circulation of 730,542 and the *Post* 436,544 for the six months ending March 31.[*,40]

That year also saw Rupert Murdoch and his son Lachlan recruit a brash Australian editor named Col Allan to run the *Post*. Later, Lachlan conceded to *New York* magazine the peculiar criteria that had governed their search. "I needed to find someone who didn't think I was crazy when I said I wanted to beat the *News*. Col was the only person who was as crazy as I was."[41]

Crazy, indeed. The late Steve Dunleavy—the ex-*Post* columnist—told me Allan had a penchant for drunkenly firing people in the wee hours of the night. He once apparently so fired his copy chief, via voicemail, and when the man didn't report to his post the following day, Allan called him at home to inquire why he had not. It was at this point the stunned copy

---

* The *News* terminated *Daily News Express* within days of the September 11, 2001, attacks on lower Manhattan.

man informed Allan what had transpired the night prior. Allan, Dunleavy said, had not recalled doing so. Interestingly, Col's capacity to drunkenly confound his employees apparently expanded over the years and in league with advancing technology; once Apple introduced the iPad, his wont became adjourning to one of several local bars around the *Post*'s Sixth Avenue headquarters to fiddle with the front page from a bar stool. "The poor guys on the copy desk—they had to decipher his drunken instructions as he relayed them from Langan's Pub," said former *Post* photo editor Jeff Christensen. "And the clarity of what he told them to do got worse as the night went on, until finally it was just gibberish! Sometimes, they'd have no idea what he was trying to say! Those poor people." In light of such tales, perhaps it's not surprising that Allan had earned the nickname in some corners "Col Pot."

But it's also not surprising the Murdochs gave Allan a wide berth. This was, after all, a tabloid, generally, and the *New York Post*, specifically. And he was, after all, fulfilling the terms of his original mission brief. Within five years and aided by the 25-cent price cut, Col Allan remarkably grew the *Post*'s circulation to 662,681, or just 25,903 shy of the *News*.[42] As *Bloomberg Businessweek* put it, Allan "cut story lengths, doubled story counts, devoted more space to photos (especially color ones), and upped the *Post*'s daily quota of sex, celebrity and scandal." Then, in October 2006, these efforts finally overhauled the *News* for the first time in both papers' histories. From April 1, 2006, to September 30, 2006, the *Post* sold an average of 10,629[43] more copies than its arch-rival, a fact it trumpeted on both its front page—"Circulation Stunner . . . THANKS NEW YORK! *Post* Makes History: Beats *News*"—and a Times Square billboard. But while Allan had, at last, caught his "white whale,"[44] he still lacked the capacity to place the victory into any context other than the *Daily News*' allegedly shady circulation practices. As Allan told the *New York Times* in an interview, the *Post* would have notched even greater circulation victory over the *Daily News* had it not been for all the bulk sales to third-party sponsors (hotels, nursing homes, schools) his rival had included in their final circulation tally. Meanwhile, Martin Dunn, by then the *News*' editor-in-chief, crowed that the *Post* won only through sales in Las Vegas and Los Angeles and giveaways in New York City. Also, he added, the *Daily News* was still the leader in New York, the only "place that counts."

And Allan's triumph achieved a final result as well, making an already pitched battle with the *News* even more ferocious. Now and for the first time, the two papers were neck-and-neck. As *Bloomberg Businessweek* put it, "the newspaper war was [once] as common as the mayoral election or the crosstown high school football game. [But] the inexorable decline of newspaper reading has left even most big U.S. cities with a single daily. The glaring exception is New York City [where] the huge circulation gain logged of late by . . . the New York *Post* has escalated its arch rivalry with the *Daily News* into the sort of apocalyptic struggle not seen since William Randolph Hearst and Joseph Pulitzer locked egos a century ago."[45] On any given day, victory was a toss-up. Allan's success raised the stakes for everyone, and every twenty-four hours the great game reset. And at that point, we were fighting against more than just ourselves.

Through the 1990s and until 2004, total U.S. newspaper circulation contracted, although less than 1 percent annually on weekdays and under 0.5 percent on Sundays. But in 2005, the decline accelerated. Circulation fell 2.6 percent daily and 3.1 percent on Sunday, year-over-year.[46] Then in 2006, the industry bled 2.8 percent daily and 3.4 percent on Sundays.[47] Tens of thousands of readers vanished. As the *Times* noted on October 31, 2006, "The circulation of the nation's daily newspapers plunged during the latest [six-month] reporting period in one of the sharpest declines in recent history."[48]

Some of that circulation was surely bulk, or junk, as papers retreated to their core coverage zones and the cost of acquiring new subscribers roughly tripled with the 2003 advent of the National Do Not Call Registry.[49] The introduction of free dailies attacked the incumbents' circulation, perhaps contributing to the overall statistical decline. (The circulation of such free dailies is counted as "bulk" and is thus not included in overall industry figures, the Alliance for Audited Media's Susan Kantor told me.) In New York City, the inauguration of two free dailies over four months—*amNewYork* on October 10, 2003, and *Metro New York* on March 4, 2004—wrought havoc upon the *News'* and the *Post's* business models, which rely on newsstand sales to commuters who suddenly had a free alternative to the *Post's* 25-cent and the *News'* 50-cent price. By May 2007, *amNewYork* and *Metro* claimed print circulations of roughly 315,000 and 310,000, respectively.[50]

And, of course, there was America's march online. By October 2006, the *New York Times*, a useful industry surrogate, announced that more people read its digital edition than its print edition.[51] More broadly, 57 million people had visited newspaper websites during the third quarter of that year, a 24 percent jump over the same period in 2005.[52] And the trend only continued as smartphones and other mobile devices proliferated. But while readers moved online, newspapers did not monetize them. They gave their product away for free, while online ads commanded only a fraction of those published in print. Shockingly, from 2003 to 2009, newspapers shed

$20.1 billion in print ad revenue, or 55 percent. Meanwhile, their digital sites added back only $1.5 billion in online sales. As two Wall Street analysts put it, "When print advertising moves to online, newspapers typically take in only 20 to 30 cents for each print dollar lost." They were probably being generous. Another analyst said that newspapers were trading digital dimes for dollars lost.

Staffs were scythed across the country. And as Tom Goldstein, dean of Columbia University's Graduate School of Journalism, put it, "Unless they urgently respond to the changing environment, newspapers risk early extinction."[53] Seemingly everywhere, advertising and circulation losses sparked a retrenchment, if not an outright retreat—except in one place and concerning two rival tabloids already hell-bent on each other's destruction. In New York City, the arrival of digital had brought into focus the existential war that Rupert Murdoch's visionary eyes had spied all along. Stakeouts on the ground endured for weeks and, in several cases, more than a month, often for no reason other than the opposite side refused to go home. Runners crisscrossed North America. They flew to Europe. Africa. South America. On December 25, 2007, a tiger escaped its pen at the San Diego Zoo, killed one patron, and wounded two more. The *News'* then–city editor initially passed on covering the story on the ground but, according to one of his deputies, later dispatched a runner/shooter team to California after learning that the *Post* had sent a team of its own.

Interestingly, it was never revealed to me how the *News* discovered that the *Post* had tasked its own team to San Diego, although the question does raise an interesting point. The intel probably was offered innocently from some loose-lipped *Post* shooter, whose counterpart at the *News* then reported it back to his desk. But there are other, more cynical methods of appraisal. At least one shooter on the street, admittedly discredited, swore to me that the newsrooms of either side had been infiltrated, that some mole squeaked on their respective city desks. Such an arrangement would not have been unprecedented. Ex–*Post* photo editor Jeff Christensen told me that the *Post* bribed a traitorous *News* delivery driver to provide copies of the *News'* first edition before he began his delivery route, or as soon as he got his hands on them. "It's was pretty comical," Christensen told me, continuing,

> A guy would go out and meet this mysterious delivery driver and come back with ten or fifteen copies. The *Post* had later deadlines and could change copy easily until 2:30 A.M. Meeting the driver gave the

desk just enough of a sneak peek at the *News* to quickly match scoops. They didn't do it often; I remember four or five times they made big changes after realizing they had missed something. The thinking was that if we did it too much, the *News* would realize they had a mole.

At the time, the *News'* editorial accountant was a quintessential New York City Italian named Joe Abramo, who loved conspiratorial conversations and especially those conducted *sotto voce* and liberally laced with profanity. Rarely did I enjoy an interaction with him that didn't begin with "This fucking guy." For a while, I knew who filed for overtime in half-hour increments and who hounded Joe for reimbursement checks.

But it was my professional association with Joe that speaks to my larger point about the *News* and the *Post*'s going to the mattresses in the age of digital. Even with the army of staffers and perma-lancers fielded by the *News* to do battle with the *Post*, the paper still enlisted staffers in seven-day work weeks, the two off days remunerated at time-and-a-half. At points between 2006 and mid-2008, I had 200-plus hours of overtime banked and awaiting disbursement. The reason for this was that Joe believed paying out OT in a lump sum was to incur more tax exposure than if dispensed at a trickle. I never questioned Joe. I simply consulted him on the Monday of a pay week and acceded to his authoritative-sounding advice. Some weeks he almost mystically felt 30 hours was a good number, others 40 to 45. I assumed these deviations were a function of the total accrued. Strangely, I never asked. And around Christmas, the amount Joe "pushed through," as he put it, doubled or even tripled. The *News* didn't pay holiday bonuses. No paper did. But Joe gave you a *de facto* one, regardless. Among the many staffers who had also accrued outrageous sums of unpaid OT, these seasonal bumps were called "Abramo bonuses." In 2007 and 2008, some runners worked 1,000-plus hours of overtime each year.

Many years before, John Morton had told the *Times* of Murdoch and Zuckerman, "It's not about money. It's about image and being the publisher of a major newspaper in the world's most important city."[54] But at that point in the history of papers, there was clearly more than simply ego at stake. When I arrived at the *News* in October 2006, people on the street gossiped openly about end-game scenarios. Who would stand after the radioactive cloud of digital had lifted? Many said New York City wasn't big enough to support both papers. I argued the opposite, probably romantically, saying it was impossible that the *Post* or the *News* could shutter.

They're too entrenched, too valuable as brands, too much a part of city life. But the counter-argument made sense, too, and the city's newspaper graveyard was littered with titles once thought unassailable. One tabloid— if enough pressure was applied—might just fold. And yet, one thing was for certain: For anyone employed by either the *News* or the *Post* at that point, failure was totally untenable.

3

"Ford to City: Drop Dead"

Daily News headline, October 30, 1975

WHEN I JOINED the *News* in August 2006, I had no idea runners existed—had not even heard the term—despite having been, to that point, in the business for seven years. A reporter went out, got the story, came back, and wrote it. The idea that one person would go out and get it, then hand off, or more likely call in, what he had obtained to someone else struck me as absurd. Moreover, it seemed to undermine something important about the process.

But in New York City, geography required it. The city is 305 square miles, and so runners often had to travel great distances and overcome logistical hurdles—traffic, tunnels, bridges, ferries, bus and subway schedules, but mostly traffic—to get wherever they were going. Geography made getting the story and then returning to write it impractical—especially given deadlines. Then, too, rarely was it as simple as going to a place, collecting the information, and leaving. The competition with the *Post* ensured as much; even if the person you sought was home and agreeable to speaking, that didn't mean the person wouldn't have something better to say later on; and if a shooting had occurred, a victim's family member might come outside, later in the afternoon and, say, swoon. It wouldn't do to have the *Post* get that sort of detail and not the *News* just because the *News* runner had returned to the office to write up their notes.

Specialization was also an end unto itself, as it served the *News* and the *Post* to station its best writers in the office, on the rewrite desk. (And its most gutsy in the field as runners.) It was these rewrite folks to whom runners most often called in their field hauls using, first, pay phones and then, by 2006, mobile. Conversely, runners didn't need any special facility with words. They needed *cojones* and cleverness—and in such quantities that might elude reporters who were, say, good with words, assuming those on the rewrite desk would even be willing to get their hands dirty with a door knock, or sneak into a hospital, or infiltrate a Manhattan high-rise where a liveried doorman stood sentry outside.

Then there were situations where the people for whom you were searching weren't initially available. Maybe they weren't home or had refused your first request. Depending on their importance to the story, a runner would then await a more agreeable moment. If you were hustling to the newsroom to beat deadline, you couldn't do that.

During my job interview at the *News*, the city editor, Dean Chang, made a noteworthy statement that was followed by an equally revealing question from his deputy, Jere Hester. Chang said that while I would be expected to "learn to write in the *News*' style," such facility wasn't, at once, necessary since I was to be "an adrenaline junkie, running from scene to scene." This statement horrified me, although I didn't have much time to consider it, since Hester asked me a question on which I understood rested the outcome of the interview. "What are you going to do," he asked me, "to help us beat the *Post*?"

I didn't know how to answer at first, but then something occurred to me—something revelatory about how some runners routinely achieved success. I told him that while the *Post* brought nothing to door knocks, I had, over the prior weekends I'd been freelance running for the *News*, brought cake, and usually Entenmann's. I told him it was important, I'd found, to make the people who answered the door feel as if you cared, even if that concern was theatrical. The *Post* didn't do this, or didn't bring cake, or cookies, or any prop. Being of Italian heritage, I had found it unusual, from the start, to approach a death house without some such offering. In this way, I'm convinced my early success as a freelance runner—the success that allowed me to win a formal interview—had more to do with my Italian heritage than with any skills I had acquired over my prior years as a reporter. Then again, running bore little resemblance to anything I'd done before.

Unlike the *paparazzi*, mercenary in hunting celebrity, I have never heard a runner cite money as motivation. I know most cared about writing, and some profoundly so, and of this group a few harbored literary ambitions. A smaller share had published books. Some believed, implicitly, in the glory of the endeavor and saw it as a suitable means of making a name for oneself. I certainly did. Some ran because of the thrill of the *News–Post* competition: the freedom it offered from routine, the wisp of adventure, or as a means of escaping office life. Some—and especially certain freelance shooters—were not suitable, I'm convinced, for any other job aside from a life of crime. A small minority actually believed in the importance of covering a story *vis-à-vis* its utility to society and the vitality of our democracy. But, as I said, this last group was the exception rather than the rule. What we believed in—universally and like cultists—was the "get," a term of art referring to an interview, or a photo; as in, *I got him!* Or, *that's a good get* . . . a tough get . . . an impossible get, a dream get, an exclusive get, or a woodable get, meaning one worthy of the front page. And no one believed in the get, and the pursuit of it, quite like Kerry Burke.

At the time of this story, Kerry was the king of the runners—a short Irish-American in his forties with wispy blond hair, crooked teeth, a Boston accent, and a habit of calling everyone "Brotha"—even women. (*"Brotha, I couldn't get words!"*) Kerry didn't have a car, so he mostly relied on subways to run to scenes. But he still routinely arrived first—a human HopStop with Hagstrom's *Five Boroughs* in hand. "I was the first staff reporter in New York City to not have a car," he once said. "Having a car was just taken as gospel; it was a condition of one's employment. But my thing was, one, you're not paying me enough . . . and two, I can get there first using public transportation or a cab. While my colleagues are busy looking for parking and stuck in traffic, I'm on the subway. Basically, if you're late, you're dead."[1]

Yes, he spoke in movie dialogue. In another press interview, Kerry referred to his beat as anything that concerned "murder and mayhem." He also elaborated without humor, irony, or insincerity: "If it's got blood and dirt on it, it's my story." He called the people with whom he came in contact at scenes "them cats," or, "this cat." Everyone was "a cat," and, as coincidence had it, Kerry, for a while upon arriving in New York from his native Dorchester, had kept company with the city's strays, slumbering on rooftops before securing digs of his own. It was all enough to engender a cynicism in some quarters over the authenticity of this wildly inflated persona. *This guy? Is he for real?*

But he was. He truly believed—not only in the glory of the get but also in its utility to the society he served with Jedi-like devotion. Some haters believed him a flagrant propagandist, committed to his own legend—and Kerry certainly furnished them with ample ammo. But as I got to know him, I came to first doubt this assessment of his outsized character, then ultimately view him as he likely views himself—the most ardent of believers in the holiness of the get. Some would argue otherwise, but to them

I offer up the night in 2011 when the runner caught the hand job assignment* of covering Beyoncé's introduction of her new branded perfume at the Herald Square Macy's in midtown. It was a dog-and-pony show, and normally the *News* would never have touched it, but the paper had such a robust advertising relationship with the retailer that, an editor once told me, it quashed a story about employee-related thefts there. We used to joke that if Macy's ever pulled its ads from the paper we should all just as soon go home that day. Now, some runners might have mailed in such an assignment. Not Kerry, who attacked every "job," as if he were reporting out† the Watergate break-in. No one was safe from Kerry—and certainly not a pregnant Beyoncé. Sniffing a scoop, he steamrolled the publicist-approved questions lobbed at the singer by lightweight bloggers and trade journalists.

"What are ya gonna name him? Is it a boy or a girl? You can't duck me, Beyoncé!"

The pop star did not reply—but looked at this white-and-black-clad curiosity as one might view a dish served in a foreign land. Later and after he'd returned to the newsroom, Kerry told me, "I tried, brotha. I really did. But that cat just wasn't talkin'."

The first time I saw Kerry Burke was on a Bravo Channel documentary called "Tabloid Wars," in which camera crews followed *Daily News* editorial personnel as they performed their duties. To say Kerry took over this show is probably understating the matter. There he was riding a subway en route to a scene, the tracks click-clacking audibly as he answered a producer's question: Don't you ever get tired? Kerry responded as if his reply had been scripted: "I'll sleep when I'm dead!" There he was running, again: "There are times I've gone to doors and started kicking them and either that door is gonna give or the person on the other side is gonna answer, because I need that quote!"[2] In fact, the very ease with which I am able to produce this quote is testament to Kerry's successful performance. It is now memorialized on his Wikipedia page, an odd phenomenon for a city tabloid reporter. I did a quick search. None of my other former colleagues

---

* *News* and *Post* reporters and shooters often referred to assignments as "jobs," especially shooters. They might say, "I'm working a job out in Queens tonight." It thus follows that some of us occasionally referred to irrelevant assignments, or those we thought of as such, as "hand jobs."
† The phrase "report out" usually described the act of collecting the quotes, color, and information that would constitute a story—the legwork—whereas the act of telling that story was the "reporting" itself. One wouldn't say, "Kerry's in Bay Ridge reporting a homicide," but "Kerry's in Bay Ridge reporting out a homicide."

seem to have Wiki pages. That Kerry does speaks volumes—and also explains why Bravo flew him out to Los Angeles for the premiere.

For a young journalist, "Tabloid Wars" was, indeed, appointment TV. There was *News* editor-in-chief Michael Cooke swaggering to Bravo, "I get up in the morning, buckle on the sword and go out and fight the *Post*. They have no mercy, those people, and neither do we. We put our foot on their throat every day and press down 'til their eyes bulge and leak blood. And still they won't die. We'll just have to keep at it until they do die. And die they will!"[3]

Ironically, by the time Cooke's words aired on "Tabloid Wars," he'd been rendered a casualty of the very battle he'd so dramatically described. Cooke served as *Daily News* editor-in-chief from January 2005 to December 2005. Filming for "Tabloid Wars" wrapped in 2005 (autumn), and by the time the show aired in 2006, Martin Dunn had already replaced him.

The *Post's* Keith Kelly documented this palace intrigue in writing that Cooke invited his ouster by "pushing his apparent penchant for women's feet on to the daily's pages" and using out-of-town freelancers because he had "few friends in the Big Apple." Kelly's mean-spirited piece also noted the brevity—and diminutiveness—of Cooke's farewell gathering. "Yesterday," Kelly wrote on December 3, "Cooke took two top editors out to Uncle Jack's, a West Side steak house, but the meal, like Cooke's tenure, was brief. By 1:45 P.M. it was over."

But "Tabloid Wars" was also interesting for reasons other than its dramatization of a job infrequently dramatized. In fact, there was just a touch of conspiracy about the whole thing concerning its almost exclusive focus on the *News*. While the creators of the show have long insisted that they intended to portray only one of the city's tabloids in action, it was never definitively settled in many people's minds just why the *Post* was so rarely featured. But regardless of what actually transpired—or what may have been the reason—the *Post* took it as an opportunity to have a little fun on the *News'* account. In its TV guide insert, the *Post* labeled "Tabloid Wars" "Paid Programming" or "Special Olympics."[4]

The *New York Post* is located between 47th and 48th streets, along Sixth Avenue in a forty-five-story skyscraper that suggests—because of its column-like façade—a mini–Twin Tower. The address also housed, at the time of this writing, 21st Century Fox and other U.S. News Corp.

properties like "Fox News." Since 2007, or after Murdoch paid $5 billion for Dow Jones, the *Wall Street Journal* also called the building home. It has a courtyard, where Fox News personalities and print and TV reporters smoke and kibitz. Beyond the courtyard, along Sixth Avenue, is an NYP, or New York Press, zone where—on any given day—Geraldo Rivera might park his gaudy Rolls-Royce.

New York Press plates, I should say, are one of the most treasured perks of a runner. They entitle any vehicle so outfitted to be parked in marked NYP zones, usually located near the headquarters of a media outlet, but well dispersed throughout Manhattan. That one cannot otherwise park in Manhattan without outlandish difficulty is the reason why they are deemed so valuable. That being said, it's still laughable that Geraldo would attach an NYP plate—this emblem of shoe-leather journalism—to a Rolls-Royce. It's also reflective of a quirk in the plates' administration. While New York state's DMV required semi-annual review of a journalist's running bona fides in order to maintain the plates, New Jersey's did not. In fact, I once attended the funeral for a long-retired *Daily News* staffer who—like Geraldo—also lived in New Jersey. Abreast his coffin was an old-time typewriter—and his cherished NYP plate. The fellow, I believe, had been in his eighties, and his NYP number was something vintage, like "NYP 0016." It goes without saying that this retiree's running days had, like Geraldo's, long since concluded. Now, as an aside, I will confess that while it's been several years since I have run on any breaking New York City news, I am also from New Jersey and thus still enjoying—like Geraldo and the *Daily News* retiree—the NYP plates' benefits. I would, however, offer in my defense that my NYP plates are more tastefully attached to an early-model Nissan Pathfinder rather than anything so gaudy as a Rolls-Royce.

The *Daily News* lived less augustly than the *Post*, or at least in 2006. Until 1995, the tabloid was headquartered at the eponymous skyscraper on 42nd Street, off Second Avenue, which incidentally served as the model for the *Daily Planet* in the original *Superman* movies. It was for this reason some *Daily News* runners loved boasting to their *Post* counterparts that they ran for "Superman's Newspaper," and one actually wore the famous "S" T-shirt from time to time. In 1995, the *News* moved to West 33rd Street and Tenth Avenue, two avenues from Madison Square Garden on Manhattan's far West Side. It was a desolate area at the time, except for when the Jacob Javits Convention Center hosted an event, like "Comic Con" or the annual auto show. Today, Hudson Yards is gleaming, there, but back in the '90s former *News* shooter John Roca said hookers would brazenly assemble and flash their wares to motorists and pedestrians like a perverted version of the Rockettes.

Inside, the *News'* lobby, on the building's third of sixteen floors, was the size of a one-bedroom Manhattan apartment, or a large studio, at the far left of which a pair of glass push doors preempted a long, blue-carpeted hallway. Two somnolent armchairs, set at conversational angles, separated those doors from a security desk.

Through the push doors was a long portrait hallway lined with blow-ups of famous *Daily News* front pages, arranged in chronological order, beginning with the paper's first in 1919. That cover—it had something to do with World War I—yielded to the 1927 photo of Ruth Snyder's final moments. The Queens housewife was executed in the electric chair in New York state's Sing Sing prison for murdering her husband. The headline screamed "DEAD!" along with a caption describing the photo as "perhaps the most remarkable exclusive picture in the history of criminology." Interestingly, the method by which this photograph was captured is instructive in suggesting that the *News'* do-whatever-it-takes culture dates to its earliest days. Knowing that Sing Sing officials had banned photography in Snyder's execution chamber, the *News'* editors essentially outsourced the matter to a ringer whose face would be unknown to the prison's vigilant guards. Tom Howard—like an early-model Todd Maisel—was summoned from the *News'* sister paper, the *Chicago Tribune*. Then—and leveraging some tabloid artistry that seemed to inform runners' modern-day hijinks— he pulled off the impossible. Prison officials allowed Howard to witness the execution under the condition he not photograph it. So, Howard belted a miniature jury-rigged camera to his ankle and—seconds before the proverbial switch was flipped—hiked up his trouser leg to allow him a clear, successful, and surreptitious shot. The *News'* front-page photo was the result.[5]

After that and on the right hung the most famous modern-day *Daily News* front page, depicting a sour-faced President Gerald Ford under the bombastic headline, "FORD TO CITY: DROP DEAD." Ford had inspired the headline by conveying if not those exact words then the sentiment to New York City officials during the 1970s in denying their request for federal aid to mitigate a fiscal crisis. Somewhere near that front page hung the one the *News* published on September 12, 2001. The photo showed United Airlines Flight 175, or "the second plane," evaporating into a fireball upon collision with the World Trade Center's South Tower below the headline, "IT'S WAR!" Farther down, a front page showed an orgiastic Mark Messier hoisting the Stanley Cup in 1994 from the Madison Square Garden ice, moments after the New York Rangers had won the championship for the first time in fifty-four years.

Then the front pages yielded to plaques commemorating the *News*' ten Pulitzer Prizes. (It has since won its eleventh.) I always got goose bumps looking at the one for Mike McAlary's in 1998 for his Abner Louima columns. It showed McAlary squinty-eyed and mustachioed, like a Wild West gunslinger, and it must have been taken months before his death from colon cancer. As a former *News* writer and McAlary pal told me, the columnist had been facing death when he received the tip about a Haitian immigrant sodomized inside a Brooklyn NYPD squad house, and the resulting columns had lent him a measure of solace in the end.

Beyond the Pulitzers and at the hallway's end was a frosted-glass wall, beyond which was the conference room where editors convened for twice-daily editorial meetings. During the meeting's morning edition, that day's assignment editor presented to his colleagues the day's "sked," or schedule, of potential stories that reporters were pursuing. Editor-in-chief Martin Dunn was typically not present. But in the afternoon, when Dunn did attend, a whole other, more intense dynamic dominated. It was then that one of several editors presented the polished "sked," or menu of stories ready for publication. Around the time of my arrival, the job was performed by a young editor named Greg Gittrich.

Gittrich was an interesting case. He was in his early to mid-thirties and had rocketed to a position not even close to accordance with his age on the strength of a strong showing during 9/11 and an oversupply of ambition on the order of a comic book villain. He'd been a borough beat reporter before the attacks, covering education out of the Bronx, until he was repurposed full-time to 9/11 and its aftermath. He slept, I heard, in WNYC's downtown offices at 1 Centre Street that first, terrible night, filing dispatches by cell phone, and then couch-surfed for weeks, rarely going home. Afterward, and by the time "Tabloid Wars" aired, he helped run the city desk,and got so much airtime that the website Gawker referred to him in episode recaps as, "The Metro Muffin" or "This town's official working class hottie." (For the record, I'd describe Gittrich as a passable Edward Snowden—an impression that, oddly enough, is aided by the fact that they both speak with the same cadence and tone.) Maybe it was Gittrich's confidence that made Gawker think him sexy. He had enough of it to fill Yankee Stadium. And it was the best kind: quiet and seldom articulated. And I don't think it was necessarily misplaced. He routinely seemed one step ahead—and so much so that I began thinking of him as "the Great Gittrich." As the war with the *Post* progressed and digital eroded both tabloids' footholds, he'd make a decision that seemed stunning at the time but prophetic in retrospect. But back then, it was the little things Gittrich did that made him seem so clever. Tabloids, for instance, are usually despotically run enterprises over which the editor-in-chief presides like a tin pot dictator. Knowing this, Gittrich insisted that he—and he alone—present the "sked" to Dunn at the P.M. news meeting, around 3 o'clock, from which the top editor chose the stories that would constitute the following day's front page. He did this despite others in the room having overseen those stories during the day. (One would presume that they were thus better positioned to explain their nuances.) But by commandeering the process, Gittrich became a palace chamberlain through which information flowed to Dunn. He could thus subtly emphasize the merits of one story over those of another—and show favor to its editor while everyone else fumed at the slight. The matter came to a head when one editor insisted on making the case for a story to Dunn, herself. It was at this point that I and other rank-and-file reporters became aware of the situation.

At the "T" formed by the conference room, one could walk right to the features and business departments or left to the city desk, the walls of both passages ornamented with black-and-white photos of the *News* during its salad days. There were men in slacks; white shirts; big, wide scarf ties that looked more like the sort of napkin you'd tie around your neck when eating pasta; spit-shined shoes; suspenders; and slicked-back hairdos with enough pomade to hold down an elephant. They looked serious, they smoked, and there were no women. In one photo, Clark Gable, looking as debonair as a man ever looked, toured the presses. In another, John D. Rockefeller handed out nickels to children.

The *Daily News'* newsroom was as big and high-ceilinged as the six terminals at JFK Airport. Window film blocked natural light, so it felt a little like a casino, where they don't want you too aware of the time of day. A wooden clock hanging above the city desk that had stopped keeping time accentuated this sensation, and I later learned it had been ferried from the old 42nd Street digs and hung as a totem emblematic of the paper's storied past. The city desk was a horseshoe of desks where editors sat, although Dean and Dunn had glass-walled offices along the walls. Beyond this horseshoe was another laden with speakers. They crackled with white noise and the clipped voices of civil servants discussing the sort of tragedies that often involve dead people. On my first day at the paper, a baby-faced man sat behind this desk. He wore a three-piece suit and a matching fedora with a press card flush under its band. This was shooter Marc Hermann and, taken with the clock, he made me feel as if I had somehow fallen through a wormhole to the 1920s. In retrospect, that impression was appropriate, if not prescient, given all that would transpire over the coming twenty-four months and how those events would render us living anachronisms.

In one of those glass-walled offices I interviewed with city editor Dean Chang on October 18, 2006, seven years after beginning my career at the conclusion of university. I was twenty-nine years old and had passed my career anonymously to that point at smaller dailies in the wilds of New Jersey: an eighteen-month run at *The Jersey Journal* in Jersey City; a five-year stint at the *Press of Atlantic City*; then finally the break for which I had long hoped. A former editor at *The Jersey Journal*—a Greg Wilson—had some years earlier made the leap to the big-time city dailies and by that point he had attained a posting as an assistant editor on the *News'* city desk. He petitioned Chang on my behalf. Now, a bit of context. The city editor of the New York *Daily News* is an august title in the rolls of American journalism—and one that carries an even greater footprint in the city of New York. It was once said that the mayor—I don't recall which—had phoned the desk on some matter and requested its chief, only to be told roughly, "He'll have to call you back." And so it was that for many months I petitioned Chang through snail-mailed clips and résumés in full expectation that it would take considerable toil in order to grab his attention. Once I arrived in New York in May 2006 with a posting as a staff editor at a trade magazine, I resumed the assault by phoning him at the city desk at exactly 12:30 P.M. every Wednesday, or when I had neurotically calculated he'd be least occupied. He never took the calls, and for twelve consecutive Wednesdays I left voicemails. I didn't know whether he listened. It just seemed like something to do, so that one might sleep well at night, years later, knowing he had done everything possible to achieve an ambition.

But, as it happened, Chang was listening. On the thirteenth Wednesday, I forgot to call only to realize my oversight later that evening. I rang the city desk about 6:30, now more out of habit than hope. But this time, Chang answered—and with a cheerful "Hi, Mike," even though I had not yet introduced myself. I stammered through asking him how it was that he knew it had been me when we had not yet spoken. He replied, "I've been listening to your voicemails for three months and I know the sound of your voice." Then he did something strange: He rebuked me for calling later than my usual afternoon time. I laughed at what I interpreted as an obvious joke. But Chang did not laugh in sympathy.

After that, the editor offered me a weekend billet as a runner, and I clearly recall my "try-out"—a weekend audition that began with pre–8 A.M. calls to the city desk on both Saturday and Sunday. On the first, assistant city editor Sal Arena dispatched me to Manhattan's St. Vincent's Hospital on a quest "for words" from a DVD bootlegger stabbed the prior night. The *News* had run a brief that morning, but now Sal wanted the bootlegger's account. Now, I should note here that sneaking into a hospital was not a method I had seen applied to that point, although I didn't question it. Truthfully, I would have snuck into an Army base had Sal asked me. It was just that sort of Bud Fox moment—the one where Charlie Sheen's character is waiting outside Gordon Gekko's office. Almost personally existential.

And it worked! I gave the hospital guard my name and was rewarded with Wayne Buckle's room number. I still recall the relief I felt when I entered his room and discovered a *Daily News* on the table. Clearly, he was a reader who would love to talk! Not so. The man screwed up his face, folded his arms—as much as his wounds would allow—and demanded a correction. What, I asked, was wrong? "I am *not* a DVD bootlegger!" he roared. "I am a filmmaker . . . and I've worked with Martin Scorsese." Quickly, I did the mental arithmetic that yielded an obvious answer. Buckle had read the paper that contained the brief in which the *News* had referred to him as a "bootlegger," and this had offended his professional pride. But I also knew that the *News* would never publish such a correction, and I hardly wanted to begin my try-out with such an outlandish request. So, I promised him earnestly that I would "do my best," and this proved enough to encourage him to provide the sought-after account. I should say I never did ask Sal for that correction—or even mention Buckle's protest.

I was still running in this weekend freelance capacity by early October, when on the 11th, the Catholic blog *Whispers in the Loggia* published an anonymous letter that was just then circulating among New York City Archdiocese priests. The letter was nothing short of a bombshell, calling for a no-confidence vote in Archbishop Edward Cardinal Egan. By Saturday, or three days after Loggia's account, no New York City media outlet had managed to get a single city priest to confirm its accusations on the record. Then on Sunday, October 15, both the *Times* and the *Post* quoted a Monsignor Howard Calkins as endorsing its central premise: that Egan's tenure had been marred by "dishonesty, deception, disinterest and disregard," as the letter had put it. *News* assignment editor John Oswald seized on this get in ordering me to Sacred Heart Church in Mt. Vernon, where Calkins acted as parish priest and regional vicar for thirteen Westchester County parishes.

Calkins did not want to speak with me. But I convinced him to do so on the strength of my Catholic past, including service as an altar boy, and a Catholic education that included a single year at Notre Dame. (I embellished this to four years in convincing Calkins.)

Calkins did speak—and said too much. He excoriated the cardinal in far harsher terms than he had in either his *Times* or *Post* interviews. He linked the letter to Egan's handling of the molestation scandal then roiling the Church. Then, realizing he had said too much, the priest appealed to the same Catholic heritage I had leveraged in convincing him to speak. He pleaded for me to censor the interview. Calkins, even then, knew or had an inkling of the consequences of what he had said. I accommodated him, but only superficially and without sincerity. When it came to the really juicy quotes, I told him, "No."

On Monday, the *News* published its story and Calkins tendered his resignation as vicar to Egan. Egan, meanwhile, held a meeting at St. Patrick's Cathedral, after which top priests issued a scathing condemnation of the letter. That same evening, Oswald invited me to formally interview with Chang in the glass-walled office two days later, on a Wednesday. I did so successfully, and after I had obtained my aim, a full-time job with the *News*, I called Calkins to see if he was okay. I felt bad. He was not available, and I left a voicemail. He did not return the call, and I have often wondered what became of him.

4

"Cops Shoot Groom Dead"

Daily News headline, November 26, 2006

THROUGHOUT OCTOBER AND NOVEMBER of 2006, the *News* and the *Post* battled in the boroughs—and beyond. "'SERIAL' SLAUGHTER—STRANGLING EYED IN 4 SLAYS AS ATLANTIC CITY STEPS UP HUNT"; "WHO GUITARIST SIRIUS-LY TICKED, WALKS OUT ON STERN"; "FALAFEL SLAY STUNS KIN. 'I FEEL EMPTY,' SEZ VICTIM'S BROTHER."

On October 14, *Post* runner Jana Winter snuck into Apt. 41FG of the Belaire high-rise on East 72nd Street and snapped photos of the ashen, twisted havoc inside. A week earlier, a small plane piloted by Yankee pitcher Cory Lidle had crashed into the unit. "INSIDE FIREY CRASH HELL; SCORCHED RUIN & RUBBLE WITHIN HIGH-RISE HOLE." Two weeks later, on October 30, the *Post*'s "Page Six" reported that New York state's married Comptroller Alan Hevesi had been caught "canoodling" with city Councilwoman Melinda Katz. The next day, the *News* ridiculed the *Post*'s account. "*POST* LASHED FOR ALL-WET 'CANOODLE' . . . CONTROLLER, POL DENY AFFAIR STORY." That rebuttal quoted Katz as saying she had to look up *canoodling* to grasp how badly the *Post* had gotten it wrong.

The headlines continued: "'SUPER BIGOT' . . . NAOMI 'ATTACK' MAID: SHE HATES ROMANIANS"; "WHEN YOU GOTTA GOYA, YOU GOTTA GOYA—BANDITS GRAB ART AS MOVERS MAKE 'P' STOP." On November 18 a "crooked Westchester lawyer" who lived three doors from Bill and Hillary Clinton fatally shot his wife—then claimed that a mysterious gunman had ambushed their car. "W'CHESTER WHACKER—LAWYER DECKS TV MAN FOR ASKING: DID YOU KILL HER?" "BURB-SLAY ATTORNEY BLOWS TOP. ATTACKS REPORTERS OUTSIDE W'CHESTER POLICE STATION."

51

Then on November 25 came "a story to stop the city," as Mike McAlary had written in the final line of his initial column on the 1997 Louima assault. Police outside a Queens strip club killed an African American man named Sean Bell on his wedding day. He was twenty-three, unarmed, and celebrating his bachelor party. The facts, as they drip-drip-dripped into print over the overwrought and occasionally dangerous winter, indicated that a fight outside the Kalua Club between Bell and another man preceded the shooting. An undercover NYPD officer, part of a prostitution probe into the club, heard Bell say, "Let's fuck him up," to which Bell's pal, Joseph Guzman, allegedly replied, "Yo—go get my gun." One cop warned his colleagues, "It's getting hot on Liverpool [Street], for real, I think there's a gun."[1]

At this point, Bell, Guzman, pal Trent Benefield—and possibly a fourth "mystery man"—disengaged en route to Bell's 1999 Nissan Altima. Two undercovers confronted them. The cops claimed they brandished a badge. Guzman and Benefield disputed this account—and said they believed they were carjackers. Bell never spoke, because after roaring from the curb, brushing one officer, slamming into an unmarked police van, reversing course, then slamming into a building, reversing again and driving toward the van once more, he was hit with four of a total of fifty shots fired by five officers. Guzman took nineteen shots and Benefield three, but they survived. Afterward, the NYPD's Giscard Isnora claimed that Guzman had reached for his waistband, possibly to retrieve a gun, while Bell peeled rubber.

From November 26, 2006, until New Year's Day, the *News* published forty stories, fourteen columns, and four op-eds on Sean Bell, and the *Post* thirty-eight stories and four columns—almost as if the two opposing papers kept score as a function of ink spilled.

"MEET THE COPS BEHIND BULLETS" . . . "QUEENS SHOOTING RULES TALK-SHOW AIRWAVES" . . . "BRIDES'S FAREWELL: 'NO, NO, SEAN!' SHE CRIES AS PROTESTORS RAGE IN QNS" . . . "SEEDY CLUB'S LONG HISTORY OF SLEAZE" . . . "POLICE ON GUARD AFTER DEATH THREATS" . . . "KIN WEEP AMID HOLY HELL FROM AL & JESSE" . . . "PROBERS HUNT GUY NAMED MO: ROUNDUP FOR COP-SHOOT '4TH MAN'" . . . "WE WANT ANSWERS." KIN, MIKE TALK; "FIANCE SHOPS FOR RITES DRESS" . . . "REV. AL'S RALLY CRY: REMEMBER DIALLO."*

---

* Four plainclothes NYPD officers fired upon and killed Amadou Diallo on February 4, 1999, in a hail of forty-one shots outside his Bronx home after mistaking the unarmed twenty-three-year-old for a serial rapist.

News and *Post* runners foraged for gets at Jamaica Hospital, where Bell's body was brought; at the Kalua Club; in the Queens projects where the NYPD hunted the "mystery man"; at Bell's parents' home and that of his would-be bride, Nicole Paultre; at Community Church of Christ, where Nicole and Sean were to have wed. Runners attended Sean's wake. We braced mourners. We catalogued details—the suit in which he was buried (black, pinstriped), his casket (black, open, and engraved with an inscription). *Post* runner Doug Montero lingered over it on the prayer line to note its eternal message from his would-be widow and two kids: "Love always, Nicole, Jada, and Jordan." The *News* runner got it, too—and noted the red carnation pinned to the deceased's lapel. A tabloid stalemate.

We collected "money quotes" about racial injustice at the 103rd Precinct, where the New Black Panther Party rallied and jeered cops. Shooters photographed—"made" in the parlance—Nicole going into Brooklyn Civil Court to legally change her name to "Paultre-Bell." Two *News* and *Post* runners were there to document the drama—and coax quotes from our damsel.

We waited outside Queens' Mary Immaculate Hospital while Guzman and Benefield mended inside. There, a column of news trucks perpetually idled curbside, poisoning the fall air as if their drivers harbored a shared and secret objection to shutting off the engines. The becalmed caravan measured a city block; and in the evenings, a benighted polyglot of TV reporters decamped to stand under oval lights for 6 and 7 o'clock "live shots." On those nights, you *felt* the city's axis turning on the story and felt as if you stood at the pole—even though the *News'* and the *Post's* runner–shooter teams mostly passed time, warily sitting in cars, leaning on cars, reading the paper, smoking cigarettes, laughing with hilarity born from tension. Running is often waiting. You run in place. This is the tabloid stakeout.

The concept of a stakeout is foreign to most papers, but the *News* and the *Post* were different. They possessed not only the resources to station runner/shooter teams in a single place for days, weeks, and even months at a time, but also the existential fear of losing that is an equal prerequisite for such madness. I say this because I know that securing a scoop was often the secondary goal of a stakeout—subordinate to guarding against the rival tabloid's obtaining one. In a vacuum, neither paper would have employed the method with such regularity or absurd commitment. But amid a tabloid death match, editors far preferred having to explain a misallocation of runners than a bad beat. No one lost their job because they'd left a reporter to languish—even for weeks! Editors *were* dismissed because they'd yielded an exclusive to the "enemy" because they hadn't kept a runner in place.

Runners often felt on such assignments as if they'd fallen into a Twilight Zone quasi-existence—the "Tabloid Zone," as we put it—of watching the same house or hospital for seven, fifteen, even forty-five days running, the house often occupied by an uncooperative resident or, worse, empty of anyone at all. And only because the *Post* or the *News* was there, too, and some editor feared the impossible might happen. It was the cold part of our otherwise white-hot tabloid war—and cause for *News* shooter Joe Marino to humorously riff on a line from *The Hunt for Red October*. In the movie, the defector Soviet submarine captain Marko Ramius, played by Sean Connery, describes the actual Cold War in saying, "Forty years I've been at war. A war with no battles, no monuments . . . only casualties." But Joe—especially while on stakeout—would subtly adapt this phrase to the *News–Post* showdown and the duration of his own tenure at the paper: "Three years I've been at war. A war with no stories. No quotes. No photos . . . only stakeouts." He'd say as much, of course, while speaking in a Brooklyn-laced Connery brogue.

But just because a stakeout lacked logic doesn't mean it didn't have rules. Because even the *News* and the *Post* recognized the necessity of sleep, runners relied on sportsmanship to conclude a day's stakeout until returning for another. It worked like this: You would call your desk and plead with your editor to allow you to go home. The editor would hem and haw and then reluctantly oblige—but only on the condition that your counterpart agreed to do so as well. Then you broached "a deal" with the other paper's runner, who repeated the process with their own desk. Once consensus was reached, you shook hands—"You actually did it!"— and vowed, with degrees of solemnity, "not to return until the following day." Some runners, of course, violated the vow—but the taboo carried its own punishment. You were never trusted, again, to make such sanity-saving deals—and so would have to remain at the next stakeout, theoretically forever, or until relief arrived, which often amounted to the same thing.

Outside Mary Immaculate, the first days after Bell's death were filled with fleshy quotes from relatives, friends, ministers, hangers-on, passersby, and whoever the *News* and *Post* could corral. But afterward, the story devolved into journalistic trench warfare. Quickly, the hospital got wise to the *News* and the *Post* sneaking upstairs to search for Benefield's and Guzman's recovery rooms. Security tightened, and so we contented ourselves with daily updates on their conditions, the early ones rendered by a Dr. Cooper and later ones by Rev. Al Sharpton, or his attorney Michael Hardy. In the absence of facts, speculation prevailed. One morning, I reported that Guzman was on a respirator. By afternoon, the friends who liberally afforded themselves the title "family spokesperson" said that he'd recovered. Another afternoon, we debated whether Bell's almost-widow had discarded her engagement ring in favor of a wedding band. (She'd visited but had been photographed at such a range we couldn't tell.) There was a thirst for news—and little in the way of fact to quench it.

My counterpart was *Post* runner John Mazor. He was late-twenties handsome, blessed with swoon-worthy biceps, a world-class jawline, and a Kirk Douglas dimple. Up top, he wore stylishly mussed dark brown hair of the like gel companies would love to have you believe is an easily achieved effect. And he had a drawl, one that conveyed long afternoons swathed in seersucker on Victorian porches—or until he confided that he was from the Northeast.

His photographer, most days, was Ellis Kaplan, peculiar even by the inflated standards of peculiarity applied to city tabloid shooters. He was an aging Jewish man who lived with his mother and spoke with a nebbishy Brooklyn twang that should be recorded and preserved in some archive as the model on which all replicas are based. He had a shock of gray-blond hair combed across a fallow scalp and wore big, thick, Coke-bottle glasses that seemed so flamboyantly unstylish as to be an intentional repudiation of style—and thus stylish. But it was Ellis's outrageous rebellions against the type that set him apart. He drove a Hummer! And he had guns! Lots of guns! I'd never asked him about his arsenal, but it was legendary through the reports of runners he had told, or those who had seen it.

The *News* alternated photographers. Some days it was Joel Cairo, a tall, slim shooter suggestive not only in body type—but disposition—of those wild inflatables with the waving arms posted outside auto dealerships. He loved to quote *Mad Max 2: The Road Warrior*, feeling, I believed, some sense of strained kinship with a man who also drove maniacally in desperate pursuit of a commodity in limited, yet great demand. *Gimme your petrol! I mean gimme a quote!* He also occasionally wore a gorilla mask on prolonged stakeouts. Other days it was Nick Fevelo, a twenty-something Staten Island Italian cursed with artistic ambitions, who brooded and looked like he moonlighted in a boy band. Together we passed the time like retired men—reading papers, smoking, and prattling. One night, I played Hangman with a *Times* staffer who had crashed the stakeout for only a single day. I went first and picked "EMERGENCY ROOM." She guessed it before the guy on the scaffold wheezed. Then she chose a ten-letter stumper—"PERFIDIOUS"—that would have hanged an octopus. Cairo, ensconced languidly in the front seat, annexed my outrage.

"I've never even heard that word! What does it mean?"

"Evil," the *Times*woman interjected, to which Cairo grimly replied, "Yeah? Like someone who would choose the word 'perfidious' in Hangman?"

Haw! Haw! Haw!

And so it went, day after day, the stress of remaining perpetually in a cobra's coil, on the precipice of action, growing until you'd laugh like a hyena—like a madman—at anything at all. Or until I ended it all with aid of stray observation made by—of all people—Ellis.

December 3, 2006

Mary Immaculate Hospital looked like Resorts Casino in Atlantic City—or some other grand, early-twentieth-century hotel. It was seven stories of brick fronting 89th Avenue with two crocodile arms and small, boxy windows arranged, symmetrically, at short intervals. Except for the first floor. That was stone and gothic with a *House of Usher*–looking crest hovering, ominously, above an arched threshold. It had Latin engraving and stained glass and looked, suspiciously, like the adornment to a mausoleum, or some horror-filled nineteenth-century asylum. It was nothing you would want to see if you were being wheeled into the facility—and certainly not if you were visiting a loved one there.

Ellis Kaplan stood across the street, on 89th Avenue, and mulled the shooter's dilemma. He had to pee—but couldn't risk going to a restroom in case a shot presented itself. Usually such conundrums were solved by one of two solutions—either rely on the *News* shooter to cover for you, or a pee cup. In this case, Ellis was being snobby about the pee cup and Cairo was acting cagey about covering, although probably just to toy with Ellis to pass time.

Then he looked at me—and only me—because Cairo and Mazor were ten or so yards away. He said, "I wonder what that door is over there." He nodded. I followed his chin. It went to a spot to the far left of the hospital, or to the modern annex that seemed glued on to the old brick building by a *porte-cochère*. It was set back from the street by a weedy forecourt. Ellis didn't pursue this train of thought likely because he was occupied with more urgent, personal matters. I did and filed away the detail for reproduction once Mazor went foraging for dinner that evening and left me alone.

I crossed the forecourt and opened the door with a pneumatic whoosh. It was the ambulatory clinic—and once inside I passed a reception desk, decisively and with aplomb. (Runner's tradecraft: Always look like you belong and *never, ever* give them the chance to stop you.) I entered a hallway and wandered until finding the main lobby's elevator bank. I saw the security desk and its guard. But I was staring at her from behind and she, sublimely, did not turn around. I pushed the "up" button with fugitive desperation. An elevator opened and I entered. Nobody ever willed a door to close so frantically.

I knew the floor on which Benefield roomed. One of his posse had betrayed the number during negotiations that had concluded, comically, with a demand for $10,000—or "10 stacks," as he put it, for a photo. Upon arriving, I found his room as the fourth on the left after entering a ward through a pair of push doors. He and his posse had it to themselves. They got silent. Quick. It was the Blue Oyster Bar scene from *Police Academy*.

"What are you doin' here, white boy?" one mockingly asked. I told him I'd been strolling the ward and chanced upon Trent's room. I said, "Trent," like we knew each other. *Haw! Haw! Haw!* One laughed. But he quickly got quiet before a wall of reproachful stares. I then explained how long I'd been in front of the hospital and how badly I—and the rest of New York— wanted to know what "Mr. Benefield" (I switched to the formal) had to say.

"You bring the 10 stacks?" It was the same "advisor" with whom Fevelo and I had negotiated. I mumbled, "Not really," then told him I wanted to first hear what he would say. But the kid must have worked on the school newspaper. He said, "Sure," but, "everything my man has to say has to be off the record." And while I would have agreed, Benefield would have none of it. He reared up in bed and told me, "Fuck off, cracker." To come back with the 10 grand. The rest of the room took his cue and grew hostile. I willed myself out.

Back at my car, Mazor asked where I'd been and I tripped over an explanation of going for coffee; then a labored apology for not having asked if he'd wanted one. It sounded the way apologies do when you lie to a beggar about not having any change. Then I kept to myself. I had to. We sat next to each other in the gloaming as if nothing had changed and me, half-knowing and half-hoping everything was about to.

December 4, 2006

Eighty-ninth Avenue never looked so empty as it did early the following morning when I got out of my car and trundled across the no man's land pavilion separating the street from the ambulatory clinic door. It wasn't day and it wasn't quite night, an inky, blue-jean sky with clouds that looked like bruises. The clinic was electric-lit. This time, I risked a smile to the receptionist. She smiled back. I continued to the elevator and then to Benefield's floor.

When I got to the room, it was empty and the index card with his name was gone. I searched down the hall. No Benefield. But something better. When I first saw the name on this index card, I didn't believe it. I stood there, suspicious, and imagining the scene to come. Then I entered the room. The card had, miraculously, read, "Joseph Guzman."

He lay in bed with a sheet pulled to his chest. His eyes were closed and he looked peaceful. It was him, all right. But also not him, as I'd seen him in photos. He looked drawn. Two others were in the room. One—Eboni Browning, his pregnant fiancée—hovered at his bedside. She looked cheerful with a wry grin nestled between chestnut cheeks. The other woman perched her equally large girth on the ledge below the room's lone window and glared. Browning spoke first. She asked, "You snuck in, didn't you?"

I launched into my pitch to Guzman, basically a lot of improvised pleading. I told him the city was on edge; things "looked awfully bad out there" and "the situation might spiral out of control." Could he appeal to the people? Settle things down? Eboni Browning answered for him. "Yes," she said, provided no photos were taken. I nodded and sat opposite her, across from Guzman's bed. I asked if he had a message for those who would take matters into their own hands. He rasped, "I don't want any violence. No violence, man. No violence. Not in my name." I asked about Sean Bell and he reached, dramatically, over the nickel mesh sides of his bed, took my clammy hand in his own, and said, "You could put this in the newspaper: I took 16 shots,* but a superstar died that night . . . A superstar. I loved him."

"Joe," I said. "There's one thing everyone wants to know. It's the biggest thing. Did any of those cops I.D. themselves as officers? Did anyone show a badge?"

"No way, man. Never! No one showed me shit and anyone who says differently is a liar."

When I got outside, Sal Arena, an editor, answered my call to the city desk.

"Sal, I got 'em!" I howled.

"You got who, Mike?"

"Guzman!"

"No kidding? Was the *Post* there?"

---

* Guzman's tally of "16 shots" was three shy of the reported figure.

"Got him alone!"

"Great," he said and then added something I hadn't expected. "Were you with photo?"

The question hit me like a cocktail in the face. It took me ten seconds to mumble what should have taken two.

"You have to go back," he said.

"That was one of their conditions," I mumbled.

"Conditions?"

I feebly told him. He cared as much as a traffic cop when you tell him it's an emergency. They're going to write the summons. It's just a matter of how much dignity you're going to waste before accepting the ticket and they say, "Thanks. Drive safely."

"Hold for Corky," Sal said. "You'll dump to him. Photo will be there, shortly . . . and don't tell anybody. Keep this quiet the rest of the day. Don't say a word about it at all."

I muttered something about the possibility of arrest, but the line was already dead. So, I stood, there, on 89th Avenue, seemingly staring at the phone, until Cairo arrived, grinning. When he saw me, the laughter he'd been nursing came pouring out of his nose.

"Jacko! What's the scene? Or do I not want to know?"

I started to comply, but he interrupted by ask-declaring, "Ya know what we should do? Kidnap Guzman. We could *make* him talk."

I told him that wouldn't be necessary, that Guzman had already "talked."

Cairo frowned his disappointment, although it proved only a momentary discouragement. He nodded vaguely toward the rear of his vehicle and advised, "We need to create a diversion to get into the hospital. I got Roman Candles in my trunk. How 'bout that?"

At this moment, Cairo's face looked like one of those caricatures they draw in Times Square for $15—the features comically distorted.

"Save the candles," I told him. "We need a picture. I already got words and a way in. You got a point-and-shoot?"

He nodded and showed me the small, nonprofessional camera hidden in his coat pocket. He showed it to me the way TV characters do the butt of a concealed gun. I briefed him on both our mission and what I'd already done, although describing it made it seem a lot more dramatic than it actually had been. When I had finished, Cairo pondered, then asked: "So . . . Guzman doesn't want a photo, but we're gonna shoot him, anyway, after he gave us a scoop?"

Then Cairo punctuated his own question with more guffaws. *Haw! Haw! Haw!* "I still think we should kidnap him!"

After that, we crossed the weedy forecourt toward the clinic door. For a moment, I felt disembodied and as if I was watching myself from above.

The room was just as before, only now the second woman was eating a pork chop. Why anyone would eat a pork chop in a hospital, much less that early in the morning, is beyond me—although this detail, in subsequent re-tellings, has assumed an oversized importance relative to its actual role. It's not that I spent too much time considering the pork chop. I was too absorbed telling Eboni Browning and Joseph Guzman that while I knew I wasn't permitted to take photos, I would have to nonetheless. At this point, Cairo burst into the room with his point-and-shoot and "blasted" Guzman, like a Hollywood blackmailer photographing a star with his pants around his ankles. I'd gone in first to ensure that Guzman was still in bed and no one else—say, a nurse—was present to interfere with our stratagem.

What happened next was ridiculous.

The second woman dropped the pork chop and yelled, "Oh no you didn't!" Eboni Browning looked stunned and Guzman raised his arms, as if to hoist himself out of bed, although he was still too weak to do so. Cairo yelled, "I got it!" and we hustled through the ward. The second woman waddled after us, holding the pork chop. She was pointing it at us and demanding, "Stop them! They're getting away! Don't let them get away!"

Matters came to a head at the elevator bank, where Cairo and I found none open. A nurse caught up, as well as our pork chop–toting pursuer. The former requested an explanation; the latter excoriated us while emphasizing her disgust with—of course—the chop. She waved it and poked Cairo with it—all the while demanding our arrest. The nurse asked who we were, and we identified ourselves as journalists for the *Daily News*.

"Wait here," she said and returned to the ward. We didn't wait. I booked into a stairwell and took flights four steps at a time. Cairo followed, although we were separated for reasons that now elude me. I found him, though. He stood on the sidewalk, off the hospital's property line, with a look of atypical seriousness across his comedic features. When I asked him what was wrong, he replied, "I told you we should have kidnapped him."

Two hours afterward, the majority of the interim spent standing next to my car with Mazor, I labored to look as if nothing had transpired that morning. It was hard work. He had conveniently arrived twenty minutes after all the shit with Cairo had gone down. Now, Cairo called and I stepped away with the excuse that it was my desk. Cairo said four words and hung up. *Jacko, I got it.* The photo had been taken with a camera that did not allow for the evaluation of photos without the aid of a device. Cairo had returned to Manhattan to see if our hijinks had succeeded. He told me the photo was good.

The following day's story was a two-page spread on pages 4 and 5. It ran fifteen inches under a 20-point headline that blared, "PAL OF SEAN BEGS, 'NO VIOLENCE.' SURVIVOR OF POLICE SHOOTING CALLS BELL A SUPER-STAR." The lede read, "Whispering from his hospital bed, police shooting survivor Joseph Guzman yesterday called on New Yorkers outraged by the death of his pal Sean Bell to refrain from violence." The story ran under a large, grainy photo of Guzman in bed, shocked and with arms outstretched for reasons that were, thankfully, not articulated.

5

▪▪▪

"N.J. Miss in a Fix Over Her Pics!"

New York Post headline, July 6, 2007

THAT MARCH, the deadliest fire in New York City in seventeen years killed
ten people, including nine children, after a row home went ablaze in the
Bronx. For weeks, the *News* and the *Post* documented first the horror—the
charred rubble, the charred corpses, witness accounts of children hurled
from top-floor windows—then, later, its aftermath: funerals, hospital vigils,
anecdotes about the dead. Both the *News and* the *Post* sent runners to
Mali, the immigrant victims' native West African country. The tabloid war
was the story behind the story, the one the public never read.

Tabloid madness bookended the fire. On February 5, NASA astronaut
Lisa Nowak was arrested in Orlando for the attempted kidnapping of a
romantic rival. She'd driven 900 miles from Houston—allegedly wearing
"space diapers"—to enact the crime. "LUST IN SPACE . . . ASTRO-NUT
FACES SLAY-BID RAP . . . SHOCK TALE OF TRIANGLE." The day that story
broke, Anna Nicole Smith died in Florida—sending both the *News* and
the *Post* on a month-long odyssey from her death scene in Hollywood to
her burial site in the Bahamas. Days afterward, Britney Spears alighted on
a made-to-order tabloid meltdown highlighted by the public shaving of her
head and the assault of a car with an umbrella. "SHEAR MADNESS . . . BALD
BRITNEY A BUZZ KILL." Then the fire. Then the indictment of three of the
Sean Bell cops. A day after a grand jury handed up the true bill, the *Post*
tailed Detective Mike Oliver, one of those indicted, to a Madison Avenue
eatery and exclusively reported he'd "dined on truffles and downed bottles

of $875 wine." "RAP PARTY . . . '50 SHOT' COP IN $4,200 BASH AFTER INDICMENT." The *News* ate crow.

Then, on April 30, the Audit Bureau of Circulation (ABC) issued the first of its two biannual industry trade group reports on the circulation of the nation's largest newspapers. The numbers revealed that the *Post* had notched a weekday circulation of 724,748 for the six months ending March 31. That represented a 7.6 percent year-over-year jump, enough to maintain its unprecedented edge over the *News*. The *News*, meanwhile, posted a 1.4 percent increase and weighed in at 718,174. Serious advantage to the *Post*.[1] But, typically, the victory wasn't good enough. The *Post* needed to kick its rival while it was down. On May 2, Keith Kelly—the *Post's* media columnist—published a story accusing the *News* of juicing its figures with "bulk sales" to third-party sponsors, as well as schools, which would then give the paper away for free as handouts or class materials. This sort of "junk" circulation, Kelly charged, was used to conceal a "single-copy sales disaster" in the *News'* paid circulation. "BULK FICTION—DAILY SNOOZE'S USE OF BULK SALES MASKS DROP." Graciously, if not a touch late, Kelly confessed in the second-to-last paragraph that the *Post* had also incorporated such "bulk copies" into its own circulation—only less than the *News*.

That same morning, April 30, the *News* proved that tabloid turnabout is fair play. Days earlier, it had gotten wind from loose-lipped distributors that the chest-thumping *Post* secretly intended to emphasize its impending circulation victory by concluding the long, grinding price war it had begun with the *News* in September 2000. That day, the *News* learned, the *Post* would double its newsstand cost in Manhattan to 50 cents, the same price for which the *News* sold. Now the *News* preempted the *Post* with a blindside slashing of its own price to 25 cents.[2] The result was disastrous for the *Post*. Over the eight weekdays it sold for 50 cents and the *News* for 25 cents, its sales at high-volume Manhattan outlets dropped 20 percent. Meanwhile, sales of the *News* spiked 30 percent over the same period.[3] On May 10, the *Post* capitulated, returning to 25 cents. The *News*, victorious, returned to 50 cents. Col Allan tried to save face, insisting, "The *Post* strategy is well calculated and is working as we had expected it to." But wiser observers knew better. As *Crain's New York Business* noted, plenty of people like the *Post*, but "thousands of readers like the paper only well enough to pay a quarter for it."[4] Martin Dunn, the *News'* newly installed editor-in-chief, was less diplomatic: "We did seven years of [their] being half our price, and they could barely give it seven days. All of a sudden they're squealing like a pig stuck on a skewer."

June 10, 2007

New York City in the summertime can have a pleasantly vacant feeling. Everyone is out of town, gone to the Hamptons, the Jersey Shore, even Virginia Beach. You can stroll Fifth Avenue without your eyes locked in front of you for fear of colliding with the person a stride ahead. You can obtain a reservation at a fashionable restaurant and even, once there, a good table with a window. You can make it crosstown in under ninety minutes and—if the stars align—successfully hail a taxi in a less-than-obvious place. The bars are empty, the club lines short. Sometimes, on a weekend like that, you'll actually come to feel sort of lucky at having stayed behind and don't much mind not having boast-worthy plans in some faraway place. And sometimes, you can even approach a very beautiful girl in Union Square Park for absolutely no reason at all and not be met with a contemptuous and scornful reply that will haunt you. I missed all that running for the *News*. And I never felt its loss for even a second. I was involved in a war with a real enemy. And I was chasing gets.

On Sunday morning, June 10, I found myself on the third floor of a mausoleum in St. John's Cemetery in Queens, sitting not forty feet from the crypt containing John Gotti's remains. An editor once said three things reliably move tabloid product in New York: the Giants, the Yankees, and Gotti. The don had been dead now five years—to the day—and the *News* still thought spying on whoever came to pay their respects would make an outstanding story.

The room was a good one to pray in, although I only pretended to do so after saying a few obligatory words to Gotti. I told him I had read books about him and enjoyed them. There didn't seem much else to say, but it felt odd to stand before a famous person's crypt without saying anything at all. I'd brought the *News* and stole peeks in between fake prayers. The room was the size of a city bus with vacuumed forest-green carpeting and a divan bookended by ornately carved end tables on which sat the sort of lamps you'd find in the main branch of the New York City Public Library. Soft light—and not much of it—fell on marble walls engraved with the names of the interred and their lifespans, in John's case 1940 to 2002.

Outside, The *News'* north Brooklyn shooter, Debbie Egan-Chin, waited in her *News*-issued Chevy Malibu, parked far enough from the building that anyone coming to see Gotti would not suspect the *News* runner waiting inside. She was, however, parked close enough to "make them" going in with her long lens.

Deb was a mother of two young children who looked as Irish as her maiden name suggested, with pale, freckled skin; red-blond hair; a contagious smile; an easily evoked laugh; and eyes that twinkled. She was good. Very good—and coveted among runners going on contested out-of-town jobs—and often tapped by the photo desk to do battle with the *Post* far afield of New York City. She was among the female minority in the *News'* and the *Post's* street corps. I'd say the percentage ran 80–20 percent male, although, frankly, one's gender was never discussed. In three-and-a-half years on the street, I never heard a runner or shooter reference another runner's or shooter's gender. It didn't matter. What we did discuss—often and obsessively—was competency, as in ranking the top five runners and shooters on the street, or playing the stakeout game of "If you're going out of town to fight the *Post* (or the *News*) what shooter are you picking to go with you?"

Most of the women on the street dressed in a gender-neutral fashion. Denim. Sneakers. Shorts. (Shooters could dress more casually than runners, because they didn't have to interview anyone.) Deb often wore Crocs. In the winter, she wore a snow suit. Female runners and shooters didn't discuss boyfriends, husbands, beauty, or anything like that. It was for them as it was for all of us—all about running. All about the job. All about beating the *News* or the *Post*.

About forty minutes passed, and then the woman for whom I had been waiting sat across from John's crypt. She wore a black dress, black jacket, tortoise-shell sunglasses, and enough hair dye to poison a reservoir. She didn't bless herself and I didn't see her mouth moving. Whatever Victoria Gotti had to say to her late husband was communicated through her thoughts alone. Not once did she look at me. Then she got up and walked toward the stairwell, through an arched passageway. I followed and approached her only after she got outside and chatted with Deb and a late-arriving *Post* runner who had been waiting outside the crypt as well. The city desk's plan, hatched the night before, to arrive long before the *Post*, infiltrate the crypt, and exclusively spy on Victoria, had worked. When the *Post* had arrived, Deb played dumb over her runner's whereabouts. Now, she feigned surprise that I'd been upstairs. It was a minor victory—but wins over the *Post* were made of less.

The win, albeit a small one, was welcome considering recent events. On June 7, *Daily News* editor-in-chief Martin Dunn had fired city editor Dean Chang. Few had seen it coming, although *Post* columnist Keith Kelly had reported that Dean had clashed, of late, with executive editor

David Ng after Ng passed on a photo in May of married Yankee superstar Alex Rodriguez (known as "A-Rod") "cavorting" with a blonde at a Toronto strip club. The *Post* bought that same image and made it the paper's May 30 front page. "STRAY-ROD . . . PHOTO EXCLUSIVE . . . ALEX HITS STRIP CLUB WITH MYSTERY BLONDE . . . PAGES 2–3." Ng had, apparently, mistaken the woman for Rodriguez's wife, Cynthia, also blond.

Kelly, too, noted that Dunn's contract was expiring and that Dean's ouster—along with that of national editor Mark Mooney—was a "last-ditch" attempt by the editor-in-chief to show Zuckerman he had a plan to raise circulation—and especially considering the *Post*'s recent gains. And while Kelly left this angle unsourced, the theory was supported by Dunn's choice for Dean's replacement, ex–*Post* city editor Stuart Marques. Kelly, of course, framed Dean and Mooney's firings in the context of a newsroom in crisis. The story ran under the headline "DUNN WRONG: NEWS BOUNCES 2 EDITORS" and quoted one insider as saying, "It's bleak. Dean and Mark were sort of the heart and soul of the newsroom. Most people's loyalties flowed to those guys much more than to Martin Dunn or David Ng."

Another anonymous source quoted by Kelly added of the A-Rod fiasco, "It was Ng's call and he blew it. That was a flat-out scoop—and nobody sees any ramifications there. . . . It's safe to say everyone was angry and upset . . . [Dean] is a class guy, a well-respected guy and a talented guy with three young kids who was just treated very shabbily."

Meanwhile, Stu's return was a homecoming. He had been a *News* reporter before joining the *Post*, where he had been fired by Col Allan in 2001 in a spectacle that has become part of New York City tabloid lore. Allan's arrival in the States was preceded by a legend that he had once urinated in a sink during a news meeting at his former Australian newspaper. When he arrived at the *Post* in 2001, Stu—and a few other editors—winkingly welcomed their new boss with the gift of a urinal. Not long afterward, Stu was fired, along with others involved in the joke. Apparently, Col didn't think it was funny.[5]

The following month—and for the second time since January—both city tabloids chased a beauty queen. The first involved reports that Miss USA Tara Conner snorted cocaine, danced on nightclub tables, and dabbled in lipstick lesbianism with Miss Teen USA Katie Blair.[6] Pageant owner Donald Trump gave Conner an ultimatum of rehab or surrendering her tiara. Conner opted for rehab, and once she dried out, I spent a frosty February week staking out the Trump Place apartments on Manhattan's West Side in hopes of spotting her. Five days of chasing blondes into elevators—"*Is your name Tara Conner?*"—while binge-watching

"Simpsons" episodes on a shooter's laptop made me feel weird and, yet, privileged to be doing something so absurd for pay.

The second chase involved New Jersey's nominee for the 2007 Miss America Pageant. New Jersey judges had crowned Amy Polumbo, twenty-two, Miss New Jersey on June 16 in Ocean City. Nineteen days later, on July 5, a Thursday, the story broke at the Paramount Theatre in Asbury Park. Polumbo revealed at a press conference that a blackmailer had lifted "compromising" images from her Facebook page and then mailed them to her with a demand that she abdicate her state crown ahead of the national competition. Neither Miss New Jersey, nor her lawyer, Tony Caruso, revealed at the presser the photos' contents, but Polumbo provided plenty of dramatic quotes.

The story, I should say, wasn't a huge one, but for the *News* and the *Post* personnel who ran on it, it would come to feel that way. Everything, frankly, came to feel that way. Viewed through the prism of our tabloid war, even a bullshit burglary seemed of vital—even existential—consequence. It was how the United States conducted foreign policy during the Cold War. Lose here—no matter how far-flung or snake-infested the jungle— and the whole war would be lost. And so we ran—as the *Post* did—on every story as if it were the last one we'd ever cover. Here's how that day—and ensuing ones—unfolded, as the *News* and the *Post* battled in the field over a beauty queen, the runners giving no ground, although covering lots of it.

Noon to 1 P.M.

Miss New Jersey conducts her presser. Her stone-faced parents flank her on stage. Grandma sheds camera-friendly tears. Friends bob signs reading, "We Love Amy Polumbo." Everyone is spangled with buttons emblazoned with her likeness. The Associated Press, the *Asbury Park Press* (a regional daily), News 12 New Jersey, and WCBS (New York's channel 2 affiliate) are all in attendance.

1:36 P.M.*

The Associated Press, or AP, publishes a 472-word story on the scandal to its state and local wire. The story is written out of its Mt. Laurel field bureau, about seventy miles from Asbury Park, but only seventeen from

---

* Times of broadcasted and published reports are accurate to the minute. Others are estimates.

Philadelphia. The AP will add an abbreviated, 262-word version to its entertainment news wire at 3:15 P.M. Now, a word here on how the AP works. The AP is a cooperative of 1,700 American newspapers and 5,000-or-so radio and TV stations that, together, fund a global network of journalists. Smaller papers and even big-city metros, like the *News* or the *Post*, can't maintain bureaus in, say, Rome, Italy. But if the pope said something noteworthy, his remarks might still require coverage. AP reporters filled in those gaps and posted reports to the "wire." Member outlets could then publish that content as they saw fit.

In the *News*, such reports, if published unchanged from their wire form, ran under the byline "News Wire Services." In other papers, they typically read, "AP Report." But AP reports are usually written in such stolid, humorless prose they'd make even Joe Friday seem colorful; and more often than not, a *Daily News* rewrite reporter needed to renovate them with tabloid verve. In that case, the rewrite reporter would typically smack their own byline onto the story and demote the AP to a tagline, or credit that appeared at the conclusion of an article. And for years, this was accepted practice, or until 2007, when Stu Marques lured away the AP's top rewrite man in New York, reporter Larry McShane. After that, the AP's New York bureau chief issued a passive-aggressive mandate to Stu saying that *News* rewrite reporters weren't sufficiently overhauling AP stories to justify smacking their own bylines on them. So, for a while, we all operated under the edict of ensuring that every phrase from AP stories was completely rewritten, even if that meant reorganizing sentences so we used the passive, rather than active, voice.

3:24 P.M.

A *Daily News* editor spots the AP report during a periodic scan of the wires and orders the tabloid's "library" to run Polumbo through "Accurint." Both the *News* and the *Post* have such libraries, although they weren't really libraries, or hadn't been for many years. At the *News*, books did line the walls—encyclopedias, zoning maps, city registries, council meeting minutes—but by 2006, the Internet had rendered them mere props. The library's real purpose, and that of its researchers, was to hunt for people through databases compiled by LexisNexis. The *News'* favored tool was called Accurint and allowed you to input a person's name and obtain a report of their current and prior addresses; phone numbers—home and cell—e-mail addresses; political affiliation; employment and criminal histories; bankruptcies; liens; hunting, fishing, and boating licenses; and relatives and associates and their phone numbers, addresses, etc.—anything included in a person's paper trail. The library's reach was astounding. An Accurint report could include distant cousins, ex-roommates, former co-workers, people who hadn't spoken to the party involved in a decade. And because the *News* and the *Post* both used Accurint, runners often chased the same door knocks. It was just a matter of who ran hardest—and got there first.

3:42 P.M.

I am staked out—speculatively, as I occasionally am—outside the Bronx morgue. Sometimes, I'd sit there in my car, on the parking lot's edge, off Jacobi Hospital, watching for new arrivals bearing the unmistakable signs of distress. (Not the dead, but the kin who came to identify them.) Then—and if their hysteria suggested the demise was untimely and fresh—I'd approach and inquire about the means of death and, if it *was* newsworthy, continue along usual lines. Occasionally by doing so I'd score quotes about a shooting or motor vehicle accident before the desk became aware the incident had occurred.

But now assistant city editor Greg Gittrich was calling. He orders me to Amy Polumbo's last known address, as unearthed through Accurint. He relays the story so I will know what to ask, then instructs me to keep him posted. I roar south and west toward the New Jersey Turnpike, hoping I can escape the city limits before rush hour gets going.

3:44 P.M.

The photo desk orders Nick Fevelo to the same place. He'd been "sitting on the scanner" in Staten Island, waiting for something to run on. Nick is a freelance shooter and harbors artistic ambitions. It's just a job for him—neither a crusade against the *Post* nor an addict's obsession over the next get—and he can thus be relied on to expend, perhaps, three-fifths of the effort of, say, Todd Maisel, although sometimes that's not a bad thing.

5:05 P.M.

WNBC, New York City's channel 4 and NBC affiliate, includes a brief "anchor script" at the top of its 5 o'clock news show on the scandal. "The new Miss New Jersey says someone is trying to blackmail her," says the anchor, almost certainly reading off a teleprompter words that had been written by some intern, low-level staffer, or part-timer.

5:12 P.M.

Gittrich calls to question me about my progress. The *Daily News* routinely monitors the 5 o'clock news broadcasts of city affiliates, and the WNBC segment on Polumbo's presser has elevated his interest in the story, if not the story's ranking on the daily sked. I advise him I am snagged in traffic just off Exit 11 on the New Jersey Turnpike. He grunts and rings off.

5:36 P.M.

Newhouse News Service, another wire service, publishes a 415-word Miss New Jersey story to its "Lifestyle" wire headlined, "MISS NEW JERSEY CLAIMS EXTORTION ATTEMPT."

5:39 P.M.

News 12 New Jersey, a twenty-four-hour New Jersey news channel, airs its first report on the presser. It will re-air that same report at 6:11, 6:39, 7:29, 8:29, 9:29, and, finally, 10:09 P.M.

6:10 P.M.

WCBS, New York City's channel 2 and CBS affiliate, airs a Polumbo anchor script on its 6 o'clock news with video of the presser it collected in Asbury Park earlier in the day.

6:17 P.M.

By God's grace, I arrive at Polumbo's would-be development inside of three hours. It looks like a thousand other prosperous New Jersey exurbs, with ranch homes with Chemlawn yards and paved driveways. I see no other media, and a wave of ecstatic relief washes over me. The library-provided address has a footpath from front door to sidewalk. A man hefts a Hefty bag over it to the curb. I know at a look he isn't going to be easy. Coin-slot eyes. Pursed lips. A brooding face that didn't even have to say, "Fuck off." It was implied. Of course, I walk him to his door—"*I wonder if you can help me. I'm looking for a young lady named Amy Polumbo."* He slams the door, first the storm one, then the composite one behind it. Given that I hadn't brought my battering ram, I pound until he answers.

"What is it with you guys?"

"You guys?"

"WNBC. They were here this afternoon. They asked the same thing. Not as obnoxiously as you, but close. Anyway, there's no Polumbo here."

A freight train of interlocking thoughts barrels through my mind: "Where is the *Post*? Where the hell is Polumbo? Where the hell is the *Post*? What am I missing, here?"

6:31 P.M.

I hassle a 411 operator for Polumbo's lawyer. The request yields three Anthony Caruso, Esquires, in New Jersey. The first number is the charm. Reception parks me in Muzak purgatory, and Caruso answers after enough time has elapsed to ensure I know who holds the ace-high flush. He tells me the national Miss America Pageant has punted to its Garden State chapter on whether to disqualify Polumbo. He insists she is *not* resigning, there are a total of twelve photos, and he hasn't any idea who stole them, although he does rule out jealous and/or jilted boyfriends. No nudity. No drugs. I ask, "What the hell is she doing? Picking flowers?" That *almost* represents the conclusion of the call.

> ME: "Hey, wait! Have you gotten any calls from the *New York Post* today?"
> CARUSO: "Yeah, they called earlier."
> ME: "Did you, by any chance, get the sense they know more about this story than I do?"
> CARUSO: (Chuckling) "No."

6:47 P.M.

Fevelo arrives. The *Daily News* library dictates the contents of Polumbo's Accurint. I hit the phones, first calling grandma in Florida. No answer. I call a potential aunt in Pennsylvania, a Hail Mary unknown in Ohio. Nothing. I leave a voicemail for the Garden State chapter of the Miss America Pageant and then catch a break. A young man pulls a bicycle into the driveway next to The Great Scowl's home. Stephen Bottiglieri says Polumbo moved a year ago, "to the other side of town." He recommends checking for homes registered in her mother's name: Jennifer Wagner. He says her Facebook photos mostly portrayed her time as a Walt Disney World park actress. She did Ariel from *The Little Mermaid*.

"Maybe they show her having a few drinks, but what college-age kid doesn't drink?" he asks.

It is now less than two-and-a-half hours to first edition, the *News'* Metro edition. Room for error is dissipating. The stakes are rising. And God— and the *Post*—only knows what the latter has amassed. I need something. Anything to feed the desk so it doesn't devour me instead.

7:09 P.M.

Directory assistance yields a Jennifer Wagner in nearby Freehold. Fevelo inputs the address into his GPS. No go. We try MapQuest. Same result. I call the Freehold P.D. and request directions.

DISPATCHER: "Who's asking?"
ME: "What's the difference?"
DISPATCHER: "Because I know who lives there and I know they would rather not be bothered."

I argue a little. I plead a little. But getting him to spill was like swimming through a sea groin.

7:18 P.M.

I phone the library and ask for Wagner's Accurint. It confirms the address and phone number already rendered by 411. It *also* gives me those of her neighbors. I call them, one by one, and request the directions the cop wouldn't give. Nothing doing.

"You're trying to talk people into helping a tabloid reporter come to their home?" Fevelo asks skeptically. "You might as well tell them you want to bury a body in their backyard."

7:31 P.M.

Desperate, I call back a neighbor I'd cynically categorized as a soccer mom. I tell her I need to get home to my wife and newborn child (I have neither) and my editors will not allow me to do so until I, at least, knock on Miss New Jersey's door. I infuse my voice with distress. It works. She says the development is so new, it doesn't appear yet on maps, or GPS.

She gives me directions.

7:47 P.M.

Nick and I pull into a townhouse development so new an entrance sign directs us to a model unit. The streets are freshly paved and the lane markers so bright I might get wet paint on my tires. But not a single soul is out and about. It's a Potemkin village, a Hollywood set, a contrivance. If I stub out a cigarette and look away, it might not be there when I look back. Miss New Jersey's townhouse is white with gables and charcoal roof shingles. It fronts lush, Crayola-green grass. That ends with a two-lane road. Then a hedge row, then an earth-churned farm. I knock on the door, then peek into its windows. Nothing.

7:56 P.M.

I door-knock Polumbo's next-door neighbor. A mid-sixties egret with scarecrow hair the color of moonlight answers. I explain my mission and watch shock distort his bony, beakish features.

"You mean *she's* Miss New Jersey? Jesus Christ, that's the best we can do? This is what happens when they start mucking up the contest with questions about war, peace, and the environment. They should just stick to swim suits and high heels!"

Back to the cars—and the stakeout that awaits us, ever so patiently, there.

8:03 P.M.

The air is still. Electric lights click on above us—and buzz like live wires. Time passes. The desk doesn't call. The *Post* is nowhere. North Jersey— and New York City—feels very far away, indeed. Nick and I are two lonely sentinels manning a far-off forward observation post awaiting the tripwire alarm of something resembling motion. We read the papers. The *Post* wooded that day with a tabloid trifecta of celebrities, scions, and New York Governor Eliot Spitzer's ongoing spat with State Senate President Joe Bruno. "DIDDY DISS . . . GAL PAL WALKS OUT" . . . "GORE KID IN DRUG BUST . . . "POLICE STATE . . . GOV SICCED COPS ON JOE . . . EXCLUSIVE." The *News* countered with July 4th fireworks—"RED, WHITE AND BOOM!" and Al's wayward kid: "GORE KID'S HIGH-BRID . . . POT, PILLS FOUND IN SPEEDING ECO-FRIENDLY CAR."

We talk through open car windows, two lollygagging cops on a highway median. Night falls. Crickets chirp. The farmland across the two-lane buzzes with unseen life.

9:30 P.M.

The *News'* first edition, Metro, closes. I've added nothing but Caruso's retread quotes.

10:15 P.M.

Fox 29 News in Philadelphia, WTXF, airs a fifty-one-word anchor script during its 10 o'clock news broadcast. The story has, officially, gone regional.

10:20 P.M.

WPIX, channel 11 in New York, does its own Miss New Jersey report on *its* 10 o'clock news.

10:30 P.M.

The *News'* national edition closes.

10:40 P.M.

Fox News' Greta Van Susteren does a report on Miss New Jersey. The story is, now, national and evidence of how even a small story can mushroom in New York's larded media market.

11:08 P.M.

Headlights fill my rear view. I remind Fevelo, again, not to shoot until we have words. We already have a photo from the presser. It's an explanation that is required.

A minivan slides into a spot and we both make a big show of ourselves. The minivan disgorges passengers. It's quickly apparent that Miss New Jersey is among them. My impression: She's shorter than I imagined. And she wears little, or no, makeup, and that makes her look far younger than the photos snapped earlier that day. Her hair is mussed and complexion ruddy. She wears shorts and a T-shirt, stands shyly behind her mother, and smiles girlishly. Her teeth look as white and perfect as display window dentures.

Jennifer Wagner shoos her daughter into the house, forces a crooked smile, and stonewalls my questions until I broach my chat with Caruso.

Sure, I say. We got on. He told me to find you. She isn't buying it, so I phone him, hand her the cell, and listen, vaguely, as he vouches for my bona fides. Even still, the forthcoming interview is unspectacular, worth perhaps one-eighth of the effort Nick and I have expended to obtain it. But the *Post* is not there and so any words, I know, will be deemed doubly valuable by the desk.

Wagner tells us Amy spent the day at Great Adventure, an amusement park. She is very proud of this subterfuge, saying, "All of these people were looking for my Amy and she was getting her picture shot on a ride." For Fevelo's sake, I ask if they purchased the photo. Wagner says, "No," reiterated the innocuousness of the Facebook photos and adds this nugget about who stole them: "We think it was somebody inside the pageant." *You mean like another contestant?* "I don't want to comment," she says.

It is over as quickly as it had begun, and Nick and I are left standing in the lot like two awkward teens at a ninth-grade dance.

11:29 P.M.

WCBS re-airs the story at the end of its 11 o'clock news, just before the anchor teases "The Late Show with David Letterman" and that night's guests: Jane Fonda and Kelly Clarkson.

11:30 P.M.

The *News* closed its Racing Final edition, so named because it contains the horse-racing results from local tracks.

11:33 P.M.

I dump my notes to the desk. Without apology, Gittrich orders me to return to Polumbo's home by 8 A.M. It is fifty miles back to North Jersey, but I didn't have it nearly as bad as Nick. He'd have to pay the Outerbridge toll to get back onto Staten Island.

July 6, 2007

1:30 A.M.

The *News'* final edition for July 5, Sports Final, closes. It's the beginning of a new news day.

8:06 A.M.

Polumbo's parking lot jeers me as I pull in only nine hours after having departed. My spot is close enough for competent spying on her front door, yet far enough away that the home's occupants won't notice me unless they are looking. I inventory vehicles, matching license plate sequences to the one I'd lifted from the family minivan on Thursday night. (Runner's tradecraft: Always copy the "tags" of pertinent vehicles—even if there is no immediate and obvious need to do so.) No matches. Examine the *News* and the *Post*, which played to a draw, although I give the *News* a slight edge on the strength of the Bottiglieri and Wagner quotes. The *Post* scored a big zero in the field. Ronica Licciardello, the New Jersey pageant runner-up who would inherit Polumbo's crown if she abdicated, or was disqualified, told the *Post* she hoped for a speedy resolution to the scandal. Those quotes *could* have been obtained via door knock, but they *feel* like the work of a phoner.

Austin Fenner wrote the *Post* story, one of his first since defecting from the *News* in June for what was rumored to be a big raise. Persistent, ancillary rumors—perhaps jealousy-born—suggested motivations for the *Post*'s alleged largesse: The *Post* fields few African-Americans, and Austin, who is black, stems off a lawsuit. The *Post*, long decried as racist (at worst) and racially insensitive (at best), is weary of *News* victories every time the Rev. Al Sharpton shovels a scoop. Austin, who penned a series in March reporting that some of Al's ancestors were slaves owned by former South Carolina Sen. Strom Thurmond's forebears (unbelievable, but true!), has major pull with the Rev. Or Col Allan delights in fucking with the *News* and stealing its staff. Or Austin is, simply, worthy and wanted.

The *Post* splits its wood between the blackmail plot and Spitzer's State House scandal: "BEAUTY QUEEN IN SECRET PHOTOS BLACKMAIL" . . . "DIRTY TRICKS . . . JOE DEMANDS A 'CRIMINAL' PROBE OF GOV." The *News* goes big on the beauty queen: "BEAUTY QUEEN BLACKMAIL . . . THREAT TO RELEASE PRIVATE PICS STUNS DEFIANT MISS NEW JERSEY," while a pair of "skybox chips" teases Albany tension and "100 GREAT SUMMER TREATS." I finish the papers, smoke my fourth Marlboro Light of the morning and focus on Polumbo's front door. (Runner's tradecraft: The moment your attention wavers will be the moment your quarry appears.)

8:47 A.M.

Shooter Mike Schwartz joins me in the parking lot. A poor man's Dustin Hoffman with a sapphire stud in his left ear, he is also an ex–*Post* staffer among those fired when Murdoch broke the paper's union. He still refuses to say the mogul's name, like "Lord Voldemort" in Harry Potter. His extreme antipathy will, I know, guarantee excellent effort.

Together, we assume our positions, as stage actors who had rehearsed a play. Mike ducks behind his vehicle and trains his lens on Polumbo's front door. I make the short, yet mentally long, walk to said door and introduce it to my knuckles. A long pause. Listen for motion. The tension always the same. The questions, preconceived, scramble in my head. Emotion takes over. Yet, there is nothing. Back to the car and a call to the desk.

"Jaccarino for Sal."

A news clerk relays the call. Sal assumes the line: "Yeah, Mike."

I tick off particulars. No answer to the door knock. No minivan. Sal asks, "Where's the enemy?"

"No sign."

"They weren't there last night either, right?"

"Nope."

"Okay. Give it 'til 11, then head to the lawyer's office. Stake it out and see if she shows. In the meantime, do your best to find out where our friends are lurking. We need to know."

"10-4."

I play a hunch, call Jana Winter, often my counterpart in the field for the *Post*. She is a short, hyper-competitive girl who would steamroll you for a scoop. She is ego-driven, relentless, and perpetually unhappy. And she is also very, very good. It takes four rings for her to answer, and when she does, I hear ambient sounds suggestive of commerce, someone making change, another asking, "How much do you want?" Jana quizzes me on *my* whereabouts and what I'd gotten. I evade her questions, buying time to zero in on those sounds. Finally, I ask, "Jana, where are you?" But she answers by demanding of me the same question. I ask if she'd gotten anything, and when she refuses to answer, I all but plead.

"Fine!" she barks. "I got a family friend this morning."

Totally unnerved, I conclude the call. Schwartz demands a brief on what little Jana has revealed. I comply, then relay Sal's order to head to Caruso's Princeton office at 11. Mike is not happy. *News* freelancers are not recompensed for mileage, and the gas allocation will cut severely into a day rate already depleted by the cost of running his vehicle's air conditioning. I invite Mike to my car until 11 o'clock—staffers *are* recompensed—although both of us are cheap and prefer the swelter and savings to comfortable air.

1:25 P.M.

Irritable and sweaty, we arrive at Archer Greiner's law offices, tucked into a corporate park off Route 1. Two brick buildings bookend a parking lot and a goo-covered still-water pond. We introduce our cars to the hundreds sunbathing on the asphalt hot plate, then enter the law offices. Double glass doors and a fifteen-step hallway decorated with mail-order modern art lead us to a bottleneck reception desk. Behind that and looking consciously professional is a willowy, wan-skinned woman with anemic lips and a withering gaze. She is wearing black horn-rimmed glasses and a rigid suit over an equally starched white shirt. You could get a paper cut from just brushing its collar.

"Mr. Caruso is not in," she says, her voice like the Pathmark freezer aisle. I ask if she's sure. She says, "I'm aware of the whereabouts of the firms' lawyers at all times."

I resist the urge to laugh, then ask if this applies after-hours, too. She snarls and I give my name, number, and media affiliation in that voice that's supposed to inspire fear in figures of authority everywhere. Mike and I then walk beyond the double doors and make ourselves into a nuisance. We ask everyone coming and going for quotes about Polumbo. It takes more than ten minutes but certainly less than fifteen for Caruso to come outside.

He looks less like a lawyer than a Lord & Taylor advertisement. Polo shirt. Deck shoes. Pricey tan. He informs us there will be a presser at 5 o'clock, and I ask why the receptionist couldn't have just said that. He smiles humorlessly. We ask if Polumbo is coming. He says he'll know later. We ask if he'll reveal the photos. He says he will not. We ask if he will elaborate on their content. He says he will not. We ask for "one good reason why we should wait around all day for this presser." He says, "You'll have to come to find out." It is a reply worthy of contempt—but I just let Schwartz go to work on him. Ten questions later, Caruso looks peaked and I had extracted my pound of flesh by proxy.

At that point, it becomes a waiting game. We shuttle between air-conditioned cars and shade. All around us, the world works. Lives. We wait for news to happen.

2:34 P.M.

Sal calls for an update. I explain the situation and the scene inside Archer Greiner that preceded it. Sal is not amused. He would rather I had concealed myself and covertly staked out Archer Greiner's offices in hopes that Polumbo would unwittingly appear. At minimum, Schwartz could have "gotten her" as she entered the building. Now, as he points out, she knows to avoid the location. He's right, of course. But that doesn't discount the fact that I shouldn't have dilated on my conversation with Caruso. (Runner's tradecraft: Tell the desk only what it needs to know, and nothing more, unless you have good news, in which case elaborate freely. Verbosity engenders criticism because editors will always have an opinion about how they would have done it differently.)

4:10 P.M.

Jana pulls up. She is wearing her customary street gear: jeans, comfortable blouse, Tory Burch flats, a look of contempt for everything around her. When she sees Mike and me at a picnic table, she accessorizes with a Cheshire cat grin. Has she gotten something more than she'd allowed that morning? She won't say. I attack her redoubt with questions, or until Mike pulls me aside and—with a Harrison Ford–like intensity I did not think him capable of—growls, "Don't ask her anymore. Whatever you do, don't give her the fucking satisfaction. Fucking *Post!*"

Caruso is a disappointment. Over numerous calls, he remains noncommittal on Polumbo's attendance. Then—at 4:45—he postpones until 6, a decision that proves transparently intended to allow a TV affiliate an opportunity to arrive. Then and once all anticipated affiliates and print reporters have convened, he informs us Miss New Jersey will, in fact, not be showing. It had all been an elaborate bait and switch.

At the presser: We ask our questions, but Caruso is implacable. Jana's last is whether he at all feels bad about having summoned us to reiterate what has already been said. Caruso gives Jana the same wan smile that Mike and I had seen earlier.

6:21 P.M.

The desk orders me back to Polumbo's house to get the money quote Caruso didn't provide. Since I recognize this as a fool's errand and unlikely to result in a quote, I selfishly inform Jana, knowing it will assure me the company of at least one other person on the excursion. (Schwartz is, mercifully, allowed to return to New York.) It is the petty act of a small man. And I compound it by telling Jana, "Sucks for you."

8:15 P.M.

The Polumbo house is dark and empty—just like I feel inside. It is now fourteen hours after I began my day—my second in a row of such duration and stress. I make it longer by pressing Jana about her "get."

"Aren't you miserable enough?" she asks.

I let it slide. She has a point.

Dusk comes quickly—a Monet-like blur—and then all at once, clouds that had glowed angelically mottle into bruises, and the twinkle of stars replaces the embers of another dying day. The zapper-like street lights buzz on—just as they had the night before—and, for just a moment, I feel as if I'd fallen into the "Tabloid Zone." I ask Jana if she is hungry. She ignores the question and replies with a rhetorical one about Miss New Jersey's whereabouts. It is a measure of my disgust that I, at once, reply, "Who cares?"

9:30 P.M.

The desk tells me to suggest a deal, although I am not going home. Midnight will kick off the seventh day of the seventh month of the year 2007, or 7/7/07, and because I am already "conveniently in New Jersey," as Gittrich puts it, I should go to Atlantic City to interview gamblers about wagering on such a "lucky day." I inform Jana and she asks, "Is this a ploy?"

I reply that neither I, nor anyone else working for the *News*, am so clever as to concoct such a ridiculous rationale for leaving.

"You're really going to Atlantic City?" she asks. "Wow! Sucks for *you*."

We both laugh. Jana gets permission from her desk to make the deal. And then together—two runners in the New Jersey wilderness and sometime just before 10 o'clock—we ritualistically shake hands, warily enter our cars and motor away, each hoping the other doesn't double-back to fuck the other. We drive in single file as far as the Garden State Parkway, then split up, me grimly heading south and Jana en route back to New York.

July 7, 2007

12:05 A.M.

I spoon-feed quotes to gamblers outside the Taj Mahal (the Trump property in Atlantic City, not the mausoleum in India). It's easy pickings. *Sure.*

Sure. It's the luckiest day of the millennium! The minute I heard, I hit the Turnpike! All I can think about is sleep.

6:33 A.M.

I awake in Atlantic City's Sheraton Convention Center Hotel abreast the A.C. Expressway. For a fugue-like moment, I can't place my location. Then it floods back and my only impulse is to find a *News* and a *Post* and learn how badly Jana has beaten me.

7:05 A.M.

Outside a bodega, I read. The *Post* woods, again, with State House intrigue and blackmailed beauty queens. Its front-page photo shows Polumbo in much the same pose Edvard Munch portrayed his subject in *The Scream*. It is a complete con job. Although Polumbo looks appropriately anguished in the image, she was, at that moment, crying tears of joy after winning a pageant. "BEAUTY QUEEN CATFIGHT . . . COPS PROBE RIVALS" . . . "ELIOT SPITS . . . GOV CURSES BRUNO AFTER DUST-UP." The *News* counters with WCBS-FM's return to an oldies format after switching to a youth-oriented one called "Jack." "WCBS-FM ADMITS IT DON'T KNOW JACK AS IT BRINGS BACK REAL DJS AND MUSIC." Eva Longoria's Paris wedding to NBA star Tony Parker rounds out the *News* wood: "HAPPILY EVA AFTER."

The *Post*'s Polumbo story notes law enforcement's interest in Miss New Jersey's runners-up, quoting this to an anonymous source who singled out second-place finisher Ronica Licciardello as "a person of interest." The source adds that cops plan to interview all five runners-up that weekend. The story does not claim a single source willing to put their name to their quotes, other than Licciardello's mother, Rosario, who denied her daughter's involvement. The *Post*'s lede, meanwhile, is tabloid gorgeous—saying the scandal had taken "a Tonya Harding–style turn," a dig at the Olympic figure skater whose ex-husband had conspired to have her rival, Nancy Kerrigan, "clubbed in the knee" before the '94 Games.

The *News* counters with tabloid sleights-of-hand and obvious filler. Its story leads with a Miss New Jersey board member's saying that Polumbo had been summoned to account for the photos at a meeting the following week. It nakedly, yet artfully, dramatizes Caruso's explanation for Polumbo's absence at his silly presser by reporting she was "in hiding with her family." (Caruso had said she was spending "necessary" downtime with them.)

All in all, it's a drubbing. It's the story of the day—the wood—and we, I, had been soundly beaten.

8:10 A.M.

I prepare to take licks, which Gittrich, indeed, dispenses in that quietly irate way so much worse than when someone actually screams at you. He inquires how I had been so badly "mauled"—that's the word he uses—and when I tell him I don't know, he orders me to find out "before Martin calls again." After that, I retrieve a New Jersey map from my glove compartment and chart sensible routes to the homes of Polumbo's runners-up. After *that*, I start running.

8:19 A.M.

Krista Richmond lives forty miles south of Atlantic City in Cape May. No one is home. I double-back northwest along Route 47, toward Millville and Ashleigh Udalovas's abode. Door knock. No answer. I head sixty miles north up Route 55, until I am just outside Philly, then turn northeast toward Mount Laurel. I arrive at Ronica Licciardello's home with an empty notebook, a stress headache, and $60 in accrued mileage reimbursement.

The 2007 Miss New Jersey Pageant's second-place finisher resides in an ellipse-shaped subdivision with fifty or so colonial-style homes. It is off a wooded north/south road punctuated with takeout shops and gas stations. Licciardello lives off one of two cul-de-sacs in a white colonial with fieldstone trim, a two-car garage, wide lawn, and two hedgerows along the property lines. I rap on the door, ring the bell, then head across the street for neighbors. They tell me Ronica has been in pageants all her life, her mother is a schoolteacher, and her brother has some sort of disability, likely Down syndrome.

12:33 P.M.

I call Caruso to stand up the *Post*'s story. He says it's unfounded and explains that nothing should be construed by cops' interest in Polumbo's rivals. Furthermore, he explains how "deeply distressed" Amy is over the *Post*'s account. I sense an opening, tell him the *News* had had the same info (we hadn't) but chose not to run it without an on-the-record source because "it would have been wrong to smear those girls without one."

"Well, you did the right thing," Tony says.

"I know, but I'm catching hell because of it. I'm fucked, here, Tony. Help me out."

"What do you need?"

"You know what I need."

"I can't do it."

"Why?"

"I just can't. Or not yet."

(Runner's tradecraft: Reporting is transactional. Yes, the *News* did not have the referenced info about cops' interest in the runners-up, but Caruso didn't know that. Telling him we did—and chose not to run it— engendered sympathy and cast the *Post* in a poor light. It's a bluff and one that, as you'll see, paid dividends down the road.)

12:51 P.M.

Behind me, three cars pull up, single-file. Fevelo; "Killer" Bill Farrington, the *Post*'s go-to shooter on big stories; and Jana exit their cars and size up the nabe. I get out of mine and ask with a self-confidence I didn't feel, "What took you so long?"

Bill shakes his head. He is short, thinly built, and understated—with a blond Marine's buzz cut, gunslinger eyes, and a face as Irish as a 2 o'clock happy hour. *News* runners call him "Killer Bill" because of how often he'd massacred us on the street.

I congratulate Jana to pry an opening to appease Gittrich's bloodlust for information. She accepts the kudos, skeptically, and parries questions about the unnamed source upon which her "get" had been founded.

"Ah, no chance, Jaccarino."

Bill aloofly studies the list of penny stocks he carries around in his pocket. Bill has a "guy" whose touts are transcribed there. I know enough about the "pink sheets" to know they are once-removed from a lottery ticket—and so does Bill—but he likes the implied legitimacy of Wall Street, as opposed to buying a Pick 5 at a bodega.

1:00 P.M.

The four of us knock, again, on Ronica's door. Nothing. We return to our cars and dig in for a stakeout, the trench warfare of tabloid journalism. I ply Ronica's Accurint and call would-be relatives as far away as Florida. I call the Monmouth County Prosecutor's Office. I call back Richmond, then Udalovas. On the latter, I get lucky *and* a quote to serve up as an offering to the angry news gods in New York. In the car behind mine, I spy Jana dialing for quotes, as well, and likely the same people I'm phoning.

1:44 P.M.

Gittrich phones and asks in his android monotone, "What do you got?"

I reply with a concise summary that is really a long-winded way of saying, "Not much."

"Now, let's talk about yesterday," he says, ominously. "Martin wants to know how this happened."

"Greg, I really don't know," I say. "Caruso says it's a lie, that law enforcement's interest in the runners-up is standard investigatory procedure. And Udalovas just told me she hasn't been contacted by cops. I'm efforting the prosecutor's office now."

"Didn't Polumbo's mom tell you the first night she suspected someone inside the pageant?"

"Yes," I mumble.

Gittrich is silent before the rare display of humanity. He tells me, "It's OK" and that I "should do a better job working on the [anonymous] source level."

He's right. At the end of the day, Wagner had pointed me in the right direction, but I'd forgotten to follow up. Knowing this—and damning myself for it—I exit the car and ponder the sky. Jana sidles up to me, her face dominated by a Joker-like grin.

"What's your problem?"

"Not now, Jana."

"Come on. What's the matter?" This time different, soothing. I'd never heard her talk like that before.

"I just got stomped on by my desk."

"My story?"

"Yeah."

She sighs, draws her Parliaments, shakes one loose, and offers me the pack. I take it. She lights it. She does the same for herself. Silently, we smoke. It is the first time we stand in each other's company and do not try to one-up each other.

"Here's how I did it," she says, and then adds, "if it helps at all."

I tell her it does, and she explains how *Post* reporter Jeane MacIntosh (Pronounced Jean*nee* and informally known as "Jean*ee* Mac") had told her that in order to get the scoop in any New Jersey nabe, a runner should head to the local Wawa, one of a chain of 7-11–like convenience stores dotted around the southern and central portions of the state. Jeane Mac would know. Like me, she lives in New Jersey. Jana says she headed to the Wawa down the road from Polumbo's house and soon got one of Jennifer Wagner's pals, who gave her quotes and the name of the cop handling the case, who—in turn—gave her more quotes. Some of those quotes had concerned cops' interest in the runners-up.

"Were you there—at the Wawa—when we spoke in the morning?"

"Yup."

I nod and consider how such a location would have accounted for those ambient sounds of commerce.

"Jesus," I say. "Wawa, huh?"

"Wawa."

"Fucking Wawa."

"Fucking Wawa."

"Come on," I add. "You want to give Ronica another shot? Maybe we can convince them to let us go home before 10 o'clock."

"Wouldn't it be pretty to think so," Jana says.

I chuckle over the Hemingway quote, adding, "I thought you only read tabloid newspapers."

2:21 P.M.

Together, the four of us stalk up Ronica Licciardello's driveway to her porch. The shooters flank us and ready their cameras. I knock. Nothing. I knock again. Same result. I ring the bell—and then just as I turn away, I hear rustling.

"Maybe you knocked over a dish with all that banging," a smirking Fevelo says, although the sound had definitely been a someone and not a something. Farrington speaks for all of us when he says, "There's someone in the house."

I knock again, then peek through the window. The living room is a desolate doll house. We decamp the porch and head for our cars . . . but halfway, the garage door clacks open and a Chevy muscles down the drive. Fevelo and Farrington bookend the backseat like Mafia hitmen. *Pop! Pop! Pop!* Shutters whir. Flashes explode—and then something awful happens. Hands beating on the windows. A boy with Down syndrome, screaming with each flash.

"Cease fire!" Jana screams and the car hurries down the block.

"She wasn't in the car," Jana says as Fevelo and Farrington check their images to confirm.

We return to our vehicles and resume the stakeout.

2:47 P.M.

The Chevy returns and we allow it to proceed into the garage without incident.

3:04 P.M.

A grown man—the one who had been driving—comes outside the house and glares. We approach. Ronica Licciardello's father tells us we are upsetting his son, that things are difficult on even the best of days and could we please show some decency and depart? I don't hesitate, tell him that is impossible, but that should he make his daughter available we can reasonably ask our editors to consider his request.

"So, you're going to hold us hostage? My son hostage? Unless my daughter talks to you?"

I shrug. There's no good answer to a question like that. He sighs his way back into the house.

3:13 P.M.

Ronica Licciardello holds reluctant court in her front yard. She is gym-fit with chestnut eyes and a shoulder-length curtain of hair. She doesn't wait for questions but alights on what sounds like a rehearsed statement: "I wish only the best for Amy and her family at this time."

Blah. Blah. Blah.

Jana asks about the blackmail plot, but Ronica says only, "I have not been contacted by law enforcement."

I inform her of our need for a more personal denial. I add for good measure that we both attended the same university—a fact I'd read in one of that morning's stories.

"Come, on, Ronica," I implore. "We don't want to be out here bothering your brother. But our bosses aren't going to let us leave until we have something on this point."

She sighs. Again, the brother—the wedge that makes her dance on our string.

"If I answer this question, will you leave?"

We all silently agree. If Gittrich still wants a stakeout, he can come down from New York and do it himself. I tell her as much and she gives us the needed three-word denial of blackmail: "No. I did not."

"Great," I say and cheerfully ask Ronica, "So, how did you like Penn?"

Without thinking it over, she glares at me and says, "It's time for you to leave."

3:33 P.M.

Back in my car, I brief Gittrich. He asks: "Did the *Post* get this, too?" I say, "Yes," and he tells me he needs something exclusive to stanch the bleeding from Jana's get. He orders me back to Polumbo's house and concludes, "Get me something from Miss New Jersey on the record. Anything." I ring off and feel like someone punched me in the gut.

4:47 P.M.

I call Caruso from Miss New Jersey's house and put a fresh coat of desperation on earlier pleas for a Polumbo sit-down. He states the obvious: "They don't give you guys a break, huh?"

Fevelo loiters in a car hard by my own. Jana and Bill had returned to New York—a shocking departure from *News–Post* SOP, yet indicative of their tabloid's comfort with its lead. I inform Caruso of my whereabouts. He says he'd love to help, but "I don't know where they are right now. Hey, maybe in hiding?" He says this last part with sarcasm, and I chuckle at the obvious reference to how we'd dramatized his remarks in print.

"Maybe I can give you something, though," he finally adds. "A second package arrived today at the New Jersey chapter's headquarters from the blackmailer."

I smell scoop—and tabloid redemption. Caruso elaborates on the package's contents: a threatening letter and possibly a photo.

"Hey, Tony," I say. "There's a simple way out of this."

"Yeah . . . what's that?"

"Just e-mail me the photos and all of this—all of it—goes away. If they're truly as innocent as you say they are, then you got nothing to worry about."

He laughs, then says, "Nice try," and not for the first time I wonder about his motivations.

6:20 P.M.

Fevelo and I await the Polumbos in the parking lot, again talking through open car windows. We talk about the story, then the paper, then colleagues, then our own lives, each passing hour of the stakeout peeling away formality and banality. We play the game "What did we do to deserve this?" Nick says he should never have indulged artistic ambitions. I say I should have enrolled in Wharton Business School. Nick says he made a "fat kid" cry in fourth grade. I admit I once made promises to a college coed, then snuck out the backdoor of a bar the following day under the pretense of using the bathroom. Fevelo roars. *Haw! Haw! Haw!* It is lightweight confessions as idle banter. Two Catholic kids passing time. Our real crimes go unspoken. The stakeout drags on.

8:47 P.M.

Headlights light up my car. It's Thursday night all over, again. Eerie tabloid *déjà vu*. The Polumbos, again, are dressed as if they had spent the day camping. Again, Jennifer Wagner hustles her daughters into their house before we can pose a question. It's all happened before—except for one difference: This time Wagner requires no prompting to speak.

"The *New York Post* printed lies!" she howls as if having waited all day to say that sentence. *Are you referring to law enforcement's quoted interest in the runners-up, or the blackmailer's assertion of lurid living by your daughter?* "Both," she says, and vehemently so. "Why would they print such a thing? Whoever this source is, they're not telling the truth."

9:21 P.M.

I phone Gittrich, who takes the feed and orders me to return to the house by 8 A.M. I inform Fevelo, but he lingers. He adds one more thing to our earlier game. One last sin before going home. *What do you think about what we did to that kid today?* He means Ronica's brother. I sigh. It's as good a reason as any to explain being trapped on stakeout.

July 8, 2007

10:20 A.M.

Jana smokes her tenth Parliament of the morning and I do my best not to broach what Wagner had said the night before. Once more, we stand in the Polumbos' parking lot under equal circumstances. Jana is jumpy. I am resigned. Our task is to get words from Miss New Jersey, although Jana's desk has turned the screw. They got wind that Polumbo will appear the next day, or Monday, on the "Today" show in New York for an interview with Matt Lauer. They want Jana to tail the quarry into Manhattan and discover where she will be lodging overnight. The information, we both know, will permit shooters, and perhaps a runner, "to get her" coming out the following morning going to 30 Rock. My desk made it clear that if Jana gives chase, I am to, as well.

The morning trudges on. It is again hot and muggy, a hard day for fat men. Incrementally, our game faces falter under the tedium and the sun. What follows isn't quite the *bonhomie* of yesterday but still an upgrade. We toy with a hypothetical day of hooky at the Jersey Shore. They'll never know, I say. Jana's reply: What happens if WCBS shows up?

The *Post* wooded that day with a dramatic photo of a tour helicopter moments after it crashed into the Hudson River. "CHOPPER DOWN . . . EIGHT SURVIVE IN HUDSON CRASH . . . PAGE 3." The *News* countered with an exclusive interview with Governor Eliot Spitzer in which he denied "trash-talking" Senate President Joe Bruno. "SPITZER TELLS NEWS: 'IT AIN'T SO, JOE' . . . GOV DENIES CALLING BRUNO DIRTY NAMES."

Both papers run Polumbo stories, but inside. Tabloid box scores to runners. A review reveals a nominal *News–Post* draw, both stories leading with the second blackmail package, although Jana got a Licciardello neighbor to give up her neighborhood nickname: "Queenie." The get chafes . . . and, to my mind, embellishes the growing narrative of my defeat. Secondary analysis: Caruso, at best, dramatized the second package as exclusive to the *News*. At worst, he lied. Caruso is playing everyone.

11:15 A.M.

I excuse myself from Jana under the pretense of calling the desk, then call Caruso. I articulate indignation and trowel the mortar of manipulation. Caruso greets me with Sunday cheer: "How are you this morning, my friend?"

"Annoyed! You knew I was fucked for helping your client, Tony, for doing exactly what you had hoped the *Post* would do, but didn't, for sitting on that crapola about the cops and the runners-up. And what do I get? I get you telling the *Post* the same shit about the second package you told me was exclusive. I thought that was my saving grace. Come on, Tony! I mean, I was out in front of the house last night! Amy's mother was hysterical over what the *Post* wrote. I can read you my notes, if you want. I'm sitting, here, trying to do right by you *and* your client, and it's getting me nowhere."

"All right, all right," he says. "How can I get you off the hot seat?"

"You know what you can do. You've known all along."

"OK," he says. "I have to finesse this. We have exclusivity agreements with Lauer and O'Reilly.* It's not as easy as just letting you have at her. But I'll try to work something out. How 'bout you meet me at 30 Rock tomorrow after the 'Today' show?"

"Done."

"See . . . I'm not that bad a guy. I'm looking out for you."

"Sure," I say. "Sure you are."

1:10 P.M.

Inside her car, Jana is dialing for quotes. I wonder whether to feel guilty about having bluffed Caruso into a Polumbo sit-down. A quote occurs to me, something I'd read: *If diplomats lie in service of country, politicians in service of career and Casanovas in service of love . . .* I finish the quote . . . *then what do tabloid reporters lie for?* I don't answer, not with spoken words. And, really . . . I don't have to; I need only look at this woman, phone to her ear, scribbling notes, to know the answer. Would she have done the same? Competition—and actions taken within the context of as much—can justify a lot. And, besides, I don't feel guilty. More like I'd just executed a coup, having traded on a lie, on a pretense to having possessed—and suppressed—the same information on which Jana's dubious yet effective Wawa exclusive had been founded. But the subterfuge? The bluff? It was getting me places, much better places than if I'd played it square.

I return to my car, unaware that none of it would matter, unknowing that something was just then ticking its way down the New York City news

---

* Polumbo was to appear on Fox News with Bill O'Reilly following her "Today" show appearance with Matt Lauer.

transom that would dwarf Miss New Jersey—and unmask it for what it really was: a good tabloid tale, perhaps even the biggest news of the day, but insignificant relative to real news. Yes, the *News* and the *Post* had fought over the story for four days as if it were both papers' last stand. But they contested everything that way, as a point of "This far and no farther." I was just too green to realize it or to know when it really counted. But I'd learn and within only fifteen hours, when my phone rang at 4 A.M. and Sal's shockingly alert voice barked, "Head to Brooklyn!"

6

⣿

"2 Cops Shot During Traffic Stop"

Daily News headline, July 9, 2007

AMONG KERRY BURKE'S memorable pronouncements was "When a cop gets shot in New York City, it's like Pearl Harbor!"—a declaration that had less to do with the official response to such a catastrophe than the hysteria it ignited among the city's media corps. But the phrase's durability isn't rooted in its drama or even how Kerry delivered it like a wrestler vowing to win the belt. Like all enduring phrases, it's lasted because it's true.

Around 2:30 A.M., as Miss New Jersey rested for her "Today" show appearance (and I did the same, in anticipation of meeting her afterward) a twenty-three-year-old NYPD rookie named Russel Timoshenko and his partner, Herman Yan, spotted a black BMW X5 SUV cruising in Crown Heights, Brooklyn. The license plate was registered to a 2007 Mitsubishi Outlander. They pulled the SUV over. Timoshenko approached it from the passenger's side; Yan, from the driver's. Inside, three men waited, two armed to the teeth and one behind the wheel. All three had felony records, and two had a pair of felonies each. If those two were arrested, again, they'd likely trigger New York state's Persistent Felony Offender law, or "Three Strikes Rule," exposing them to life sentences. One, Dexter Bostic, was out past the curfew stipulated by his parole. In other words, none of them had anything to lose. The next seconds would occupy the collective consciousness of New York City for the next ten days, as Bostic and Robert Ellis, both thirty-four, opened fire, the fusillade slicing Timoshenko's spinal cord and hitting Yan in his forearm and chest. Amazingly, Yan returned fire—at least ten shots—as the SUV fled eastward, toward Kingston Avenue.

Sal ordered me to the scene before 4 A.M. over my protests that I was to meet Polumbo at NBC Studios later in the day.

"Forget that. This is way more important," he replied.

I stifled outrage. After all that hustle—and hard work—a bigger story had nullified everything. Or seemed to.

The "scene" was two blocks east of Prospect Park, where Brooklyn's gentrified coast concluded and its untamed interior began. There, an African American majority, occasionally militant, resided in uneasy peace with a Jewish Orthodox minority. Four-story pre-war apartments cascaded into three-story row homes. Ground-floor retail was a hodgepodge of barber shops, nail salons, Chinese laundries, Szechuan takeouts, an auto parts dealer, a revivalist congregation, pizza parlors, and a bodega. Cornices of dentil crown molding married the buildings into a seemingly single contiguous edifice. At the scene's beating heart was Timoshenko and Yan's radio car—eerily motionless where Rogers Avenue met Lefferts Boulevard. Cops mulled about it, like ants on a fallen picnic sandwich. Some loitered while others measured and probed amid, perhaps, a dozen billfold evidence markers. Catty-corner to the car was a daycare center with a fire-engine-red awning. Most urgently, I saw no sign of the *Post*, although a mob of other media was present.

(Runner's tradecraft: Upon arriving at a scene, a runner's first job is to attain a rudimentary understanding of the who, what, when, and where of what's happened, which will then be transmitted to the desk for the composition of sked lines and online briefs. This is straightforward. Either witnesses are present, or not. Then comes the decision: Do you stay with the pack? Or do you go it alone? Reporters typically work in bunches, ensuring that no one gets beat but also that no one obtains anything exclusive—and thus glory. Good runners become lone wolves. They break off. They hunt for the remarkable. There is risk in doing so. While a runner is off hunting, the pack may obtain a key witness, or crucial detail, and a runner's absence will look all the worse for everyone's having gotten this information while they did not. It takes guts and confidence to go it alone. Kerry Burke echoed this requisite in describing his approach to breaking-news scenes:

I see the pack of reporters, and I don't follow the pack. I try to go off in a different direction. I keep an eye on them—I understand that playing defense is a part of every game—but I don't just hang around waiting for the Deputy Commissioner of Public Information [DCPI], the [NYPD's] press liaison on crime scenes, to give me handouts. Basically, what they give is [the] cop version. Very often, they don't show up at all. And very often when they do, they don't talk. I respect what they do, but frankly that's not where you get stories. If you're just going to produce all the same stuff as everybody else, how good are you at your job?)[1]

The *Post's* Josh Williams: "You have to take chances on the street and go outside the box. If you don't, you get what everyone else is getting or nothing. Certainly not enough to beat the *News*."

Williams recounted a compelling story to illustrate his point. He said that on November 11, 2005, he was one of three *Post* shooters who were working the biggest story of the day against an equal number of shooters from the *News*. A month or so earlier, a Queens woman had vanished and her four-year-old daughter was found barefoot and alone on a Forest Hills Street. On October 6, the woman's body had been fished from a Pennsylvania landfill. Now, she was being mourned at the Brooklyn Funeral Home in East New York.

Obviously, the shot everyone wanted was the kid coming to mourn her mother. But the cops didn't want us getting it. They wanted to protect the little girl. So, they stuffed us in a press pen in a vacant lot across the street from the funeral home. We were climbing over each other, using ladders. But it was no good. Next to the funeral home was a gated entrance and from the pen, you couldn't see the lot behind it. Once the car was in, there'd be nothing you could do to get the shot. You were done. So, everyone is looking forward and I look up and see these guys in an apartment looking out a window, down on the parking lot. I sort of backed away and made a hand signal. Then I went inside and met them. The place was a mess. A dope den. Needles everywhere, people on mattresses. The guys were zombies. But as soon as I got up there, the car came and made for the gate. I made the kid out the window. The only shot. My editors told me not to say a word. I can only imagine what the *News* shooters thought when they saw the *Post's* front page the next day. God, I loved kicking their ass.

On-scene, the NYPD had sequestered eight square blocks around Rogers and Lefferts with yellow police tape, making thorough coverage impossible. I had to pick a spot and hope the *Post* didn't score on the other side. I drifted to the corner of Bedford and Lefferts and meshed with a scrum of spectators, media, and uniformed cops. Reporters grabbed anyone who answered "Yes" to some version of the question "Do you know what happened?" Crowd members pushed and shoved for their moment on camera. Kerry Burke, again, on crime scenes: "Very often it's absolute chaos. But, you know, I've been doing this for a while, and I read scenes to figure out what's happening when the world's gone mad. I realize, okay, these detectives are the actual case detectives and those detectives aren't. Okay, that's family. Okay, the shots had to have come from over there. You figure out what happened just by looking at the lay of the land and everybody involved."

I did so, now. People congregated on stoops, on the sidewalk, in the street. It was a nice day and they seem to crave some measure of community. Even without questioning, they replayed the events, some because their knowledge conferred a short-lived authority. Mostly, though, people picked it apart and imposed logic on the illogical. If it could happen to that cop, it could happen to anybody. I learned to approach groups with care and with my notebook stowed. I learned to listen for a good long while before making an introduction. I learned that the best information often comes without one's ever asking a question, and humility goes a long way, especially in a neighborhood like that.

The initial canvass complete, I dumped my notes to Alison Gendar, who headed the *News'* bureau at 1 Police Plaza, the NYPD's Manhattan headquarters. Every local paper—and some wire services and TV stations—had such outposts, allowing for the face-to-face conversations necessary to get anything more than a grimace out of the cops. All these "shacks," as they are called, were about the size of a large walk-in closet and honeycombed in the same corner of 1PP. The walls were thin and because of this, reporters like Alison often whispered in a campfire murmur when discussing exclusive content, or when taking field feeds. She thus spoke as I dictated my notes for the *News'* online story. The story would contain the basics, and exclusive gets would be held in abeyance for the print edition, so the *Post* could not steal what we'd digitally published for their own tabloid brew.

Afterward, I checked my cell—it was still several hours from the appointed time to call Caruso. I hadn't given up yet on Miss New Jersey, having informed the attorney of my redeployment while en route to the scene. He'd said to call back at 1 P.M. So, I loitered near the police tape and listened as a burly guy with a Johnnie Walker tan and Jimmy Durante nose spread bombast around the block like salt before a snowstorm. He had blondish, graying, close-cropped hair and wore dark suit pants and a cream-colored golf shirt with a U.S. Marshal–like five-cornered badge embossed over the breast. He was asking the journalists, "What do you guys need?" and acting, generally, in a way that made me think of the police captain Michael Corleone whacked during his meet with the Turk. This was Lt. P, or so I was soon told, the most belligerently nasty fuck to work in DCPI, the NYPD's Orwellian media office.

Now, a word on DCPI. All NYPD-related media inquiries had to go through DCPI, and if a runner so much as spoke to an officer at a scene— or anywhere—the pro forma reply was, "Call DCPI." The joke among runners was if you had been shot and asked an officer for help, but wore your press card, you would be told to, "Call DCPI." Despite this, older runners spoke of a more accommodating time—when you could get close to a corpse—that ended once Rudy Giuliani and his second police commissioner, Ray Kelly, took power. After that, information was tightly controlled and strategically dispensed. More than once, DCPI released a report about a police officer's arrest ahead of a thin Saturday paper on Friday at 11 P.M.

Ostensibly, DCPI was a single person, the deputy chief of Public Information. The NYPD's top PR guy. But the abbreviation also referred to the department he oversaw. In 2006, Paul Browne occupied this lofty station. Browne had once been a New York Statehouse reporter but became an NYPD company man who wrote typically stilted press releases in bad, passive voice–heavy prose. He was widely despised among New York City reporters for suppressing information. When Browne announced his retirement in 2013, the cheeky New York City website Gothamist published a story with this headline: "LYING NYPD SPOKESMAN PAUL BROWNE TO STEP DOWN (UNLESS THAT'S ALSO A LIE?)."

Now, reporters peppered Browne's on-scene surrogate with questions, most of which the fellow answered obliquely, if at all. The exasperation this engendered was exacerbated by the fact that not twenty feet away a ponytailed reporter was scribbling furiously in a notebook while chatting with Gene White, the lieutenant who occupied the No. 2 spot at DCPI. Finally, I asked Lt. P, "Who's that reporter over there with the ponytail?"

"Why do you want to know?" he asked, his nice-guy façade suddenly melting like an ice cube in the scotch I surmised would accompany his lunch. Its subtraction left a hard cop's glare.

"Well, he's walking with Gene White," I said. "And I heard Gene say he was going to give him a ride back to 1PP."

"So, what if he is?"

"Well, that makes me nervous. It's competitive out here and I don't want him getting something I'm not."

"I'm shocked you said that. Shocked!" he replied, and turned to Carmine Aloisio, a WNBC cameraman. Carmine was a vet's vet, a guy who lugged his camera around with perpetual good cheer. "He's shocked you said that, too," Lt. P said, nodding his swollen, vein-filigreed nose at Carmine. I looked at Carmine, whose expression hadn't changed. I asked him if he was, indeed, shocked, and Carmine feigned hearing someone calling him from afar.

After that, I disengaged from Lt. P, and Carmine returned to my side and whispered of the ponytailed man: "That's Tom Hays with the AP. He's sourced up the kazoo."

"Who's that guy?" I asked, nodding toward the NYPD officer with whom I had just spoken.

"That's Lt. P. He hates reporters and hates having to release information to them. And where does he work? DCPI. What a world we live in."

Carmine punctuated this wisdom by deadlifting his camera to his shoulder, then waddled off in search of B-roll. I watched him shortly aim his camera at the radio car like a bazooka, then melt into the crowd. My cell phone rang. Michael Schwartz was calling from Rockefeller Center. He said he'd just made Polumbo leaving "Today" and that although "my friend from the *Post*" was on site, no words had been given or gotten. "I don't think they like her," Mike said. "Polumbo got into the car and Jana kept asking questions. She was pissed and got aggressive but they just shut the door." I congratulated him, allowed that I had something up my sleeve for later—if I could only get away from this shooting. After that, Mike concluded the call in the same endearing way he did all of them: "Bye-bye."

From there, I reconnoitered the police tape, probing for weakness and aperture. Action and movement overcame anxiety. Action if only for action's sake. Action to ward off worry over the *Post*, still unseen, yet certainly lurking. At Empire Boulevard and Rogers, I ducked under the tape while a woman inquired of its sentry when residents could return to their homes. He requested her driver's license to validate claims of local residence, providing opportunity for tabloid incursion. While walking, I did not look at the cop, nor did I look over my shoulder, although I very much wanted to out of anxiety he had seen me. I only looked during the moment before I entered an apartment building adjacent to the radio car intersection under the pretense of assisting an elderly woman who was trying with difficulty to maneuver a push carriage of groceries over the threshold.

Once inside, I found the building suggestive of dozens I'd infiltrated for stories, typically proceeding door-to-door, knocking on each one, waiting that seemingly long interval that is really only seconds, when you strain to hear whether your knocking has prompted motion, and then somewhat eager and somewhat anxious of the asking to come and the reception that asking will bring. *Did you know so-and-so? What sort of person were they? When did you last see them? What's in your heart now as I inform you, begrudgingly, of the tragedy that has befallen them? Do you have any photos? Do you know where I could obtain one? Do they have any kin who live in this building?*

Most of the buildings, pre-war, looked the same, regardless of the borough, with ornate lobbies, artfully crafted tile floors, often checkered and forming a pattern doubly impressive when viewed from the second floor, if a staircase allowed for such macro viewing. There were woodwork cornices and sometimes staircases on both sides of the lobby, like in the dining room of a cruise ship. And somewhere a bank of mailboxes with unit numbers—and if you were lucky—names of the residents, as well.

In this case, I was not looking for someone, but anyone who had viewed the shooting. I started on the side of the building where the units might have windows facing the relevant intersection, knocking on each door, noting the ones where no one answered so the next runner to conduct a canvass—surely there would be a second one on such an important story— could revisit the units where no one had answered. Shortly, I knocked on a door that opened to a young black man with veiled eyes resonant of recent sleep. He wore a robe over his naked torso. On his sternum, the nub of a scar protruded as large as a nose and I fought against looking, although I could not help but look and he saw my looking and I felt ashamed and compounded the mistake by asking, "Did you get shot?"

He shook his head and said, "Nah, stabbed," and I asked what had happened and he replied, now grinning, "I don't even know, man. Some guys tried to rob me. Halloween a few years ago." I nodded gravely, and said, "Jesus," and he replied, still grinning, "He had nothing to do with it. Listen, I gotta roll. First I heard of the shooting was on the news."

My canvass, or the remainder of it, proved equally unproductive, and when I concluded on the top floor I ascended a stairwell that led to the roof. Shortly I was outside, looking down at the crime scene, eight stories below. John Doyle, a *Post* runner, and Gary Miller, a *Post* shooter, stood near the radio car. They'd breached the tape and moved candidly inside it. John spoke to a police official and Gary stood abreast him, and I felt worried and gloomy, so much so I hustled down the eight flights to find the same official. But when I exited, I saw neither John, nor Gary, nor the official and so made my way past the radio car and down Rogers Avenue, where I resumed my canvass.

I continued without success until around 1 o'clock when I called Caruso, but he did not answer and so I returned to Bedford and Lefferts, watching a *Times* photographer working frankly and unapologetically, there and within the tape, while an NYPD sentry stood nearby. I assumed the sentry would not interfere with my doing the same and so abandoned my efforts toward subterfuge and subtlety. But as I knocked on the second door—the cop approached and asked roughly, "What do you think you're doing?"

He was a uniformed cop, maybe twenty-five. And when I informed him I was with the *News*, he reacted to my violation of the tape as a personal affront to his authority.

"Get . . . behind . . . the . . . tape . . . now!"

I became ferocious, a product, I suppose, of too little sleep; worry over the *Post*; anger over having lost, or possibly lost, the Polumbo interview; and too much repressed nervous energy from sitting too long on stakeout. Or maybe it was just a live wire in my brain, long malfunctioning, that goes haywire when anyone in authority acts with ignorance or carelessness for the theoretical underpinnings of that power, or as an abuse of it. Many journalists have this same defect. And so my reply was a big, fat, ugly sneer: "I'll do what you want—tough guy—but there's no reason to get all 'NYPD Blue' about it. In fact, you should probably lay off the TV. From the looks of it, you're getting too much."

Normally, I think, he would have arrested me. But I had my press pass around my neck and so was—within the boundaries of a certain measure of insubordination—inviolate. I knew it; so did he. So, when he asked me why I had to "catch an attitude," I sneered, again: "Because those who show respect, get respect, and you ain't showing me or my job any!"

"Get off my block!" he roared.

"*Your block?* This isn't your block. This belongs to the people of New York, who pay your salary, but that ain't much, is it? What are you out here for? Twenty-five grand a year? Keep grinding it out, tough guy. Now I know why you're so pissed off."

It was an ignorant remark—and one that I regret now with age and hindsight and especially after learning that the wounded cop, Russel Timoshenko, was making only $100 more than the quoted figure. My regret does not concern the edge it provided to my competition, for at this point, Pablo Guzman, a WCBS channel 2 reporter, sidled his sure-I'll-have-another-helping girth over to the cop, snaked his boa constrictor's arm around his shoulders, and with "I'm cutting the line at Walt Disney World" nerve, apologized for my poor behavior.

"I'm, *so, so* sorry about that," he cooed in a honeyed baritone. "You, frankly, deserve better."

"See, Pablo!" the cop cried. "That's the difference between a professional like yourself and a low-budget reporter."

Pablo Guzman nodded with four-alarm-fire gravitas. Momentarily, I saw—but couldn't hear—him pumping the cop for details about the shooting and scribbling notes.

"See, kid. That's how it's done."

It was Aloisio, again, clearly my crime scene Jiminy Cricket, schooling me on a how a crime scene was a crime scene but also a journalists' jungle and I had played squirrel to Guzman's owl. "We'd eat each other alive out here if it meant a get," said Carmine. "Thank god I just gotta shoot the camera."

Carmine was sympathetic, and that gave me an opportunity. I had, by then, called Caruso twice, to no avail. He was screening calls. I asked Carmine if I could borrow his cell. The hunch played. Caruso greeted me first with surprise, then ludicrous affability.

"Good to hear from you!"

"What's the scoop?" I asked.

"Mike, things are unraveling. I'm getting bombarded."

"What's that supposed to mean?"

Edginess and indignation laced my reply. Carmine frowned. I slathered Pablo Guzman–esque honey over my voice:

"Pardon me, Tony . . . What's going on?"

"It means I'm not sure I can help you. She came out after the 'Today' show and I let Mike shoot photos. But some guy got in her face with his own camera."

"Who'd he work for?"

"That's just it. I don't think he worked for anyone. He didn't have a professional camera. And Amy got rattled."

"Come on, Tony. Don't leave me high and dry."

"All right. What do you need?"

"Three minutes . . . that's all."

"I can't do it. She's shook up, Mike. If you get anything, it'll be you walking with her in the lobby or to the limousine and you get to ask one question. Something like, 'Hey Amy, how do ya like New York?' and she'll say, 'Great. Great. I'm having a good time.'"

"All right, but if I only get one question, let me ask something that will give me a response I can turn into a story."

"What do you have in mind?"

I considered angles. I needed something that would make news, something on which a story could be hung. Polumbo, I knew, would be made to account for the photos at an emergency meeting of the Miss New Jersey chapter's board the following week.

"All right," I said, "how 'bout I ask what she'll say to the board on Thursday. And her answer will be, 'I deserve to keep the crown.' In fact, if that were her answer I could work with that."

"All right. I'm not promising anything. She's her own woman."

"You gotta come through for me, here, man. I know Bill O'Reilly and Matt Lauer . . ."

"Mike, stop whining."

"I'm not whining!"

"I'll tell you what. I'll ask her stepfather. He's here with me in the hotel room."

Muted voices, then a rustle of words, then Tony resumed the phone, then the assent for which I'd fought.

"All right," Tony said. "'I deserve to keep the crown.' That okay with you? Her dad says it's okay, so that's one person in your corner."

"Cool."

"Where are you now?" he asked.

"I'm in Brooklyn."

"All right, be prepared to be in Manhattan within the hour."

"What hotel you at?"

"I'm not telling you yet. Come to midtown, then call me at 4 and if anyone asks how you got this quote, you can't tell them that I arranged it for you. Is that understood?"

"Sure," I said, then relayed the gist of the agreement to Sal, who dispatched Kerry Burke to relieve me in Brooklyn. Sal instructed me to hold position until Kerry's arrival—then informed me that a group called "The Committee to Save Miss America" had assumed responsibility for the Polumbo plot and could I ask Caruso about them? I told him I would, then waited, although Kerry did not arrive by 3:30, or the time I had marked as the deadline to abandon the scene. Insubordinate, I returned to my car and drove into midtown.

At 4:15, Tony called and said without preamble, "All right, let's go over this. No cameras. No one else. One question. If I see anyone else, the deal is off," and I told him okay even though I would have very much liked, at that point, to tell him—and his client—to jump in a lake.

But I did not and abstained from any outbursts, and so Tony identified the hotel—the Muse Hotel, located on 46th Street.

"We're going to come out at 5," he added, to which I replied I'd await him in the lobby.

"No!" he barked. "That will look too obvious. People will think I told you to wait there," and I asked him to clarify what seemed, to me, an impossible concern over potential witnesses. He replied with exasperation I felt was wholly undue, "I can't be seen to give the *News* preferential treatment over the *Post*. It will come back on my client," and although this mollified me, this clear articulation of the risk, however small, he was assuming on my behalf, I still thought such OCD-like precautions ridiculous.

"There's no chance Jana will be there," I said.

"Even still."

"Tony, let me ask something, but you gotta promise not to tell Bill O'Reilly or Jana. We got wind the people behind this mess are calling themselves 'The Committee to Save Miss America,' and those photos—the latest batch—are only the second of twenty-six sets."

"I know," he said. "They're the signatories of the letter."

"So, you know?"

"Yes, of course."

"Well, can I have a quote about it?"

Tony commenced, saying, "I don't care what they call themselves. There is no such thing . . . ," but then stopped and added, "Strike that . . ."

"Listen," he dilated, "if I give you a quote, then I have to call Jana back and give her one, too. She's called three times over the last hour asking for an update."

"But that's ridiculous," I said. "I'm about to talk to Amy exclusively."

"Mike, you're only getting that one question and you assured me you'd say it was an accident if anyone asked how you got that quote."

"Yes, of course," I said, wearily.

"So, what do you want to do?" he asked.

"Forget it," I replied, not giving the matter thought but acting from my gut and the animosity for the *Post* that dwelled there. "I'd rather have no quote and keep Jana in the dark than have one and risk them getting the bit about the committee, too, if they don't already have it."

"Wow!" he said. "You guys really hate each other, huh?"

"You have no idea."

"Good enough," he said and rang off.

I opened my car door and melded into the rush-hour crush. The pedestrians on Sixth Avenue moved quickly and purposefully and with that urgent single-mindedness Manhattan commuters possess when fleeing work, each passing second drawing more workers from their posts—and into the street—and thus extending the duration it will take those already there to get home. Navigating this, I went one block south and turned west on to 46th Street and found the Muse Hotel midway on the south side of the street. The façade had two glass doors with decorative iron door pulls as big as cricket bats, both doors bookended by miniature conifer trees ensconced in Ali Baba vases with black and tan stripes. Above the entrance and jutting out as far as the curb was an oblong marquee with a lot of lights, not yet illuminated, that wouldn't be too big of an injustice for a Broadway play. It had "MUSE" scribbled on it in an undeliberate hand and the words, "the" and "new york" above and below it, respectively, in lower case and a more traditional font.

Inside, the lobby was breaking its back to look contemporary. There were black Italian leather divans and ottomans and cylindrical end tables with copper finishes; a glossy floor of clouded marble trisected by black columns running from the front door to the reception desk; dark-paneled wood that wasn't mahogany but looked it under the muted, recessed lighting; albino *bonsai* plants; a marble-tiled mosaic; and a flush mount light fixture, above it all, that looked like the top of the transporter room on the starship *Enterprise*.

And there was blue light—lots of it—and a typical Manhattan lounge off the lobby where a young man would have little trouble finding an older woman of a certain type after 10 P.M.—and especially on a weeknight. She'll have a very definite European air, or seem exotic, and will smoke long, thin cigarettes of an obscure brand sold at only a single Upper East Side importer, although she will seem shocked when you don't recognize the brand's name. She might wear headwear, although not definitely, but if so, it would be a fedora, tilted rakishly so you could not too easily comprehend her expression, other than a mysterious smile, from far away. She would have liberally applied fire-engine-red lipstick and lavender eye shadow, as well as mascara in such quantity her lashes might resemble a garden rake. She will drink a complicated cocktail, served in martini stemware, and say something like, "I always drink these when I'm in New York," although much later in the evening she will jokingly confess she is from Gravesend. And when you break down and can resist no longer, she will uncross her legs and reveal French-cut black stockings and garter straps and no underwear and there will be a moment of almost ecstatic comprehension of what is before you and what is imminently to come; and for years, when you are alone in bed, aching, you will think of her, regardless of faults now recognized, and seize upon the embers of the yearning you felt at that moment and the heights she later took you to.

I grabbed a Perrier from a table full of them off the front desk, strolled over and asked its heroin chic attendant if any other entrances or exits were located off the lobby.

"Well, this is the front lobby," she replied. I nodded, seethed, and stalked outside, the minutes passing palpably and as if audibly through the ticking of an enormous, unseen clock. 4:30. 4:35. 4:40. 4:45. Then, Tony rang my cell and I fumbled it before answering.

"All right, we're going to come out at 5:15," he said. "Are you here?"

"I'm in front."

"No cameras?"

"No cameras."

"Listen," he said. "If you see anything suspicious, give me a call."

"Suspicious?"

"Other media."

"Will do."

I clicked off and noted stray details that would permit Corky to embellish a lone quote into a plausible story. I reminded myself, again, to take note of Polumbo's hair, clothing, and demeanor, knowing he would request such granular details to lard the piece. Then, incredibly and around 5 o'clock, I saw something Tony might consider "suspicious."

It was a camera crew! But not just any! The cameraman wore spiked hair, a Megadeth T-shirt, leather pants, jackboots, and a silver, hooped eyebrow ring. The reporter was, perhaps, 4'10", and wore a blond pixie haircut streaked with green highlights. She wore a gray hoodie, jeans, and shit-kicker Doc Martens. A third woman, perhaps the producer, was only slightly taller, with vampire porcelain skin, crow-black hair, and a crescent of diamond studs along the rim of one ear. This wasn't NBC. It wasn't even WPIX. But it might alarm Caruso. I asked the reporter for her affiliation.

"No one," she said.

"What's your assignment?"

"We're with a German TV station, making a documentary about young artists in New York."

Of course! The answer seemed almost comically self-evident once rendered. I phoned Caruso and left a panicked voicemail beseeching him to "Not get freaked out when you see them!" then all but barricaded the front doors so there would be no chance I could miss them on the way out. Finally—at 5:30—they exited. Miss New Jersey was followed by her mother and Caruso, who wore a dark suit, white shirt, and orange tie. Polumbo wore a white sports coat over a fuchsia dress and pearls. Her blond hair was made up and parted off-center, and she was no longer the girlish youth I had seen outside her home—but the woman from her first press conference. And yet, when I yelled, "Hey Amy. Mike with the *News*," a goofy smile lit up her face and overcame the artful effect of the makeup and returned her, again, to the ingénue I'd seen five days earlier. I continued, "What are you going to say . . ." although I was not able to finish before she replied, like a bad actress, "I deserve to keep the crown!" and she giggled and slid into an SUV that quickly pulled away, leaving me in front of the hotel with her mother, Jennifer Wagner.

"Long days, huh?"

"You have no idea," she replied, staring vacantly at the unoccupied parking spot. "Be good to my Amy, huh?"

I nodded and said I would, although I knew I couldn't promise anything. And yet nodding and promising as much—in that moment—seemed like the right thing to do.

Simultaneously and in Crown Heights, *Post* shooter Gary Miller[*] and Kerry Burke battled for surveillance footage of Timoshenko's shooting. Gary, like many *News* and *Post* shutterbugs, staff and otherwise, had a colorful origin story. Before joining the *Post*—before, in fact, any career in photography—he'd worked fifteen years with the NYPD, ten of those as an undercover narcotics detective in Brooklyn. Gary, who is black and rangy and looks like a menacing version of the singer Seal, wore his head shaved and spoke in a low rasp that sounded, at times, like a hiss. His career with the NYPD concluded prematurely after he was accidentally hit by a motorist while en route to an undercover drug buy, although he remained on the city rolls as a provisional Bronx public school teacher. Within months of beginning his new gig, he assigned his students the writing of a play that would later be performed as a school production. I'll let Gary—at this point—pick up the narrative as it was once relayed to myself during the long stakeout hours when the fodder of our pasts became a convivial means of passing the time.

When the show was over, I asked this kid, Stanley—who was like the school hoodlum—to help me put all the equipment I'd rented for

---

[*] While Gary's Christian name is, in fact, Gary, he uses the byline G. N. Miller to honor the first and middle initials of his daughter.

the play back in my truck. Stanley refused. So, I took the stuff down myself and left the kids in the classroom with the pizza I'd gotten to celebrate. So, now I'm downstairs discussing something with another teacher, when one of the kids runs down and tells me Stanley is going berserk. He's throwing pizza and fucking everything up. So, I run upstairs and I go, "Stanley, what the fuck?" And Stanley doesn't say anything but runs outside and I'm chasing him and when I finally catch up, he's outside messing with my truck and I know my service revolver is in a locked box, inside. The hood is open and so is the passenger door and I'm thinking he might have my gun. So, he takes off and I chase him. I chase him for, like, fifteen blocks and when I catch him, I drag him back to the school, literally drag him, because at several points, he goes dead weight on me. Well, someone must have seen all this and called 911 because the cops were there when I got Stanley back to the school. Stanley was arrested, and the media got wind of the whole thing and it made headlines the next day. Now, my name wasn't released—or published—but I was put on leave and had this administrative hearing scheduled to explain myself. So, I was killing time and I'd always had this interest in photography. You know, amateur, like. And one day I'm out taking pictures and I see this dog drowning and the [NYPD's Emergency Service Unit] saves the dog. Well, I took some shots and they got published. By the time that hearing rolled around, I was already getting shifts at the *Post* and so I just said forget it. Later on, I made staff.

With this context in mind, I'll now resume the narrative of the events that occurred in Crown Heights while I elicited a contrived quote from Miss New Jersey in Manhattan.

The way Gary told the story, he noticed during the morning that several surveillance cameras were affixed to the façade of the daycare center at Rogers and Lefferts—the same daycare center with the fire-engine-red awning next to where the firefight had occurred and Timoshenko and Yan's radio car had stopped. He said he first saw the cameras while shooting with his long-lens camera. Then, around 11 A.M., while I was still on-scene and perhaps even just before or after I had watched in horror, from the rooftop, as he and Doyle talked to the police official, he saw the daycare center's owners return to their place of business and be permitted by the cops to go inside. He said he followed them, found a janitor, and was directed to said owners. This might explain why I saw neither Gary nor Doyle after having rushed down the eight flights.

Once, again, allowing Gary to assume the narrative: "I said the *Post* would be interested in buying the video. You know, getting some frame grabs, and then she showed me the tape and I said to myself, 'Holy shit! This shit is great!' So, the desk told me to give her a price. They didn't tell me what to offer. They just said to say a number, so I threw out $5,000. They agreed and I left to get my computer so I could transmit the video to the desk and in the meantime the owner was going to draw up a contract. I think she was talking with my desk, but when I came back Paul Martinka* was there, sitting on the place until I could get back to make sure the *News* didn't barge in while I was gone."

But as it happened, the *News* didn't barge in, or at least not until after Kerry spied Gary returning to the center from having retrieved his computer. Kerry, who'd relieved me shortly after I arrived in Manhattan around 3:30, told me he had been standing outside the police tape when he "saw Miller follow that other cat Martinka into the center, and yeah, there was a cop, and the tape was still up, but at that point, there really wasn't any other choice. I just pulled up my necktie and told the cop, 'I gotta get into that daycare center!' And the cop didn't reply. I walked by him too fast for him to say anything."

Added Gary in retrospect: "Kerry was on the street and I think he knew I was finagling something, so I tried to sneak in through a side door to the daycare center on the way back with my computer, but he saw me and he came in behind me as I went. The janitor didn't want to let him in, but Kerry told him he'd spoken to the owner over the phone and the guy moved aside. At that point, that's when the negotiation occurred."

What happened next has become New York City tabloid legend— conveyed orally and embellished over time. Everyone has their own version—varying minutely although consistent and appropriately dramatic as concerns the broader strokes. Part of the problem is Kerry, who remains—to this day—so deeply chagrined he refuses to discuss the details.

"It got ugly in there. That's all I'm going to say," Kerry explained when I asked him. "Gary said some things in there and he'll have to live with them, although I suspect it's easier for him to live with them than it would be for others. You know what I mean, brotha?"

As for Gary, the cop-turned-tabloid shooter proved both more forgiving of what happened and voluble in relating the specifics. Perhaps this is attributable to who concluded the day as the victor, although the reason for Gary's candor remains unknown.

---

* Paul Martinka was another *Post* staff shooter who primarily covered Brooklyn.

So, I got in there [Gary said], and the *Post* had upped the figure, in the meantime, to $7,000 and we had, you know, a verbal commitment. Their lawyer had contacted our office and spoken to our lawyer. Either the *Post*'s lawyer or someone at the photo desk was going to e-mail a contract to her lawyer. The final contract had not yet been signed and shipped. They'd done it verbally—like a handshake. So, as I go in there and started talking about taking the tape—and they were already dubbing a copy for me at this point—Kerry starts telling her he wants the tape and the *News* will pay more.

First I said, "Let's go half-and-half on this, Kerry. No one is gonna win. No one is gonna lose." But Kerry said, "No!" He wanted the scoop. So, I said, "No! They can't have it! This is exclusive," and I got on the phone with my office and I gave the daycare owner my phone and she spoke to someone there, whoever was on the desk. A brief conversation. I could see her face was stressed. Whatever was said, it was tense. Then my office called her lawyer. All this while Burke was saying he'd pay $10,000. And then finally she told Kerry, "OK. We'll give it to you." And I said, "No! You have a contract," and she said, "No. We never signed it." But I reminded her that it was a verbal thing and all the while Kerry is pulling out his checkbook—he was fucking walking around with the damn thing in that stupid book bag—and as he's writing the check, I said, "No, you can't!"

But Kerry did. He traded a check for $10,000, scrawled out on the spot, in return for the critical video. Some accounts have Gary, at this juncture, decrying the check as fraudulent—"Don't take it! It's a fake!"—while others have Kerry quitting the center in a more decorous fashion. On this point, neither Kerry nor Gary will elaborate, although Gary did contradict Kerry's notion that he might find it hard to "live with himself" by explaining that, whatever actually occurred inside the daycare center, he sleeps just fine at night.

Regardless, Kerry then negotiated a ride from the daycare owner's assistant, which—in the final accounting—proved to be not only his undoing, but the *News*', as well. For as he was being driven back to Manhattan, sitting in the vehicle, the *Post*'s lawyers threatened to sue the daycare center owner for breach of contract, even though it was only a verbal agreement and the actual contract had not yet been signed. "I think we scared her," Gary now opined. "We were putting the screws to her in a big way after Kerry left."

And it worked. Because somewhere over the Brooklyn Bridge, the assistant was ordered by the center's owner via mobile to return with the tape, which was then given to the *Post*. And while much conjecture has been expended by various parties about how they would have comported themselves in that situation—one *News* shooter said he would have grabbed the video from the assistant and jumped out of the moving car while in motion over the Brooklyn Bridge—Kerry said there was nothing he could have done.

A few things, however, are certain: Upon learning of the setback, Stu Marques hurled a phone across the city room, nearly hitting another editor, after which he retrieved the phone and remarked, "I thought these things were supposed to break when you threw them," and Kerry and Stu wouldn't speak for months. And that was just the superficial fallout. The real consequences didn't come until the next morning.

July 10, 2007

Much is made—and appropriately so—of the importance of a newspaper's front page, and no more so does this emphasis apply than when it comes to tabloids. There's a reason: Unlike broadsheets, which predominantly circulate through subscription (home delivery), tabloids rely, overwhelmingly, on newsstand sales. And when a prospective reader, usually a pedestrian, passes a newsstand, it is more often than not a tabloid's front page that tempts them to surrender the price of ownership. It is for this reason that responsibility for creating a tabloid's front page falls directly to its editor-in-chief. That, in fact, could be said to be his or her primary duty. And more often than not in tabloids, it is only a single story, or some combination of two or three, that occupies the front page.

Different newspapers have their own jargon for the front page. *The Jersey Journal*'s staff called it, simply, "the front page," while *The Press of Atlantic City* branded it "A1" in reference to its page number. At the *Boston Herald*, staff called it "the splash." But at the *Daily News* and the *Post*, the front page was rigidly referred to as "the wood," an allusion to a bygone era when wood engravings were still used to create it. In fact, so fetishized was "the wood" at the *News* and *Post* that when Kevin Convey—the *Herald*'s editor-in-chief—replaced Martin Dunn in 2010 and began referring to it as "the splash," it fell to Rob Moore—the managing editor—to quietly apprise him of the appropriate local nomenclature.

A good "wood"—constituted, ideally, by a good story, dramatic photo, witty headline, or some combination thereof—could translate, alone and independent of what content was published inside, into a powerful victory over the competition. But the wood was more than that, at least for the *News* and *Post* runners and shooters who'd competed to obtain the information and photos that constituted it. For what was the wood but the most tangible representation of who had won the prior day, either the *News* or the *Post*? You might think I'm crazy, but there was nothing quite like going to bed after obtaining a monster exclusive, knowing that in only a few short hours you would not only be able to see and touch the physical manifestation of your triumph but measure the scale and grandeur of your victory by how greatly the *Post* lacked. The only thing to which I can reasonably compare the feeling was the childhood expectancy that accompanied Christmas Eve, when I still believed Santa Claus would come during the night.

All of this said, I never saw a more profound disparity in the *News* and *Post* woods—and thus a greater victory, and corresponding defeat—than in the two days immediately following Timoshenko's shooting. It was so bad, in fact, that the *Post*'s street corps seemed to universally defer to the *News* runner, Kerry, most involved in that defeat by abstaining from the gloating that characteristically accompanied such triumphs. In fact, I now recall how *Post* runners spoke, over those two days, about anything *but* the woods. They spoke about the Yankees, the shooting itself, or some other trivia, but not about the woods.

On July 10, the *Post*'s front-page screamer blared, "AMBUSH," over an image of Yan and Timoshenko, paces beyond their radio car, striding toward the SUV, unseen aside from its rear. The two cops, identified by arrows that culminated with their department mugshots, presciently had their right hands flush with their holsters. Below that main image was a smaller headline that read: "HERO COPS CAUGHT ON TAPE MOMENTS BEFORE BOTH ARE SHOT." To the right of this headline, a text box read, "PHOTO EXCLUSIVE" and contained the story lede and a tease to additional coverage on "PAGES 2, 3, 4, 5."

On July 11, the *Post*, again, bludgeoned the *News* with the daycare center footage, splashing three numbered frame grabs across its wood showing Yan heroically returning fire after his partner, Timoshenko, had been shot. These grabs ran to the left of a photo, taken on the 10th, of a convalescing Yan, dressed in street clothes and sporting his arm in a sling. Above this garish layout ran the massive, 140-point headline "SUPERCOP," as well as the secondary headline: "WOUNDED OFFICER KEPT ON SHOOTING." A text box teased additional coverage on pages 4, 5, 6 and 7. As for the *News*, it feebly relied on a piece from its top news columnist, Michael Daly, describing the video, as Kerry recalled it from memory. The *News*' front pages on the 10th and 11th aren't worth mentioning.

I don't remember much about the 10th, that awful, horrible second day. Bostic and Ellis were in the wind, and while the NYPD hunted them, every *News* city desk employee, it seemed—even Mike Daly—searched for some shred of footage not already purchased by the *Post*. Maybe my editors sensed what was coming on the 11th, after the defeat of the 10th, and wanted something—anything—to hold back the onslaught. But it was, as I said, a lost day.

My share of this hunt was based in a deduction that would leave me, by day's end, smelling of cooking grease. The NYPD arrested Woods hours after the shooting following the discovery of his fingerprint on a box of Popeyes chicken left in the abandoned BMW. To Gittrich, that suggested the trio had visited one of the dozen-plus Popeyes Chicken franchises in Brooklyn prior to the shooting. It also followed that surveillance cameras may have captured the group as they awaited the fulfillment of their order. My directive was clear: Find the footage, discover whether the NYPD had seized it, and determine if a copy remained for sale. And while I, ultimately, wasn't successful, Kerry Burke did, indeed, obtain the sought-after video—an ironic bit of redemption he referenced years later in finally revealing what he carried around in "that damn stupid book bag," as Gary put it.

> Everywhere I go I got this container of yogurt and muesli. I also carry cameras, flashlights, binoculars, notepads, pens, unread mail. I got bills in my bag and a newspaper to read. I have an iPad, which, in theory, I can file stories on, but that's been a bad investment because the iPad connection just doesn't really work when you need it. I have a charger, some plastic gloves, a Hagstrom map of the five boroughs, an umbrella and a checkbook, because the dirty side of the business is that sometimes I have to buy pictures. One time I got in a bidding war with the New York *Post* for footage of two police officers being killed. Another time I bought security footage of these killers. Before they went out to basically kill people, they went to a Popeyes Chicken. I went to that location and let's just say I bought $1,000 worth of chicken.[2]

Separately, the *News* hoarded one more trump, although the tabloid wouldn't play it for a week to come. While both papers stationed reporters at Kings County Hospital, where Yan recuperated and Timoshenko remained in a coma, only the *News* employed a runner—Veronika Belenkaya—who spoke the native tongue of the more severely wounded officer's parents. That fluency with Russian led to a rapport that, in turn, led to a scoop on July 17 in which Timoshenko's father, Leonid, spoke his first words to the press since his son's shooting: "They should be torn apart," he told Veronika, of Bostic, Ellis, and Woods.

This is not to say the *Post* didn't see it coming. As Veronika's familiarity with Leonid and his wife, Tatyana, became clear, the tabloid hired a Russian-speaking freelancer in an ultimately vain attempt to counter the *News'* edge. But by then, Veronika had gotten too close to the grieving parents. The resulting front-page story, published on the 17th, was a great victory and still more evidence of the *News'* dramatic recovery in the wake of the Burke surveillance video fiasco. I say "more" because, by then, the *News* had already stolen away the momentum from its crosstown competitor through what turned out to be a lucky break scored in the wooded wilds of Pennsylvania.

7

﹟

"Tracked Down and Busted in Pa. Woods"

Daily News **headline, July 12, 2007**

WHILE *NEWS* AND *POST* runners skirmished throughout New York City and beyond—"Pearl Harbor!" indeed—the search for Bostic and Ellis shifted to the Poconos, that lightly populated rustic region in eastern Pennsylvania. As it would later be reported, both fugitives had paid a pal to ferry them there in order to hide out. But upon arrival, they instead ordered him to continue on to South Carolina, where Bostic had kin. Indignant, the driver returned to New York and reported their whereabouts to police, who by Wednesday morning had converged upon the Poconos for an ultimately dramatic manhunt.

The Poconos is a straight shot from the city on I-80 West, the highway that begins at the George Washington Bridge and runs clear across the country to San Francisco. I drove it for seventy-five miles, the first thirty dull and scenic, the final forty-five frantic and a blur, as Gittrich called with updates about the pursuit. "Some shit newspaper in the Poconos is reporting Ellis and Bostic are hiding in the woods behind a Circuit City," he sneered, then conveyed an address on Gertrude Street in what turned out to be the borough of Stroudsburg. "Call me as soon as you get something."

I dialed Todd Maisel, the staff shooter the *News* had dispatched to meet me. Todd, as I've already said, was running personified: kinetic, relentless, and devoted to the get with a lama's purity of purpose. Years later, a colleague posted an open inquiry on Facebook asking how to avoid Memorial Day traffic when driving from New York City to the Long Island

Hamptons. One shooter's reply: "A hit of speed, Todd Maisel and off-road tires!" Now, Todd answered my call in that amped-up, nebbishy, voice that sounded so much like Woody Allen after a hit of meth. "You're joining the manhunt, too! That's just what they need: Two crazy motherfuckers!"

I found Gertrude Street and knew, at once, I had the right place. Four unmarked police sedans and a Pennsylvania State Police cruiser straddled the roadway. Big, prosperous colonial homes overlooked a thick, boundless thatch of brown reeds. Wading through those reeds were large men outfitted in bulletproof vests—gold and silver stars pinned to the shoulder straps—toting shotguns while combing the rolling, windblown mystery. In the distance, I heard the yelps of unseen dogs and theorized over the desperate, fugitive panic of two assuredly mud-crusted men on the run from the law.

Atop the crown of the hill, a grandstand of journalists, all local, stood behind the obligatory yellow police tape—tied from the back fender of an idling cruiser to a tree. The *Post* followed five minutes after my arrival—first in the form of an editor who lived nearby and then as Austin Fenner, the newly minted turncoat from the *News*. Together, they convened a sidebar about ten yards from the group, their hands veiling their mouths, as NFL coaches do when relaying calls from their sideline to an on-field quarterback. I suppose they feared I might be capable of reading their lips if they had not done so.

After they had concluded, I sidled abreast of Austin and inquired what it was like, "to work for the enemy." His reply was both memorable and revealing. Through chuckles, he said, "Same but different. It's surreal at first, like all the guys you've been competing against are now your teammates. Like you're on a basketball team and you've switched jerseys."

Then all at once, the cops ran from the brush to their vehicles, leaving man-sized swaths of broken reed stalks in their wakes. Then flashing lights. Then burning rubber. The manhunt had moved on; all except a potbellied local deputy who leaned against an idling cruiser. He studied the white exhaust spouting from its muffler and remarked, dubiously, how "It keeps away the mosquitos." Then he spat robustly and discussed remedies for engine overheating with a local reporter. I had no such luxury. Austin had moments before spoken on his cell, hopped into his car, and then peeled out, urgently, while avoiding my stare. I felt panic, then a sense of impacted energy, like you might during the tenth hour of a transatlantic flight. *What do I do?* But if Austin had an angel directing him, I had Seamus McGraw, the local freelancer whom *News* photo director Mike Lipack had hired to assist Todd.

"The search has shifted," Seamus said, without melodrama, or pre-amble, before blessedly giving me the location to which the cop army, formerly of Gertrude Street, had gone.

"How do you know this?"

"Contacts," he said and hung up.

A few minutes of harried driving later, I found the location. It wasn't an address but the wooded median between the east- and westbound lanes of I-80, about two miles east of exit 293, its junction with I-380. As I'd soon discover, the I-80 lanes distended here, like an artery with a blockage, leaving a marshy, wooded bubble in the middle, about three-quarters of a mile long and a quarter-mile wide at its largest point—enough room, as it turned out, for a man to hide from hundreds of police officers for a good long while before giving up the fight. It was rugged, thicketed terrain on the northeast corner of 4,000 miles of State Game Land 38, just west of Camelback Mountain and Big Pocono State Park. If Bostic and Ellis somehow made it into *those* wilds, I might have made even more overtime than I did. As it was, I, Maisel, and everyone else covering the story were in for a long night.

It was around 6 P.M. when I drove the ten miles between Gertrude Street and I-80. The sun was still high above a wooded horizon, although now orangey and no longer stridently bright. I parked on the westbound shoulder, perpendicular to where the median's tree line commenced, aban-doned my car, and joined dozens of officers on a grassy ridge. There was not yet a police tape, and I mixed easily with the cops at the ad hoc staging area. But then came news from Todd that Bostic had been captured. He called and relayed this information excitedly and with jubilation—"They got him!" he cried—although his voice grew dejected, perhaps even mo-rose, when I asked if he had made the shot.

"No," Todd replied.

I asked if the *Post* had made him.

"I don't think so," Todd said, although now with concern accompanying his gloominess.

Hearing this, I tried to reassure him and said: "I'm certain they didn't get him, Todd," although I did not, at all, know if this was true and was saying as much only to assuage his fears. I added, "It was a shit show up there, Todd. No one made him," and Todd answered, "Yeah, but they got him!" and this time he meant the NYPD, and not the *Post*, and he had said it with all the boisterousness of the first thing, because Todd, I real-ized at that moment, actually cared about Bostic and Timoshenko, while I, honestly, cared only about the story and felt nothing more than a sporting interest in who was caught beyond its description as a dramatic narrative suitable for print.

After that, I looped to the eastbound arm of I-80 and pulled into a rest stop. But I did better than get a breather. I got the last civilian to see Bostic and Ellis before Bostic was caught. I was looking for the men's room when I saw an olive-uniformed maintenance man. He was chewing tobacco, enough to make his cheek protrude as if distended with air. David Paynter was seventy-eight and a witness to Ellis's using a pay phone while a winded Bostic caught his breath on a bench. "He was sweating like the dickens," Paynter told me. "I said, 'You look overheated,' and he said, 'We walked about a mile and a half in the dirt.' He was sweating, and he looked like he walked as far as he could walk. He said, 'Our car broke down, and I'm trying to call someone.' Then he said, 'I'm too old to run.'"

It was a good get and exclusive to the *News*, since I did not see Austin at the ridge or at the rest stop. Finally, we were on the scoreboard, although Todd, individually, was not. He came pulling in to the rest stop, still pre-occupied with the *Post* and concerned over any photographs its shooters may have made of Bostic's arrest. He came pulling in, in one of those gray Chevy Malibus the *News* loaned out to all their staff shooters.

Previously, I've made some description of the modifications and con-tents of Todd's Malibu—the improvised console, the police scanner, the prayer cards, the roof mount, the phony police light—and even the bulletproof vest that was actually the flak jacket he wore while embed-ded with U.S. GIs during the second war in Iraq. It was now that he re-trieved the vest from the Malibu's trunk, put it on over his photographer's/ fly fisherman's vest, and told me the reason for this improbable—almost fantastical—sartorial prop: "Because when you go to war, you have to bring the right equipment."

Todd had taken the *News'* recent front-page losses to the *Post* per-sonally, perhaps more so than anyone other than Kerry Burke, who had wonderful cause to take those defeats personally but probably would have, anyway, even if it had not been he most embroiled in the daycare video scandal and the returning from the Brooklyn Bridge.

"We have to stop fooling around with these people," Todd now said, meaning the *Post*, as he paced the rest stop. "We have to send our best people on big jobs, like this one, and stop fooling around. We can't lose, here, today." He spoke as much to himself as to me, and I tried to calm him with a reference to "our" earlier get of the highway attendant. I was careful to use the plural possessive, although Todd said it wasn't enough—"not nearly enough"—and we "needed something big to send those bastards from Sixth Avenue back to New York with their hats in their hands."

Todd's anxiety persisted overnight, as we hunkered down at the rest stop with competing journalists and the Pennsylvania State Police and NYPD and other cops involved in the search for Ellis. There were generators and space heaters and TV vans and a big white truck that looked like an R.V. from which the Red Cross dispensed coffee and hamburgers out of an aperture on its side, as do the drivers of ice cream trucks. And there was the repeated spectacle of a helicopter taking off from and landing at the rest stop's western edge, the rotors whirring and the grass around it windblown from the whirring. And there was much rumor and expectancy, as well as false reports, about Ellis's capture, and press briefings rendered throughout the night by a State Police major about the search's progress. But there was no *Post*, neither Austin nor another runner, nor any shooters, and this absence made Todd very nervous, as I said, over the night.

Todd huddled with a scanner tuned to the frequency utilized by SWAT officers combing the woods. They wore black cargo pants and bullet-resistant vests and night vision visors and riot helmets. They had automatic weapons and microphones running into those helmets. I'd watched them suit up before entering the median and then listened on Todd's scanner as they spoke to one another, clinically, while conducting their search. "I have motion," one said, as the journalists around Todd's vehicle collectively held their breaths. "Copy, what do you have?" came another voice; then the long pause, filled with static, before the anticlimactic answer: "Negative, it was only a deer."

Between these episodes, I slept and Todd worried. Several times, I awoke in my car's backseat and asked the other reporters for Todd's whereabouts. Each time, they told me he'd driven off without explanation. But he always returned thirty or so minutes later, looking haggard and strung out. Once, I asked where he'd gone and he replied, vaguely, about "checking things out." I understood. The *Post*'s absence worried me, too, but deadlines acted, in my favor, as a bulwark against excessive worry. If the *Post* scored overnight, I'd have a whole day to regroup. But Todd had to be present to obtain the shot. There would be no second chances for a shooter.

Sometimes I awoke to the helicopter's whirring rotors and would dutifully trudge off to ask the major for an update. The last time I did this—around 4:30 A.M.—he told me there would be a press conference at 11 o'clock. But it never happened. As the appointed hour approached and the journalists convened, we were first told the major was unavailable and then that we should wait because "We might have some good news."

Todd didn't wait. For him, those words were the starter's pistol on what became a mad chase. He sprinted to his car and pulled onto the highway.

I called his cell but got only his ridiculous voicemail: "This is Todd Maisel. I'm either at a homicide or a fire. Leave a message." Then—and after watching other journalists follow Todd's decisive lead—I ran to my own car. From the rest stop, it was, perhaps, a mile eastward to a service road bisecting the median and connecting both sides of I-80, one of those theoretically off-limits to civilian motorists, but which the journalists employed to loop-the-loop back toward Ellis's probable extraction point off I-80W. The belief was that the fugitive—at that moment—was being fished from the median, or would be imminently, and the goal became one of locating the exact spot so as to witness the event. The runners needed to see it to describe it to rewrite; the shooters, like Todd, needed to obtain the crucial shot.

But it wasn't easy; the State Police ensured as much. Deducing our intentions, the more officious followed to prohibit us from loitering along I-80 West's shoulder. First, they herded us on professionally and then, once we disregarded their authority, under threat of arrest. And so we motored westward on I-80 to the next exit, got off, and then circled back onto I-80 eastbound. Once there, we raced past the Ellis target point on our left (although no longer visible through the trees), passed the rest stop on our right, and once more on to the service road; then another loop onto the westbound side, hoping . . . hoping . . . hoping the State Police did not see us as we employed it, and then slowing the vehicle to a crawl during another pass of the area of most police activity, waiting . . . waiting . . . waiting . . . to see if they brought him out during those frantic moments, and then, when we could no longer view the likely extraction point, first from the driver's-side window and then in the rear view mirror, not regarding the roadway as we looked, we gunned it again to Exit 293 to repeat the process. We did this as one among, perhaps, twenty journalists, each in our respective vans and cars, or all those who had remained overnight at the rest stop. That included WNBC, WCBS, WABC, Fox 5, the *News*, the local media as well as some city runners and shooters who had not slept at the rest stop, and notably *Post* shooter Jason Nicholas, who also went by the alias Nick Brooks and who had killed a man with a shotgun in 1990, he claimed in self-defense,[1] and was as determined in his pursuit of the get as Todd was in his.

Now, a brief word here on our opposition. Nick Brooks—for that's how I knew him—was at the time of this story freshly paroled. And this improbable fact made the wild bronco abandon with which he ran doubly exceptional. Yes, most of us risked arrest in some fashion. But Nick? He didn't act as if a bust could return him to prison for the remainder of a six-year term. He acted as if he didn't give a fuck, or at least about anything other than the get. I should also say that this nightmare scenario of re-incarceration nearly came to pass twice within three days two months later in September. In the first instance, Nick ran on a suspected pipe bomb detonation outside a Chelsea film studio. When police allegedly ordered him not to employ a flash for fear it might detonate a second, hidden device, he did so anyway, lest he miss the shot. In the second case, he climbed to a Bronx roof to document the killing of a man by transit offi-cers on a subway platform below. As Paul Browne—yes, DCPI's—later told the *Times*, "the landlord had signed an affidavit allowing the police to arrest trespassers without receiving specific complaints." Brooks claimed he'd been invited to the building's roof by its residents. In that same *Times* story, Nick said, "It is a privilege to photograph this city. If Homer were alive today recording the deeds of men, he'd be a photojournalist."

On I-80, I drove like a maniac, and was oft-threatened with arrest— *One more fucking time and I'm cuffing you!*—and then saw Todd on my third lap, idling on the shoulder despite the troopers' warnings. "I don't give them a chance to give me an ultimatum," he said, after I'd pulled abreast. "When they come, I just drive away. Never give them a chance to threaten you with arrest! Then you're free to pull over again."

This sage advice rendered, we both saw Nicholas motor wildly by in his jeep, the soft top down, one hand on the wheel and the other holding his camera, his head turned dangerously away from us and toward the divider. Todd was off after him! And then it was over and neither I, nor Todd, had been in position at the critical moment; although Nicholas had been and, in fact, had obtained the exclusive shot—that of cops dragging Ellis from the woods. It felt as if a piano had fallen on me when Todd called to say as much. "Yeah, they got him," he said. "They have a shot of him in the grass. You can't really see his face, but they got him. There's nothing I could have done. I did all I could."

He had not said this disconsolately but with resignation and acknowl-edgment of the indispensable role of luck in our odd trade. I gave Todd credit, not only provided Lipack's likely reaction but the un-fulfillment of his own ambition. But, as it happened, fortune was about to smile on both of us.

I don't know why I pulled in to the rest stop, again, following those *Mad Mad Mad Mad World*–esque antics. I'd like to embellish the decision by calling it a hunch. I'd like to say some sixth sense pulled me there. More likely, I needed a place to cool down, call the desk, and relieve myself after the lunacy of those prior twenty minutes. Regardless, I found a cadre of NYPD cops removing body armor and prepping for Miller Time. The captain, like his troops, was cheerful with success. Things had worked perfectly! Two apprehended. No casualties. And so when I pleaded my case, telling him of our setbacks and describing how we had "been there every step of the way, from Monday in Crown Heights to the overnight at the rest stop," he overcame his reluctance and allowed me to phone DCPI on my cell, explain the situation, again in overwrought terms, and then hand him the phone so he could also inquire on my behalf. And then, when DCPI told him he could not speak, that to do so would represent a violation of the NYPD's centralized dissemination of public information, he grinned, held up a single finger and told me, away from the phone, "I got one more card." And it wound up being a trump.

After more conversation, the captain returned my phone and told me that although he was not permitted to speak, he knew someone who could. Over his shoulder, he called, "Danny. Danny, come on over here," and promptly a stocky white guy approached, with drab green eyes, a goatee, and a mullet that wouldn't have done an NHL forward much disservice. He wore a white T-shirt that was working hard to contain his chest hair under a blue windbreaker embossed with an elaborate seal on the left chest. To my delight, it read, "U.S. Marshal," as did the silver star that dangled from a chain he wore around his neck.

This was Danny Potucek, who was bound by none of the NYPD's closed-mouth edicts and, incredibly, the first man to find Ellis cowering in the woods. He quickly warmed to the notion of playing the hero in print. "Nothing makes me feel better than helping another officer and his family," he said, adding with obvious amusement that while most of the cops on the hunt were accustomed to city streets, "I don't mind the woods."

I phoned Todd, who raced to photograph Potucek as he regaled us about Ellis's capture. He said that shortly before 8 A.M., he'd been part of a skirmish line making an eastward sweep of the median in an area where a bloodhound named Scooby had picked up Ellis's scent. He inexplicably had an instinct to advance beyond the vanguard and shortly thereafter spotted the fugitive huddling in the lee of a tree, his face shrouded by the hood of a brown sweatshirt. "I pointed my gun at him. It was a .40 caliber," he told me. "I said, 'Show me your hands' three times and he sort of cowered and yelled, 'I don't have a gun. Don't hurt me. Don't hurt me.' After that, I started yelling, 'I have him. I got him!'"

Potucek said he'd been awake for thirty hours to that point but felt no weariness in the moments after the collar, a time during which, he said, dozens of cops cheered, hugged, high-fived, and handcuffed Ellis with Timoshenko's own cuffs. As he spoke, Todd shot and no other media were present aside from a *Staten Island Advance* reporter who'd sheepishly asked if he could "listen in." I didn't care. The *Advance* didn't count. Only the *Post*.

I called the desk, and assistant city editor Jill Coffey greeted the get with typical ebullience. Jill always reacted with almost irrational enthusiasm—a kindly counterpoint to Oswald's grim bloodlust. Todd and I still believed, however, that we'd been whupped. Only two hours later—after Gittrich reviewed my notes—was I informed otherwise.

"This is good shit," the normally stolid Gittrich gushed, before asking with equally uncharacteristic diffidence if I didn't mind the material's going to a Michael Daly column.

After that, it was *gar-bage* time. We were up by 40 in the fourth—Todd had seen Nicholas's photo and pronounced the wound cauterized. It was grainy and taken at a bad angle. One could barely, he said with giddiness, make out the fugitive's face. Only Martin Dunn remained unappeased. In a fit of Stalin-esque paranoia, he ordered his ground troops to tail the paddy wagon conveying Ellis to New York—just in case of a Richard Kimble–like escape. Martin wanted to be there for the most improbable of gets should it present itself. Even Oswald felt these orders required an insubordinate annotation.

"Hey! Ya never know," he said in conjuring the New York Lotto's motto.

Only Todd agreed with Dunn.

"If anything happens, we'll be ready," he said grimly. "We're so close. We can't let those fucks steal it away."

And so commenced one of the shortest car chases in New York tabloid history. I drove. Todd and Anthony DelMundo accompanied me, cameras poised for the impossible. The convoy departed the local courthouse where Ellis had waived his right to contest extradition. But, honestly, I didn't try. I thought the orders were FUBAR. And so when the cops ran the first red light they encountered, I remained in place. As I asked Anthony: "Do you think the *News* will pay for my insurance surcharge?"

"I wouldn't chance it," Anthony replied, as Todd malevolently cursed my lackluster effort.

But even Todd cheered before too long. For appearance's sake, I drove fifteen miles on I-80 in search of the lost caravan before calling not Gittrich but Lipack to advise.

"How's Todd?" a surprisingly cheerful Mike inquired, to which I told him: "Disappointed. It was tough out there."

Mike chuckled, then said, "Tell him not to worry. You guys got the wood tomorrow."

I was flabbergasted. Despite Gittrich's uncommon enthusiasm, I still didn't believe anything we'd gotten merited the wood. I thought Mike was making a joke. But then he explained how Todd's best photo of Danny Potucek was to go under the headline "HOW I GOT HIM." And then suddenly, everything seemed to make blissful sense.

Later that night, after I had returned to my apartment in Hoboken, Michael Daly called. He thanked me for my notes and seemed self-conscious about having written a column based on someone else's reporting. I joked about how I had been trying to give him actionable notes for eleven months, and each time he'd found something better. He ignored the quip, then criticized Stu Marques for having had the gall to rewrite his lede.

"He started the story, 'It was 8 A.M., when U.S. Marshal Danny Potucek spotted a man sitting against a tree.' What was 8 A.M.? You can't find a single example of good writing where the story begins with, 'It.' Jesus Christ! I'm having a hard fucking time with this."

Inwardly, I thrilled over Mike's conspiratorial tone. He was the paper's top news columnist and someone I revered. It was also funny. He was a Yale alumnus and truly torqued that Stu had fucked with his copy—never mind he'd had the poor grace to begin a sentence with the word "It." But after a while, I no longer followed him, and so asked about Timoshenko. Mike was close to the cops. And I'd been out of the loop in Pennsylvania.

"He's not gonna make it," Mike said. "Horrible thing. And by any account, he was a genuinely nice guy. They should shoot these fucking mutts."

Mike had said this in his characteristic half-mumble, so ironic given his great facility with speech and as if he saved all of his powers of articulation for copy. Then he moralized a little more and then he was gone and I stared at my computer for what seemed like a good, long while. The video game I'd played was no longer fun. I just sat and stared. The next day, Saturday, Russel Timoshenko was pronounced dead from his wounds, the *News* clobbered the *Post*—Nicholas's photo got little play on page 5—and New York City's tabloid war moved on to the next battleground. I didn't even get a day off. Within a week, it seemed as if the whole thing had been only a long and lurid dream.

8

"Sports' Worst Nightmare"

Daily News headline, July 22, 2007

ON FRIDAY, JULY 20, six days after Russel Timoshenko died, the *Post*'s Murray Weiss broke a front-page scoop about an NBA official's wagering on—and possibly fixing—pro basketball games. The story was headlined "FIXED!" and quoted FBI sources as saying authorities discovered the scam through an unrelated Mafia probe. That day, the *News* dispatched me to Weill Cornell Medical Center. Two days earlier, an underground steam pipe had exploded on Lexington Avenue, and a tow truck driver from Canarsie, Brooklyn, had been badly burned and placed in an induced coma. I spent the day scanning faces in the lobby, approaching smokers, outside. *Do you know Gregory McCullough? He was in that accident two days ago on Lex.*

By 4:30, Gittrich informed me that our sources had identified the unnamed referee as Tim Donaghy. He ordered me to his former home in West Chester, Pennsylvania, and said court records indicated a legal dispute there with an ex-neighbor named Pete Mansueto. Three hours later, I arrived in West Chester as a blood orange sun hovered above a horizon of black oaks behind Mansueto's McMansion. It was a lot of house and even more lawn. The *Post* was already there. Tom Liddy was a twenty-something *Post* copy kid* with a mop top and wary eyes. His shooter was

---

* The title "copy kid," I should say, was by then a vestige of an earlier time that had outlived its original job description. Historically, a newspaper reporter would cry out, "Copy!" after having finished a typed-out story. A copy kid would then retrieve this draft and hustle it, as well as

123

Matt McDermott, a cheerful biker dude with a linebacker's build and roguish scruff. He was garbed as always—jeans and a sleeveless denim vest, one that provided good exhibition of his muscled, tattooed arms. Blessedly, they agreed to await DelMundo's arrival to door-knock the Mansuetos.

The cul-de-sac was a select one, and there were only four homes. I followed Tom to the first one on the left after entering. It had a high-pitched roof with a single gable window and a chaotic jumble of roof lines and dormer windows. At the lawn's edge, a privacy garden of purple crab-apples shaded some nicely formed boxwood shrubs. More oaks flanked the driveway, along with red carnations and a periwinkle. I guessed the resident would be a gardener, but then saw the neighbors' yards just as lavishly—and assuredly professionally—done.

We walked up a long driveway to the house at its conclusion, door-knocked, and waited. In turn, a goose of a woman answered. Veronica Crabtree* was on the other side of middle-aged, or that time in your life when you begin to take an abnormal interest in the affairs of your neighbors and other things that shouldn't concern you. Being that her suburban soap opera had an intimate cast, she knew plenty about everyone, the perfect runner's source. In almost every way but one. For Veronica Crabtree would make us earn our get.

She'd come to the door like a lot of people did—with just the appropriate amount of decorous, yet ultimately hollow, compunction. She wanted to talk. She knew she wanted to talk and you did, too. You just had to make her feel decent about it, like an accountant encouraging you to cheat on your taxes by saying his last four clients did so. So, we obliged her, spinning tall tales of the story's urgency—and the importance of her perspective to our final account. She obliged us and told us how the Donaghys were such "wonderful people," then threw the Mansuetos savagely under the bus. "I think the bigger person had to move away from the situation because it wasn't a calm one," she said. Then, she embroidered the Donaghys' portrait with a few more stray bits of goodwill and concluded with this capstone: "There are two sides to every story. Remember that." I scribbled hurriedly, although it would prove urgency borne from an unfounded fear. For Ms. Crabtree would perform multiple encores for other, late-arriving reporters over the course of the night.

---

carbon copies, to the city desk editors, rewrite reporters, copy editors, and other newsroom staff through whose hands a story would pass en route to its publication. By 2007, most, if not all, papers had long since digitized this process—and eliminated the copy kid position—but the *Post* retained the title for junior employees, like Tom, who weren't quite interns but also not quite staff reporters, either.

* Out of politeness, I have changed the woman's name.

We crossed the street to the Mansuetos' McMansion. DelMundo was still driving and I could hold the *Post* off no longer. There, Lisa Manseuto came to the door pregnant and bloused in enough fabric to rouse a becalmed ship. She referred us to her husband, saying, "He's on his way from the club." Shortly thereafter, Pete Mansueto pulled up: plump, tan, and fragrant of happy hour. He wore khaki shorts, an Izod golf shirt, and a ball cap over an otherwise fallow brow. He greeted us boisterously and with that eagerness to please strangers of which I'd long ago learned to be suspicious. He then asked, chivalrously, to permit him a few moments to check on his "pregnant wife." So, I stood there, wondering if this man was worthy of my contempt, although I didn't get to wonder long. Pete Mansueto had been waiting a long time to tell his side of the story.

He soon rejoined us at the curb and asked us what it was we would all like to know, then and without waiting launched into a fiery account. He told us he had waged a years-long feud with Donaghy based on small and petty slights. Donaghy had called the police after Mansueto's son threw mud balls over his fence. He claimed Donaghy tried to set his house on fire, crashed his golf cart, flipped his wife the bird, and stalked her. Then he gave Tom and me copies of a lawsuit charging Donaghy with having threatened two mailmen. "It's unfortunate," Pete Mansueto said with such rueful sorrow as to imply a rehearsal. "We all have choices to make. He made his."

All in, it was some performance, and one I was almost sorry to see conclude. But, as it was, I had two mailmen to call. From my car, I phoned the library and requested numbers for both men, explaining how a *Post* reporter—*"no more than 100 yards away!"*—was imploring his own researchers to do the same at that very moment. The researcher, Shirley, reacted as if the last five requests had come laden with equal urgency. It was 9:30 P.M.

Five minutes later, Liddy appeared at my driver's-side window and asked if I wanted to hit Radley Run Country Club, where Mansueto had promised we'd find more Donaghy dirt. I told Tom I was dumping my Mansueto notes to rewrite. Then I phoned Dennis Van Zandt.

"This could bring down the NBA!" I howled. "Are you watching TV?! It's on every channel!"

But the first mailman wanted no part of the story aside from what he'd seen on CNN. So I called Charles Brogan and performed an encore. This time, the mailman regaled me with a tale so ludicrous it made what Pete Mansueto had said seem reasonable.

"I knocked over his recycling bucket and he freaked out," Brogan said of Donaghy. "He came out of his house hollering, 'Get the hell back here and pick that up!' I just kept on in the mail truck. But he got in his car and cut me off. He jumped out and threatened me. I kept driving, and he hopped back in his car and cut me off, again. He wouldn't let me deliver the mail! He kept cutting me off at every house on the block!"

Liddy returned and asked, "You ready yet?"

"Fucking rewrite," I told him. "They took the whole feed and the computer crashed."

Tom reluctantly stalked away, and I returned to the call. Brogan continued: "He wanted to fight me. . . . He kept saying, 'I'll have your job. I'm a public servant and he's the big NBA ref. I called the police and when they got there he told them he had been golfing with Michael Jordan that day."

"Did they arrest him?"

"No. But the next day, he called the post office and asked for my supervisor, then had Michael Jordan get on and say what a great guy he was. He wanted to talk to me, but I didn't take the call."

I dumped my notes to rewrite and absently watched as Pete Mansueto retrieved something from the edge of his lawn. Momentarily, I got one final glimpse of him when he turned to wave goodbye. He is frozen that way in memory, unburdened, redeemed, and no less ridiculous, finally at peace with having won his dirty little war.

The four of us—for DelMundo had arrived—drove to a pub, where McDermott flirted aggressively with our waitress, Mandy. I pretended to be in good humor but found it difficult dining with the competition when I planned to treat them as such, and especially after the deception I had perpetrated on Tom. I excused myself early and found a motel.

July 21, 2007

The *Post* wooded with a photo of Donaghy and the headline "THE 'FIXER.'" The *News* also wooded with a photo of Donaghy and the headline "DISGRACE!" That morning, I found my Honda mummified in toilet paper outside my motel. A note stashed under the windshield wiper read, "Sorry you left so early. Mandy." McDermott! And, yet, Matt's *bonhomie* made Friday's prevarication—and plans for Saturday—doubly difficult.

A call to the desk directed me to Brogan. They wanted a photo and more detail. I phoned him. *Sure! Come on over. No, no one else has called. Should I expect anyone? Okay, I'll stick with you if they do ring.*

Anthony and I found him enjoying his working man's backyard in a lawn chair. Only one anomaly impeded a clean get. Fourteen hours had made his memory ambiguous on the point of Michael Jordan. It was now Michael

Jordan or Charles Barkley whom Donaghy had referenced as his golfing partner. It would prove an important point, but for now, Tracy Connor, the morning's assignment editor, was pleased with the exclusive.

"Does the *Post* have it?"

"No."

Soon, Liddy called and asked, "What are you guys doing?"

I'd been expecting the call yet was putting off how to handle it when it did inevitably come.

"We're having breakfast," I lied, the words coming easily. Far too easily. "We're heading to Donaghy's parents' house. Do you want me to wait for you there?"

In the silence, I could hear the hamster wheel of Tom's mind spinning. Finally, he said they were at the public library looking for high school yearbook photos of Donaghy, and should they unearth one, Matt would oblige Anthony with a frame. It was generous.

And, yet, the call was cause to sigh. *This* was why some runners refused to dine with their opposition on out-of-town jobs. Socializing implied collaboration. It was too hard to dine with the *Post*, then view them appropriately in the field. Not when the stakes were so high.

Still, the lone wolves—Kerry Burke, for one—proved exceptional. Most runners shadowed their opposites in the field and thereby removed the risk of a bad beat. Such arrangements were considered imperfect, yet acceptable, by both runners *and* their desks, and especially on consequential, out-of-town jobs. No one liked doing business that way, but even dogmatic editors preferred both papers' getting the same story to getting scooped. You could explain matching the competition to Martin Dunn or Col Allan. Getting beat was a whole other matter.

But while playing nice with the *Post* obviated risk, it also removed the chance for exclusives—and thus glory. Now, I was playing it both ways. It wasn't necessarily a calculation, but a matter of having procrastinated on the handling of Tom's call, knowing how I wanted to play it; and yet also knowing that the way I wanted to play it was wrong. Then, and at the decisive moment, I'd chosen not to inform Tom of our Brogan get and also coaxed him into revealing his lines of attack. After all, who knew what the *Post* had uncovered?

The library returned addresses for Donaghy's parents in Broomall, fifteen miles away, and at the Jersey Shore. Gittrich dispatched a reporter from New York to cover the latter location. On the way to Broomall, I called the ref's brother in Delaware and his grandparents in Havertown. I called back Van Zandt. Empty-handed, I pulled into a townhouse community adjacent to a lake. Not awaiting Liddy, I knocked on the library-indicated door. No answer. I tried neighbors, also without success, and now Liddy and McDermott arrived and we repeated the process. I did not advise them that I already knew the result.

I asked Tom for his agenda.

"I'm going to hit up his high school," he replied.

I told him that was cool. Anything but Brogan would be cool. And so we drove to Cardinal O'Hara High School in Springfield, four miles away.

The school had an east wing and a west wing with a conjunctive portion. The façade was three-tiered and had green-frosted windows, white stanchions, and a big cross. Next to the high school was the Don Guanella Home for the mentally challenged. We parked there, reconnoitered, found no one, and entered the office. It was papered with clippings reporting the success of a Donaghy-run basketball clinic. But no attendant. So, we searched until my phone rang. I told Tom it was my girlfriend and retreated out of earshot. I then informed Gittrich of my whereabouts and that "the *Post* [was] in hand."

"Good. Do they have the Brogan stuff?"

"No."

"You're going to have to break off at some point. If this Michael Jordan angle is true, I want it. Jordan had gambling problems and I'd like to link him to Donaghy."

"Yeah, there's a problem with that," I said and explained Brogan's change of heart. Gittrich sighed. He had very much wanted to impale Jordan on Donaghy's pike.

"Regardless," he said. "Run it down. Barkley also gambled. I'd prefer Jordan. But either will do."

By then, the *News*' first edition was "out the door" to hit newsstands around 7 P.M. The *Post* always bought it—then raced to match exclusives for its Sunday run. I did some math and thought it better to break with both Liddy and the burden of guilt I'd been hauling since my deception. If the *Post* recovered in time, so be it. I would still have gotten credit for the Brogan scoop. I recall that when I told Tom the truth we were standing in the lee of the high school's northern side, shadowed by its concrete wall. I ridiculously said he might want to sit down before I began speaking.

"Who died?" he asked.

"No one. Listen. Have you called the two mailmen on the civil suit Mansueto gave us?"

"No. That was on my list of things to do today."

"Well, I already got Brogan. It's good stuff. You may want to give him a ring."

"When did you call him?"

". . . last night, from the car."

"I thought you were on with rewrite."

". . . after that."

I had said it all with good humor. I really was giving him a hand if one thought about it. He was a *Post* runner, after all. What could he expect? But Tom didn't see it that way. His jaw clamped, his lips pursed into a puckering frown, and his eyes narrowed to coin-slot slits. I could tell he was no longer looking at me objectively.

"I trusted you."

Three words—the rest is immaterial. And, yet, there's a lot to say about those three words. The editors could send runners to embarrass other editors on their wedding days. They could call each other names in print and report when one got busted for DWI. But the runners—we had a code. Or, at least, it felt like we did. It was why the *Post* didn't rub Kerry's nose in it after Timoshenko. Why you didn't double-back on a stakeout once you'd shaken hands and departed the scene for the day. Why we gave a late-arriving runner our notes, when the interview wasn't exclusive. Or why *Post* runners showed up for a *News* runner's farewell.

We never did connect Donaghy to Jordan or Barkley. The next day, Tom's story had quotes from Brogan, too. If there was a victory for the *News* in all that, it was a very small one—and, yet, everything had seemed so life-and-death the day before.

July 22, 2007

Sunday morning in suburbia. Sparse traffic, desolate nabes, a morning for diner omelets, sleeping in, and self-indulgence. I treated myself to a 7-11 breakfast biscuit and 460 calories of regret. A chipper girl worked the counter, and she glowed when I complimented the store on having the New York dailies. The *News* wooded with Donaghy's photo abreast of the headline "FOUL PLAY." The story quoted sources as saying Donaghy might turn state's evidence. The second half dealt with the Brogan/Van Zandt civil suit. The *Post* wooded with Donaghy for the third consecutive day, also with the headline "FOUL PLAY." (*That* happened more often than you'd think.) "'FIXER' REF LED NBA IN TECHNICALS," teased a Liddy story claiming Donaghy was a "whistle happy foul freak." A brilliant sidebar by

Brad Hamilton described seven contests from the 140 Donaghy had officiated over the prior two seasons in which controversial calls had obviously contributed to the outcome. Advantage *Post*.

Anthony and I returned to Donaghy's parents' community, which, that early, seemed under an enchantment. A neighbor broke the spell, and I asked about the Donaghys.

"You're not from a collections company, are you?" she asked. I gave my clothing—jeans and a khaki button-down—an incredulous once-over. She shrugged and said, "Even repo men must get casual Sundays," then added, "Aw, hell. I know who you are."

On the desk, Rob Moore answered my call as he always did: in a lilting "*Daily News*," with a high-toned and elongated "Daaaail—ee," followed by a clipped and baritone, "*News*." It was the same way the paperboys who hawked the tabloid to midtown commuters almost sang the paper's name while they pushed their wares.

"Stay put until 1," Rob added, then rang off. It was 10 A.M., and I mulled options until I caught one of those monumental breaks you contemplate years later over beers in a bar. Pete Mansueto called and said, "I have those names you asked for."

"What names?"

I hadn't asked for any.

"Donaghy's friends. Weren't you the one who asked me for them the other night?"

"Sure," I said, knowing I hadn't and Tom likely had. We had both given him our phone numbers.

"All right. You want to get in touch with . . ." and, here, Mansueto gave me three names.

I started with Kit Anstey, the Realtor who'd sold Donaghy his West Chester home.

"There's always problems with Mr. Donaghy," Anstey said. "He sued me, the builder, and the listing agent. The man goes out of control. Anybody he can sue, he sues. Some investigation firm, you know, was asking people in West Chester about him. . . . It was between a year and a year-and-a-half ago. American Investigators, I think. I forget the name of it."

"What did they ask?"

"'Do you know Mr. Donaghy?' 'Does he gamble?'"

"Does he gamble?"

"That's what they asked."

"What did you say?"

"Yes."

"What else did they ask?"

"'Where does he gamble? At private houses? Blackjack games? On the golf course? Does he go to the casino?' You know, I never thought of what he's being accused of now. He had a wonderful life. Who would throw it all away on gambling?"

"Did they ask anything about point shaving?"

"No. It was just his gambling habits."

"Was it a man or a woman?"

"A woman."

"Can you try hard to remember the name of the company?"

"It was American something. I might have their card at my office. I can get it tomorrow."

I called back Mansueto, who told me he'd also been contacted by a P.I. in the spring of 2005. He said the woman was a "local girl" who'd informed him she'd been hired by the NBA.

"I told her I was in the throes of a legal matter with Mr. Donaghy and I had no comment. She asked who else I could call and I gave her names. She said he was at the Borgata. I believe the NBA tried to get the [surveillance] video [of him gambling] from the Borgata. I think they keep it for two weeks and they just missed it. I heard they went there to investigate. The NBA knew about his gambling. So many people were talking about it. I forgot who told me."

I called back Kit Anstey and quizzed him on what the investigator had asked him. He parroted what Mansueto had already said: "The whole gist of it was his gambling. She said, 'I'm a private investigator investigating Mr. Donaghy.' I asked her who she was representing and she said, 'The NBA.'"

Now, I had it! Two sources saying a P.I. had contacted them about Donaghy's gambling on behalf of the NBA—a national scoop! But the revelation begot questions: How many games had Donaghy been permitted to officiate while the problem metastasized?

I asked the library for the names and addresses of every P.I. firm beginning with the words "America" or "American" in Pennsylvania. I called the desk and informed Rob. He reacted incredulously and then, after explanation, enthusiastically. Two words: "Get more."

The library returned two numbers for "American Investigations," one in Ambler and a second in Glen Mills. The second looked promising: Glen Mills was twelve miles from Broomall; and one of its principals was a woman named Melanie Gormley. But I started with the Ambler firm and got its owner, Neal Spearing, who told me he'd heard of Donaghy only through the news. I scratched it and moved on to No. 2. Phone disconnected. Anthony and I raced to the Glen Mills address but found it padlocked. From there, we drove to 27 Elstone Drive, Dennis Gormley's home. Dennis was listed on library-unearthed documents as the firm's other principal and presumably Melanie's hubby.

It was a tree-shrouded property with the home set far back from the street. Lots of shrubbery bookended a long driveway. At the end of it, I found a rickety old crone and a middle-aged man about Dennis's Accurint-listed age. The woman identified herself as his mother and the man his brother. The mother spoke for both of them. "Dennis moved away," she said, elaborating how the now-divorced couple once ran a mom-and-pop P.I. firm. Melanie did the investigations, and Dennis handled the books. She said it like she didn't approve of the endeavor and added that neither of them had ever mentioned anything about the NBA.

"Any way to reach Dennis?"

"We'll call him and get back to you," she replied in a way that made it clear she wouldn't.

I asked about Melanie's whereabouts.

"She's taken up with a younger man someplace local."

She'd said it with disgust—disgust for Melanie, disgust for me . . . and even more for my questions. Interview over.

I called the library and got a possible address for Melanie Gormley a few miles away. Anthony and I raced there like our cars were on fire. But we found only a vacant home with a note pinned to the door decreeing it to be auctioned at a forthcoming sheriff's sale. I canvassed neighbors and, at once, found a woman tending a garden. She told me Melanie had moved recently to nearby Newtown Square. She now lived behind a Blockbuster Video. I asked the library to run Gormley's new address and, while waiting, had the woman call her house phone. Someone answered. Discussion. Finally, a summary judgment: "Melanie's not home. Her daughter doesn't want to talk to you."

I took it in stride. There was always the library. Always a runner's best friend. But not on this occasion. The library returned no listing for Melanie Gormley in Newtown Square. I asked for the Blockbuster, got its address, and faced an arduous canvass. To that point, success had seemed inevitable. Now only panic. It felt like the moment you realize your wallet is missing. But then an idea. If Melanie had recently moved, the library's databases—which relied on one's paper trail—might not yet have had the opportunity to log the updated address. I tried 411. It worked!

Anthony and I ran. My nerves were electric, like one of those buzzing blue-lit whackers that obliterate mosquitos on summer nights. If a bug landed on my skin, it would combust. I could feel it—a big one.

The home was a clapboard bungalow. A paved driveway straddled its left side and concluded with backyard parking. About halfway down the drive, the home had a service door. Noting this, Anthony climbed into his SUV's rear, angled his then-prone body so as to aim a long-lensed camera through the vehicle's tinted windows and at the door. The windows were not so heavily tinted so as to prohibit Anthony from effectively shooting through them, but sufficiently darkened that a subject would not realize they were being photographed until opening the paper the following day. Anthony had made these extraordinary modifications for instances such as these. Covert photography.

The door was wooden and coated with peeling white paint, and, when I knocked, I could hear my knuckles echoing through the home. I knocked again—now harder. Nothing! I tried the knob. Gently. Gently. It was unlocked, but I didn't open it. I returned to the curb, then to Anthony's SUV. I shook my head. Anthony, usually resilient and indomitable, looked disconsolate. But we were not beaten. Not yet. It just meant a long and anxiety-filled race to deadline in our cars. Racing against Mrs. Gormley's arrival while remaining still.

Nothing happened. Little often does. A robin chirped. A squirrel ran up the bough of a whorled elm, looked down at a pal, and goaded him with a nibbled acorn. The pal complied. The two played tag among the branches. A car pulled out of a driveway. A car pulled into one, and a woman conveyed groceries through her front door. A boy kicked a soccer ball. Others bicycled down the street. I waited and watched. Anthony waited and watched and stroked his camera like it was a Pekingese. I smoked. I smoked, again.

Realtor Steve Christie, Anstey's opposite on Donaghy's home transaction, called. He confirmed the P.I. firm's name as American Investigators. Gormley had phoned him, too. I informed Mark Moore, the *News'* night editor. He said the *News'* attorneys were reviewing the story—and its sourcing—at Martin Dunn's behest.

"I think it's good," he said hopefully. "Keep pushing. Get Melanie Gormley."

But I didn't. What I got was the cops.

He parked his cruiser behind Anthony's SUV and came to my driver's-side window. He demanded my license. I told him who I was, why I was there, and furnished my NYPD press cred. He looked at it with disdain, then without interest. He wanted the license.

"On what basis?" I asked.

"You're a suspicious person."

"Am I? Who says?"

"I do."

"Well, well," I replied and, here, he blurted a few clipped police codes into the walkie-talkie strapped to his shoulder.

"You can do this one of two ways," he said. "You can give me your identification or spend the night in jail. And don't think that your New York City lawyers are gonna get you out, because the chief of police is also the judge in this town."

"That's very efficient," I said. "Must make it hard for innocent men."

He responded with a languorous, sarcastic, self-indulgent chortle that seemed to go on forever; then looked down the street and then up at the sky. He studied it, nodded, took a deep, cleansing breath, and then leaned into my window frame so far I could feel his Whopper-for-lunch breath upon me. He didn't say anything but just stood there, huffing and looking over my car, like somebody mulling whether he wanted to buy it. It was a long, electric moment, and if glares could wound, we'd both have been in need of medical attention.

"Just give me the license," he said. "There's no reason for this to escalate."

I complied. I'd fought the good fight. If I'd fought anymore, I'd have gone to jail.

"Tell me why you're here, again," he said, and I told him. He said, "Stand by" and walked up Gormley's driveway and went inside. Minutes later, he rejoined me at my car.

"So, you think this woman conducted an investigation for the NBA into the referee they're saying fixed games."

"Correct."

"Well, she's not home, and let me tell you, you're not going to get arrested but you're this close," and here he held up his thumb and forefinger about a half-inch apart.

"What have I done?"

"You're harassing the little girl inside. She's scared to hell. You tried to open the door. I don't know what you can do in New York, but you can't do that here."

He swaggered back to his car after a warning to stay off the property—a big man with a small soul. That and a badge. Then, Anthony was at my window. He wanted to know why everything had to be a battle. I told him; I told him like I'd been drafting the reply for the last three hours: "Because they want us to respect their jobs. But have so little for ours. They love to read the paper. But they don't give a flying fuck about how those stories get in there, or until they have to deal with us. Then they spit on us. Then we're a nuisance and horrible, unforgivable people. But they love reading the paper with their coffee in the morning. It's a losing fight, I know. But I like fighting it and I'm going to keep doing so."

It was a good speech, one to be proud over—even though no one was going to storm any beaches because of it. That was okay. I felt good. But I didn't get to admire the rhetoric very long, because for the second time that day, I got profoundly lucky.

He was a young man. Fine-looking. Sixteen-ish with a good face. And what he had to say did nothing to change my impression. He told us he'd been inside the home the whole time, apologized for Melanie's daughter's calling the police, then remarkably said he understood our jobs. Melanie Gormley, he added, was on a boat, somewhere, with her boyfriend. He asked whether her cell phone number would be enough. I told him it would be. He gave us the number. I thanked him profusely, got in my car, and called.

Melanie Gormley answered timidly, *"Hel-lo?"*—in that way Hollywood damsels do after the floorboards creak on a dark and stormy night. I identified myself, and she replied in a tone I now recognized very intimately— that *how-dare-you!* tone that sounded as if it came down, and at me, from far atop the moral high ground. She told me I was scaring "the hell out of me and my daughter." I said her fears were unfounded and wondered what sort of P.I. she must have made. No Philip Marlowe, here. More like the mousy, mettle-less clerk who cleans up the stacks after the sterner librarians have gone home for the night.

So, I tried to calm her. I used my soothing voice. But that *never* worked. She just repeated how terrified she was in that borderline hysterical tone of the persecuted, as if David Stern* would have hitmen jumping out of her pajamas if she spoke to me.

"Listen," I lied. "I have a daughter, too, and I wouldn't want strange men knocking on the door, either. But if I print you worked for the NBA and it's wrong, I could lose my job. Please help me."

But Melanie Gormley was unmoved; she was the obstinate jetty upon which the waves of my desperate entreaties were beaten back into the surf. And so I tried a journalistic gag play. I told her I was going to count to ten and if she was still on the line by the time I finished, I'd presume it

---

* David Stern was the NBA's commissioner from 1984 to 2014.

confirmation that she worked for the NBA. It was the ploy Dustin Hoffman's Bernstein had employed in *All the President's Men*. But she hung up on me before I even got to "two." Somewhere, Melanie Gormley went back to being afraid on a boat, and her daughter remained fortified behind no-longer-unlocked doors.

But it didn't matter. Mark Moore told me the story was the wood. Whatever the *Post* had planned, it wouldn't top this scoop. Donaghy was becoming the *News'* story—and no longer the *Post's*, all because Pete Mansueto had mistakenly picked up the Post-it note on which he'd scrawled my number—and not the one on which he'd written Tom's.

July 23, 2007

That morning, the *News* wooded with the Donaghy/Gormley story—"NBA KNEW! PRIVATE EYE INVESTIGATED ROGUE REF 18 MONTHS AGO." The story, inside, ran with a photo of Donaghy looking out of a window of his Bradenton, Florida, home. The *News* and the *Post* were staking out the home, 'round-the-clock. Both tabloids deployed runner–shooter teams in twelve-hour shifts. So far, Donaghy had declined comment and activated his front-lawn sprinklers if they came within range. The *Post* wooded with Donaghy's family's urging him to enter the federal Witness Protection Program. "BASKET CASE . . . 'FIX' REF GETS DEATH THREATS." An inside story put Jana Winter at Donaghy's parents' house on the Jersey Shore. She'd gotten quotes from neighbors but nothing approaching the news value of the *News'* scoop. But without it, we would've been beat.

Anthony and I began at Villanova University, where Donaghy had attended college and some media outlets reported he'd played baseball. It was a half-hour drive from my hotel, during which I lost myself soothingly in *The Marriage of Figaro*, the overture on repeat a balm for my frayed nerves. The progressions bloomed from one to the next, like flowers opening from buds. By the time I arrived, I was doing the mock-conductor with one hand and driving with the other. I thought I did it well. I'm sure Mozart did it better at the Burgtheater.

At Villanova, the sports flack dispelled the baseball report. Next, we hit the West Goshen Police Department, where I efforted the report involving Van Zandt, the mailman. Then, Anthony was summoned back to New York and I returned to Cardinal O'Hara High School alone. There, a receptionist directed me through locker-lined hallways that were off-season empty. I eased into a closet-sized reception room, out of which the principal fetched me with a curt wave. I sat opposite him across an executive desk on which you could have laid a Rothko. He politely waited with hands folded. He was a priest and wore the standard issue, all of which seemed so starched that sitting down had to be a misfortune. He had a ruddy and clean-shaven Gaelic face, framed by a Brillo of salt-and-pepper hair; jowly but not overly so for someone I put in his early sixties. He regarded my introduction with paternal disappointment and the frank demeanor of someone who hadn't done a cheap thing since the '70s. But that could have been my Catholic prejudice.

"Mr. Donaghy graduated in 1985 and few, if any, of the staff recall him," he said, as if reciting a statement. "But why come here? When O.J. Simpson is arrested, they don't say, 'O.J. Simpson, who attended such-and-such high school.' They just say 'O.J. Simpson.' But with Mr. Donaghy, it's 'Tim Donaghy, who graduated from Cardinal O'Hara.'"

I said I didn't know, and he sighed his way into the more comfortable corners of his big Oval Office chair. I could tell he was a little annoyed for having gone off-script, but it was nothing a little Catholic schoolboy charm couldn't remedy. I told him I'd attended a school not unlike his own and then, at his prompting, described it. He was delighted and asked for an extensive description of my career to that point. We chatted a little more, and I departed with the friendly advice to talk with Donaghy's former O'Hara coaches, Buddy Gardler (basketball) and Bill Dugan (baseball). Some moments and a phone call to my library later, I had addresses for both. (Runner's tradecraft: Source work is often a matter of manufacturing sympathy and goodwill, often through the discovery of common ground.)

Plymouth Road was about a mile from the school on the other side of Highway 476. Big oaks flanked the road and made a nice leafy canopy, like camouflage over an artillery emplacement. Soft, muted sunlight filtered to the street below, and I found Buddy Gardler's home near its dead end, abutting Rolling Green Golf Club. The home was modest and boxy. It looked like a Wyeth portrait. No one answered at Gardler's door.

From there, I ran on the four possible addresses for Dugan. The first two were wrong. No one answered the third. At the fourth, I found a working-class row home with "DUGAN" stenciled onto a piece of driftwood hanging from the door along with the word "WELCOME." A woman answered and I asked for Mr. Dugan—the correct one—although he didn't live up to the sign. He proved an aging, cranky man who seemed disinclined to be further troubled by the world. Or at least not by its tabloid reporters. Of that I was made quite sure.

July 24, 2007

Donaghy's Accurint report led me to a block four miles from Cardinal O'Hara. A lot of three-bedroom homes underwritten by thirty-year mortgages, quiet desperation, and the daily grind. I'd grown up on a block like this. Tim Donaghy had grown up on this one.

The first door-knock yielded an aging woman with no cheer. When she honked me off her porch, it sounded like a flock of Canada geese being chased by a golden retriever. Other neighbors were nicer and told me what a good boy Donaghy had been.

From there, I drove to a Home Depot parking lot and listened on the radio as David Stern confirmed at a press conference that the NBA had investigated Donaghy with a local P.I. I didn't have a ruler, but you would have needed most of one to measure my smile. Then, I returned to Buddy Gardler's home, where the coach greeted me with a sort of fatalistic resignation, as if he knew I would come, or someone would. It was just a matter of when and who. I didn't even ask him for words. He just sighed me inside with a nod.

The front door led into a living room. It had bowling alley carpeting and a couch fronting a TV that was tuned to an ESPN report about Donaghy. Gardler sat in an Archie Bunker chair near the couch. He shook his head and said, "It's just amazing."

After that, it didn't take much prompting. It seemed that little else had occupied Buddy Gardler's mind in the ten days between when the story had broken and I'd showed up at his door. Speaking to me was just a segue in his Donaghy-preoccupied stream of consciousness. He said quite a bit about Donaghy and his background, but the important part came when I asked him about "these bookmakers they're saying Donaghy worked with."

"I've heard something about a Battista," Gardler replied. "Baba is his nickname. Somebody he knew in high school. I really don't know. I can't remember where I heard it. I've talked to a million people about this since it broke. Ya know, I believe in karma. What goes around . . . . Timmy felt he could do whatever he wanted and it finally caught up to him."

I returned to Cardinal O'Hara and found the principal in the same place I had left him. He smiled when I knocked on his doorframe and asked, "What can I do for you?"

I told him I wanted to see old Cardinal O'Hara yearbooks. Since Donaghy had graduated in 1985, I told him 1982-to-1986 would do just fine. He told me to wait in his office and shortly huffed his way back, laden under a leather-bound pile. Together, we leafed our way through the heavy-stock matte pages, and I felt the same almost ecstatic expectancy as when pulling up at Melanie Gormley's home two days earlier. Here, somewhere, lay another national scoop, buried, hidden among the fresh-faced, prom night smiles and tough guy scowls that would soon enough erode under the buffeting of time. Gardler, or whoever had whispered "Baba," couldn't be wrong, I thought. I didn't want them to be wrong. Page after page of graduating classes, and then finally one possible, a Carl Battista—then a silent rejoicing: "YES!"—then another, James, from 1983. "YES!" again. Neither looked like a bookmaker. But who does at that age?

July 25, 2007

On Wednesday, both the *News* and the *Post* wooded with Lindsay Lohan's early-Tuesday arrest for drunk driving. The *Post* ran her Santa Monica P.D. mug shot with a text box pointing toward her forehead. "ROOM FOR RENT," read the headline. The *News*, meanwhile, saved its best for the story's lede: Lohan, Connor wrote, "was receiving medical care last night after leaping off the wagon and hitting a new low—chasing her assistant's mother through la-la land with booze on her breath and coke in her pocket." The headline: "GIRLS GONE WILD! LILO BUSTED ON DUI; BRITNEY'S BERSERK PHOTO OP."

I leafed through addresses, compiled the prior night through a library search for every Pennsylvania-based Carl and James Battista with ages matching someone who'd graduated high school in the early-to-mid '80s. The first Carl lived in Clifton Heights, about a mile from Cardinal O'Hara. No one was home, but a neighbor said he was a hospital nurse—not a promising occupation to prove Gardler's thesis. Moonlighting bookmaker? How 'bout a Sunday parlay with your aspirin? I nixed him and moved on to a James, also in Clifton Heights. But he'd moved on and so I did, too. My choices then were James in Phoenixville, James in Pittsburgh, and Carl in Nazareth. Pittsburgh was impossible, and Nazareth was parallel with New York City. I opted for Phoenixville, thirty miles of country driving north. I arrived shortly before dusk with a stress headache and a bellyful of Battistas.

Picket Post Lane was part of a prosperous subdivision, elevated on a modest ridge overlooking the Schuylkill River to the north and Valley Forge to the southeast. It was about 150 gabled homes falling somewhere between affluent colonials and outright mansions. I didn't know what a bookmaker's neighborhood would look like, but this didn't seem to be it. Too staid. Too suburban. It offended the notions I had of the man, or rather his occupation, although these had admittedly been purchased cheaply by the cost of a movie ticket. In retrospect, I suppose this was exactly where such a man would live, concealed beneath the shroud of the mundane.

The library-proscribed house was equally inscrutable. No lights. No car in the drive. No signs of life. It offered nothing as I beseeched it for some measure of confirmation. Then the door, as I waited, there, with my neck hairs at attention and arms dotted with goosebumps. No answer to my door knock! I peeked into the windows, then beyond its curtains, but saw only shadows. I did a runner's canvass of the nabe. But no one knew anything about James Battista of Phoenixville, Pa. The man was a ghost, enigmatic and elusive. Rarely outside. Occasionally walked his dog, a statement I soon confirmed . . . .

. . . James Battista was pear-shaped with a bald head and a graying goatee that matched the one worn by the mini-Schnauzer he was coaxing to pee on the fringe of his front lawn. He wore baggy mesh gym shorts, a golf shirt, and jogging sneakers. Maybe it was the day's dying light in his eyes, but I took his squinty prison-yard glare to suggest he'd rather not be bothered. I bothered him: "You Jimmy Battista?"

"Who wants to know?"

"The New York *Daily News*."

"I have no comment. None!" he said and about-faced so abruptly it made his Schnauzer squeal with whiplash. The thing whined all the way to his front door, as I yelled after him, "Wait a minute! You don't even know what I'm going to ask you."

"Don't come on my property—*at all!*"

It was a silly way to handle things. If he'd just said, "I don't know any Tim Donaghy," I probably would have believed him after mulling the neighborhood. But, as it was, I knew I had the right fellow. His reaction was just as good as a confirmation. And although I met traffic en route to my Cherry Hill hotel, I didn't feel any of it. I could have driven to Pittsburgh—not that there was a need to any longer. The *News* had its man.

July 26–30, 2007

The following morning found me once more in front "The Sheep's"* house—only now accompanied by a freelance shooter stationed across the street in a parked car. The sun, overhead, was as angry as a sassed

---

* Later, it became clear "Ba-Ba" was only a derivative nickname rooted in Batista's real one: "The Sheep."

codger—hot enough, as it turned out, to melt even a bookmaker's icy glare. I had help, of course, as I so often did. But I don't remember another instance—and especially on such an important story—where having my dog, Jackie, in the car's backseat so adroitly played upon a reluctant source's empathy for animals. But, as I already knew, Jimmy Battista liked his dogs.

After three hours, Battista exited his front door and bee-lined for my car, frowning with a foil pan in his arms of the like you'd use to cook lasagna. He also held a thermos. When he got close, I rolled down my window.

"What do you think you're doing?" he demanded.

"What do you mean? You know very well why I'm here."

"No," he said and shifted his aggrieved gaze toward my panting dog. It wasn't the stakeout that offended him, but the fact I'd brought my dog along on such a smoldering day.

"Take this," he said. "You can't keep a dog out in this heat."

I took the pan and poured some water. I already had some, but that wasn't the point. If Jimmy "The Sheep" wanted to play canine hero, I wouldn't stop him. Then he retrieved from his pocket what looked like a carrier pigeon's note, or a Chinese fortune cookie.

"Here's my lawyer's number. You should give him a call. I can't talk—but he will."

I thanked him—more for the number than for the water—and waited as he seemed to ponder something left unsaid. But he left it there, unarticulated, with what I imagined was some measure of relief. Like Buddy Gardler, James "Ba-Ba" Battista seemingly knew one of us would come, and he was glad to have the inevitable visit over. Then I called John Marzulli in New York—our Mafia reporter—and advised him of the almost-triumph.

"No shit?" he said, as incredulous as I was. "The dog? How do you like that?"

I told him I liked it as much as a shower that never runs out of hot water. He asked whether I wanted to make the call. I asked him to do it, the scrawled number in my hand like a hot utensil. I was glad to be rid of it, and if Marzulli failed, it would be his neck in Dunn's hangman's noose. But an hour later, Marzulli called back while I remained in front of Battista's brooding abode. He had the goods. The lawyer confirmed that Battista was Donaghy's bookmaker, or at least the one under suspicion by the feds. Then Marzulli sang that sweet music so intoxicating for a field reporter: "You got the wood."

A runner's high followed—although this one had nothing to do with endorphins.

After that, I spent the next four days, poolside, at my Cherry Hill hotel, watching the stock market tank. "FEAR STREET: DOW IN FREE FALL." A harbinger of things to come. The desk didn't mind my lollygagging. The orange had been so squeezed, or at least from the field, there wasn't anything but the rinds. But I couldn't go home, not until Jana and the *Post* did. And after the Battista scoop, they didn't go easily. They didn't go easily at all.

9

"'Mayday' Last Call from Doomed Bravest at Ground Zero"

New York Post headline, August 20, 2007

I RETURNED HOME from Pennsylvania on Tuesday, July 31, after eleven days in the field. The following evening, a Minneapolis bridge collapsed during rush hour and 111 vehicles plummeted almost an equal number of feet into the Mississippi River. By noon on Thursday, Kerry Burke, Michael Daly, and I were flying to Minneapolis. I spent three days working the tragedy, mostly at the Holiday Inn where the families of those who hadn't come home the night before convened for updates. *Is there anywhere else she could be? I'm so, so sorry. Could you tell me about her? What was the last thing she said to you before she left the house in the morning? I'm so sorry.*

It was gut-wrenching, but comparatively low-stress work with the *Post* choosing to remain in New York. And it ended well, after I identified from files warehoused at the University of Minnesota's library Kurt Fhurman as the state inspector who'd signed off on the bridge's integrity every year since 1994. Kerry then staked out Fhurman's home and cajoled him to words, warning the beleaguered inspector, "They're gonna pin it on ya, Kurt! Now's ya chance to talk!" I can only imagine what Fhurman thought as he furiously tried to pedal his bicycle away from Kerry. But Kerry's approach worked. Kurt told Kerry, "Go after the designer. Go ask him why he did what he did," which gave the *News* a very nice national exclusive on a highly contested story.

On Saturday, August 4, President George W. Bush toured the wreckage in Minneapolis amid signs reading, "SUPPORT THE BRIDGES, END THE WAR." Afterward, I flew out. That night, Alex Rodriguez hit his 500th home run in a 16–8 rout of the Kansas City Royals at Yankee Stadium. The following week, I raced through South Jersey to find—and lock up—the fan who'd caught the home-run ball in the left-field seats before the *Post* could find him first.

On Monday, I got Walter "Sonny" Kowalczyk's brother, Brian, who told me Sonny would not part with the ball, valued in excess of $100,000, until consulting with local sports talk radio host Mike Francesa. He also said Sonny had gone to ground for fear someone would "A-ROB" him, as the *News* put it in its next-day headline. Late Monday, the *Post* and I tried to tail Brian from his apartment to his brother's hiding spot, although we lost him on the New Jersey Turnpike. The rest of the week, or until Friday, I staked out Brian's home, along with the *Post*, in hopes either of the Brothers Kowalczyk might appear.

On Saturday, August 11, I crashed the first of three funerals for a trio of Newark kids murdered, execution-style, in a schoolyard. The gunmen had ordered them to kneel in front of a wall before pumping headshots. At the funeral, I snuck notes as Mayor Cory Booker stood abreast the coffin and shouted, "Enough is enough!"

On Sunday, I ran to Staten Island after a stalker gunned down a forty-four-year-old woman. Her son was wounded by two shots while trying to shield her. When I arrived, he was in critical condition and unaware his mother had been killed.

From Staten Island, I ran to Queens (Verrazzano-Narrows Bridge to the Brooklyn–Queens Expressway) and got the fiancé of a woman mowed down in Ozone Park on Saturday night by a drunk driver. The fiancé gave me a very nice quote about how he'd begged his fiancée to hold on— "Honey, we got help coming"—then threatened the driver by saying, "I'm going to kill you."

On Monday, I returned to Staten Island to door-knock the grandmother of twenty-one-month-old Baby Hailey, left brain dead after her mother's ex-con boyfriend bashed her head against a playpen. The grandmother told me how she'd told the little girl how much she loved her before doctors removed life support. From there, I drove back to the forty-four-year-old's house. The son still didn't know his mother was dead, but her husband had choice words for the shooter, who had been found dead of a heroin overdose in a Newark basement. *"He's a coward. He couldn't pull the trigger on himself. He could pull the trigger on my wife and kid, but he drugged himself to die in peace. He's going to hell."*

All month, I stalked death. On Wednesday, August 15, I door-knocked Phil Rizzuto's New Jersey home two days after the Yankee legend died from pneumonia. I got his daughter—and good words for the dead. Two days later, on Friday, I crashed Baby Hailey's funeral. After that, I collected fear and loathing from the relatives of a nineteen-year-old whose two-year-old son had been raped and fatally beaten by his father in a "beer-fueled attack."

I wasn't troubled by all this death, or in any way of which I was conscious. They were just stories, and I'd long ago sloughed off any notion of the victims as real people. Most, if not all, runners did. Or those who lasted. They were characters in a hopefully dramatic narrative measured wholly by news value, and any horror, heroism, misery, death, destruction, bravery, and/or sacrifice was judged not in human terms but as raw material, as much as steel girders would be by a construction worker building a tower.

But that doesn't mean that in some un-surveyed place of which I was barely aware, or not at all, all of the suffering to which I bore witness wasn't being logged and quietly annotated. And there would be a reckoning, the wisp of which I perceived on a Sunday in August. The day before, on the 18th, two firefighters died at the old Deutsche Bank building at Ground Zero in a quite-preventable inferno that commenced after a demolition worker smoked a cigarette in violation of safety rules. The following day, the *News* dispatched me to the Brooklyn row home of one of the widows. That day, among the others, stands out in memory . . . .

August 19, 2007

I found Linda Graffagnino a quarter of the way into the street in a misting rain. She was short, slim, and slight—an adolescent's body—with dark hair pulled into the sort of vicious ponytail that could only end with a demand for aspirin. She wore sneakers, Capri-length yoga pants, and a T-shirt. She might have been Jewish, but I'd bet Italian given the neighborhood, Dyker Heights, near southwest Brooklyn's shore. She was holding a cell phone in one hand and a *Daily News* and a *Post* in the other, yelling into the phone about both tabloids' coverage of her husband Joe's death. Briefly, I considered waiting, but I didn't want to squander the *Post*'s tardiness and the chance for exclusive words. So, I made myself obvious and waited for her to acknowledge me. "Hold on," she said into the phone. "I think one of them just got here."

After that, it was like Sinead O'Connor at the Garden.* But, like O'Con-

---

* In a quintessential New York moment, the Irish singer was booed during a Bob Dylan tribute concert thirteen days after shredding a photo of Pope John Paul II on "Saturday Night Live." O'Connor ignored the crowd—just as I gamely did what, at least, felt like an equally hostile Linda Graffagnino.

nor, I was undaunted. I'd mentally composed a speech about Joe on the drive over—something about his being "a son of the city whose sacrifice meant so much to so many"—and I plowed through it like O'Connor had Bob Marley's "War." Then I held out a Pathmark bouquet. Linda Graffagnino took it and gave me a reply—but it wasn't anything I could quote in the paper. *Do you really mean that, or are you willing to say anything for a quote? I got two kids who don't have a father, but thank God Joe was, how'd you put it: A son of the city?"*

After that, she stormed up her row home's steps and disappeared behind a slammed front door. I stood motionless, staring at it for what seemed like a good long while, the acid drizzle mingling with my hair spray to form rivulets of toxic glue that first coated, then irritated, my forehead. Finally, I retreated to my car to distill something quotable from her diatribe and informed the desk that she'd been "understandably emotional."

Shortly thereafter, Debbie Egan-Chin, the *News* shooter, arrived and we settled in, like hunters on a deer stand, a half-dozen row homes from the Graffagnino abode on the same side of the street. It was a civil servant's nabe—two long rows of semi-detached brick homes facing each other across the gulf of a wide, paved street, like chessmen lined up before the opening gambit. They had none of the elegance, artistry, or charm of brownstones—and it would take at least an hour to get to midtown by mass transit. They were—often like their occupants—what they were. No frills; tough and full of utility.

I briefed Deb on the morning's action, and she approvingly noted that "the widow" was a smoker. That meant our prey would come outside often—and allow for frequent shots. Neither we, nor the *Post*, upon arrival, referred to her as anything more than "the widow." She was not Linda, or Mrs. Graffagnino, or Joe's wife, but only "the widow." Hers was the same story we often reported. Somebody had died. Somebody's spouse stayed behind. Linda Graffagnino had been rendered, by horrible circumstance, a journalistic archetype. Thinking of her in such clinical terms made it easier to do what we had to do. We all but acknowledged this difficulty in jokingly referring to ourselves as the "Vulture Squad"—the runners and shooters who daily covered death and then stalked the victims' survivors for photos and quotes. At the time of this writing, there's even a Facebook group titled as much. I guess joking about it also made it easier to bear what we were doing.

"And you know," Deb said, "she's going to be smoking a ton today with her husband having died."

It was a predatory observation, and Deb punctuated it with a nervous giggle. I added one in sympathy. She then captured "the widow" and the mourners she welcomed at her door. *Click-click-click*. To me, still smarting from *the widow*'s rebuke, the whirring of Deb's short-lens camera sounded like the awful creak of a door opening on a sleeping baby's nursery. You could hear it but prayed the sound went unnoted. But it had been . . . if not the sound, then the sight of those who had made it. Deb and I.

The man decamped Graffagnino's stoop and plodded up the block, resignedly and as if cognizant of an inevitable outcome, like a soldier storming an impossible bluff. It was the denouement I'd been expecting and—after all those evil glares—I was glad to see it finally commenced. He looked like James Rebhorn,* the actor, and when he reached us, he pondered, as if mustering his words, like reluctant troops, for the wild charge to come. I braced myself. But the scene, as I had imagined it, and known it so many times before on equally ghoulish stakeouts, never came. His approach was more subtle.

"Could you lay off *just* a *little*?" he asked as if our exhibition, to that point, had been so egregious even a minute concession would prove a monumental reduction in its total effect.

"How 'bout we go twenty yards down the block?" Deb asked. It was a stock reply. It wouldn't matter, I knew; she merely had to replace her short lens with a long one. "James" considered the offer, caressing his chin, but shook his head. He didn't know he had no leverage. He might have thought his righteousness provided leverage. But it didn't.

"How 'bout you go all the way down the block where she can't see you?"

"We can't," I said, evenly. "We have no choice."

"Well, that's just awful," he said.

"I know," I replied, believing for just a moment he had been sympathizing with what I genuinely viewed as a moral dilemma. "I don't want to be here either, but it's my job and I'd like to keep it."

"That's awful," he repeated.

This time I perceived his scorn.

"Let me ask you something," I asked. "Do you know who Mike Reilly and Howard Carpluk are?"

---

* James Rebhorn was a character actor known for playing a number of stern-ish roles during the 1990s and especially the headmaster Mr. Trask in *Scent of a Woman*. Later, he—or the roles he chose—softened, especially in the case of his vastly sympathetic interpretation of Carrie Mathison's father on "Homeland."

He didn't reply.

"Well, let me help you," I said. "Those are the last two firefighters to die in the line of duty in New York City, and even though you don't know their names, millions do. And do ya wanna know why? Because we stood outside their widows' homes, their parents' homes—even when we didn't want to, even when the neighbors came to us with their self-righteousness and told us to—how did you put it—'Go all the way down the block.' People know all about their heroism . . . and their sacrifice, just as they will for Joe Graffagnino and Robert Beddia* because we didn't pack it up in the face of people like *you*."

A long moment ensued—an eternity. Or maybe it just seems that way in memory. Then he said, "I pity you." And I know I should have just eaten it—but I don't like to be pitied. No one who believes they fight the good fight does. And so I told him to "go . . . the . . . fuck . . . to . . . hell." Just like that, with long, emphatic pauses punctuating each word.

"I am going to hell," he replied, "and I'm certain I will see you there."

At that, he turned on his heel like a toy soldier and returned to the row home's steps. Once he was there, they congratulated him! Back slaps all around! And he stood there, shaking his bowed head, assuredly disapproving of those vultures down the block to whom he had appealed in heartfelt and reasonable fashion for so little. Fuck him, I thought—and so assuredly did Deb, who gave me my own congratulations.

"Thanks!" she cried. "No one ever says anything back to them. But what if we weren't here? How would they feel if we didn't care and put it in the paper? You know how? Like they didn't matter. Like people didn't care. They would feel like they had died for nothing."

I nodded. I was glad Deb approved. And maybe she was right on some level. Linda Graffagnino's yelling about tabloid coverage certainly suggested *she* cared. But I think if I was honest with myself I'd admit that I didn't believe, even then, what it was I had said. It was just something one serves up to guilt-trip another. The truth was I probably agreed with "James" and because I agreed with him was likely why I had been so cruel. Not that I examined my feelings. Those realizations would come only later.

That day, the *Post* devoted its wood to a photo of the Deutsche Bank building consumed by smoke and flames aside from an inset containing headshots of Graffagnino and Beddia: "INFERNO . . . 2 FIRE FIGHTERS DIE IN GROUND ZERO FIRE. PAGES 6 & 7." The *News* did nearly the same,

---

* Robert Beddia was the other firefighter to have died in the Deutsche Bank building blaze.

deviating only on the headline: "GROUND ZERO HORROR . . . TWO FIRE FIGHTERS KILLED IN BLAZE AT FORMER DEUTSCHE BANK BLDG."

Not until, shockingly, past noon did the *Post* runner motor up Linda Graffagnino's block on a ninja motorcycle with sleep-filled, mole man eyes, I-don't-give-a-shit facial stubble, epic bedhead and, ultimately, a familiar, friendly face behind an ultra-cool, black visor'ed motorcycle helmet. This was Greg Mango—not the oddest oddball among the *Post*'s curious corps of freelance shooters, but also not, in any way, the least colorful.

He was a short man, likely approaching forty, if not moderately on the other side, although my impression could have been clouded by his careless living. He was witty, amiable, perpetually aggrieved, and so thoroughly a conniver you could have dropped him in the farthest outpost and he'd still procure your heart's desire. He hadn't paid income taxes in five years and believed anyone who did so on a routinely annual basis was a fool. Just wait for the amnesty, he'd told me, as if this were the most obvious financial advice. And when the city fathers opened up the planning for the Freedom Tower—now 1 World Trade—he'd submitted his own sketches, then sued when it wasn't selected. Apparently, he felt that the winner, architect Daniel Libeskind, had stolen his idea.

Now, he parked his motorcycle in front of Linda Graffagnino's home without artifice—wait until "James Rebhorn" got a load of him!—slung his short- and long-lensed cameras around his neck and across his chest, like bandoliers on a Mexican gunfighter, and marched to where we were, admittedly lying low across and down the street. To the ambivalent, even the unconsciously so, his candor felt like an unfortunate remark at a funeral.

Under one arm, he cradled his helmet, redolent of absorbed sweat and last night's booze, and when he came within hailing distance, I, at once, said, "Hey, Mango! You missed it. Some shit really went down here this morning you would *not* believe! I mean . . . maybe Deb could give you a frame, but I don't know how the hell you're gonna match it!"

"You're some shitter, Jaccarino," he replied. "That's some shit you're pulling on a brother. I mean, I obviously haven't had the best of mornings, if you couldn't tell."

"Tell ya the truth, Mango, I thought you're looking better than usual today. But, hey, I'm just looking out for you. I could have just let you read about it in tomorrow's *News*."

Mango looked at Deb with pleading eyes, beseeching her for clarity. *Hey, what gives?* Debbie first wore a stone face but then doubled over with grab-your-belly guffaws.

"Jaccarino, you suck!" Mango said. "That's all I'm gonna say. You *suck!*"

"Come on," I replied. "You show up three hours late and want me to what? Park your motorcycle? What are we . . . Bert and Ernie? You know, we're on opposite teams, right?"

"You're a schmuck, Jaccarino," Mango growled. "You were probably born one and grew up to be an even bigger one. And because of that, I forgive you. It's not your fault."

At this, Deb said, "Come 'ere," and placated Mango's pique by scrolling through her images. With each frame, though, he became increasingly agitated.

"Oh man! *I am fucked!*" he lamented. "Why would she come back out in this rain? I could go the whole day without seeing this bitch.* Oh man! I'm *sooo* fucked!"

"Relax," Deb said. "She's a smoker."

"Really?"

"Yeah. She's been out every fifteen minutes."

"No joke?"

"No," I said.

All afternoon, the stakeout proceeded like that—trading jokes, old stories, bits and pieces of our lives. Mango, anxious over Deb's head-start, stood across from Graffagnino's home and photographed it with his *"paparazzi* rig" so voguish among *Post* shooters—the metal bracket on the camera employed to provide greater space between the flash and the lens, such an arrangement necessary to eliminate shadows when holding a camera vertically, which is the standard method utilized when photographing celebrities. As one *Post* shooter told me, "You always shoot celebs vertically because you need to get their legs and their entire outfit in the photo." In this case, Mango illuminated the home with his flash's garish glow, all the while offering commentary—*Look at how beautiful this picture is! Look at the emotion!* First, the mourners ignored us, then they glared at us, and finally one shot us the bird.

A TV crew soon arrived, as well as *Times* shooter Robert Stolarik, who took up the topic of the NYPD's recent penchant for roughing up photographers who'd encroached on crime scenes. Somehow, this improbably segued into a confrontation between Mango and the TV reporter after Mango refused to move out of the way to allow for a clean live shot with

---

* One should not judge Greg Mango too harshly, and I include this passage only to portray how runners, at times, could come to view their subjects. You simply could not muster empathy for everyone after running, day after day, on tragedy and continue to work effectively. Walls had to be erected. Language, at times, was perverted. Callousness was unavoidable and, as I said, not necessarily reflective of the person who demonstrated it.

the Graffagnino home as a backdrop. Mango protested first because "the widow might appear"; then simply because he "was there first." They screamed at each other and, ultimately, had to be restrained from fisticuffs—all while the widow, I saw, was watching.

August 20–21

The *Post* split its wood today between the fire—"'MAYDAY' LAST CALL FROM DOOMED BRAVEST AT GROUND ZERO"—and New York socialite Emily du Pont Frick, "warehousing [sic] [her] ailing elderly mother . . . in a dreary nursing home in Pennsylvania." "DAUGHTER DEAREST . . . DU PONT HEIRESS STASHES MOM IN 'POOR' HOUSE." The *News* went all-in with the fire: "FATAL INFERNO AT GROUND ZERO . . . HELL ON THE 14TH FLOOR . . . SCREAMS OF 'MAYDAY' AS AIR AND WATER RAN LOW."

On-scene, again, on Graffagnino's street—the same runners from the *News* and the *Post* assembled—the day proved unremarkable, aside from the small success of coaxing Joe Graffagnino's mother, Rosemarie, who lived around the block, into the "woodable" quote of "Pray for us." I achieved this largely through buying a box of Mona Lisa Bakery crumb buns and offering it to her when she refused comment. Mona Lisa Bakery is generally regarded as one of the best places in Brooklyn—and thus the world—for baked goods and, especially, Italian pastries. So, perhaps it is unsurprising that those crumb buns, when coupled with pleading about how my job hung in the balance, moved her to the three all-important words, which briefly vied for the wood but, ultimately, did not make the story. *News* reporter Elizabeth Hayes managed a phone interview follow-up later in the day with Rosemarie from our Manhattan newsroom during which Joe's mother said, "I lost my best friend. I saw him almost every day. There wasn't a thing we couldn't talk about."

But the *Post* prevailed—as did its runner, John Mazor, who achieved a measure of retribution for the Mary Immaculate Hospital Guzman get. "BABY FOR TRAGIC HERO'S SIS," read the headline, above a story reporting how Joe Graffagnino's sister, Maria Breen, had given birth that day to a 5-pound, 2-ounce baby girl named Kate. Joe, the *Post* wrote, would have been Kate's godfather and uncle. August 20 was also Joe's birthday, the *Post* noted—and his parents had spent the day picking out a Queens mausoleum plot. (Probably before I had door-knocked them, or between when I had and Elizabeth Hayes had called them from Manhattan.) Tempering the beat was that much of this information came from Vincent Savarese, Maria's uncle, who was a *Post* delivery driver.

The *News* began the story's fourth day again in front of Graffagnino's home. It was important to arrive there early that morning, among other mornings, and lay claim to a good spot providing decisive sight lines to the house. Joe's wake was scheduled for that day, and years of covering such matters for other fallen FDNY officers had taught the *News* that the widow would play as important a role, narratively speaking, as the dead.

Only an FDNY officer did not appreciate the frankness with which I stood in front of the home. *I don't want the first thing she sees when she comes down those steps to be you,* he'd said. Some argument ensued concerning the importance of documenting Linda's anguish, journalistically, versus the hallowedness of the FDNY's ceremony. It went badly, so much so an FDNY press officer was summoned. *That* fellow told me he would phone the city desk to lodge an official complaint if I didn't abandon my position. I told him my editors were well aware of my location. He then promised me that the *Post*, which was oddly absent, would be the recipient of "the next ten fire department scoops" if I persisted. Then a compromise was struck. I told him I needed something to counter whatever the *Post* was obtaining—and he couldn't expect me to acquiesce without an alternative. I told him that if he exclusively served up one of Graffagnino's colleagues, I'd abdicate the block. He agreed. Firefighter Mike Simon soon arrived to lend some nice, exclusive quotes about Joe's dedication and unforgettable smile. After that, I left as promised, although the FDNY couldn't have foreseen that my next stop would be even more objectionable.

I jogged to Andrew Torregrossa and Sons Funeral Home only a few blocks away to get eyes on Joe's coffin. It wasn't a ghoulish impulse, but I knew from experience that certain members of the rewrite desk would want to know what type of wood Joe's coffin was made of. *Oak? Pine? Mahogany? Wicker/Willow?* Once there, I found the room—the first on the right off a corridor—eerily empty and equally quiet. Only me and the closed casket, and although I couldn't discern the wood, I did note Graffagnino's FDNY helmet poignantly placed atop it. And there were photos . . . lots of 'em. Joe and Linda. Joe and his kids. Flowers—enough to stock a solarium. And in retrospect, I shouldn't have been in such a hurry to leave because if I'd dallied even a little I would have avoided the confrontation to follow—but, as it was, I felt like a thief with my hand in the display case.

While I was on my way out, hurrying toward the front door, three firefighters walked toward me from the other end of the corridor. I ducked into a men's room. But one followed and it became clear he wasn't abiding any call of nature. He demanded my identity—*Who are you? Why are you*

Above: News shooter Anthony DelMundo covering a flood in Broad Channel, Queens, on September 10, 2010. Credit: Anthony DelMundo

Below: The author (with his dog, Jackie) and the *Post*'s Perry Chiaramonte stake out Willie Randolph's Franklin Lakes, New Jersey, home on June 18, 2008, two days after the Mets fired him at 3:11 A.M. After four hours, Willie emerged and told the runners, "I deserve better." Credit: Alfred Giancarli

Above: News shooter Debbie Egan-Chin works a "Trying to Save Lives" rally outside the Breukelen Houses in Canarsie, Brooklyn. The rally memorialized the death of Jarrel Worrel, who was shot in the back on East 108th Street, early on October 31, 2015. Credit: Todd Maisel

Left: News runner Kerry Burke dumps his notes during the "Fake Rockefeller" story of 2008. Kerry was on stakeout in Ipswich, Massachusetts, to interview the woman who had driven con man Clark Rockefeller and his kidnapped daughter, "Snooks," from Boston to Manhattan. Credit: Alfred Giancarli

Above: City shooters photograph a group of perps outside Manhattan Criminal Court on July 2, 2014. Second from left is the *Post*'s Steve Hirsch. Credit: Joe Marino

Below: *Post* shooter Tim Wiencis scuffles with two New York State Court officers outside Queens Criminal Court after a not guilty verdict for three NYPD officers who had fired upon Sean Bell outside the Club Kalua on November 25, 2006. Meanwhile, the *News*' Joel Cairo (*top right*) photographs the exchange. Credit: Anthony DelMundo

Above and below: Chaos erupts on April 25, 2008, outside Queens Criminal Court after a not guilty verdict for three of the NYPD officers who had fatally shot Sean Bell outside the Club Kalua hours before his wedding, seventeen months earlier. *Post* shooter Tim Wiencis shown amid the scrum. Credit: Anthony DelMundo

Above: *Newsday*'s Charlie Eckert and the *Post*'s James Messerschmidt photograph a perp as he is "walked" by two detectives outside the NYPD's 104th precinct in Queens. Credit: Anthony DelMundo

Below: *News* runner Veronika Belenkaya approaches Ashley Dupre on the beach at Sea Girt, New Jersey, on June 6, 2008. The *News* had gotten a tip that Dupre, the hooker at the center of the Eliot Spitzer scandal, often sunbathed on that beach. Once approached, Dupre "smiled politely" but refused to answer Veronika's questions. Credit: Anthony DelMundo

Left: Post runner C. J. Sullivan phones his desk while on stakeout on Long Island on May 12, 2008. Credit: Anthony DelMundo

Below: News runner Joe Gould stalks Derek Jeter outside Yankee Stadium in the Bronx on September 9, 2008. Credit: Anthony DelMundo

Right: The *News'* Pearl Gabel (*on ladder*) and the *Post*'s G. N. "Gary" Miller shoot FDNY firefighters as they assist a group of their colleagues trapped in an overturned fire truck in Brooklyn on October 24, 2009. Gary had paid a bystander to hold an umbrella as he shot in the rain. Credit: Anthony DelMundo

Below: Journalists perform a group door-knock at a home in Queens on May 19, 2009. Credit: Anthony DelMundo

Above: Shooters await ex–New York Giant Plaxico Burress outside the Manhattan District Attorney's Office at 1 Hogan Place on July 29, 2009. Inside, Burress pleaded for mercy after a November 2008 incident in which he shot himself inside a city nightclub. Credit: Anthony DelMundo

Below: Journalists surround friends of Kevin Pravia as they embrace outside his Chelsea home on September 1, 2008. Two days earlier, a twenty-two-year-old named Jeromie Cancel had punched the Pace University student, strangled him with an electrical cord, stuffed a plastic bag in his mouth, and, finally, smothered him with a pillow. Cancel then watched the horror movie *Saw* as Pravia's corpse lay in a bed nearby. Credit: Alfred Giancarli

Above: News shooter Debbie Egan-Chin. Credit: N. Stephen Chin

Left: News runner Joe Gould and *Post* shooter Daniel Shapiro cover the disappearance of Brooklyn woman Laura Garza in December 2008. Credit: Anthony DelMundo

Above: News shooter John Roca pops Christie Brinkley outside Suffolk County Supreme Court in Central Islip, New York, during the supermodel's 2008 divorce trial from Peter Cook. Credit: Anthony DelMundo

Left: News runner Joe Gould door-knocks Vito Fossella's extramarital lover Laura Fay's Cameron Station town home in Alexandria, Virginia, on Sunday, May 18, 2008. To that point, Joe had been on stakeout for five days. He would be on scene at least twenty-eight more. Credit: Angel Chevrestt

Above: The author at work while on stakeout in Alexandria, Virginia. Credit: Anthony DelMundo

Below: The author pleads his case with an Alexandria police officer who had ordered him, the *Post*'s Lorena Mongelli, and a *Staten Island Advance* runner to leave Vito Fossella's extramarital lover Laura Fay's street in May 2008. The author lost the argument. Credit: Anthony DelMundo

Above: Post shooter Steve Hirsch (*left*) and Reuters' Brendan McDermid (*right*) flank rapper 50 Cent outside Manhattan Supreme Court. Credit: Joe Marino

Left: Post runner Kevin Fascik stalks Alec Baldwin. Credit: Joe Marino

Above: News runner John Lauinger languishes on stakeout. Credit: Anthony DelMundo

Below: News shooter Todd Maisel flees Akai Gurley's enraged family outside Kings County Supreme Court on April 19, 2016. Earlier, Justice Danny Chun had downgraded ex–NYPD officer Peter Liang's manslaughter conviction to criminally negligent homicide and imposed a sentence of probation and community service. Liang shot Gurley in an unlit stairwell of the Louis H. Pink Houses in East New York on November 20, 2014. Credit: Paul Martinka

Above: News shooters Anthony DelMundo and John Roca and *Post* shooter Tim Wiencis scramble to photograph Christie Brinkley's ex-husband Peter Cook. Credit: Dennis A. Clark

Left: Post runner Doug Montero in action. Credit: Anthony DelMundo

Above: News shooter Todd Maisel amid the devastation wrought by Hurricane Sandy in Breezy Point, Queens. Credit: Anthony DelMundo

Below: News runner Henrick Karoliszyn (*left*) and *News* shooter Anthony DelMundo (*right*) pose for photos at a rodeo in Scottsdale, Arizona, on February 23, 2010. The *News* team was dispatched to Scottsdale amid reports that Tiger Woods had sought treatment for "sex compulsion" at a clinic located next to the rodeo. Credit: Anthony DelMundo.

The author and *Post* shooter G. N. "Gary" Miller play chess in a Waterbury, Connecticut, Irish pub as they await then–New York Governor Eliot Spitzer's televised resignation speech. Gary always traveled with a chess board for lulls in the action such as this. Credit: Alfred Giancarli *here?* I evaded with espousals of remorse. They sounded as hollow and wooden as a row of canoes. He asked again. Now, I answered defiantly. *I'm reporting the story.*

"That's disgusting. You should be ashamed."

"Over what? Doing my job?"

"What about respect? Privacy? Don't those things matter?"

I replied that years from now, when Joe Graffagnino's kids wanted to know about their father and what had occurred on this day, they could dig up the *News*' clippings.

"Oh my God," he huffed. "Keep telling yourself that."

After that, I showed myself out, then ran-walked back to Graffagnino's home, where Linda tiptoed down her steps on the arm of a firefighter in full dress blues and pristine white gloves, while a row of his comrades precisely saluted from the curbside. She entered a chauffeured vehicle and was driven to Andrew Torregrossa and Sons Funeral Home. I ran in her vehicle's wake and watched the ceremony's encore—more rows of perfectly attired firefighters in solemn salute. Bagpipes played as a sergeant bellowed instructions. All that time, it never occurred to me what honesty might have yielded in reply to the funeral home firefighter's questions. *Who are you? Why are you here?* I'm with the *News* and if I don't sneak in, the *Post* might—and I'd have to answer for it.

August 25, 2007–September 1, 2007

On the 25th, I covered a deliveryman's death as he unloaded produce into a Greenwich Village restaurant. "VILLAGE IDIOT . . . DWI SUSPECT RAMS WORKERS, KILLS DAD OF 4." The next day, I took driving lessons from a Hollywood stuntman in Giants Stadium's parking lot, part of a publicity stunt for a video game. I then wrote up my hijinks for the *News*. "*Not since Popeye Doyle tore up the city's streets in* The French Connection *has someone had so much fun in a car. Or at least, in the front seat*" of one. This sort of stunt journalism was commonplace for the *News* and the *Post*. During my *News* tenure, Kerry Burke worked as a U.S. Open ball boy; Melissa Grace drove a pedicab around midtown; Rich Schapiro cut pastrami at the Carnegie Deli; I did a stand-up act at a comedy club, barfed in a stunt plane, and pretended to steal a bus from a Hoboken bus terminal. The *Post* dispatched Frank Ryan to ambush Democrat Thomas DiNapoli with a five-question "Economics 101" pop quiz three days after his appointment as New York state comptroller in 2007. When DiNapoli, who was lunching at a Long Island café, couldn't answer how many beneficiaries were part of the state's pension system, the prior year's total portfolio return, its allocation in stocks, or its largest holding, the *Post* declared, "He's clueless." And when Nevada legalized male prostitution, the *Post* sent Mandy Stadtmiller to the Shady Lady Ranch for a $500 test run with its first practitioner—an ex-Marine named Markus. The result was an epic first-person account.

Five days after the stunt lessons, I covered a Staten Island man's ultimate meltdown. Peter Quartano drove a Cadillac through his old home after his estranged wife, Eileen, obtained an order of protection, and a judge tossed him out. "There wasn't much to it," a neighbor told me. "He lost it. The week of July 4 they arrested him by my tomato plants." Great color accompanied the great quote. Before the judge awarded Eileen possession of the home (and he drove a Cadillac through its front door), she apparently walked out and left him there, alone. This motivated Peter to create a mock grave on its front lawn, lay flowers upon it, and inform his neighbors, "She's dead to me."

That night, Gittrich told me to begin September 1 at Bookends bookstore in Ridgewood, New Jersey. He told me a man named David would be working there, and I was to tell him, "Blair sent me." At that point, "David" would wrongly sell me a copy of the Anna Nicole Smith biography *Blonde Ambition*, which was not slated for official release until September 4. Oddly enough, this was not an unusual request. The *News* occasionally dispatched runners to obtain books ahead of the official publication date, during that interval between the embargoed inventory's delivery to the store and its sale to the public. On one such instance, I offered a Barnes & Noble clerk $1,000, cash, for Jose Canseco's book *Vindicated*, which rightly claimed that Alex Rodriguez was a dope fiend five years before the Biogenesis scandal proved the slugger's undoing. The clerk refused the offer.

In this case, I followed Gittrich's instructions and David produced the book from under the sales counter. The *News'* following day's story—a scoop—quoted the text as reporting that Larry Birkhead and Howard K. Stern (Smith's attorney) were gay lovers. The *Post* did not have it. But my day was only beginning.

Once I returned to the newsroom, Gittrich ordered me to a residential tower on Manhattan's Lower East Side. Four people, he said, had died in a 4 A.M. car accident on East Tremont Avenue in the Bronx. The *News'* overnight runner Tanangachi Mfuni had beaten the NYPD to the scene—and foraged, there, amid the GMC Envoy's wreckage without police interruption.

Now, it should be noted that the *News*, at this point, employed a single overnight runner on what we generally called the "lobster shift," that shift between 10 P.M. and 6 A.M., the shift having gained its colorful nickname decades ago when the *News* owned an airplane that, when not professionally engaged, was dispatched by overnight staff to Maine to procure lobsters for breakfast in New York. The *Post* did not maintain a lobster shift runner, and this often gave the *News* a decisive head start on stories that had occurred during the wee hours of the morning, as was the case here, after Tanangachi found, amid the debris at the Bronx scene, the vehicle's registration card. Accurint put the listed owner—Maymond Baba—at the Lower East Side address cited by Gittrich. But as Connor cautioned, "Go easy. Cops haven't ID'd the vics. We're not 100 percent sure he was in the car."

"Yeah, someone could've borrowed it," added Gittrich.

"You'll know when you get there," said Connor.

"Yeah, they'll be crying," Gittrich said.

But as, it happened, no one was crying. Or at least not when I got there. Maymond Baba lived in a brick public housing tower near the FDR Drive and the Department of Sanitation garage where Naomi Campbell had completed five days of community service that March for attacking her maid. Naomi had swept floors and scrubbed toilets while New York City's media waited in a parking lot outside. Memories from the day resound. At Sal's direction, I'd asked Katz's Deli to create a branded sandwich in the model's honor—"The Naomi," they called it—and then deliver it, on the *News'* dime, to the garage in time for her lunch break. But Naomi refused the sandwich and I wound up with a week's supply of pastrami, turkey, and bacon.

It was an untamed neighborhood—one of the last in Manhattan—and a vagabond snoozed on a bench near where I parked. When I activated my car's alarm, he bolted upright and asked, "Why ya gotta do that?" I apologized profusely for fear he'd give my car the squeegee man treatment.[*]

The building was sixteen stories, but I took the stairs. Outside Baba's door, I found *Times* runner Colin Moynihan. He looked as Irish as his name suggests, with soft, soulful eyes, thick mahogany hair going gray, and bushy eyebrows. He'd been bicycling Manhattan's streets for the *Times* for years but they criminally refused to upgrade him from "perma-lance" to staff no matter how well he performed. They preferred novice, yet

---

[*] I am unaware if this is a technical term, widely used, although I am certain the experience to which it speaks is a common one. Back in the '70s and '80s, when New York City was not such a very nice place, "squeegee men" would offer to squeegee your car windshield and then proceed to clean whether you wanted the cleaning or not. Sometimes, if you refused them payment for services rendered, no matter how unwelcome, they'd break your windshield.

pedigreed, twenty-five-year-olds. And, yet, Colin kept running, or pedaling, for the right to appear in the *Times*.

"I knocked," he said. "No one's home."

A black label with the name "ERVIN" in white letters was glued to the door. Together, we knocked, again, and this time an old woman with whiskers met our summons. She stood in relief against the gloaming, shaman-like and wordless with a craggy Indian face and wiry, gray-white hair. Then, she barked a few urgent bursts of Spanish into the shadows over her shoulder and a short, shirtless man with a Havana mustache and potbelly emerged. He asked, "What's this about?"

I did most of the talking.

"Do you know Maymond Baba, sir?"

"Yes."

"Have you heard anything yet, today?"

"No."

"The police haven't been here?"

"The police? No."

I looked at Colin and Colin looked at me. He had the fear written across his face that I felt in my gut. I'd heard about such door knocks—*informing the family*, they were called, brought out by veteran runners during empty hours in the chest-puffing terms of a runner's rite of passage—although I'd skirted the necessity of performing the duty.

"They don't know," I said.

Colin shook his head, sighed, and said gravely: "I don't think we should do this."

In an aside, I asked Colin how the *Times* had gotten Baba's name. He called his desk and an editor explained that a police reporter at 1PP had learned Baba was a Con Edison employee. A *Times* runner had then learned from Baba's colleagues at the utility substation where he'd worked that he had, indeed, been an occupant in the death car. Knowing this, I told Colin we had to do it. I didn't elaborate on motivations, but I'm sure he knew them without asking. The *Post* wasn't there, and the circumstances were tailor-made for an exclusive, dramatic get. Colin, who only nominally competed with the city's tabloids, wanted to wait. I didn't blame him, although I wasn't about to sit silently by.

"Maymond may have been in an accident in the Bronx," I said.

"But we're not sure," Colin hedged.

"Is he OK?" the shirtless man asked.

"We're not sure if he was in the accident," Colin repeated. "It's not for sure."

"What happened to the people in the accident," the man asked, his face a map of worry. "Are they OK?"

"No one survived," I said. "There were four people in the car and no one survived."

I had said this calmly and reasonably and with the unintentional absence of emotion. I got like that sometimes—cruel or, more accurately, indifferent—as a rampart against sorrow. In response, the man talked to someone unseen inside the apartment. He said, "They say it's Maymond. They say he was in an accident. They say he didn't survive," to which Colin interjected, "We're not sure he was in the car, sir! We're just not sure."

I asked how the man was related to Baba and he replied, "I'm his stepfather."

He then motioned to the whiskered woman, who had remained silent and by his side throughout the unfortunate episode. He said, "This is his grandmother."

We both offered an awkward, "Hi," although this elicited a baleful stare from her smoldering, coal-black eyes. An excruciating silence followed—one I thought it useful to fill with explanation of the chain of events that had moved us to their doorstep. I began with Tanangachi's scrappy, on-scene reporting—then segued into the *Times'* deft legwork in the field. To me and in the aggregate, it sounded like an indictment against hope. To Baba's stepfather, the tenuous gaps in the narrative's logic left ample room for proof of life.

"Well, there's still hope?" he asked. "Is there not?"

"Yes," I lied. "There's still hope."

"Come inside," he said. "Come. Come."

We followed him across the threshold into a vestibule with a coat closet inset into the left wall. Beyond that—only two steps' worth—was a transitional space between a tiny kitchen and a small dining area. Further into the apartment was a bathroom and, I thought, two—or perhaps three—bedrooms. The lone window off the kitchen was heavily curtained, allowing for only dim, muted light. The home was cluttered, cozy, and obviously an American immigrant clan's tenement, a homesteader's uncertain foothold in a new land.

The stepfather asked what kind of car had been in the accident. I relayed this query to Connor, who could only say it had Pennsylvania plates. Baba's stepfather, whose name was Juan Canuelas, overheard me repeating this information. When he did so, he grew hysterical.

"Pennsylvania plates?" he asked. "Oh Jesus! Oh Jesus!"

"Did his car have Pennsylvania plates?" I asked, quite unnecessarily.

"Yes," Juan Canuelas said. "It had Pennsylvania plates."

I did not reply, and in the ensuing silence, his face became pleading, full of entreaty, as if I were the outcome's ultimate arbiter. "There are a lot of cars with Pennsylvania plates," I offered in a game tone that quickly withered when adding, "We just don't know," and then, "I'm so sorry. Normally, the police come by and tell the family."

"What color is the car?" Juan Canuelas asked, and so I called Connor again, but Connor didn't know and said I should call Jonathan Lemire at 1PP. She had said this quite angrily and impatiently, as if my asking had been a burden. So I called Lemire, who at once told me he had to call me back. But before he could hang up, I said, "No! No! Wait! I need to know the color and type of the car that was involved in the Bronx accident."

He said, "An SUV. Red."

"OK."

I told Juan Canuelas.

"That's him!" the stepfather cried. "That's his car. But it can't be! Please, God! Oh God, don't let it be him!"

He then looked at his ceiling and implored, "Please Jesus, if you can hear me, don't let it be him. Please Jesus, if you can hear me in heaven, don't let it be Maymond. Oh, God, please, Jesus!"

The man's face was taut and his teeth gritted. Then he slammed his fist down on the kitchen counter and said, "Goddamnit, Lord, if you can hear me, please don't let it be him!"

Connor called me at this inconvenient moment and requested an update. I imagined she was now off the deadline that had prompted her to impatience during our earlier call.

"They're taking it hard," I said, solemnly. "The *Times* is interviewing the family now."

"Then what the hell are you doing?" she asked. "Get in there and get some quotes!"

I joined Colin. The stepfather was now sitting at the kitchen table with the grandmother. His head was bowed and held up by his hands. His gaze was fixed below the table on his lap. Colin was asking, "Is there anything we should know? About Maymond?"

The stepfather misunderstood this question to refer to his potential criminal history.

"No," he said. "He's not in any trouble."

"No," Colin elaborated. "Good things. We mean good things."

Juan Canuelas strained; then answered, "No, I can't think of anything."

"How would you like everyone to remember him?" This was Colin again.

"Always working. He was always working. Always, always working."

"What's your name?" I asked. He gave it as Juan Canuelas and then, at my prompting, spelled it: "C-A-N-U-E-L-A-S."

He was looking at neither Colin nor me but staring blank-faced at the kitchen wall in that dazed look of people shown on CNN when they emerge from bombed-out buildings.

"Does he have siblings?"

"Yes, one sister."

"What's his sister's name?"

"She's my daughter."

"So, she's Canuelas, too?"

"Yes," he replied.

"What's her first name?"

"Leeanna."

"Lillian?" I asked.

"No. Leeanna."

"How do you spell that?"

"L-E-E-A-N-N-A."

"L-E-E-A-N-A?"

"No. Two N's."

"Like this?" I showed him my pad.

"Do we have to do this now?"

"No."

At this point, the victim's mother emerged from the bedroom, the door having previously been closed. She asked after the commotion and the stepfather replied, "They say it's Maymond. He's been in a car accident."

"Is he OK?" she asked, although she looked dazed and still asleep.

"I don't think so," he said, his face falling apart and his voice crumbling. His eyes welled with tears—the sadness he had been bravely restraining— and the woman stared at him as if dumbstruck. It was only then that I thought she seemed to fully wake.

"They don't know for sure, but I don't think he made it," Juan Canuelas said.

The mother turned her eyes upon us. They were filled with fury.

"Who are these people? Who are these people to come and tell me my son is dead?"

"They are reporters," Juan Canuelas said. "They're nice people."

"No," the mother said, a single, definitive syllable.

"We should go," Colin said. "We shouldn't be here."

"I'm not leaving," I said. "I'm not going to come and dump this on them and then leave," and while I had said this quite nobly, my motivation for staying had nothing to do with propriety or honor—but entirely for want of witnessing what would come next and obtaining the ability to relay the mother's anguish to rewrite. At this point, the mother returned to the apartment's recesses and went into the bathroom. It was on the left, just beyond the kitchen. I heard the click of a lock turning—and then crashing. I said to Juan Canuelas, "You better get her out of there. She may do something to herself."

Juan Canuelas responded by going to the door and saying softly against it—while the crashing continued—"Darling . . . darling. I'm sorry. I'm so sorry."

His voice broke into sobs and I heard glass shattering inside the bathroom. There was much ruckus as he continued, "Darling, you have to come out." But then there was no answer and only an ominous silence as the stepfather, Juan Canuelas, grew agitated and yelled, "Darling, open the door! Open this door now. Open it up!"

There was still only silence, and Juan Canuelas threatened to break the door down. It was then that a young girl in a John Jay College T-shirt emerged from another bedroom, sleep in her eyes, and the stepfather told her, "You must get your mother out of the bathroom."

Through hushed entreaties, the girl managed to dislodge her mother, who exited like a zombie—her face devoid of emotion—before falling like dead weight into her husband's arms. Together, the husband and the daughter carried the unconscious woman into the bedroom. When the girl emerged, again, I asked her if she knew Maymond Baba and she said, "Yes . . . he is my only sibling. Was my only sibling." She then retrieved a blue Con Edison helmet from atop the refrigerator, caressed it, and said, "He loved his job."

While she did this, I asked the stepfather for a photo. He said, "Now is not the time," and turned toward the bedroom, where his revived wife was now making guttural animal noises. As he soothed her, the grandmother helpfully offered me what looked like a primary school graduation photo of Maymond. He wore braces and a wide smile and was sitting with a younger version of his mother, behind him. She had a single hand on his shoulder. As I held the photo, I phoned Craig Warga, a shooter who was waiting downstairs, and told him to hurry up so that he might obtain a "studio" of Maymond.

But before Craig arrived, Juan Canuelas returned from the bedroom and again asked, "Do we have to do this now?"

I replied, "We just a need a photo."

"Not now," he said and his tone had become resolute.

From there, I went to Rockaway Beach to cover the story of a shark that had washed ashore earlier that morning. Craig never did get the studio, although the *Post*, somehow, obtained quotes from the Canuelas family later in the day. They were the much the same, I found, as I had gotten.

10

...

"The Juice Is on the Loose: O.J. Simpson Leaves Jail after Posting $125,000 Bail"

Daily News **headline, September 19, 2007**

I STARTED SEPTEMBER 14 in Hackensack on a report of two schlubs who'd so ferociously battled over the final bottle of beer that one had fallen to his death from a fourth-floor window. Sal had heard the story on 1010 WINS—New York's all-news radio station—and wanted his own account. An hour later, he called back and asked if I'd heard what had happened to O.J. Simpson. I told him I had not. Without explanation, he ordered me to return to the city and, if I had not heard from him by the time I arrived, to book a flight to Las Vegas and call him from there. He did not ask what I had gotten on the schlubs.

On the way, I tuned into 1010 WINS and listened how cops had questioned O.J. in connection with the robbery of a memorabilia dealer at the Palace Station Hotel and Casino. O.J., who was sixty, had long since retired to Florida's world-class golf, sun-drenched shores, and civil suit protections. He was living in quasi-exile, but at least he was living well. Now, Sal called as I cleared the Lincoln Tunnel. I told him the next flight was ninety minutes out.

"Make it," he barked. "Just go!"

There is only one other time I have heard the usually unflappable Sal speak with such priority. It would occur approximately two months later, after Sir Paul McCartney was spotted strolling the beaches of Long Island's Hamptons with a married Nancy Shevell. I had been staked out at the time at the Manhattan morgue, off Bellevue Hospital, when Sal had phoned me on my cell and barked two urgent words—"Drive east!"—and then hung up. We didn't speak again for two hours.

Now, while I was jockeying crosstown, Debbie Egan-Chin called and said she'd be following my progress on a flight departing an hour behind. I told her I would obtain a rental car upon arrival and she should call after landing. She sounded exuberant, albeit stressed. Apparently, photo director Mike Lipack had made the same loose ultimatum of catching the next flight as had mine. At the airport gate, four obvious media teams lugged tripods and TV cameras through the jet bridge, although I saw no one from the *Post*.

∷

The Palms was a trio of fifty-story slabs that could have only been a Las Vegas casino. It could not have been a residential tower, an office building, or even mixed use. It had a lot of shimmering glass and red-and-gold signage and spotlights that bathed the buildings in a vertical glow. A Venus flytrap for people. Deb and I parked in a free lot off the main tower and straddled its glowing façade to the *porte-cochère*. The valets had done good work. A Porsche, a Maserati, and a Lamborghini the color of gold bars all took the desert sun outside. It was a lot to look at. There was also a squad of Jason Statham–like guards with earpieces and black suits and black ties over white shirts who looked as humorless as TV reporters at a four-alarm fire. Then inside the casino and to a spot past reception and the concierge, where I called Gittrich. He told me CNN had O.J. posing, earlier, for photos at the Palms pool, and our freelancer, "who sucked," had failed to find him.

"We *need* him," Gittrich said.

I asked if he thought O.J. would talk. Gittrich huffed with a scary certainty that left no room for failure: "O.J. is one of the biggest media whores on Earth. He'll talk."

The pool was beyond the reception desk through a pair of frosted swing doors through which towel-swaddled bathers walked. I cleared the doors, saw a pool boy checking room keys, then about-faced. Deb and I agreed to check in, instead, obtain keys, and frustrate any efforts to toss us out. But the hotel was booked, so we reserved a room for the following night and got an ad hoc key under the pretense of inspecting the pool. I told the receptionist "my wife" was excited to see it after months of anticipation. The line bought me mileage. It would buy me still more.

"Hey, one last thing," I said before quitting the desk. "Could you look up a guest for me?"

"Of course," the receptionist said.

"Simpson," I said. "First name: Orenthal."

She snorted through a closemouthed smile. Her fingers danced over a keyboard. She had mirthful eyes, innocent and un-emphasized. Her chestnut hair boasted raven streaks, and she had smooth, unblemished skin and a button nose that twitched when she smiled.

"I'm sorry. There's no guest here by that name."

"Are you certain? I'm pretty sure he's been here."

"Nope," she said. Her nose was twitching.

"Have you seen him?"

"Can't say I have."

Deb was standing outside the reception queue with her right hand on her hip and all her weight on one foot.

"Did you really think it would be that easy?" she asked.

I shrugged.

The Palm's pool was a modernist milieu on which someone had spent a lot of money and someone else a lot of thought and effort before collecting. It was lush, massive, and hierarchical—and there probably wasn't a better place in America for a plastic surgeon to advertise. It was corralled by a perimeter of white-cushioned chaise longues on which luxuriated the most elaborate collection of augmented women I'd ever seen. They looked like they would rather not have been disturbed. I disturbed them. Sure, they'd seen O.J. But not for hours. They motioned to an open-air VIP deck on top of a silver-column-supported tower that sprouted out of the pool like a marble beanstalk. It looked like a nice place to spend a day—if you had $10,000 and someone else's credit card. We prowled the pool and inspected another VIP area. Empty, too. We concluded by touring redwood cabanas with bamboo thatch roofs, flat-screen TVs, and bottle service. I dodged palm trees returning inside. The casino felt like a meat locker after the pool, and I listened to the Donkey Kong–like sounds of retirees blowing their 401(k)s. I informed Gittrich of O.J.'s absence.

"Keep looking," he said. "I know it's a needle in a haystack, but we need words."

Deb frowned and asked, "What do they want us to do?"

"Find him, of course."

"It's a big city."

From there, we scarfed a food court meal and hit the scene of the crime. The Palace Station was about five miles from the strip, off the Las Vegas Freeway on South Rancho Drive. It looked gaudy and garish, like a faded housewife concealing her shabbiness beneath too much makeup.

Lots of gold neon and liveried valets made up like toy soldiers buzzed around an entry plaza lit up like a Broadway marquee. The building was designed in the Italianate style and probably marble, although you'd never know with all that neon. We stashed the car on the outskirts of five acres of parking lot, straddled an arcade to the front doors, then casually entered. To the right was the front desk, although one doing little business. We passed that, and I hovered off the casino while Deb found a restroom. As soon as she returned, we met the enemy. The *Post's* Jennifer Fermino was a small-boned woman with smart, coal-dark eyes; shoulder-length dark hair; emphatic lashes; high cheekbones; and an accent like Leah Remini's on "The King of Queens." She fussed over Deb like a cherished sister, but I detected an edginess underpinning all that goodwill—and one that crystalized in oblique questions that, if posed to an unseasoned shooter, could have yielded revelatory answers. But Deb was too canny. Then they hugged and exchanged cheek kisses—I got one, too!—and Jenn disappeared. There had been more *schmaltz* stuffed into that ninety-second exchange than *The Sound of Music*.

"Whoa! She is smooth," Deb said. "We gotta bring our A-game. She's the best they got."

"Yeah?"

"Very clever, Mikey!"

Deb slapped my shoulder and guffawed. I grinned, then groped my way through a jungle of slot machines until we found the elevator bank. But there were too many floors to methodically search for the O.J. robbery room. Instead, we began a desultory exploration of the ground floor and hoped something would turn up. It did. A houseboy pushed a mulish bellman's cart over a carpeted corridor. But its wheels kept going perpendicular. So, I got in front and pulled as he pushed. When we got to his destination, I asked about the O.J. room.

"*Porque?*"

"My wife's a big fan."

I nodded at Deb. She grinned and waved. He shrugged, and I tipped him a fiver. I was suddenly popular—and in receipt of the needed number. Room 1203 was on the shabby side of the hotel, back from the renovated portion that contained the casino. It felt like a flophouse, and the police tape over the O.J. room's door did nothing to improve the milieu. Deb shot exteriors, and I banged on doors. But no one had heard or seen anything, so we returned to the front desk and tried a ruse.

I sidled to a clerk who looked as cagey as a poker sharpie, as if she'd seen every hustle in the book. I hoped she hadn't seen this one. "You know the story about O.J. being here last night?" I asked, leaning in close—far closer than someone merely hiring a room.

"Nope."

"Come on, you must have seen the story."

"What if I did?"

"Listen, I know this sounds kinky, but my girlfriend wants to stay in the same room O.J. was in."

Here, I nodded over my shoulder toward Deb. Then, I leaned back to the clerk, shot her an up-from-under leer and let my top teeth pinch my lower lip. I was now almost whispering. "It turns her on. Don't ask me why. It's sick, I know, but she's always had a thing for him. Help me out."

The woman didn't flinch, didn't look awry, didn't pause before tapping some keys and responding in a monotone that the room was off-limits. If this is what passed for pro forma at the Palace Station, I wondered what it would take to get a rise out of them.

"We'll pay you triple the rate," I said, without asking what the price was to start.

For the first time, she regarded me with anything more than a business-as-usual scowl.

"You really want that room, huh?"

"I know, it's crazy, but if I can do this one thing for my girl. Well, you know how it is."

She chuckled but repeated the room was off-limits. I asked for the manager. She nodded without pique and entered an office off the company side of the reception desk. Momentarily, a 6'4"-ish fellow nursing a thinning combover the color of dry sand greeted me chummily. He emphasized a Carolina blue shirt and khaki Dockers with a paisley tie, and he had the thickened, tanned face of a golf course drinker. I told him my lurid tale and leered over my shoulder at "my girlfriend." He took it in stride, as if the last five requests had been laden with equal, if not more, obscenity. But there was nothing he could do, he said in the sober, apologetic tone of a concierge discussing tickets to a sold-out show.

"The Las Vegas Police Department has sealed the room. I can't give it to you at any price."

I nodded and revealed who I was and the nature of my interest. He said he still couldn't let me in. I asked after the security video and told him, "I would really pay for that."

"Pal," he said. "There ain't enough money. Whatever you can pay isn't worth the hassle from the cops. I'm sure you realize a business like ours, at times, has need for a working relationship with them."

I told him I understood and asked whether he'd be disinclined to rent us two other rooms for the night. He smiled and said, "Sure. That'll be $64.50 times two, plus tax."

When I returned to Deb, who had been standing out of earshot, she asked what all the fuss had been about.

"Well," I said. "The good news is we have a place to sleep. The bad news is they think you have a fetish for O.J. Simpson."

Deb's skin is usually as red as her hair. But I don't think I ever saw it redder.

September 15, 2007

That night, there were no clubs. No gambling. No drinking. And certainly no "What Happens in Vegas Stays in Vegas." Only dreamless, wooden sleep, preceded by worry over the *Post* and then my phone's jarring alarm at 8 A.M. Then a continental breakfast at a gas station, a call to the desk— the *Post* didn't have O.J., either—and then the scheming of the day's plans. We'd pursue Bruce Fromong, one of the two men O.J. had held captive at the Palace Station, then devote the rest of the day to finding O.J.

Fromong lived on the northern part of town, far from the strip, in the booming sprawl of strip malls and off-the-rack *hacienda* homes on quarter-acre plots, most financed by cheap money, no doc loans, shady loan agents, and the rotten Wall Street system that had deputized them. Pile drivers, pavers, and hard hats buzzed everywhere, choking the roads; what should have been a fifteen-minute drive took forty-five. Meanwhile, Deb and I watched the arid, dusty mountains that encircle the city come into stark and textured view.

At Fromong's house, an economy car with Oregon plates loitered on a paved driveway. We parked a half-block away, and Deb remained in our vehicle and aimed at his door. I felt the hood of his car. It wasn't cold, but nothing would be. The sun, overhead, felt hot enough to wither a football. At his door, a bouquet of reporters' cards were wedged into the frame— enough to rival a P.R. man's Rolodex. I removed those and stuffed them into my pocket; then left mine, alone. Then I ambled down the driveway to his car's rear. I tore a sliver from my notebook the size of a Chinese fortune, rolled it, then wedged it into the grooves of his driver's-side tire. Then I burrowed my car key as hard as I could into the point where the tire met the driveway. No one would notice, but I would know on a second visit if the car had been driven. Another vehicle pulled up. I recognized the driver. Jenn Fermino looked smooth, sharp, and well rested. And she wore the winsome grin that seemingly comes as standard on New Yorkers as leather seats on a Lexus.

I said, "Hey, Jenn," and she gave me a big wave, like a long-lost friend. She asked if anyone was home and I said no, and that I'd just knocked. She nodded and asked if I minded if she tried. I told her that was fine, then added, "If you don't take my word for it."

She laughed and said, "Of course I take your word for it," but she still knocked.

After no one answered, I convened with Deb.

"I don't think we should stake it out," she said. "We need to find O.J."

I agreed, and we swung our rental around and asked Jenn if she was staying.

"For a while," she replied coyly.

Deb and I headed toward the Palms with the undeveloped notion of re-checking the pool. But then I had an idea. It would still take us to the Palms, only not the pool. That morning's *Las Vegas Review Journal* contained a gossip blurb about O.J. dining at a Palms' *sushi* restaurant on Wednesday for a bachelor party. I asked Deb, as we inched up Martin Luther King Drive, "Most weddings are held on Saturday nights, right?"

"If you're lucky. Most people have to settle for Friday or Sunday. Why?"

"I got a hunch," I replied, and called the Palms' reception.

"Hi. I'm in town with my fiancée and we're thinking of holding our wedding reception here. Do you have any weddings today? I'd like to take a quick look at how you guys do it."

The receptionist connected me with the weddings department. Momentarily, a woman told me, "There is one wedding today, but I don't know. What did you have in mind?"

"I wanted to come by before the reception and see how it's laid out."

"I suppose so," she said, and I asked the questions to which I had been building.

"What time is the wedding tonight?"

"6:30."

"And where in the hotel is the wedding?"

"The Palms Ballroom Number 2."

"How 'bout we come by at 6?" I asked. "Mr. and Mrs . . . Ventimiglia."

"Good. My name is Valerie. You can meet me there."

I rang off and told Deb, "That's the wedding!"

"You think so?"

"Think about it. If you're staying at the Palms, chances are the wedding is at the Palms. O.J.'s friend is probably a wheel, and I'm willing to bet he scored a Saturday reception."

"Makes sense."

From there, we drove to Walmart. I bought a dress shirt and Deb did the same, along with a pair of heels. More *News*-bought clothing. I'd probably bought six shirts and an equal number of jeans on the *News'* dime. Jose Martinez, an occasional *News* runner, once told me he had twelve. With no time to pack—and jobs stretching into infinity—we often put clothes on the paper's account. We also bought a disposable camera and a fanny pack to stow it in. On our way out, Deb said, "I got one question."

"Yeah?"

"Who's Ventimiglia?"

"My next-door neighbor as a kid. Nice guy."

It was still too early to check in, and I had another idea. Before leaving the Palms the day before, I'd swiped a brochure of area golf courses from the concierge. It catalogued them by cost and quality, with graphic dollar signs denoting the first and graphic stars the second. Deb and I stopped for lunch at a greasy spoon, and I marked the upper-echelon courses on the brochure. Deb guessed my plan before I described it.

But it proved a fruitless endeavor. Most of the top courses had people answering the phones who acted like people who answer the phones at top golf courses. Only one club pro received my inquiry in the spirit it was offered. "O.J.? Oh yeah," he said. "You just missed him. He was on the back nine looking for Ron and Nicole's killer. Told me had a line on the guy and rented a set of clubs to go find him."

I kept calling, but it never got better than that. And we were due for check-in at the Palms.

It's hard to say how many questions are too many questions, how much specificity is too much specificity when pumping a source and you don't want to betray that you're a reporter. And while the same could be said of any profession demanding a modicum of discretion, it's not as easy as you'd think, for you are working against yourself, your own desire for information. My failing was that I always believed if I asked one more time, or phrased the question just a little differently from the one preceding it, I might obtain the sought-after answer. But it's at that point you usually cross over the intangible, yet still very real, threshold of what seems like casual conversation into something engendering suspicion.

I did that at the bar on the Palms casino floor, and I was lucky it didn't cost us. We were, there, around 5 o'clock, killing time. I was drinking Coca-Cola and Deb white wine. Most casino goers don't drink socially in the afternoon, and so I had plenty of elbow room to pump the bartender. He'd seen O.J., although he was coy about it. Here and there. Doing this and that. Then he politely moved to the other end of the bar. When he returned to offer Deb a refill, I asked again. He gave us a long, searching look. Then he said a memo had circulated among staff warning about journalists and "people asking too many questions." Then he apologetically asked if the memo applied to us and would we kindly produce our room keys. A day earlier it would have meant the big *adios*. But, as I said, we were lucky. And it was a good thing, because five minutes after this exchange, the moment happened. I wasn't even looking for it, but one could no more easily miss a fire engine.

O.J. swaggered across the casino in a tuxedo worn over a dimpled sharkskin vest and matching graphite tie. He wore the tie in a Windsor knot over a white-collared shirt with a rose pinned to his lapel, like the Godfather at Connie's wedding, only his was white. He completed the ensemble with two Bond girls. One on each arm. The dark-haired one wore a coal-colored cocktail dress with a plunging V-cut that showed a lot of bust. The blonde needed no such tricks. I'd put her at a DD cup but that was likely an injustice. She oozed out of a metallic, blue-and-silver bandage dress that, had its Pollack-like pattern been committed to canvas, would have looked splendid on some Manhattan financier's wall. It was all as gaudy as an '80s rock anthem but gorgeous after so much worry and work. I was off my stool and abreast of O.J. before you could say, "Kato Kaelin."

"O.J., Mike Jaccarino with the New York *Daily News*."

"Hey, *Daily News* . . . and good-looking guy, too. Good for you!"

"Hey, thanks," I said. He had his arm around my back. We were buddies, but I had, at most, fifteen seconds before reaching the casino's door. And then I saw something that shocked me. On my right was Jenn Fermino, asking O.J. questions, too.

"Listen, I spoke to Alfred,"* he said. "As far as I'm concerned, it's over. The two of us are friends and this has been blown way out of proportion—a big misunderstanding."

"What about the robbery? The cops . . . they questioned you, right?"

"Robbery? Who said anything about a robbery? I was meeting a friend of mine to collect a few things that are really mine. That's all. You know how the media is."

I nodded. I knew how the media was, but I couldn't give it much thought. I kept yelling to Deb, who was facing us and walking backward, shooting with the disposable camera as we approached the door. "The real camera, Deb! Shoot him with the real camera!"

---

* "Alfred" refers to Alfred Beardsley, the other memorabilia dealer O.J. held up.

Deb stowed the disposable and whipped out the big gun. *Pop! Pop! Pop!* The flash lit us up like a strobe light. But I knew we'd gotten him, and that made it all fine. Then we were outside, and I felt all the tension dissolve into euphoria. I high-fived Deb and yelled, "We got 'em!" But it was good she'd kept her head because she noticed a single, stray, yet all-important detail I had missed. As O.J. assisted the Bond girls into a ghost-white limousine idling under the Palms *porte-cochère*, Deb's face went equally white.

"Mike!" she cried and pointed to a taxi behind the limo. I looked in its backseat. Jenn Fermino was hiding there with her body prone. She'd been hoping we wouldn't notice! I hailed another taxi—good thing the cabbie was there too!—and jumped into its backseat with Deb. Then I said those words at once so familiar, yet rarely heard outside of a Hollywood lot.

"Follow that cab!"

Our driver snorted his reluctance, although the promise of a triple rate persuaded him to action. But O.J.'s party never tried to outrun us. You could have called it a "slow-speed chase," but that seemed a little trite, the parties involved considered.

The Crystal Chapel was a U-shaped building arranged around a paved courtyard, and we screeched into it as if chased by a runaway bride's father. The place was as honkytonk as Boss Hogg—yet somehow had prospered as a profit-making proposition for fifty-plus years. Paul Newman and Joanne Woodward had gotten hitched here. Michael Jordan, too, a fact now advertised on a roadside billboard offering the "Michael Jordan Package." Jenn hopped out and made a beeline for O.J., who was posing for photos with the betrothed. The local Fox and NBC affiliates were on-site, as well, and their camera-toters hurled themselves like bowling balls into the crowd.

"Congratulations," O.J. joked. "The media's here for your wedding!"

Then a heckler passing by on the sidewalk cried out, "Hey, O.J.! What's it like to be a murderer?!" and all hell broke loose. The groom, Thomas Scotto, stormed over two flower girls. "Get over here!" he hollered. "I'll throw ya head into the pavement!" O.J. retreated toward the chapel as Jenn and I peppered him with questions. He answered calmly and willingly and as if oblivious to the mayhem around him. (Media whore, indeed!) "Hey, I guess what happens in Vegas doesn't stay in Vegas," he joked, and then Jenn asked if he'd gotten in any golf.

"Not today, but I'm hoping tomorrow."

Here I asked if he was "guilty," not intending the question to refer to anything more than the Las Vegas hold-up. Poor choice of words because then, and for the first time, O.J.'s eyes narrowed to coin slots as he icily responded, "Come on, man. Give me a break," and only then did I realize he had mistaken my question as an allusion to Ron and Nicole. But just as quickly as the veneer had evaporated, he again grew jovially voluble, or at least until a chapel official informed him that his party was second in the wedding queue. "But, man, we gotta get in there!" O.J. cried, nodding toward the ruckus. The woman—he'd called her "man," only incidentally—about-faced and was shortly thereafter followed back into the courtyard by a second wedding party, the bride of which looked distraught.

"You can't do this!" she shouted, shaking a bouquet at the chapel official. "We paid good money—just like him!" (The bride now aimed the flowers at O.J.) The official whispered something to O.J., who corralled his group, including the still-irate Scotto, and led them inside. I, at once, went for the bereaved bride, who was by now shedding mascara-stained tears.

"What happened?"

"We've been bumped!" she said, like some B-list talk-show guest. "O.J. ruined my wedding!"

Now I searched for a Scotto party member on which to glom. Outside the chapel loitered one of the Bond girls, the super-endowed one with bottle-blond hair and teeth like polished ivory. She smoked a cigarette. She smoked it in short, nervous puffs and didn't appear to enjoy it. I bummed one and asked if I might squire her inside.

"Oh, I can't. I'm with O.J."

This was Christie Prody, O.J.'s better half. I'd be seeing a lot of her in the days to come.

After that, there wasn't much to do. What daylight—and euphoria—remained slowly ebbed, and I found myself under a darkening sky, emotionally drained and desirous of drink. I rarely wanted one but felt now as if I deserved some celebratory dispensation. So, we dutifully waited for the Scotto wedding to conclude, saw the white limo off, and then went our own and separate ways. Deb and I headed to the Paris, a French-themed menagerie hotel across from the Bellagio in the heart of the Strip. It was gaudy, garish, and expensive. Maybe even more so than the headline we'd earned that day. Maybe.

September 16, 2007

The *Post* wooded that day with a story about a city-wide shortage of donated sperm from Nordic countries and the "panic" this paucity induced among affluent, would-be parents. "SPERM BLANK . . . CITY SHORTAGE CAUSING PANIC." The *News* countered with a murder-suicide in Brooklyn: "'MOMMY!' 4-YEAR-OLD BEGS MOM TO BREATHE AFTER SHE'S GUNNED

DOWN BEFORE HER EYES." O.J.'s Vegas shenanigans merited a skybox chip: "O.J. TO *NEWS*: VEGAS SPAT SETTLED. PAGE 2."

Down on the Strip, Sunday morning was lurid with the echo of the night before—like a hot-sheet motel room with the sheets strewn and ashtray overflowing. I passed staggering gamblers; delirious "bro" club hoppers; a working girl click-clacking on clown stilt heels; zombies begging for handouts. And a lone jogger doggedly keeping routine. I passed all this until I stood before the Bellagio's forecourt pool. It wasn't for swimming, and calling it a mere pool seemed ungenerous. It was more like a mini-lake. I wanted to see it before going home, which seemed possible if you took O.J. at his word. But as I stood, there, watching its fountains propel fingers of water skyward at geyser-like intervals, Gittrich called and said I'd be sticking around for the foreseeable future. It seemed that if I had taken O.J. at his word, the cops had not. They were questioning him again that morning.

"Find him," Gittrich said, like Darth Vader. "And score an exclusive interview."

After reuniting with Deb—and a gas station breakfast—we raced to Metropolitan Police headquarters. Deb drove, and I phoned dispatch. An operator told me suspects were often questioned at the relevant substation. Duh! If a suspect were questioned in New York it would be at the precinct, not 1 Police Plaza.

We pulled over to the shoulder prepared to change course. Only now, my cell phone GPS was on the fritz! It rarely worked, I found, when the stakes rose, as if reliability corresponded in the inverse to a moment's importance. Finally, after a twenty-minute ride that should have taken ten, we found the substation shuttered. I now seriously felt the pressure. Strange and uncomfortable thoughts flit through a runner's mind when they are stymied by and confronted with competition and the expectations of editors. I envisioned the *Post*, poised for words from O.J.

"Where do we go?"

"I don't know," said Deb.

I called back the cops.

"I'm desperate! If O.J. was questioned on a weekend, where would it be?"

"Robbery? This *was* a robbery, right?"

"Sure was."

"Try there—the robbery squad. 4750 West Oakey Boulevard."

It turned out to be three-and-a-half miles of furious driving, off a six-lane highway with an off-white concrete median that sprouted palm trees at car-length intervals. The building was a boxy, four-story affair with bands of mirror-coated glass layered over sandstone. It looked like an architectural lasagna. On one side was an ARCO am/pm gas station and on the other the Sandpiper Apartments, which advertised a $155 "Move In Special," on a low-slung, roadside billboard. Across the street, a Costco-like building housed a swap meet. It had a khaki-colored stucco exterior and a dull adobe-hued roof sporting block white letters that read, "GET IT . . . FOR LESS."

Inside the robbery squad lot, four news trucks idled abreast two SAT vans with their dishes pointed at 45- and 315-degree angles. Local print reporters and shooters loitered around early-model American sedans. Most important, Jenn Fermino scribbled in a notebook in the driver's side of a rental with a cell in her hand.

Gittrich called and coldly said, "CNN's reporting O.J.'s under arrest. Where are you?" I told him. His first question was not whether O.J. was, in fact, there, or why I had chosen that location over any other. His first question was, "Is the *Post* there?" and only once I informed him I had "the *Post* in sight" did his voice relax and he asked whether I had confirmed O.J. was, indeed, at the building—and what chain of logic had led me there.

"Has he already been 'walked'?"* Gittrich asked.

"Anything's possible. You know as much as I do."

"Funny that considering I'm in New York," he said sourly.

I let it slide and listened as he instructed me to "make a deal" with the *Post* to temporarily pool resources to check both the courthouse where O.J. would be arraigned and the city jail where he'd presumably be held before that arraignment. Still, convincing Jenn—or any *Post* reporter—to accept a *détente* would require finesse. Come across as overconfident and the pitch might be inferred as weakness. Project diffidence and she would reach the same conclusion. I needed to appeal to practicality and the wisdom of extending me trust. This last part was crucial. Although it happened infrequently—and less so with staffers—people had been burned making such deals before.

I found Jenn still engrossed on her phone. She had the car windows up and her engine idling. I leaned against her back door and politely studied a SAT truck. It was so hot outside that I could feel the asphalt through my sneakers. Then Jenn lowered the window, and I felt the coolness of her car—and her demeanor. She had her notebook in her lap, filled with notes. I looked without looking. I couldn't help it.

"Don't bother, Mike. I'm trying to figure out where to eat tonight."

---

* More explanation of the perp walks can be found in ensuing pages.

"Oh, sure."

"What's up?"

"What are you hearing?" I asked and, before she could reply, added,"My desk thinks he's under arrest."

She nodded vaguely. I decided clarity of intention the best approach. I laid it out clinically. I sloughed artifice. And it worked. We agreed she'd cover Robbery while Deb and I hustled to the courthouse and jail. But I had to sweeten the deal. Jenn said if Deb got images of O.J., the *Post* needed a frame.

"That's a little much," I said.

She shrugged.

"I mean, Jenn . . ."

"You want to do it or not?"

I was getting steamrolled. But Jenn had waited until the decisive moment to play her trump. She knew I'd protest but not walk away. She'd played me like a fiddle.

But none of it mattered. Shortly after we got to the jail, Jenn phoned and confirmed O.J. was at Robbery. Deb and I hustled back and saw that the horde had tripled. And it was no longer the usual suspects. Interlopers had engorged the scrum. They dressed more casually than even New York City runners. They had longish hair and goatees and looked vaguely French. Some rode scooters and cradled visored helmets. This was the *paparazzi* press.

I was occasionally called a *paparazzo* while at the *News* and typically during stakeouts concerning some celebrity affair. It bothered me. The *News* and the *Post* were anything but the first rough drafts of history. But they went through the motions. These pseudo Frenchmen looked slovenly in all but their stubble beards. And they worshipped the god of commercialism. You'd never hear a New York City runner judge a get by how many more newspapers it sold, but only its value as a story. The *paps*—especially the reliable ones—didn't care about anything else. O.J. was a pelt to be sold, turned in to their agents in return for a percentage of syndication, or a flat rate. But I come to this appraisal only after parsing the revulsion I felt on that day. If you'd asked me then why I disliked them so, I'd simply have said they lacked manners. Deb absorbed their elbows as she wormed into the two- and three-deep human wall thirty feet from Robbery's exit on the east side. Only a metal fence kept the shooters at bay. From the door, it was ten paces to the ground floor of a four-story parking garage, where two SUVs and four motorcycle cops idled in what the consensus believed would be O.J.'s convoy to the city jail. Some shooters employed step stools and one a painter's ladder. There was much pushing and invective—all complicated by the Las Vegas heat.

(Runner's tradecraft: I, too, had to decide where to stand, positioning often being the most important element to running. Whether someone gives you a quote is usually beyond your control, but you can put yourself in position to collect whatever words are yielded. Years later, when both the *News* and the *Post* received a Saturday-night tip that Tiger Woods had holed up at the Trump International Hotel, off Columbus Circle, during the height of his sex scandal, both papers fielded five shooters-a-side to cover all exits to the hotel. In this case, I didn't have that many doors to cover but was limited by manpower. So, I reconnoitered the building and opted for the only choice I had—join the scrum in front. I could have been contrarian and waited out back, but it was a question of risk/reward. I could score an exclusive—and play the hero for a week. Or, I could stand with everyone else and ensure I got whatever they got and that I had a job to go home to.)

The runners and shooters did have one thing in their favor. The cops likely wouldn't hide O.J. but would parade him before the horde in a well-choreographed manner suggestive of when a fisherman comes ashore with a prize catch. This is called the "perp walk," and it is standard operating procedure for the cops and media after a noteworthy arrest. Most times, a suspect's first stop is a precinct, where they are questioned and, if arrested, "processed," a euphemism for fingerprinting, mug shots, and the filling out of forms. This could take hours or more than a day. They are then held at a courthouse until arraignment, or the formal reading of charges before a judge, who determines bail. But because cameras are not permitted in most courtrooms, it is that seconds-long "walk" from the precinct door to the vehicle that will convey them to the courthouse that represents the media's only opportunity to obtain a photo before a suspect disappears into the "system."

(Runner's tradecraft: Early in my *News* career, I was given some advice about handling such walks. The trick, said the veteran, is not to shout obvious questions, like 'Did you do it?'" that are too easily ignored. A runner, he said, should, instead, endeavor to push buttons, bait, coax, even wheedle. *Are you the baddest man alive? Did she scream for mercy? Any words for your kids?* He also added a dubious corollary to this general rule. If you don't get anything, he said, think of the most provocative thing you can ask and shout *that*—even if it has no grounding in the facts of a story. The veteran, here, offered the example of yelling: *Did you have sex with the body?* Then added, "Even if he says no, that denial could make for a nice headline!")

Usually, it didn't matter what you screamed. Most perps silently concealed their faces with a hoodie, so they'd come out looking like Kenny from "South Park." There were exceptions: Carlo Gambino and John Gotti both wryly smiled. Dominique Strauss-Kahn looked at the horde with European contempt. Vinny "Chin" Gigante wore pajamas, slippers, and a dazed expression to prove he was mentally incapable of leading a crime family. Russell Crowe wore sunglasses and a smirk. Lee Harvey Oswald screamed in agony.

In O.J.'s case, he wore something approaching Gambino's caterpillar grin. He did so while led to the motorcade by plainclothes detectives. He wore a blue short-sleeved golf shirt, jeans, and handcuffs. Deb made him. And although the motorcade was pursued by moped-borne *paparazzi*, we decided it wasn't worth our while to join them.

September 17, 2007

Monday began with a breakfast worthy of our labors the day before and one of three loaded code phrases runners employed to justify outlandish meal expenditures on the road. *Breakfast with a source. Lunch with a source. Dinner with a source.* It was a running joke that any one of those three phrases, scribbled on an expense sheet, translated to, "I had a meal exceeding the *News'* $5 breakfast, $10 lunch or $20 dinner allowances and have no other way to rationalize it." This farce worked because of a quirk in our ethics. If Judith Miller* went to jail rather than disclose her sources to a judge, we weren't expected to reveal ours to Joe Abramo—not that Joe asked. In fact, he encouraged us! In this case, Deb and I had Eggs Benedict, which absurdly cost $33 at the Bellagio bistro.

Now, between sumptuous mouthfuls, I told Deb, "There's no way O.J. held those guys up. And don't tell me a guy that personable could almost decapitate his ex-wife, either. He came across as too nice a guy. I felt real warmth. Is it possible he's that schizoid?"

"You just like him because he said you were handsome," Deb said.

She was glum. After all her toil, the *News* published O.J.'s mug shot, provided by Getty Images, rather than her own hard-won photo. "O.J. IN THE CAN . . . COMPLETE COVERAGE PAGES 6–7." The *Post*, for its part, published a wire image as well, although this one from the AP and

---

* Judith Miller was a *New York Times* reporter who went to jail in 2005 rather than testify at a grand jury convened to investigate who had leaked the classified information that Valerie Plame was a CIA agent.

portraying O.J. during his perp walk. "O.J. IN A CAN . . . ARRESTED IN VE-
GAS HEIST . . . STORIES, MORE PHOTOS ON PAGES 4 & 5."

Meanwhile and overnight, the downtown district surrounding the
Regional Justice Center had assumed a carnival-like atmosphere. Where
the streets had been empty, they now swarmed with media. I knew from
experience that this touring national news caravan would move on in a
week's time, onward to the next story *du jour*, the next town, the next news
cycle. *Plane crash in Montana! School shooting in Nebraska! Sex scandal
in Miami!* But that week, it was Vegas. With O.J. arrested, the nation's assignment editors committed their chips, and a bucket brigade of news vans
now snaked along South 3rd Street in front of the brick-and-glass building
where O.J. would be arraigned. CBS, NBC, ABC, CNN, Fox, MSNBC,
"Inside Edition," Court TV, and "Entertainment Tonight"—all had staked
claim to such prized real estate in the form of, if not a homesteader's flag,
then taped-out rectangles denoting where their spot ended and the next
crew's began. Occasionally, minor turf wars flared, with adjacent networks
and shows arguing over their boxes' borders, like hostile nations in a ter-
ritorial dispute.

Augmenting the national media were the big-city local affiliates with
enough money to send their own teams. Jeff Rossen, then of WABC in
New York but destined for NBC News and "Today" show fame, shot the
shit with Charles Leaf, the Fox5 New York reporter who would astoundingly be convicted of child molestation years later. I knew Rossen from assignments we'd handled in New York, and you could tell even then he had
that ineffable, fast-talking quality that makes for successful TV newsmen
or wealthy used-car salesmen. He greeted me and said, "Guess I'm late
to the fun." I told him he'd missed a lot. He congratulated me on my work
at the wedding, then returned to massaging his hair.

Inside the courthouse, a media liaison directed me to the courtroom
where O.J. would be arraigned after being held without bail on Sunday
night. I followed his instructions and found a female judge presiding there
in a purple sequined blouse under her judge's robes. There was a Judge
Judy quality to her that seemed an awfully long way from the indifferent machine of Manhattan Criminal. To my right, Greta Van Susteren sat
scowling with her crew. I waited a half-hour, then Deb called and said our
reinforcements—John Roca and Nancy Dillon—had landed at the airport
and I should come outside to meet them.

Nancy had been the 8 A.M.–to–4 P.M. reporter who'd preceded me on
the city desk. She'd quit to marry a California man but had lately returned

as the *News'* west coast reporter. She had a reputation as a sweet person and a pro's pro. She was heavily pregnant.

Roca I'd never met, which isn't to say I hadn't formed a mental portrait of the man. He was the staff's senior shooter and a legend whose exploits were produced during stakeouts in the same way as Kerry Burke's. Cairo told a story about how Roca had once pulled up in a convertible at Peter Cook's Long Island Hamptons home after the architect had cheated on Christie Brinkley with an eighteen-year-old office clerk. Cairo said he'd been staking out the house with the *Post* for a week when Roca arrived. "He had a blonde next to him and another one in the backseat," Cairo said. "He asked if I had everything under control, then told me he was going for lunch. Fuckin' Roca!"

John maintained homes in the Hamptons and Manhattan—heady stuff for a tabloid shooter. He flew planes as a hobby and was wired into the celebrity world so powerfully that he made a lucrative side living off of exclusive photographs of various stars. Years later, he told me he'd named the third floor of his Hamptons home "The Lohan Loft," because syndication rights to Lindsay Lohan photos had paid for its construction. That week, John was celebrating his thirty-seventh anniversary with the *Daily News*. He'd covered "the Troubles" in Northern Ireland, Studio 54 during its Ian Schrager salad days, and a million other stories of consequence over an illustrious career. He was in his mid-fifties now and wore khaki slacks, dress shoes, and a shirt with the top two buttons jauntily undone. He showed a lot of chest hair and was short and Brooklyn-swarthy. And when he spotted me, he shoved out his hand and yelled, "Jacko-bazzi! What's up with this hand job?" I didn't correct him, and he'd call me "Jacko-bazzi" for the next four years.

I'd formulated an introduction based in curiosity about how John had obtained one of the summer's biggest scoops. He'd shot exclusive photos of Paul McCartney nuzzling both Christie Brinkley and Renée Zellweger in the same night at a $3,000-a-ticket Hamptons fundraiser. The photos had been the August 26 wood, although they were peculiar in their granularity and under-exposure, aside from colored light, red in the case of the Zellweger photos and purple for those featuring Brinkley. But as I listened to John describe how he'd made the shots, I realized I'd mistaken tabloid cunning for artistry.

"Kid," he said, "it was something else. The publicist only let me into the party with a minder. So when I saw McCartney making out with Christie, I told him to go get us some drinks. While he was gone, I popped 'em. If

I'd used a flash, the whole place would have emptied out like someone had yelled, 'Fire!' But I still needed light so I timed the shots to coincide with the colored lights on stage from the Tom Petty and the Heartbreakers show!"

I asked him how much he had made in the secondary market, or once the *News'* exclusivity rights ran their course and his agency syndicated them. At this, he frowned in disgust. "That whole job was as bad as a *mortadella* sandwich," he said. "I used to shoot for the *News* for eight hours, and whatever I got after my shift was on my own time. Now, with those two photos, the *News* changed the game. They tell me I'm on overtime. So, all I got was time-and-a-half instead of the big bucks. They own me! No matter what time I shoot, they own it. And I need that money. That's my getting-laid money. You know . . . back in the day, I could do it with my looks. I can't do that no more. Then . . . I used to do it with candy," and here he clutched his chest. "I can't do that anymore, either. So now I gotta buy 'em things: clothes, jewelry, perfume. And I'm not a spendthrift. I got girls all over the country. I'm flying them around," and here he snapped his fingers back and forth to presumably denote all the women he had airborne at that very moment. "Anyway, you know what I mean." I told him I did, and after that, we segued to discussion of the story.

Our plan, it emerged, was to stake out the city jail during visiting hours—8 to 10 P.M.—and await Christie Prody. It was a move borrowed directly from the *News'* and *Post's* local playbooks. In New York City, both tabloids routinely efforted jailhouse interviews, although such operations were speculative. Arrestees did not agree to the interviews beforehand; did not, in fact, know a runner was coming to interview them until the moment they were frog-marched into the visiting area, sat down in one of its plastic grammar school chairs, across a tiny desk, and the runner identified him- or herself as a journalist. This dynamic often created unfortunate spectacles, since your visit, even if it was refused (after the frog-marching), still counted as an inmate's daily allotment. One prisoner had to be restrained after I identified myself. He screamed about how he wanted to see his child but could no longer do so because of "that asshole," which, of course, meant me. Perhaps once per every ten attempts at obtaining a "jailhouse tell-all," a runner got words.

New York City primarily imprisons inmates in a 413-acre prison island off northern Queens known as Rikers Island. To get there, one drove through Astoria's quaint row-home streets, over the Grand Central Parkway, until those homes yielded to warehouses, junkyards, scrap metal shops, fuel importer/exporters, a police equipment depot, a check-cashing storefront, and desolate streets. The joke was the jail was located so close to LaGuardia Airport, an escapee could turn stowaway after a brief swim across the Rikers Island channel. (Runner's tradecraft: Because the New York City Department of Corrections allows inmates only one daily visitor, it is imperative to queue before their family or, less benignly, the *Post*, arrives. If one arrives late, or after the inmate has already logged their lone daily visit, a runner will then pass an agonizing twenty-four hours awaiting the next day's *Post* to learn if that visitor had been, say, Doug Montero or the inmate's mother.)

When it came to O.J, the logistics were simpler. Because he'd made out a visitor list of whom he was willing to meet, there was no point in the shenanigans employed in New York. We only had to stand outside the jail and await whoever did arrive. Then the same dynamic applied as at a perp walk. We'd shout provocative questions and hope to elicit a response. And even if we didn't earn a reply, we could always rationalize an emotional state from minor—and often irrelevant—details. For instance, whether Christie Prody had a downcast gaze might be attributable to her desire not to be blinded by photographic flashes. But because she didn't pause to explain herself, you could write that she looked cowed by heartbreak. Along the same lines, if she hurried past the media outside the jail, it was likely because she didn't want to be in our presence any longer than necessary. But you could write she appeared hell-bent on coming to O.J.'s aid.

That evening, I stood outside the Palms waiting for Christie Prody to alight to the jail. The plan was for me and Roca to cover the casino and Nancy and Deb to cover the lockup. Deb wasn't pleased with the arrangement. She felt it bad *juju* to tamper with our team. I cared, but not as much. To me, Roca and Nancy's arrival meant the willowy limb on which I'd been teetering for five days was just a bit thicker, and should that limb now collapse under the weight of a *Post* exclusive, there would be more people to fall with me.

As I loitered alone outside the Palms, ducking the Statham squad, an NBC van pulled up before the entrance. I pleaded with the producer to employ discretion.

"Who cares?" a cameraman huffed. "We're fucking NBC!"

He told me they'd been tipped that Christie would come out this way. I called Roca, who was yet to join me. No answer. I called again. Same result. Finally and frantically, I asked Deb to abandon her post at the jail and drive back to the Palms. She arrived furious and postulating Roca in all manner of hedonistic pursuits. *He's at the bar, three sheets to the wind! He's at the pool! He's sleeping off a hangover! He's at the craps tables!* An hour later, Roca called back. He'd gone directly to the jail and "made" Christie and O.J.'s sister, Shirley Simpson-Baker, going in. He'd had a "hunch" that that would be the best place and had unilaterally scuttled the plan.

But we still needed words from O.J.'s family. Neither Christie nor Shirley Simpson-Baker had spoken at the jail. Christie had looked distraught and Shirley had glared. I called the Palms and asked, again, for "Orenthal Simpson's room." Again, a receptionist chuckled. But I had a trump. Thomas Scotto—the bridegroom—had tipped me earlier that O.J.'s daughter Arnelle was coming to Las Vegas. That gave me another name to request from reception—and the *Daily News* library, which advised me Arnelle hailed from Miami. Then I made the call. Reception put me through to "Arnelle Simpson's room."

Arnelle answered with a peremptory "no comment." But I was prepared. Armed with the knowledge supplied by the library, I told her, "I know you probably don't remember, but we met . . . years ago, in a South Beach nightclub. We talked and had a drink. Listen, I've been on the ground, here, in Vegas since the story broke and interviewed your father before the arrest. Can you please just give me something toward his state-of-mind? I'd appreciate it—if for no other reason than you were once kind to me when we met all those years ago."

A moment of silence ensued. Then, she answered: "I don't recall meeting you but I'll tell you this: It is what it is. His spirits are good and he's positive things will work themselves out." The quote served as the kicker for Tuesday's story. And if she didn't remember me, there was good reason: We'd never met. (Runner's tradecraft: Empathy and goodwill, even engineered under false pretenses, are powerful tools to employ in obtaining the "get.")

September 18–20, 2007

The following day, Tuesday, the 18th, was a lost day in terms of what transpired in the field. O.J. was behind bars, the world awaited his arraignment, and I spent the day doing TV appearances, including one that concluded with an on-air argument with Chris Matthews.

Very often, I should say, cable TV personalities like Matthews relied on print reporters to augment their coverage of a national story. It worked well for all concerned. The TV show got a free field update from the scene and the paper an opportunity to burnish its brand, so long as the reporter involved acquitted themselves adequately on air. In this case, Matthews asked me how it was that Las Vegas cops were so certain O.J. had, indeed, brandished a gun. I answered evasively and as if he'd asked what Christie Prody had said on the matter—the standard approach to such questions when you don't know the answer. Matthews, perhaps unsurprisingly, was not appeased. He told me Prody was a "straw man" and repeated the question. Now, I smiled broadly and responded to his diatribe by answering, "I don't know, Chris. How do you like *that*?" and for many months, afterward, I received what passes, I suppose, for fan mail for a reporter, from untold viewers of "Hardball" who were pleased someone had finally, as one put it, "given that wind bag his just due."

The following day, the 19th, was the arraignment, and I suppose some explanation is required here of this arcane legal procedure. After one's arrest, the arraignment is the accused's next stop through what is commonly referred to as "the system." They appear before a judge, hear their charges, enter a plea, and learn the terms of bail. But for runners, these events provide a crucial chance to glimpse the evidence and get eyes on the perp. Are they cocky? Cowed? Worse-for-wear? It's also an opportunity to meet the lawyers, obtain a quote, and lay the groundwork for future gets. And if you are very lucky, a relative or pal of the accused has come to lend support and will give words. Like most of the criminal justice system, these events are stylized and scripted affairs. But like much of O.J.'s Las Vegas visit, his arraignment proved anything but ordinary.

The day began around 6:30 A.M. outside the Regional Justice Center. We'd already been told officials would hold a media cattle call there at 8. They were offering seats for O.J.'s arraignment on a first-come, first-served basis. I loitered and read the papers.

That morning, the *Post* split its wood between the Federal Reserve's half-point rate reduction and another Mets historic autumn collapse. "WELL FED! STOCKS SKYROCKET DIZZYING 335 PTS" . . . "METS AT A LOSS." The *News* opted for Day 6 of the Anucha Browne Sanders trial of Knicks general manager and coach Isaiah Thomas and Madison Square Garden. "WHY SHE HAD TO GO . . . DOLAN: I FIRED ANUCHA AFTER SHE ALLEGED SEXUAL HARASSMENT."

Finally, around 8:10, a Metro Police officer herded us inside. I sat in front of Christie Prody. Marcia Clark, the L.A. prosecutor who'd handled O.J.'s 1995 double-murder case, sat on the gallery's opposite side. She now worked as a TV talking head—and was blond! O.J. soon shuffled into the courtroom bookended by two Metro officers. He wore a navy blue, V-neck prison jumper and stainless steel handcuffs—and he looked old.

Sometimes, I've found, a man can age slowly through the passing of years and sometimes rapidly and irrespective of how much time has elapsed, and so it seemed with O.J. Compared with our first meeting five days before, he now looked haggard and squeezed by circumstance, as much drained of life as a grape withered by the sun. He croaked monosyllabic answers, and his only emotion—a frog-eyed double take—came upon hearing the kidnapping charge read. Then it was over. Christie wept, and Yale Galanter, O.J.'s attorney, said he'd be holding a presser on the courthouse steps.

I went outside even though it seemed beside the point. Whatever happened would be televised and thus watched by rewrite back in New York. But I'm glad I did. Just as Galanter began speaking, a man wearing an "O.J. 07" sweatshirt tried to high-five him and then howled, "Don't leave me hanging, bro!" This interloper was later unmasked as the Jimmy Kimmel provocateur Tony Barberi. Unfazed, Galanter warned us O.J. would not do interviews, which also seemed beside the point. Gittrich had already ordered me to chase O.J. wherever he went—all the way back to Florida. *"When he sleeps, you can, too."*

Now, it just became a matter of making sure I, or Nancy, was on the same flight as he was.

Occasionally, *News* and *Post* runners got into car chases. When ex–NYPD Commissioner Bernie Kerik appeared before a U.S. Magistrate in White Plains, New York, on corruption charges, I awaited his departure in a chase car stationed outside. Kerik had been chauffeured to the courthouse by a doppelgänger who wore the same mustache, shaved head, sunglasses, dark suit, and red tie as his boss. I suspect Kerik had hoped to confuse the press. It didn't work. After his hearing, we chased him— both Keriks—for thirty-five miles of mostly highway driving, conducted at dangerous velocities, from the courthouse to his Franklin Lakes, New Jersey, home to ensure we could report, accurately, what he did after his appearance.

In June 2008, Hillary Clinton conceded the Democratic Party's presidential nomination to Barack Obama, making it the *Daily News* and *Post*'s mission to obtain the first photograph of her in defeat. Would she appear defiant? Or cowed? As Oswald had put it, "If she frowns over her lettuce at the deli, I want to know about it. Let nothing escape you."

It was a complicated assignment given the Clinton compound's height and depth from the public roadway, its foliage, and the Secret Service's having obstructed its perimeter with a tall white fence and, beyond that and into the cul-de-sac, crowd-control barricades. Hillary would not be visible, even to a long-lens shooter, until she exited the property, although she had no scheduled appearances and seemed disinclined to leave the house.

The *Post*'s Perry Chiaramonte and I decided the best—and only—chance of success would be to closely pursue departing vehicles, hope Hillary was an occupant (although one couldn't tell at once because Secret Service SUVs had opaque windows), and make her after she stopped and hopefully got out in what would be a public place. But this plan presented complexities, too. The Chappaqua home hosted a lot of traffic, and the vehicles' tinted windows prohibited knowing which ones carried Hillary, which ones Bill, and which ones only agents. We passed the stakeout's first day mostly chasing SUVs occupied by agents making deli runs into town. But then Bill gave us a clue. It was humorous, really. Even for tabloid personnel laying siege to his home, the famously affable ex-president couldn't help himself from rolling down his window each time his vehicle passed and waving. His doing so allowed us to discern both when he was in the car—and not Hillary (they didn't travel together once)—but also a pattern. When Bill traveled, his vehicle was accompanied by least two other SUVs. We quickly stopped pursuing vehicles departing the home that were not part of a caravan. We also knew that when three SUVs departed about 4 o'clock with no greeting from Bill, it was likely Hillary, and that suspicion proved correct.

Perry and I bolted for our cars. But while he lost her, I continued at the motorcade's rear. We entered the highway, and one broke formation to come up behind me. The driver affixed a flashing yellow light to his vehicle's hood, and a moment of indecision ensued. I called Oswald.

"Are there any real cops?" he asked.

I told him, "No."

"Well, they can't pull you over," he replied. "They can shoot you, but I'm fairly certain they can't pull you over. Keep going until a real cop stops you."

So, I pursued the motorcade to the Triboro Bridge toll plaza, where I lost it because I did not have E-Z Pass and the caravan had gone through an E-Z Pass lane. My efforts did, however, bear fruit. After going that far, the desk correctly surmised Hillary was destined for either JFK or LaGuardia airports. Shooters were dispatched to both. The *News* made her going into the airport looking more annoyed than anything else, although I suspect her frustration at that point had little to do with the primary's outcome.

Yet neither of these chases approached the adrenaline or danger of the one I'd undertake that day, the second, lesser-known and higher-speed of O.J.'s public car chases.

The media mob outside the justice complex had swelled into the hundreds after O.J.'s arraignment, and that didn't count nonprofessional onlookers who were there only to catch a glimpse of tabloid history. One man bobbed a picket sign reading "Free O.J." Others riffed on the same theme with their howls. The rolling bedlam dragged on for three hours, as we waited for O.J. to make bail, change into street clothes, and exit. On one side of me stood a Reuters reporter and on the other a German writer who spoke pidgin English. "Das O.J.," the German said, "zis as Amerikan as you get, eh?"

Our plan was for me to document O.J.'s exit, then reconvene at Nancy's room at the Palms. Nancy would pursue O.J. from a chase car idling a block north on Casino Center Boulevard. My own vehicle was stashed in a loamy lot a block south. Then and as the horde throbbed, "Free the Juice!" and, "No Justice! No Peace!" Galanter parked a silver Dodge Charger curbside by two metal swing doors out of which O.J. would exit.

A piston-like poise supercharged the crowd. O.J. exited. The pistons fired. A shooter stumbled and landed on his camera with a shriek. No one stopped. We were tabloid soldiers storming a hill. Everyone shouted questions. None were addressed. Someone yelled about Ron and Nicole, someone something else about guns. My cell phone rang. It kept ringing. I ignored it, until finally some god-sent instinct made me answer on the caller's third attempt. Nancy. The cops had blockaded the street. She couldn't get through. "You have to chase him!" she cried. "I'll make it another way."

Then, I was running. Running. Running. Then inside my car. Then my foot on the gas and racing out of the lot. A caravan gave chase. I slotted into the rear and needled my way in, capitalizing on colleagues' mistakes and indecision. It was like the Lincoln Tunnel approach at rush hour. We took S. Casino Boulevard to E. Charleston Boulevard and got on the Freeway. A helicopter hovered overhead—"Goodfellas" style. A moped-riding *paparazzo* pulled even with the Charger and aimed a camcorder into its window. A van straddled me on the left. A tripod camera mounted to its roof recorded the sequence. I white-knuckled my way to the pole position. Galanter made a rubber-burning right off the Freeway at West Flamingo Road. A sedan with a shooter dangling out of its passenger window overshot the exit, then revved up a grassy embankment in pursuit. I phoned the desk and screamed for Oswald. "John! I got 'em! I got 'em, John! I'm in the rental behind the silver Charger."

"No shit? We can see you on TV," then, "Don't lose 'em. Don't even think about. . . ."

From Flamingo Road, we pulled into the Palms, did a semi-circle around the building's east side, and were stopped by a wall of cops. Galanter whizzed through the roadblock, and O.J. vanished into the casino's rear doors. I was irate. Belligerent. Vindictive. Unreasonably, I pursued Galanter as he looped around the police and into the casino's garage. I tailgated. Slowly, we loopty-looped toward the garage's rooftop. Then Galanter parked, exited, and screamed: "What the fuck do you think you're doing?"

A motorcycle cop dismounted and asked the same question. I explained who I was and for whom I worked as Galanter huffed into an elevator. After that, I moped my way to Nancy's room and found her, Roca, and Deb preparing for a speedy departure. While I had won—and lost—the chase, my colleagues made ready to transfer our pursuit to the air. Nancy had discovered two modes out of Las Vegas: one commercial, one chartered. The latter was staged out of a private hangar at McCarran Airport. Deb and I drew commercial; Nancy and Roca would infiltrate the hangar. It was 3:40 P.M., and the next commercial flight to Fort Lauderdale was a US Airways flight departing in seventy minutes. Our chances of making it were slim.

The drive was a blur of angry horns and unfortunate gestures as I weaved in and out of traffic, first on West Flamingo Road, then the Freeway and finally East Tropicana Avenue. I made a screeching right onto Paradise Road and barreled down the airport service causeways to short-term parking. Deb and I fled the car as if it were about to explode and raced for US Airways' terminal. It was after 4 o'clock when we reached the ticketing desk and discovered the flight was booked and O.J. was on it. A slumping "Entertainment Tonight" crew, nearby, relayed the bad news. I pleaded with a ticketing agent. *My wife's going into labor in Florida! I'll miss the birth of my son!* She could do nothing.

But then the news gods intervened, and spectacularly. A CNN producer for whom I'd done a live shot the day before inexplicably informed the agent she could no longer take the flight!

"That's my ticket!" I howled. Then I meekly inquired: "Is that possible?"

"Baby, huh?" the agent asked. "Sure, it's possible. What you guys will do for a scoop!"

I looked at Deb.

"Go head," she said. "We really rocked this week, huh?"

"Sure did."

I conveyed my room key and a request she fetch my luggage. I had nothing with me. No toothbrush. Nothing. She said she would take care of it—and I gave her the rental car key, too.

"I'll see you in New York," she said. "Good luck, Mike."

It was 4:10 and I had ticket in hand.

Since I had no bag and was on the verge of missing the flight, some bemused TSA agents hustled me through the first-class line. I asked if they'd seen O.J.

"Sure," one said. "Just missed him."

I reached the gate ten minutes before takeoff. Most of the manifest had boarded, and the gate was swarming with enough police to take custody of an extradited drug kingpin.

"You made it," a man said as I caught my breath and asked if O.J. was there.

"Sure. He's already on the plane."

"You saw him?"

"Yeah, we talked."

"What did you say?"

"I said, 'You had a tough week' and he smiled and said, 'At least I didn't lose any money.' I told him he'd done better than I had because I did lose money and then he paused and said, 'On second thought, I did lose some money.' Then he boarded. He was in high spirits, or appeared to be, considering everything that's happened."

Then I queued, flashed my boarding pass, and proceeded down the jet bridge and through the plane's riveted, shiny door. It didn't take long to find O.J. He was there, all right, standing in the aisle, astride the fourth row of economy class and yucking it up with a flight attendant who—by design or coincidence of close quarters—rubbed her derriere on O.J.'s chino'd crotch while cramming a carry-on into the overhead. Already seated in 4E, the middle seat of the leftward grouping, was Christie Prody, who didn't seem to mind the exhibition. She was smiling, too. She smiled even wider when she saw me.

"My man!" I yelled, hoisting my outstretched palm toward O.J., who grinned and high-fived me. Cell phone cameras popped all around us.

"Hey! What's up, my man?" O.J. asked and turned to Yale Galanter, who I only then saw was seated in the right-hand grouping. O.J. added, "You better watch this guy. He's a reporter."

Galanter rubbed his forehead, as if suffering a brain freeze, then yelled, "Don't talk!"

"Ah, come on, Juice," I said. "Can't you give me some words for your fans?"

"Nah, I can't. Lawyer's orders."

With a bottleneck growing, I proceeded aftward. I didn't mind. Five hours on a plane was a long time and there would be chances, although, as it happened, I wouldn't be the only one to take them. As I settled into my seat, something struck me—the gray, bushy pompadour of the man seated directly in front of me. I thought I recognized it. It's hard to know a man from the back of his 'do and, out of context, I probably wouldn't have placed it. But as it was, I was on the lookout for the *Post*.

Steve Dunleavy was the *Post*'s version of Michael Daly, although only insofar as he was *their* main news-side columnist. He didn't write like Daly—he wrote, as Pete Hamill once said, "like he was double-parked"— and approached stories with the tabloid flair of, say, the *National Enquirer*. But he was legendary, and I greeted him with the reverence I thought his reputation deserved. *Mr. Dunleavy.* At first, he betrayed surprise—we'd met only once, during a smoke on the Timoshenko story. Then he placed my face.

"Glad you're in this mess, too," he said in his Australian accent.

I asked, "What's the plan?" and he replied, "First we're going to have a cocktail."

I told him I didn't want a drink. He reiterated the wisdom of one. I told him I'd have tomato juice. He said, "Well, okay," as if disappointed, then, "We're going to wait until cruising altitude and then make our play."

Something in the way he'd said it made me nervous, and I wondered over the consistency of "our play." He elaborated: "We'll wait until cruising altitude because it will be harder for the pilot to land and have us arrested. Then we'll go up and ask O.J. for a quote."

"On second thought, I'll have that drink," I said and he replied that he was glad I'd come around.

Later, as the cabin lights went dark and dusk hovered over a downy horizon, Steve and I advanced toward the cockpit, him in front and me following. O.J. looked asleep, his golf visor pulled low and his head nestled into Christie's shoulder. Steve whispered to him: "Any words for the New York press?" and before O.J. roused, ol' Yale shut it down. Afterward, Steve said, "Figures a guy named Yale would have a stick up his ass. But you never know until you go, eh?"

A mob of journalists awaited us at Fort Lauderdale International Airport—the crush so intense Homeland Security officers had to frog-march O.J. out of the terminal. The *News*' Florida stringer, Angela Mosconi, was among the scrum and relieved me as both Dunleavy and I hustled to pay phones to relay color to rewrite. It was about 12:20 A.M. local time—less than a half-hour to deadline. But we'd made it; the *News*' story was recast and included the line "O.J. gleefully high-fived passengers as he jetted out of Sin City last night."

From there, Dunleavy and I went to a South Beach café to await the morning editions. I drove after he sheepishly explained at the airport that he hadn't possessed a driver's license for many years, since he'd plowed a vehicle into an uptown Manhattan bodega. We sat outside on wrought-iron chairs across a white-painted, wrought-iron mesh table with elaborate legs that looked like the carved spokes of an old-time bannister, one of the legs uneven so the table rocked, although not so much that we worried about spilled drinks. I drank gin and tonics with lots of ice and lime. Steve drank bottles of beer and then switched to vodka, neat. It was cool and pleasant, and we smoked cigarettes while I listened to his war stories and opinions, until the *Post* arrived at an all-night bodega across the street. "JUICE LOOSE . . . RUN FOR YOUR LIVES! O.J. SIMPSON TAKES A STAB AT FREEDOM YESTERDAY." Steve read his column aloud and seemed to enjoy the novelty of seeing words he'd dictated hours earlier so soon before his eyes. And the whole milieu felt exciting and new, as if I were on some big, grand adventure.

O.J. never did emerge from his suburban Miami home over the ensuing days, but I still wound up spending a week in Florida accompanied by Dunleavy and Roca, who soon thereafter arrived from Vegas. Occasionally, we'd drive by the home, but mostly we ate stone crabs and drank too much (*"Dinner with a source!"*) and spent our nights carousing at Miami Beach nightclubs where Roca had many spies and connections.

11

"Preppie Killer Robert Chambers Acts Like a 'Dumb' Doper"

Daily News headline, October 25, 2007

I ARRIVED HOME from Las Vegas to a musty apartment and Martin Dunn's generosity. Every so often—maybe five times during my *News* career—the tabloid's top editor would snail-mail me a card with a $100 bill enclosed and handwritten words of thanks. "Have a drink on me," they might say, or "You did good out there." It was a nice validation of effort expended, although it occurred to me only after the fact that on this occasion, more than just pride in my performance might have motivated Martin to such largesse. For in a little more than a month's time, the *News*—along with most other American newspapers—would report circulation figures for the six months ending September 30, 2007; and the *News'* results, as Martin undoubtedly already knew, would prove sensational.

For a whole year, the *Post* had topped the *News'* circulation. Now, the *News* not had only walloped its rival—a 681,415 weekday average versus the *Post's* tally of 14,296 less—but also recouped the Holy Grail honorific of "No. 1 among New York tabloids."[1] "Proving that quality journalism will always win, the *Daily News* reclaimed its position as the fifth-largest newspaper in the country," crowed its victory-lap story under the headline "DAILY NEWS IS SIMPLY THE BEST IN NEW YORK." But in trumpeting its victory, the *News* conveniently omitted that it had recovered its crown only by losing less than its rival—1.73 percent versus 5.24 percent—of total weekday circulation. On Sundays, the losses were worse—7.0 percent for the *News* (total circulation: 726,305 copies) compared with 5.0 percent for the *Post* (405,486). Still more concerning was how both papers had tempered those losses with "junk" or bulk circulation—118,801 daily copies for the *News* and 49,481 for the *Post*.[2]

Nationwide, things weren't better, as total print circulation among 538 top daily U.S. newspapers declined 2.6 percent year-over-year on weekdays and 3.5 percent on Sundays.[3] Online audiences and revenues, again, grew rapidly,[4] but not so lucratively the Project for Excellence in Journalism wouldn't note, "Newspapers are still far from dead, but the language of the obituary is creeping in. The industry has been in declining health for some time now. It got sicker rather than better in 2007, and 2008 offers no prospect of a quick cure."[5]

Through that October, the *News* and *Post* traded screamers: "FARE DAY'S WORK: CABBIE NABS ALLEGED PERV" . . . "NIC CAGE RATTLED BY INTRUDER" . . . "ORLANDO KA-BOOM—ACTOR, PALS IN CAR CRASH" . . . "NYPD NOSE BEST! STICK OF POT LEADS TO HUGE QNS. BUST" . . . "'LOVE SLAY' JURY IS HUNG." On October 19, the *Post* ran the headline "BIANCA: GIMME SHELTER," over a story about a court's giving Mick Jagger's ex-wife's landlord the right to "boot" her out of her posh, yet rent-stabilized, Park Avenue pad. Four days later came this *News* counterpunch: "'HIGH MASS'—PRIEST OUTRAGED WHEN GOONS SELL CRACK IN BACK OF CHURCH DURING SERVICES."

Runners kept running, circling an endless tabloid track. Running, running, running. "DON'T BITE HAND THAT ARRESTS YOU—MAN BITES HAND OF QUEENS COP" . . . "SEX SUIT NEW INDIGESTION FOR CIPRIANIS" . . . "MICKEY SOUSE: ROURKE 'DWI'" . . . "CONAN'S STALKER PRIEST: LET US PREY—CREEP DOGGED STAR TO ITALY."

Then on November 17, the Saturday before Thanksgiving, the running stopped, albeit for a single night, as Kerry Burke hosted one of his "Gathering of the Tribes." A few words here. Every few months—although the timing was irregular and wholly dependent on when Kerry's spirit moved him, the uber-runner organized a social-of-sorts for New York City journos at one of a handful of Lower East Side haunts in routine rotation. Tom & Jerry's, The Magician: all sawdust dives where pints were priced cheaply and the jukebox went heavy on the Ramones. We'd pack the joint from 10 P.M. to closing, like the 3 Train at rush hour. Sometimes, the uninitiated stumbled in and gaped: *You mean you're all reporters?*

Everyone came, or as Kerry noted, "everyone in the game." WNBC. WCBS. WABC. NY1. Fox 5. 1010 WINS. The *Times*. PIX11. And, of course, the *News* and the *Post*—such heterogeneity lending the suds-filled summits their Native American–inspired name. Invitations were extended personally and through Kerry's cell phone directory of hundreds of city journalists. Most everyone got a call—some variation of the same fifteen or twenty words. "Brotha/Chief, the tribes are gathering. We're going to be at a little bar on the Lower East Side called . . . Spread the word." Such events had a whiff of one-night-only *détentes*, like the Mafia's Appalachian Meeting in 1957 or the *Godfather* scene where Don Vito toasts away the bad blood: a one-night-only chance to meet your enemy on friendly terms, toast him, swap stories, beer, and bluster. "These are the best street reporters in the city," Kerry told the *Times*. "They stink of death, but I'm honored to work the same streets as them."

For this outing, Kerry chose Tom & Jerry's; and during the night, talk was heavy on Linda Stein, the so-called Realtor to the Stars, who had co-managed the Ramones before a second career selling Manhattan's priciest pads to celebrities like Sting and Spielberg. The *News* and the *Post* had been sprinting on the story for weeks—Stein's $2.5 million Fifth Avenue murder scene; Stein's funeral; her daughter's home; suspects' apartments, including that of the assistant who eventually copped to the crime—and finally the 7th Precinct stationhouse where the "perp walk" had occurred. Some runners wanted to talk Norman Mailer, who had died November 10, but conversation always returned to Stein—and another *News* victory from October surviving in memory. I was happy to talk about that one. I was one of the two who'd been involved in the get . . . .

. . . I started October 23 on the Upper East Side. A man named Allan Stevenson had died in traffic at 73rd Street and First Avenue at 2:36 A.M. after eighty-nine years of life. A hit-and-run driver in a Mazda Miata had blown a red light while Stevenson crossed the avenue to buy coffee for his building's doorman. Upon my arrival, residents said Stevenson had beaten cancer, made it on Broadway, and roomed with Brando before Brando became Brando. Now, they said, he was at Manhattan's morgue, off Bellevue Hospital, forty-three blocks south.

The *Post* and I had run to a draw over two hours and were down to Hail Mary witnesses—people so far removed from the story we didn't think they'd seen, or knew, anything, but we had to brace, anyway, because some *Times* desk jockey might unearth a winner among them by phone. That was how I met the old man with question mark posture playing solitaire in Delizia Pizzeria at 73rd and First. He told me Stevenson, dead for nine-and-a-half hours, used to prowl the neighborhood during the early morning and then conjoined his demise, philosophically, to how solitaire was such a good metaphor for the man's life. "Think about it," he said. "The outcome is set at the deal. All you gotta to do is play out the hand."

It was a good line. I wrote it down. But not for the *News*. It didn't publish philosophy. Then I went back outside and foraged for coffee. But I never found it. The city desk called with one of those jobs that made me wonder if its editors would acknowledge my employment if I got caught. "I gotta move ya," Rob Moore said. "Maintain the scene until relief arrives. I have a *mission impossible* for you."

"Do I have a choice?"

"No."

"That's not sporting of you. Even Ethan Hunt had a say in the matter."

"Well, you don't."

The story, as Rob told me, had been hotly contested with the *Post* the day prior, October 22, when the infamous "Preppie Killer" Robert Chambers had been arrested for cocaine distribution out of a midtown apartment. "PREP KILLER CHAMBERS BUSTED." "'IT BREAKS MY HEART,' SAYS HIS FATHER." "CHAMBERS OF HORRORS."

Chambers was a known tabloid quantity. In August 1986, he'd been arrested for killing eighteen-year-old Jennifer Levin in Central Park. Because of his prep school/altar boy pedigree, great hair, and vague resemblance to JFK Jr., the *News* and the *Post* labeled him "The Preppie Killer." He did fifteen years, got out in 2003, and was now back in trouble for running coke. "Get into the apartment," Rob said. "We want photos and as much detail as possible."

"The apartment? It's an NYPD crime scene!"

"Don't worry," Rob replied, then added that phrase I'd heard so many times when other "missions impossible" were concerned: "We love it when you get arrested."

357 East 57th Street was twenty stories of pricey drabness on the corner of 57th Street and First Avenue. The tower's façade was smog-smeared white brick badly in need of a power washing, with enough sidewalk out front for a tennis match. A long, narrow finger of midnight-blue awning protruded from the doorway to the curb and over 57th Street. I arrived before my shooter, Andrew "Theo" Theodorakis, found legit parking in midtown like some act of God, then probed the building's exterior for weaknesses.

On the tower's east side, along First Avenue, I found an $11.99 one hour-in–one-hour-out garage. I descended a modestly graded decline and located the attendant's booth. It was empty. I rounded a corner and saw a liveried Latin man doing some very elegant goldbricking abreast a wooden desk under which he jangled keys. He played dumb, so I rubbed a dollar bill between thumb and forefinger and got blown off as if I'd asked a *Michelin*-rated maître d' for a walk-in table. I retraced steps and found a driver who looked like he might know. He said there was no way into the building from the garage. From there, I hoofed it streetside and passed ground-floor retail to the corner, made a hard right on 57th Street, and saw Theo parked on its north side in one of the gray *Daily News*–issued Chevy Malibus the paper loaned to all its staff shooters. Theo told me the doorman was forty minutes shy of lunch and we should await his "clueless" substitute. Theo was good, among the best, possessing a large quantity of that ineffable, indispensable something mandatory for successful running: *cojones, chutzpah* . . . nerve. I sidled into his Chevy and sensed, rather than counted, the minutes: the immutable red-green-yellow–red-green-yellow loop of the traffic light at 57th and First, the $965 click-clack of Manolos on the sidewalk, the honking protests of stalled traffic, the gunshot staccato of a jackhammer, the ebb and flow medley of Manhattan in the early afternoon. Then we saw the doorman, liveried and as humorless as an English headmaster, march out of the building and head west on 57th. It was time to make our play.

Always, there was a moment before such ludicrous incursions that felt so much like those you experience while click-clacking to the top of a roller coaster, just before the downward, groin-tickling plunge. I don't know what I was afraid of—I'd pulled at the sheet covering that ghost so many times—but I could never pull hard or fast enough to unmask it. But I could guess: It was the bat wing specter of failure that hovered over me whenever I covered a story of consequence for the *News*—the fear of informing the desk I had failed.

I looked at Theo; studied his face. He looked as calm as a man sitting in a *shvitz*. He got out, sauntered across 57th, and made for the door. We walked through it like we owned the place—big men projecting one thing: We belong—then passed a rostrum that wouldn't have made Toscanini think twice. The man behind it wasn't liveried but wearing a maintenance man's jumpsuit. I threw out a random number and added, "Chambers' place." The guy didn't blink; in fact, he corrected me with the right apartment and added, "Have a good day, officers." It was one of those sublime moments when the Lotto balls fall into place.

An elevator oozed us up to the right floor, where we found Chambers's door padlocked after the NYPD's forcible battering-ram entry. It was crisscrossed with yellow police tape. A check for security cameras proved negative. We would need tools—and lots of luck.

Theo stayed behind in case I couldn't get back in and made like he was guarding the door. He had the face of a cop—but the baggy jeans and three-day scruff were a giveaway to journo. I checked the time—12:22, seven minutes since the doorman went on break. I probably had thirty-eight more—maybe fifty-three if lucky—until he returned.

I hustled downstairs and cheerfully told the substitute that I'd soon return. He tipped his cap. Outside, I walked calmly until First Avenue, then sprinted the five blocks and one avenue to the nearest hardware store. I bought three screwdrivers and jogged back. I caught my breath at the corner, composed myself, and returned inside. The janitor smiled, again, as I headed upstairs. It was now 12:39. Theo loitered, super-cool. I fell to one knee, sized up the screws, and applied concentration. The ensuing four minutes felt like twenty-five as the elevator dinged each floor, and we awaited the dreaded moment when it opened in full view of our shenanigans. My hands shook, but I did the job and the door creaked open. We slipped inside, then closed it behind us. It felt like the first time you get a girl alone in the backseat of a car.

We flipped on the lights and found cocaine-dusted bedlam: a nudie mag splayed open; cocaine powder on the glass coffee table, on a garish end table that looked like it belonged in a fortune teller's waiting room, on one of two black leather sofa chairs that was still right-side up. The place had been tossed. We made toward the bedroom off the closet-sized, shit-strewn kitchen and found the jackpot. Chambers—or someone—had painted two humongous serpents intertwined like a rope chain on the mildew-stained Carolina blue wall above his bed. You could almost see the two of them, Chambers and his girlfriend and conspirator, Shawn Kovell, locked in coked-out erotic excess beneath them.

On the way out, I didn't bother returning the screws. We had what we needed and things could only go downhill from there. The NYPD would know soon enough that the *Daily News*, or someone, had been inside the apartment. On the way down, I checked my watch. We had been inside Chambers's domicile roughly sixteen minutes. I hadn't even taken notes. When we hit the lobby, the substitute was still at the desk, his head buried in a ledger. We smiled at him and passed the regular doorman on his way back in. We smiled at him, too. It didn't matter anymore. He would have needed the whole staff to restrain us.

Rob Moore, ensconced at the city desk and awaiting word on his latest Corleone-esque concert of moves, greeted our success with disbelief. *You actually made it in?* I began to regale him as to how, but he quickly replied, "I don't want to know," as soon as I'd made clear the gist. It occurred to me only then that no one had actually expected a positive outcome. No matter. Ours was just one role among an ensemble effort. A reporter at Rikers "jail-housing" Chambers; another Kovell, someone working the cops, another whacking Moe Green on the massage table, and still one more Barzini on the courthouse steps. Rob, self-satisfied and unusually cheerful:

Today, I've squared all accounts. Rob, I should say, often compared his deployment of runners to the tactical moves made by Michael Corleone in the *Godfather* movies. More times than I can recall, he ended a day that had begun with a *Post* scoop by announcing, "Today, I've squared all family accounts," just as Michael had said. Rob, in fact, had so fetishized Michael Corleone, his wardrobe went heavy on the same suit vests the character donned in the movies.

That night, Gittrich called with tacit, yet qualified, praise. *Well done, although I'd rather you didn't use tools.* It was hard-earned and much-needed goodwill, considering the storm clouds that were gathering on my horizon. I'd soon be heading south for a World Series hero's undoing and what turned out to be a losing effort against the *Post*. Always the *Post*.

12

░░░

"Legend of Jim Leyritz's Swing against Braves Spoiled by His Swigs"

Daily News headline, January 6, 2008

SHOULD SOMEONE EVER HAVE cause to dial up the Westchester County mansion once owned by former New York Knicks guard Stephon Marbury on Google Earth, they would find an extraordinary image. It portrays a cascading brick home with gables and dormer windows, a white portico over the front door, and a C-shaped driveway encircling a thatch of leaf-strewn lawn. But it's what's across the street that merits conversation. There, four *News* and *Post* runners, all dressed casually for early winter, are portrayed on stakeout, shivering out not only each other but the AWOL Knicks guard.

That Stephon's home is so memorialized in cyberspace is appropriate given how the infamy of that November and December still poisons his memory in New York. Once lauded as a Brooklyn legend who rose from poverty to the NBA, he'd sullied that gold-plated image by vanishing from his hometown team three times over the two-month span. Part of the unrest concerned his father Don's death on December 2. But most was a pouty reaction to his coach's benching him on November 13, prompting the first of three Houdini acts.

By December 27, the situation had so decayed that the coach/general manager—Isaiah Thomas—said he didn't know if Marbury would rejoin the team that season. Up to that point, Stephon had been missing seven days. Enter the *News* and the *Post*, which gleefully fomented the drama by vigorously searching for him, like cops on a warrant squad, including a prolonged stakeout of his home in Purchase, north of the city. "HAVE YOU SEEN ME?" read one inspired *Post* headline over a photo of Stephon on a milk carton. "IF SEEN, PLEASE CALL KNICKS GM ISAIAH THOMAS AT 1-800-BAD-COACH."

On the 28th I drew Marbury mansion stakeout duty, although out of necessity I took a more furtive approach than the runners portrayed by Google. By then, the cops had begun running reporters off, claiming the subdivision was private property. So I hid beneath the eight-foot privacy hedges skirting the backyard of the home across from Stephon's. Shooter Alfred Giancarli was on his belly, as well, holding his long-lens camera aimed at Stephon's kitchen window in a vigil for movement. We had an unobstructed line of sight, and I was acting as a sort of sniper's spotter, advising Alfred when I detected signs of movement. I had been so engaged for four hours when Rob Moore phoned and ordered me "on to the next flight humanly possible to Fort Lauderdale." Only after I agreed did he ask if I recalled Jim Leyritz, the ex–New York Yankee who had recently retired from a journeyman's career that included several well-timed postseason home runs. I told him I did, and Rob said Leyritz had killed a woman around 3 A.M. that day while drunk driving.

As it happened, my itinerary stalled during a connection in Charlotte, and I didn't deplane in Fort Lauderdale until after 1 A.M. to the whirring of a vacuum cleaner waltzed through the terminal by a maintenance man. My body felt as knotted as salt water–pickled dock rope as I shuffled down the same corridor I had three months earlier in O.J.'s frenzied wake. I marked the same pay phones where Dunleavy and I had dumped our notes, then bused to the airport's rental car kiosk. An attendant there asked how long I'd need the car, and I said, "Better make it a month." She looked at me like I was loony.

After collecting the car, I swung back to the terminal and collected Nick Fevelo, the *News* shooter who'd arrived on an even later flight. Together, we checked into the same Collins Avenue hotel in which I had stayed that September. When I looked at the clock, I felt a long way from the prior day's morning. It was 3:44 A.M. I bedded down and brought the rolling inertia of my mind to a begrudging stop. If I slept at all, I didn't feel it.

December 29, 2007

December in South Florida felt like April in the Northeast. You could work up a sweat, but you'd have to earn it. I retrieved my rental, a Toyota RAV4, from its spot off Washington Avenue and motored to the lee of the hotel. There, the wind sounded as if fired from a leaf blower, while overhead, the clouds hustled over the horizon as they do in time-lapse videos. Then

Nick came outside, mussing his still-wet Jonas Brothers hair. He'd taken an ocean dip to work out the airline kinks. I should have done the same. My body still felt as if it had been run through a pasta maker. When we reached the corner of Collins Avenue and 4th Street, the trade winds buffeted the car like angry storm waves on a jetty. Then, we drove thirty miles north up I-95 and the Florida Turnpike, along the finger of inhabitable land between the Atlantic Ocean and the Everglades, into Plantation.

Three east–west highways—all of them running eight miles to Fort Lauderdale's beach district—trisected the town. The southernmost was Peters Road, a six-laner with a grassy, dogwood-lined median out of bloom. At some point near SW 66th Avenue, an off-white, smooth-finished concrete privacy wall interposed the sidewalk and homes. This was Beaumont Estates, a twenty-nine-home subdivision of ranch-style single family homes done up like *hacienda* guest houses with lots of pastel-colored exterior paint. We drove inside and found a peninsula of grass jutting into a circular four-way crossing. On it stood the home formerly inhabited by Fredia Veitch—Leyritz's victim. It had a cross gable roof with coffee-colored shingles and a matching, gabled single-car garage. The home was otherwise squash-colored and haphazardly concealed on the south and east sides by an inverted "J" of willowy palms and palm ferns, dogwoods, and other tropical growth. Overhead, the trade winds still herded the clouds across the sky as if by invisible cowboys, but the ground air had wilted in the now-100-degree heat. Moving felt like wading through syrup.

It was too early to knock, so we did a slow drive-by, saw the home locked up like a Cape Cod bungalow in mid-January, noted the *Post's* absence, and parked in a cul-de-sac. Jimmy in the library dictated Accurint reports for Fredia and hubby Jordan Veitch. Fredia's showed three associates, which could mean anything from an ex-roommate to the Realtor who sold her the house; eight relatives; a protean living history numbering thirteen Broward County residences since 1996; a 2004 small-claims judgment for $1,231; a single AOL e-mail address; and one criminal offense from 2005 for aggravated assault with a deadly weapon. Jordan's, meanwhile, indicated three residences since 1999; no bankruptcies or liens; three cell numbers; co-workers in two businesses called The Veitch Group and Top Line Representation Corp.; an arrest out of Tallahassee for driving with a suspended license; two busts for cocaine possession and another for trafficking in amphetamine from 1998; a Florida fishing license, many times renewed; a declared political affiliation listed as "other"; and relatives and associates exceeding in number those of his wife.

I began with a Jack Veitch, whom I guessed from his 1952 birthday to be Jordan's father. I left a sincere-sounding, although completely spurious voicemail: "Mr. Veitch, this is Mike Jaccarino. I'm an editor with the New York *Daily News*. I am so sorry. I can't even imagine how you must feel at this moment, and forgive me for calling. But I flew in from New York and I wanted to touch base. I know what you're thinking, but before you decide not to call me, I want you to know my family has been touched by drunk driving, too, and I wanted to personally come down, instead of just sending a reporter. I wonder if you would help me."

I left my cell number. Nick looked at me with a raised eyebrow and asked, "None of that was true, right?"

"Well, I did fly in from New York."

Nick said he would never believe another thing that came out of my mouth. I asked if the voicemail I'd left had sounded sincere.

"Yes! Very sincere, and that's why I will never trust another thing that comes out of your mouth."

We laughed.

"Why tell him you're an editor?"

"Might make him feel important. White glove treatment."

Nick gleefully snorted.

"Tabloid poetry," he said.

Now, I understand some people will find this sort of lying objectionable, if not despicable. And I am inclined, in retrospect, to agree. I am also aware that there are those who will point to such prevarications in the service of gets and see cause to disregard this account as a teaching tool. I get where they're coming from, too. Kerry Burke once told *The Awl*'s Paul Hiebert,

I impersonate no one. When I go into a place, I do my best not to answer any questions, but if someone asks me who I am, I tell them. If you lie to people, your leverage is gone. Why should they tell you anything if you're a liar? I know people who've done the impersonation thing, who've lied to people about who they are and what they're doing, and they're malignant. Decent journalists have to repair the damage they've done. Don't get me wrong: People have looked at me and seen a detective. I don't rush around telling people I'm *not* a detective. But I let everybody I speak to know who I am. Sometimes it's at the beginning of the interview, sometimes in the middle, and sometimes at the end.

I agree with Kerry, not only now, but then. I never told a source I was something other than a journalist to prompt them to words. That said, I did, obviously, bend the truth within the parameters of acting as a reporter; and I recount my methods truthfully and factually and with the intention of no catharsis, but rather to provide an equally honest portrayal of the pressure placed upon runners by the *News–Post* war. That doesn't excuse me, I know, and I am not advocating for these methods—and especially when lubricating a widower's father. It, simply, is what it is; and at the time I felt I had no choice.

Normally, I'm of the mind that there are no haunted houses in Florida. You can, for instance, drive down any street in New England and, depending on the time of year, feel as if every third home has played host to some unspeakable tragedy. In Florida, though, I never got that sensation. All the homes are all pastel and sun-drenched and landscaped with lush tropical flora that, at least, lends the illusion of vibrancy. But not the Veitch home. Not now. Now, it looked as foreboding as Boo Radley's front yard. But I also knew that to delay knocking—and thus squander the *Post's* tardiness—would only make matters worse, later.

With effort, I willed leaden legs toward the front door, rang the bell, then opened the storm one and knocked on that. Eventually, Jordan Veitch opened the door, looking about as sad as a stuffed animal left out at the curb. He wore black mesh gym shorts and a loose-fitting white T-shirt, untucked and draped over a beer leaguer's body. He had a boyish face he was dragging into early adulthood with coyly styled eyebrows and a close-cropped beard, a look that I knew from aborted experience required work. Lots of work. He hadn't worked on it and now the hair crawled over his cheeks like untended ivy. And he had a plunging lantern jaw that looked like the prow of a transatlantic container ship and a cinder block for a head that suggested its cargo. I grueled my way through the CliffsNotes version of the spiel I'd already given his father, then concluded with the most sincere apology I could muster. It sounded as hollow as an undertaker's remorse. But Veitch accepted it graciously and replied he had two kids who'd cried themselves to sleep the prior night. "They want to know what happened," he said, "why their mom didn't come home."

I asked him if he'd told them. He offered the whisper of a shrug and said, "They have an idea."

I considered asking him to elaborate but found myself constitutionally unable. Instead, I said, "Listen, I just want to tell the world what a wonderful woman and mother Freddie was."

And he did, and when he was done, I rushed back to the RAV4 as if it were a getaway car and I'd just robbed the City National Bank of Florida. Dueling emotions: contrite over the act; exhilarated over the success. I checked my watch. It wasn't yet 10:30 and we had a big lead over the *Post*.

I informed Connor, who was delighted by the Jordan Veitch get. Then she asked if the *Post* had it, too. "No," I replied. But before I concluded the call, I'd had to inform her they'd just arrived. "Keep them away from the house!" she cried. "Do what you have to!"

The *Daily News* and the *Post* often contracted freelancers to "hold the fort" on out-of-town jobs until staffers arrived. The urgency of the first hours of a breaking-news story demanded it. In this case, the *Post*'s was a stout, forty-ish woman with a ruddy complexion, shoulder-length red hair, a smile that looked just a little forced, and a face that reminded me of any one of a number distant aunts I saw exclusively at wakes, christenings, and communions. She introduced herself and informed me she typically wrote for *People* magazine. I told her I'd knocked and Veitch had said his father would handle media inquiries later in the day. That was sort of true. She asked if I'd gotten words. I said, "Not really," and, when she continued to the door, I added, "There are no scoops out here, Julie."

"But shouldn't I knock?" she asked and I winced, far more from a reluctance to revisit the widower Veitch than a desire to preserve my scoop. I told her we should "Give the poor man some peace," and she asked, again, if I'd gotten words. I shrugged and she advanced toward the door. I made a final, futile effort to stop her and she now turned on me with fury: "I know how it works out here!" I followed in tow, until her desk mercifully called and ordered her to await photo's arrival. I returned to the car and read that day's papers. The *Post* split its wood between Leyritz—"RUN DOWN . . . EX-YANKEE LEYRITZ HIT WITH DUI SLAY RAP"—and the assassination of Pakistani Prime Minister Benazir Bhutto. "ASSASSINS ON TAPE . . . THE BHUTTO SLAYING." The *News* did the same, although, unlike the *Post*, put Leyritz above the fold. "BUSTED! EX-YANKEE LEYRITZ CHARGED IN DUI MANSLAUGHTER" . . . "KILLERS' BOAST . . . TERROR DUO BRAGGED OF BHUTTO ASSASSINATION."

After the woods, I examined the *News'* and the *Post*'s first-day Leyritz coverage as if doing one of those "Spot the Differences" puzzles in the back of the *National Enquirer*: In this photo Julia Louis-Dreyfus has a pin in her hair. In that one, she doesn't. Both papers, I saw, had played to a draw on the facts: The *News* put the time of the accident at "just after 3 A.M.," the *Post* at 3:20 A.M. Neither specified the intersection, although both, I was sure, possessed the information and had generalized for an out-of-town audience. Both had Fredia heading home after a barmaid shift, although the *Post* identified the workplace as the Original Steakhouse. In both accounts, Leyritz blew a red light and slammed his Ford Expedition into Fredia's Mitsubishi Montero, causing the Montero to flip and Fredia to fatally hurl from her vehicle. The *Post*, however, artfully attributed this fact to "at least three witnesses [having] told cops" as much, while the *News* lazily relied on the time-tested "police said." Unlike the *News*, the *Post* included the vehicles' editions and colors—Leyritz's 2006 and burgundy and Fredia's 2000 and green—although that was likely a decision rooted in space and taste, rather than any exclusively obtained information. In the *News*, a police spokeswoman said Fredia was "days away from quitting her job," because Jordan didn't "like the fact she worked late hours." The *Post*, meanwhile, attributed her imminent resignation to a fatalistic disinclination to drive at night. Both cited Leyritz's "red watery eyes, flushed face," odor of alcohol, and failure of field sobriety tests.

Both papers noted unsuccessful attempts to contact both Leyritz and the Veitch clan. The *News* also had staked out the Broward County Jail ahead of Leyritz's release, which, the story noted, came eleven hours after the accident. Such diligence yielded a nugget: Leyritz, Connor wrote, "appeared shaken and close to tears" when he did, finally, emerge.

The *Post*, meanwhile, had three nice, exclusive gets, one of which would dominate Saturday and a second one showing how the coverage would unfold over the coming week. They included: (1) A "source close to the former slugger" said Leyritz and Veitch had known each other through a mutual friend; (2) Court documents indicated Leyritz had "been busted for speeding and driving with a suspended license" in 2006; and (3) a first-hand account of Leyritz's actions prior to the crash. In reporting this last get, the *Post* quoted a Leyritz pal named Erica Chevillar as saying the ex-jock had "sipped" vodka tonics at his forty-fourth-birthday party at a Fort Lauderdale nightclub called Automatic Slims.

And if you think I was splitting hairs, consider that Martin Dunn had assuredly completed the same obsessive exercise—and likely Col Allan, as well, both to determine a victor and a loser, generally, and to whom credit or fault was due on each respective staff. Martin, I knew, read both papers from home and sent a memo to the morning assignment editor outlining the gets on which the *Post* had trumped the *News*. Sometimes, these gets concerned something as granular as a single stray (and maybe even insignificant) quote.

Besides, I had an ulterior motive beyond simply keeping score. I needed leads to pursue in the field, and the *Post* was just as good a place to dig as that day's *News*.

The journalist horde outside Jordan Veitch's door had swelled. Nick and I joined the scrum: the *Sun Sentinel*, the *Miami Herald*, a local Fox affiliate, a *Post* freelance shooter, and Julie. Warily, yet politely, introductions were exchanged. We followed the *Sun Sentinel* to the door and formed a semi-circle. He knocked. I didn't feel as bad this time; there was emotional safety in numbers. The door opened and a bronzed specimen greeted us. He wore a worsted pale blue suit the hue of the ocean as we like to imagine it, with pink pinstripes so fine you could miss them in anything but the best of light. He had manicured nails and golden blond hair the color of angel food cake. It seemed as lush as a suburban retiree's front lawn. He introduced himself as Todd Templeton and said he was "handling P.R. for Jordan."

"Why does he need P.R.?" the *Sun Sentinel* asked.

Todd Templeton replied with an arrogant smile that seemed to convey: *You simpleton*. He said Jordan would "address [us] at 1:30 P.M. in the presence of his lawyer"—and he would not take questions. He concluded with a throaty and rhetorical "All right?," clapped his hands like a quarterback concluding a huddle, and did a modified pirouette back into the house.

"He's going to address us?" the Fox reporter asked. "Is he a widower or Abraham Lincoln?"

"Lot of professionals around a guy who's a victim," added the *Herald*.

"What's a guy like Todd Templeton make?" Fox asked.

"Whatever it is," the *Herald* retorted, "it ain't enough."

When I was back in the car, the desk called. Connor asked if I'd seen the *Post*'s Erica Chevillar get. I told her I had and she asked if I'd "Accurint'ed her yet" as if the Lexis tool were some kind of medieval contraption on which I'd strap a source in order to produce quotes. I told her Jimmy was working on it. She opined that Chevillar might have photos of Leyritz's party and the *Post* had either been "too stupid or too cheap" to obtain them. "It was a birthday party!" she cried. "There had to be photos, right?" I said, "Totally!" called Jimmy, and instructed him that if anyone asked, I'd requested Chevillar's Accurint forty minutes earlier.

"Connor?"

"Best I don't say."

He chuckled, retrieved her Accurint in real time, and gave me numbers for her as well as six of her relatives. The first was disconnected. The second got me the voicemail of a Colombian tour operator. On the third, I got lucky. Erica Chevillar's grandmother sounded like one of those ageless seniors who prune azaleas, or go canoeing, in Cialis commercials. She sounded as if she wouldn't mind being flirted with. I flirted with her—said I didn't think she'd sat out too many dances in her day. She loved that one—but not as much as she loved the Leyritz narrative, in total, which she listened to like good, juicy clubhouse gossip.

"Oh my!" she cried when I regaled her about Erica's role. But I could tell she was pleased.

"You know she was in *Playboy*?" she asked, then giggled her way through the sort of schoolyard laugh usually prompted by talk of something dirty.

"No kidding?"

Another giggle.

"I know I shouldn't say this because I'm her grandmother but she looked wonderful."

Erica Chevillar wasn't nearly so easy. The first time I called, she hung up. The second time, I left a message. Then I brooded for ten minutes and called her from Nick's cell. She answered. I steamrolled through my pitch—and she warmed after I told her about her "lovely grandmother." Finally, Erica told me her night with Leyritz had begun at a Fort Lauderdale bar called Blue Martini. She said a friend had, indeed, snapped photos, although that friend had since left for the Bahamas. She had a call out to her. I asked why she'd bothered to make that call and if anyone else had already inquired. When she didn't answer, I asked how she knew Jana Winter. It had been a shot in the dark—but it found the mark.

"We have a mutual friend," she said.

"Has the *Post* asked for the photos?"

"Yeah, they have."

"Have they offered you money?"

"I don't want to say."

"Erica, you take whatever the *Post* has offered and I'll double it. I'll triple it! I don't care what it is! Just triple it and call me back."

"OK."

"Do you promise?"

"Yes."

I informed Connor, who without deliberation or conference authorized me to spend as much as $2,000, then added, "Oh, and find out if she's willing to pose for photos. Tell her we'll even airbrush the bejesus out of her, just like they did in *Playboy*!"

Meanwhile, my colleagues mustered at Jordan Veitch's driveway like spectators for a public hanging. Then—and at 1:40—Jordan exited. They had done good work, but he still looked like a condemned man. There was Templeton, a personal-injury lawyer named Richard Abramowitz, and David O'Keefe, who introduced himself as the father of Fredia's first child. They all talked; then Jordan recited a statement. The *Post* asked if he'd told his kids about Fredia's death. Jordan repeated the line he'd already told me, then added about one of his sons, "He has a lot of questions. He asked me why Mommy wasn't going to come home; why Mommy was in the grass and who's going to take care of him."

I called it in for second edition, then briefed Gittrich with a bias toward pursuing the Chevillar photos. Gittrich was wary about my leaving the scene with the *Post* on site. But I persuaded him the danger presented by Jana—and her connection to the *Playboy* model—far outweighed the potential Jordan Veitch would re-emerge and burnish his account.

I then called Jana, who answered on the first ring.

"What's going on down there?" she demanded. "Do you have Leyritz?"

"Yes," I replied. "We're having coffee. He ordered his laced with brandy."

"Asshole."

"Listen," I said, "I'll answer your questions if you tell me about Chevillar's photos."

It was a calculated offer. I could tell it *hurt* Jana to be working the story from a desk in New York and not the field. Predictably, she took the bait, elaborating that Erica's Bahamas connection was returning stateside on Sunday and would supply the photos in person, if not already furnished via e-mail. She asked if I had Leyritz, if I had a chance at getting Leyritz, what Jordan Veitch had said, who was on-scene at Jordan's house—and even what the house looked like. Phone sex for a becalmed runner. After that, Nick and I drove the RAV4 thirty miles to Boynton Beach to see an ex–*Playboy* model about some photos.

Erica Chevillar lived in a community hewn from swampland. It was bordered on two sides by muck-covered veins too anemic to be brooks and too robust to be irrigation ditches. Strip malls suggesting the Marseilles waterfront guarded its flanks. One had Arabian arches over a shaded arcade, blue-and-white-striped awnings and showpiece balconies. But that was from across Congress Avenue. If you crossed the street, it looked like an Epcot Center re-creation of the south of France. Behind the stores was Renaissance Commons, a bunch of concrete containers cut into condos beginning at $195,000 each. They occupied plots the size of square city blocks and had names like The Raphael, Villa Lago, and Monteverde, even though they looked as Italian as an Olive Garden. The streets were post-Rapture empty, aside from grounds crews whirring around in golf carts. Their engines murmured with electric hums, and the crews looked like World War II GIs on jeeps. The drivers drove the carts like children do bumper cars.

Erica Chevillar's container was 1660 Renaissance Commons Boulevard. We prowled its exterior and found a man-child to unlock the door. He wore gray khaki cargo shorts, Skechers, low-rise socks, and a ball cap with the bill turned backward. He was confidently shirtless and as bronzed as a bust of Julius Caesar. I handed him my NYPD press cred. He was suitably impressed. We climbed an open-air stairwell to a landing and followed a balcony on the left. Apartment 2308 was halfway between two stairwells and shaded by an eave. I knocked, then tried the chrome knob and got nothing but frenzied canine barking.

Together, Nick and I squatted on the stucco balcony until security arrived. He was Latin-looking and had sad eyes veiled with sleep. He took his turn at the door, said, "Security," and was rewarded with an opened sliver of dimness; then a wall of mussed blond hair. Her frightened eyes were big, oval, and very white. But they didn't stay that way. When I introduced myself, they narrowed to coin slot slits that bore into me as she yapped as furiously as her toy dog. She held it back with one foot through the still-cracked door.

She looked like her *Playboy* spread but only vaguely. In the photo, she'd looked 6'2" with 5'5" of that being long toned and tanned legs. She'd had bedroom eyes and a balloon-like bosom. Now, I saw her in her Saturday afternoon I-don't-give-a-fuck best: 5'4" and sweat clothes. "I already gave my statement," she fumed. "Besides, I don't have your rotten photos." I reiterated my cash offer but she grew theatrical.

"I'm not giving Jim up!" she cried, and then, "You need to leave."

The guard, who'd remained silent throughout the unfortunate affair, shrugged. Erica closed the door.

"She owe you money, man?" he asked.

"Yeah," I said. "Lots."

"*Mujeres*," he replied. We all walked downstairs.

From Chevillar's, Nick and I slogged back to Fort Lauderdale. Blue Martini, where Chevillar had said Leyritz began his night, was on East Sunrise Boulevard, off a shopping mall called The Galleria. It was the sort of lounge that frowns on domestic-beer consumption and buys olives in bulk. We waded through wooden cocktail tables, bar stools, *sotto voce* conversations, a fog of menthol cigarette smoke, and moody blue light. Lots of moody blue light. We sidled up to the backlit showcase bar, bought Bacardi and Cokes, and let the bartenders get accustomed to us. After a while, I asked about Leyritz. The barmaid shook me off and checked with her co-worker. Rey had more to offer. He'd served him.

Rey wore a blue body halo from the back lighting around a sub-30-inch, backup dancer's body. He explained how Leyritz and ten pals had convened around 11 o'clock. He said the ex-jock had been the "Father

Rooster" of the group. "A couple of the girls were drunk and [Jim] told me, 'That's enough for them,' Rey told me. "He's been here before and always the same M.O. Comes in, has a few, switches to water." I asked about photos and video. Rey said, "I'll have to check," then handed me a card. I told him money was involved. He said, "That goes without saying," then added, "Gotta pay for med school somehow."

After that, we crossed over Sunrise Boulevard to a Chinese restaurant called Jade Palace. We got a highway-facing table to monitor Blue Martini—and if the *Post* arrived. We ordered and I called "Killer" Bill Farrington, who Julie had said was flying in from New York to replace the *Post*'s freelance shooter. I asked Bill if he planned to hit Automatic Slims, the watering hole mentioned in the *Post*'s account. Bill said, "After the Giants game." They were playing the undefeated Patriots that night.

From there, Nick and I drove west along Sunrise Boulevard to US 1, then cut south to the city's riverfront shopping district. It was a number 7–shaped canyon of boutiques, bars, burger joints, spas, and salons. We parked without difficulty, entered at the base of the "7," then ambled toward its crown and the lapping Tarpon River below, one of the vine-like tentacles that crept inland from the Atlantic Ocean toward the Everglades. On one side of the "7's" stem was a sixteen-story office tower with a two-story appendage full of ground-floor retail that ran most of the block. Canopy awnings shrouded second-floor windows. On the opposite side was an outdoor retail arcade anchored by a movie theater. At the "7's" crown, we turned left and walked until we found Slims on the ground floor of a three-story building. It had a white fieldstone façade; shallow-set, opaque windows; a very locked chrome door; and no signage. Nick and I stood there, tugging at the loose threads that had piled up in our minds like scraps on a tailor's floor.

Without discussion, we backtracked toward the arcade and under a block-lettered arch that read, "LAS OLAS WATERFRONT." We crossed into an open-air, red brick pavilion with a four-tiered fountain in the middle like you'd once have found in a Roman senator's atrium. Off the pavilion were two flights of long, electric-lit retail arcades with ceiling fans. We started our canvass on the ground floor. I didn't know what I was looking for. Sometimes you don't know until you find it. I had photos of Leyritz and Fredia Veitch and two questions. Did you work two nights ago and, if so, did you see either of these people? It was a hell of a way to search for scoops, but sometimes the best. That said, a portrait of the mental lottery ticket I held in my mind looked something like this: An ornery and drunken Leyritz stumbles out of Slims looking to cure the munchies. He gets into a shoving match with an equally inebriated Yankee hater who both recognizes and heckles him about his ball-playing days. Leyritz huffs to his car, blows the red, and kills Veitch. "LEYRITZ'S DRUNKEN FIGHT BEFORE DEATH!" Or . . . Leyritz grabs a nightcap at one of the arcade bars. A barmaid says, "Jim . . . let me call ya a cab." The ex-Yankee waves her off like the catcher he once was on a pop-up. The barmaid, now tragic, tells the *News*, "If only I'd insisted, she'd be alive today." "BARMAID'S REMORSE: SHE COULD HAVE SAVED FREDIA!" Of course, it didn't happen, either way. It rarely does. What I got, instead, was a surly barmaid at a place called Crazy 8's filled with more shadows than customers. She had a wan smile as welcoming as yesterday's dishes, and when I got out my notebook, it looked even more wan. "You just messed up," she said. "Messed up big-time."

"What?"

Her tone was so grave I didn't know, at first, what I'd done wrong. So I transcribed notes from memory—a nice morsel confirming the *Post*'s nugget about Leyritz's having known Veitch. The Crazy 8's barmaid had said she knew Veitch and Veitch had once served the ballplayer. From there, we rode an escalator to a seafood joint. They seated us in an *al fresco* area overlooking the Tarpon River. It was dark, and the river looked inky and inscrutable. It lapped gently at the shoreline below, and from a party boat I heard stemware tinkling and the sounds of far-off laughter. We asked the waitress if she'd seen Leyritz to justify our expenses, logged the negative, and paid the check. I didn't want to leave. I was as weary as three sled dogs in a Jack London novel. But that was the thing about contested stories on the road—always one more place to hit, one more door to knock on, one more document to parse, one more call to make, one more lead to follow up on—and always the same ruthless, uncompromising logic pushing you forward—that place, that door, that document was the one the *Post* would pursue—and use to bury you if you didn't get at it first.

Begrudgingly, we willed ourselves over to Automatic Slims and found a queue now formed of costumed clubgoers so much like the bus line back to New Jersey on a waning Manhattan evening. I joined them and hoped the bouncer wouldn't mind Nick's camera. He didn't. Inside, Slims was more sociable than its exterior: whorled oak bar, square-shaped and surrounded by wooden stools on which you might have found wadded-up gum. The barmaids slung drinks like a choreographed sister act: They were all pale and outfitted in fire-engine-red lipstick, go-to-hell expressions, and death-by-chocolate hair. I obtained two Heinekens and watched the Giants milk a 28–23 lead over the 15–0 Patriots. Finally—and with the

Post in mind (they weren't there)—I scorched the Earth so if I didn't get quotes, they wouldn't either. No cunning applied: *Did you see that ex-ballplayer who's in the news, here?*

Within fifteen minutes, a paunchy thirty-something came up behind my shoulder and asked, "You want to know about Leyritz?" in the almost-whispered tone of a pusher. He looked like a second-year frat brother with an untucked, faded, blue T-shirt, sandpaper hair, and old jeans. But he wasn't soft. He had the unsmiling eyes of someone accustomed to commerce—or crime. I told him, "Sure," and he asked if we were on the record. I made a fussy show of looking offended. "Come on," he said. "You're not exactly incognito."

I told him, "Okay, ya got me."

He said he was the bar's owner, and "the official comment is I don't know if he was here and if he *was*, no one noticed."

"OK," I said. "How 'bout unofficially?"

He repeated himself.

I said, "If that was the case what difference did it make if we were on the record or off?"

He said he could never be too careful. I told him I had just had two more questions, really a question and a request. He prompted me with a nod. I said that in a little while a light-haired photographer of modest stature—and possibly a reporter, too—would likely be asking similar, if not the same, questions and was there any chance they might get different answers. He said, "Not a chance," and then, "What else do you want?"

I said, "What gives with the barmaids?"

Straight-faced, he replied, "They're dropping 'em off here by the busload. We got our pick."

December 30, 2007

Day 2 of the story felt like Day 10, the Florida sprawl of strip malls, strip clubs, sports bars, lounges, chain restaurants, and ranch homes bleeding into one sun-drenched blur. I called Rob early, saluted a proposed stakeout of Leyritz's house—then found the town of Davie west of Fort Lauderdale and south of Plantation. I found SW 42nd Court about a half-mile down a reedy, two-lane road abreast a still-water creek glistening as if covered with petrol. Off that road, Nick and I found 11020—a tidy, prosperous home for a bus driver or tradesman, but not an ex–Major League ballplayer and certainly not one only seven years removed from his final at-bat. It was a modest, algae-stained ranch house, not more than three bedrooms, on perhaps an acre of sun-scorched grass. Mr. Leyritz had forgotten to employ his sprinklers. From the look of it, he'd forgotten to do a lot of things.

It was pasture country; I knew that from the cows grazing in a nearby fenced-in field and a *Newsday* reporter whose story noted the area's zoning—but had neglected, it seemed, to probe other, more consequential angles. It was a quiet, peaceful nabe. And it would be as welcoming to reporters as a homeowner to a colony of carpenter ants.

I parked the RAV4 down the block so Leyritz wouldn't see me. Across the street, a woman who looked like Alice from "The Brady Bunch" sheared her front lawn with a push mower. It sounded like ten fat men snoring off Thanksgiving dinner. I asked if that was Leyritz's house, nodding at 11020. She frowned. It was the frown of a Dunkin' Donuts counterman when you ask for a fresh pot ten minutes before closing time; of a supermarket bagger when you note the eggs put in too delicate a spot; of the clothing store attendant after you've left too many pairs of unfolded shirts in the fitting room. It was a frown that would have been there with or without me. Only, maybe I made it deeper. Maybe.

"Why do you guys have to be here?" Alice whined. "You're scaring my children."

I told her there was no reason for fear, and when she conceded as much, I asked why she hadn't explained the truth to her children and, perhaps, made it a teaching point.

"You know," I sneered, "don't drink and drive or tabloid reporters will end up on your lawn."

She snarled at that and gave me a look that felt like a tarantula crawling up my shoulder. Then she mumbled something about someone's having knocked on her door just before midnight the night before. That could have been the *News* or the *Post*. After that, I had much the same luck up and down the block. So, I hid in the RAV4. It was white-colored, but five minutes without air conditioning still turned it into an oven. I lowered the windows, blasted the air conditioning, and stained my fingertips with the *News*, the *Post*, the *Miami Herald*, and finally the *South Florida Sun Sentinel*—in that order. The *Post* wooded, again, with the Bhutto killing: "GUNMAN . . . VIDEO REVEALS BHUTTO 'ASSASSIN.'" Above that ran a skybox, "*16–0 . . . *GIANTS CAN'T STOP PATRIOTS' 'PERFECT SEASON.'" Meanwhile, the *News* went big on the Giants below two skybox chips— one, "BLOOD FOR BLOOD . . . OSAMA VOWS WAR ON ISRAEL," and the other, "'WHERE'S MY MOMMY?' YANKEE VICTIMS' FAMILY DESTROYED." On the Leyritz stories inside, no one had beaten anyone—skirmishes as a prelude to the main battle—even though Rob Moore had declared our effort a "clear victory" over the *Post*'s during our morning call. On stories like that, it felt more like judging Olympic figure skating.

It took an hour for Farrington to arrive by taxi. Sam Goldsmith, who'd joined the *Post* in the spring, soon followed. He was tallish, yet not tall; thickset, yet not fat; casual, yet not careless, and as bald as Big Sur. He had a moon pie face with remote eyes and a stubble growth that was two— maybe three—more missed shaves from a full-on beard. But I didn't think he was going for it; it was just another prop to show how much he didn't give a damn. He was probably thirty but somehow looked forty-five, and he wore khaki shorts, a T-shirt, and flip-flops. And although I was willing to extend him the benefit of the doubt, something—a niggling intuition— told me it was not going to work out: he and I.

From there, the stakeout commenced. Ostensibly, its purpose was to get words from Leyritz, or guard against the *Post*'s doing so. But he wouldn't talk—and so we logged stray details from which reasonable assumptions could be drawn. Such was the stuff that made passable follows in lieu of more tangible gets. For instance, we never saw Leyritz in the eleven hours we spent there, but it was reasonable to assume he was inside the house because of the family and friends who visited. Research found that the Ohio plates on a teal sedan in his driveway came back to a Donald Leyritz of Ohio. Leyritz's Accurint showed his father as seventy-three and from Ohio. If we needed more proof, a silver-haired man took the teal car for provisions. "Any booze in those bags?" asked Rob Moore upon his return.

At another point, a buxom blonde with two kids in tow pulled up in a Corvette with Florida tags. We ran those, too. They came back to a Mickey Cochrane. Research fed that name into Accurint and came back with only one hit in Florida—a sixty-six-year-old man with local addresses in Miami-Dade and Broward counties. He also had a Karrie C. Leyritz and James Joseph Leyritz listed as relatives. Given that Leyritz was a public figure, we easily learned that his ex-wife was named Karrie. And Fevelo, just to be sure, asked her. She confirmed.

All these details made it easy for Bill Hutchinson in New York to craft this lede for the following day's account: "His stellar reputation shattered by an alleged drunken-driving crash that killed a hardworking mother, former Yankee slugger Jim Leyritz remained secluded in his Florida home Sunday, distressed and desperate for a good lawyer. With his worried parents, children and ex-wife, Karrie, providing comfort, Leyritz privately contemplated his spiral from pinstripes to the possibility of serving 15 years in prison stripes."

Now, did we know for sure Leyritz was inside the house and, furthermore, mulling his misdeeds? Of course not! He could have been playing checkers and swilling gin-and-tonics. But we obtained facts through observation, inferred reasonable generalizations from them, and then crafted a plausible, fairly dramatic lede, given the rather bland events of the day. It was another victory, at least according to the sunny Rob Moore.

December 31, 2007

New Year's Eve: We got to Leyritz's house before 9 and found Farrington and Goldsmith already on-scene in a sleek Pontiac, the former behind the wheel with a camera in his lap, eyes the slits of a gunslinger and trained on the home, the former reading the *Post* with a smirk. We said hello and asked if there'd been action. Farrington did not answer, continuing to stare at the house as if the question hadn't been asked. Sam answered but didn't, saying, "It's been quiet." That left room for a photo of Leyritz, and although I could tell Nick wanted to ask, I touched his arm and shook him off.

That morning, the *Post* ran an old photo spread of Leyritz at the Playboy mansion and a story about how he "enjoy[s] a good night on the town, especially when flanked by beautiful women." Sam had written it, and even obtained a quote from the photos' owner, an Angela Bates, who had posted them to Myspace. And while Rob had said neither he, nor Martin, cared, it still showed that Goldsmith was playing our competition close to the vest. I'd been in his company on Sunday for eleven stakeout hours—more than enough time for him to mention it. *That* was enough to make me edgy over their plans for the day.

We pulled up behind the Pontiac, and Nick and I switched seats to give him a clean line of sight to the home. Then I started dialing for quotes. I called Leyritz's father, Leyritz, Karrie Leyritz, Jordan Veitch, Jordan's attorney, Jordan's father, and everyone on Jordan, Fredia, and Leyritz's Accurints. (Runner's tradecraft: I didn't think anyone would give me a quote. But on a contested story, you needed to check the boxes in case the *Post* unearthed a lottery winner doing the same. You needed to earn the right to tell Martin Dunn the next day that you'd made the call and Leyritz's uncle in Oshkosh had spoken to the *Post*, and not you, out of some quirk in the cosmos rather than your neglect. Otherwise you got creamed. But checking those boxes required time—time much better employed foraging over fertile ground, or thoughtfully considering angles, or running and being creative. You just had to do it and as quickly as possible.) I left a message for the Fort Lauderdale P.D. lieutenant who handled media inquiries, then got out of the car and paced.

Around noon, Goldsmith said he was getting lunch. I said I'd join him. The plan was to bring takeout back to the house for everyone. Nick and Farrington would cover in the interim. It took ten minutes to work this out. Things were getting awfully cagey on SW 42nd Court. Usually, going to lunch with the *Post* was *pro forma* and convivial. Runners worked too many stories and spent too much time in close quarters for overt competition. We had the same jobs, the same reference points. We knew one another well. Our rivalry was treated more like drivers do traffic, always there and disregarded foolishly, yet still, mostly scenery. But that morning—that luncheon—felt like playing poker at the Taj. It only tangentially had to do with hunger. My goal was to get a handle on what I faced.

The luncheonette was a polished chromium boxcar that looked like a 1950s camper. An obsolete, rusted-over pickup truck parked out back and nearly overtaken by weeds mostly confirmed the suspicion. The boxcar had likely been the truck's final cargo. Out front, a chalkboard advertised lunch specials for $6.99. We entered through a white-painted screen push door set dubiously into an unpainted frame. On the left was a retro, white-and-black-flecked diner counter with mounted stools. On the right, separated by a bowling lane's width, five tables looked much like patio furniture. We sat at one across a red-and-white-checked tablecloth. There were no windows but plenty of shadows. They prowled the floor like wraiths. The wall, to my left, was the corrugated metal of porch overhangs and backyard sheds, and I could hear what very little wind there was softly play upon it.

Sam moved the napkin dispenser and salt and pepper shakers around the table like a general mapping strategy. He avoided eye contact and spoke in that hollow-solicitous tone that is possible only when one spouts artifice underpinned with ill intent. I suggested we stay for lunch. He agreed and shortly took a call from Dan Mangan, a *Post* rewrite man, in New York. They spoke in code, although I could tell they wanted to convey to me the emotional gist, if not the content, of their conversation. *Great! Really? That's fantastic! Good. That'll play well.* Clearly, the *Post* had scored, and my mind went into hamster-in-a-wheel mode. It was thus spinning when Sam told Mangan, "Sure, I'll take down her number" and committed digits to a napkin. Carefully, secretly, I watched. By the time he finished, I had the ten numbers memorized. Then, when we were done, or rather he was—I was too preoccupied to eat—I adjourned to the restroom and transcribed those numbers onto a napkin of my own. Then we returned to the RAV4 and drove back amid a ponderous silence as heavy as the humidity.

What had I missed? Who hadn't I called? What am I going to eat? I must have said this last part out loud because Nick, now in the car, looked at me, then asked if I hadn't just eaten lunch. I mumbled something unintelligible and retrieved the now-crumpled-up napkin. It looked as significant as an ageless amulet. I fingered it for a long while—then put it back in my pocket and did not make the call.

Occasionally, *News* runners got beat by the *Post*—and vice versa. It was as unavoidable as a baseball strikeout. But rarely did they know it would happen before the papers come out. And if you were to ask me now which way I'd rather have it—knowing what I know—I'd much prefer the ignorance of waiting. But on this day, that's not how it happened.

Around 2 o'clock I got out of the RAV4. It must have seemed like an invitation to Goldsmith because he exited the Pontiac, too. We stood across from Leyritz's house, staring.

"You're making a lot of calls?" Sam asked.

I nodded. "You're no stranger to your phone, either."

I'd tried to inject it with a little something extra that touched on his Playboy mansion story. But if he caught the drift, he pretended not to. He said, "You getting anything?"

"Here and there. You?"

He must have been waiting for me to ask, because he said the following decisively and as if rehearsed: "Yeah, the stringer got something. The desk didn't tell me because they were afraid I might tell you."

I nodded but didn't avert my gaze from Leyritz's house. It seemed as long as I held it, I could refrain from an unfortunate reply. And it worked— one of the four, maybe five, times in my life where I actually won that battle. After that, Goldsmith returned to his car, as I did to mine. This was a new low for the *Post*. Sure, we always went at each other like stray alley cats in heat, but the fighting was done graciously and mindful it could very easily be you on the short end of the stick the following day. This was different. This was as ugly as a sucker punch or a fistful of sand. I called Rob. He quizzed me on what calls I had made, and we concluded with a promise to touch base later. Then, I called the library and asked Faigi Rosenthal, who ran it, to "tear Leyritz's life apart—down to the color of his socks."

Then it was back to the phone, until a police car rolled up behind the Pontiac, its party lights flashing, the cop on the radio, then exiting, one hand on his sidearm while strolling in that nature-walk amble so common that one suspects it's part of their academy training. He had a Brillo of brownish-black, yet oddly blond-streaked, hair. The blond looked salon-contrived, although the rest of him looked so un-suggestive of salon patronage, I concluded it had to be quirk of nature. He looked like the husky blue-collar Joe on the last stool of the local Irish pub, eyes glued to an aging analog RCA mounted in the corner. The pub would not have outdoor signage, and the bartender could give you a name, if you were so inclined, to get a bet in on something. . . . Or, he would be the too-drunk guy on your wedding video talking about something the groom would rather not have publicly disclosed.

He looked twenty-four, although maybe younger, and he had a smooth, porcelain face, ruddy in the cheeks in that way children's are when they come in from the cold. It was a face to smile at, and not one to scare any-one, which is what it was trying to do now.

"Party's over," he said, as if turning on the lights in a nightclub before closing time. I heard, but didn't see, Sam's reaction—a cackle that sounded like Ms. Krabappel's on "The Simpsons." Then, Sam sneered, "You're going to have do better than that." The cop flushed—as red as a King-high heart run—and Sam dilated on our right to be there. *If the city paves and cleans it, you can't remove us.* But the cop was unmoved. *You gotta go.* I could tell he wasn't often challenged and certainly not with logic and/or legalese. His constituents would either be cowed, at once, or require a SWAT team.

Some argument ensued until finally a compromise: We could remain on the block—so long as we parked outside the subdivision. But Farrington didn't like it. *What's the point of being out here if we can't chase him?* Some complex tabloid bargaining followed, after which it was decided that one reporter and shooter per side would remain on the block—and one shooter and one reporter would stay with the cars just outside the de-velopment. Then—and if Leyritz drove off—the two on the block would call the others' cell phones and advise them to give chase. Any photos or quotes would be pooled. It fell to Bill and me to go to a loamy outcrop off the mouth of SW 42nd Court.

Once there, I called the Broward County courthouse and requested fil-ings for a stalking charge Leyritz had earned in 2003 (dismissed, 2005) and which Faigi had unearthed, via Accurint, in New York. Karrie Leyritz was the listed victim. Now, a court clerk answered and told me the document's retrieval from storage would require several days, then asked if I wanted any other Leyritz-related documents. Her records indicated a Karrie and Jim Leyritz divorce file. Joyfully, I told her to add it to my tab. She began filling out forms. As she did so, Goldsmith rang. I knew, at once, why he was calling, but ignored him in favor of finishing my transaction. Momen-tarily, I saw the teal sedan with Ohio plates zoom by. It seemed Farrington would be deprived of his coveted high-speed chase.

When I concluded with the clerk, Farrington stood at my window. He wanted to know why I had not answered Goldsmith's call, thus allowing

Leyritz "to escape." I told him I had been on the phone with my desk and couldn't, at that moment, take the call. He huffed angrily and returned to his car. Fifteen minutes later, he returned and told me he had to go "shoot somebody," and would be gone no more than an hour. I asked, "Bill, is this something I should be concerned about?"

He replied with a cold stare—and words just as icy: "You should be concerned with all aspects of the story."

Then he pulled away in the Pontiac.

If I didn't know it already, I knew then. I was beat. It was almost 3 o'clock and the only thing I had to offer was my by- and datelines. After that, the page would be a blank. In thirty minutes—maybe a little more, perhaps less—Martin Dunn would convene the afternoon news meeting. Gittrich would tell him Jaccarino had struck out. He might even warn him that the *Post* was planning something big. It would look bad. Very bad for Jaccarino.

I couldn't just sit at Leyritz's house—not with the ex-slugger *and* Farrington in the wind. I needed movement and action. Anything. At least the illusion of headway. I needed a get. I found Nick mulling Leyritz's house with Goldsmith. I told Nick how I felt and what Farrington had said. I told him I would take the RAV4 and he should stay behind and "hold the fort."

"Do you know where you're going?"

"No," I told him.

"Good luck."

After that I felt my fears over the *Post* dissolve in the RAV4's motion like sour mix in stirred whiskey. I turned off at the Riverfront and parked. Automatic Slims was as big and brooding—and locked—as it had been on Saturday afternoon. I stared at it and thought. I took out the GPS and input an address—really just an intersection—and started to drive, again. It wasn't quite a half-mile away, only four-tenths by the odometer's count, just a quick right on West Olas, then a quick left on to SW 2nd Street, then a straight shot down a two-lane road that was palm tree–lined in some places but concrete in others. I went over the Florida East Coast Railway, past the Broward Center for the Performing Arts, and then to the light. It was red for me, too, but I—unlike Leyritz—didn't run it.

The intersection of Southwest 2nd Street and South Avenue of the Arts looked like it might once have been prosperous. No more. Whatever commerce justified that impression had died to a whimper three blocks north. It would be a desolate roadway at 3 A.M. It was desolate now, as I stood, transfixed by the light. Red. Yellow. Green. Red. Yellow. Green. Red. I heard the metal box whirring—maybe a loose wire?—and then a semi-dramatic "click" just before the color changed. It was the sound of a roulette wheel in motion. I re-created the accident in my mind's eye, noted the blank spots where what had happened was as-yet unknown, or at least unpublished. Those would give me questions. Where was Leyritz after the accident? What did he do? Did he say anything? Did Veitch? Was she conscious? Her last words would carry weight. A lot. They might even save me from the *Post*.

Across the street, the stores were fallow and graffitied and the sidewalk jagged and weed-strewn. Beyond all that was a collection of modest two-family ranch homes. They were composed of two bungalow-sized boxes with pyramid roofs connected by a single gabled rectangle. They were set well back from the sidewalk by tennis court–sized concrete aprons that flared out on both sides with enough room for six cars to park, in total. At the first one, I turned left, covered a short path to a shower-sized patio shaded by a robust eave. The front doors to both units faced opposite each other. The doors were composite, and the one on which I knocked first was pockmarked, as if it had been shot up with BBs. An old woman answered. She wore a threadbare, white cotton nightdress with a pattern of pink daises that somehow looked wilted amid the wrinkles and dried-out coffee stains. The woman wore her skin flaccidly and like an oversized dress that no longer fit her. But it's her phlegmy voice that persists in memory. The words sounded as if they gurgled up through molten lava and then bubbled into half-formed speech. Sometimes I shiver about it, even now, years later.

No, she hadn't seen the accident, but said her neighbor did. I asked her to remain at the door while I knocked on the opposite one. She did so and lent entrée to fifty-nine-year-old Mike O'Farrell. He was shirtless above black mesh gym shorts and leather, open-toed slippers. An angry, nubbed scar covered his sternum. He hadn't seen anything, either, but said he'd walk me to where Veitch's blood was soaked into the ground. I took him up on the offer.

It was a patch of white gravel circled by fluorescent paint sprayed by the cops. Catholic prayer cards clung to a telephone pole and unlit votive candles gathered at its base. "It was only a matter of time," O'Farrell said. "People run that red six times a day. I begged them to do something—but . . ." He let the thought trail off. The red splotch on the gravel finished it for him. I asked if anyone had been with Veitch after the accident. He said, "Yes," and together we walked past his house to another of the same modesty.

At the door, a woman answered and told me her husband, Bryan, was showering. We sat opposite each other, she on a burlap couch under two big bay windows with interior wood shutters. I sat in a tan, distressed leather easy chair and bucked the urge to eject the footrest. I sipped lemonade and watched *First Knight* on TV. Richard Gere's Lancelot was stealing Guinevere right out from under Arthur's nose. One of their two dogs—a toy one with big, needy eyes—jumped into my lap and nuzzled my chest. He was happy. More so than I. Then Bryan Palaceo entered and offered me coffee. I smiled and said, "Mr. Palaceo, there ain't enough!" He snorted, listened to how earnestly I wanted to memorialize the tragedy in the service of civic change. He replied that if any good came from the story—"if they fix that damn light"—it would be time well spent. Together, we returned to the splotchy gravel. Then Bryan spoke without prompting: "It sounded like a car banging into garbage cans. So, I ran out and found her—sprawled out here. Her breathing was uneven and blood flowed from her ears. Thank God she was unconscious. I kept telling her, 'It'll be OK. It'll be OK.' I don't think she heard me. She was pretty much just gasping for air."

I asked if he had seen Leyritz. He said, "Yeah, but only for a moment. He had his hands on his head. He was distraught and muttering, like, 'Oh my God!' I couldn't make out what he said."

I thanked him, walked him back to his door, and then returned, alone, to the crash site. It was near 8 o'clock. I knew it wouldn't be enough. Not nearly so. The accident was four days old, and Veitch's death, while poignant, and Leyritz's reaction, while interesting, would not save me from whatever the *Post* had planned. Then I had an idea! I reached into my pocket and found a napkin. It was crinkled and much the worse for wear— but the digits were still clear. I dialed them. A female voice answered. *Hello . . . this is Julie?* Briefly, I considered telling the *Post* freelancer I was an editor from New York and needed clarification on what she had discovered earlier in the day. It might have worked. But it also wasn't worth it. Quietly, I said, "I must have the wrong number," and rang off.

January 1, 2008

The Fort Lauderdale chain hotel in which I passed a fitful Monday night claimed only a single community computer in the lobby. So, I had to wait, almost unbearably, on Tuesday morning to learn how badly I'd been whupped by the *Post*. When my turn finally did come—after a piker in a bathing suit, T-shirt, and flip-flops had thoroughly devoured multiple NFL blogs—I discovered my defeat was worse than I'd imagined. The *Post* did a split wood. Above the fold was a story about Times Square tourists wearing diapers on New Year's Eve for want of portable toilets. "HAP-PEE NEW

YEAR." Below the fold was a bombshell about Leyritz's having accumulated seven traffic citations since 2002, including tickets for "blowing through stop signs, speeding . . . and driving with a suspended license." "HELL ON WHEELS . . . 'KILLER' YANK'S 7 ROAD BUSTS." Inside, the story quoted Mickey Cochrane—Karrie Leyritz's father—as saying the ex-slugger had been "waking up, screaming" and "having flashbacks of the lady." The story had run under Julie's byline—the *Post* stringer I'd met at Veitch's house on Saturday.

The *News* countered meekly with a story about Leyritz's offering the Veitch family his "condolences" through a statement published in the *Miami Herald*. It quoted Palaceo's color, but in the context of the *Post* exclusive, it felt like filler. I rang the desk. "This is not going to be a good day," Rob said. "Too bad, too. We had a nice paper but no one's going to care now." He added that he already had an e-mail from Martin demanding to know why we didn't have the traffic ticket story. After he said this, he asked—without humor—"Why didn't we have the story?" I stammered in search of an explanation. The truth seemed inadequate: I hadn't thought to ask Faigi to pull Leyritz's driving history, but had requested only that she "tear his life apart." It didn't seem sufficient.

After that, Nick and I raced to Leyritz's house. The *Post* followed perhaps thirty minutes behind. Sam greeted me cheerfully, a little too much so, I thought, for the circumstances. Shortly, two cars arrived whose license plates offered potential. The first came back to an attorney—David Bogenschutz—who had celebrity cachet by way of having defended Dolphins owner Wayne Huizenga's son on DUI charges. The other was owned by Hertz, although the registration was linked to a psychiatric facility in Orlando. Given what Cochrane had told the *Post*, the loony-bin angle had juice. I informed Gittrich, who assigned Carrie Melago to run down both leads from New York. I then asked Greg for permission to depart Leyritz's house in favor of other avenues, while leaving Nick behind to cover. He agreed—but reluctantly. I was glad. It seemed impossible to remain at Leyritz's home and in the *Post*'s company. Moving, searching, potentially recovering lost ground felt far more agreeable. So, I drove, first aimlessly, then with purpose, toward Mickey Cochrane's home. It was not ideal to pick over country already cleanly hunted by the *Post*, but I thought it might be a good place to start.

The home, fifteen miles from Leyritz's, was a ranch house, overgrown with vegetation, although in a tropically Florida way and not suggestive of a lack of care. Parked in front was a Corvette with a vanity license plate that read, "HER TOY." I door-knocked and then waited with the nervousness

I always felt after knocking, when all of my well-crafted speeches jumbled like tiles in a bag.

Karrie Leyritz answered. She was more casually dressed and far less made up than when I'd first seen her. She was curvy and tan and had an arm tattoo that read, "Jimbo." Her thick blond hair was knotty, and she had an impish twinkle in her eye that made it a matter of will not to flirt with her. She recognized me at once and, guessing I had come to speak to her father, said, "You're busted!" but in a joking way and without acrimony. Then, she asked, still joking, "You follow me everywhere?" and I said I knew of worse pursuits. I asked for only what the *Post* had gotten and she said, apologetically, she'd already promised Jim's lawyer there would be no further comment. I accepted this, although reluctantly—and turned toward the curb, but made it only halfway before retracing my steps and knocking again. When she returned, she was still in a joking mood. "You know this is like stalking," she said, and I replied, quite wittily, "Yes, that's why I returned."

She replied calmly that she knew Jim's 2003 arrest was going to come up and that she needed to speak to her lawyer. After that, I asked, "You busy tonight?" although in a humorous way that belied my sincere hope she'd say yes. But she dodged it and I found myself back in the car, relaying my progress to Rob, who explained that things were "Not good," and, then, after a pause, "Wait a second, Stu is asking Greg why we didn't have the story. Let's see what he says." Then, I waited while Rob eavesdropped, until he resumed the line and said, "He's covering for you. He's telling him, 'Jaccarino asked all the right questions but the library screwed up,'" and I felt an almost obscene relief, knowing that while I was safe, my safety was coming at the expense of others. Rob then added how Martin had ominously scheduled a meeting with Faigi for later in the day. After that, I called Nick and asked how things were going at Leyritz's house. He said Sam was "antsy" over my absence and asking, obliquely, about what I had. "Good," I said, pleased over Sam's anxiety, although what Nick immediately added spoiled it. He said Sam had asked him if I had been pissed off about the *Post* scoop—then tried to justify the venom of such an outrageous question by explaining it was his desk that wanted to know.

Nick told me, "I told him you were happy as a clam," and I said, again, "Good," although I was furious and bitter—even more so than during the morning. It was now 2 o'clock and a sun shower was coming down; I watched it dimple my windshield as I told Nick I would fetch him from the house, and when he asked me what we had, I replied, "Don't worry," but it came out far more confidently than how I was actually feeling.

After some driving, I found Nick alone at Leyritz's house, and he explained that Sam and Bill had departed twenty minutes earlier. We discussed this, and options—and agreed to visit Original Steakhouse, where Freddy Veitch had worked on the night of her dying. It was fourteen miles away in downtown Fort Lauderdale, inside a square-shaped mall with a penned-in parking area. We went inside and found football jersey–clad patrons watching college bowl games around a bar set off from the dining area. At that bar we saw Sam and Bill—and when I started moving toward them, Sam rushed over, grabbed my arm, and demanded, "What do you think you're doing?" I replied with a variation of the same question, although with profane flourishes, and he replied he was trying to work the bar, "incognito."

I was now at that bar, for this exchange had occurred while walking, and Bill repeated Sam's question. I told him, "This is part of the story, and I should be concerned with all of its aspects," and Bill frowned over this, and the exchange made me happy.

But there was nothing to be gotten. The staff had been poisoned by four days of media inquiries, and we were met with polite contempt. And this, added to the mystery of the *Post*'s presence and Sam's unreasonable reaction to our arrival, spooked us into believing they had obtained another get. This impression was only strengthened when we exited Original Steakhouse and saw Bill in the parking lot shooting exteriors of the restaurant.

"They've got something," Nick said ominously.

After that, we doubled down on our running, hitting strip clubs, dance clubs, restaurants, and bars where Leyritz might have drank or Veitch might have worked. But we came up empty, just as they had in New York. From there, Carrie Melago told me the psychiatric facility angle—so promising—had turned out to be an "Accurint anomaly." The desk was planning to lead—very fraily—with Bogenschutz's representation of Leyritz, unless Nick and I improbably unearthed something better from the field. We continued running—now back to Blue Martini, where the manager told us he and Rey had checked the surveillance tapes—and found nothing resembling Leyritz or his party. He said the cameras were positioned to monitor the cash registers—and not patrons. "Like a casino," Nick said, and the manager grinned approvingly and replied, "Now you've got it."

After that, we returned to the Fort Lauderdale bar district—and Riverfront area—and resumed our canvass. No one knew Leyritz—but plenty of people had known Fredia Veitch. The deceased barmaid had worked, over the years, in many places, and we collected quotes about her benevolence, loyalty, and industriousness. None of it would help. But a Hooters waitress did bestow a nugget: She said most Fort Lauderdale intersections were monitored by police cameras, and she'd wondered if one had captured the Leyritz accident. Such a video, if it existed, would be a game, set, match get. And so, Nick and I went outside and examined the nearest intersection and noted the camera mounted very plainly above it to an electric pole. At once and then giddy with possibility unrealized, we alighted to the accident scene to see if it, too, had been so monitored, although a phone call from Sam interrupted our progress. He told me, quite remorsefully, that "things" had gotten out of hand and he wanted to "make it all right." He explained that he and Bill were dining at the Fort Lauderdale vegetarian restaurant Sublime—and would we like to join them? And I, knowing I should decline, knowing fences should be mended under less duress, if at all, still said yes. I was hungry, and I suppose a little curious. I wanted things to be all right.

Upon arrival, we found Bill and Sam seated and eating cauliflower tempura. They offered some. We accepted and Sam asked—casually—if we had gotten anything. I checked the time: It was 9 o'clock and probably too late for the *Post* to recover, even if they cared about Bogenschutz. And so I told them Leyritz had hired "a big-shot attorney."

Sam nodded. I asked, also in the spirit of rapprochement, what they had gotten. Sam said, "Yeah, the stringer got something good today," and continued eating. I waited for him to elaborate. He didn't. And so came the slow burn—the anger of the duped . . . and the foolish.

We concluded the meal—but just barely. Several times, I had to resist storming out. And, after it concluded, Nick and I said our goodbyes through taut smiles, then vowed in the parking lot with the solemnity of conspirators that the affront would not go unpunished.

"Did you see that?" Nick asked.

"I sure did."

From there, we raced to the death scene, found it indeed monitored by camera—and two cops in a radio car. One told me he'd studied, "every minute of that tape" the night following the accident—but found nothing. Then pointing to the camera, affixed to the Performing Arts Center, while chuckling over his unfruitful labor, he told me, "See how it pans. It must have panned at the moment of the crash." After that, it was more running, but so much like running in place. More bars, more lounges, more barmaids, and more questions, some sneered at and some answered frankly— and a whole lot of nothing for the toil. Whatever the *Post* had gotten would remain unanswered.

January 2, 2008

The *Post* decimated the *News*, its wood a primal roar: "LICENSE TO KILL . . . YANK'S PERMIT WASN'T VALID," above a text tease reporting, "Drunk or not, ex-Yankees slugger Jim Leyritz should never have been behind the wheel . . . Records reveal that Leyritz—who was allegedly drunk at the time [of the accident]—had his license suspended on Nov. 23." The corresponding story reported that Leyritz had failed to answer a New York state summons—and Florida had suspended his license through a reciprocity agreement. It also quoted an Original Steakhouse waitress as saying Leyritz was a "known drunk" who had been repeatedly escorted from the restaurant by cops. She added that Fredia Veitch knew, and had even once served, the man who would kill her. The *News*, meanwhile, answered with a whisper: Bogenschutz and Veitch's family preparing for Wednesday night's funeral. It was a rout. The *News* was overrun by *Post* scoops.

When I returned to the hotel room from the lobby computer, Nick said, "Gittrich wants you," and handed me my cell phone. I took it, said, "Morning" in an appropriately chastened tone and awaited a lambasting that never came. Gittrich, always cool, always logical, always deadly, calmly walked me through the prior day's running, then asked for my plans. I hopefully referenced the divorce documents and stalking charge, to be retrieved from the county courthouse. He told me to drop Nick off at Leyritz's home first and to make sure to request both Leyritz's first *and* second divorces. I hadn't known there were two.

It was 6:50 A.M.

Our hotel was in Plantation, so I drove south along SW 65th Avenue into Davie, then Leyritz's subdivision. I deposited Nick on Leyritz's block (the *Post* was already there), then retraced my running north toward West Broward Boulevard. I drove that road, east, over the I-95 underpass, choked with rush-hour traffic, and into downtown Fort Lauderdale, booming with construction. The Broward County Justice Complex's architecture was a stunning example of 1970s bureaucratic indifference. Its boxy, rectangular façade occupied most of SE 6th Street. Across, the street was the standard accompaniment: bail bondsmen, delis, a DUI school, law offices, luncheonettes, and a coffee shop. I entered the courthouse and asked questions.

The criminal division was handling the stalking charge and the circuit civil my request for Leyritz's divorce. In the first case, I was told the records would not be available until after 4 o'clock. A backlog had accrued over the holiday. At the civil division, a clerk named George Soultatos gave me the same answer along with the caveat that Leyritz's first divorce had been purged from the system. Crestfallen, I pleaded with him for more expeditious delivery of the second one. He said he couldn't help—and I asked for his supervisor, who listened, wearily, as I repeated my request, this time extravagantly noting, "The *News* will pay anything the court needs to get the files ASAP."

The supervisor glared at me and said, "We don't accept bribes, here, sir."

I feigned innocence while George Soultatos moved his hands behind his supervisor's back. The supervisor stalked back to his office and I, presuming George's covert spasm to have been a tacit approval of the proposed grease, whispered, "Okay, what's it going to take?"

"What are you talking about?"

"The money, George. How much?"

He looked dumbfounded.

"George! The hand motions. Weren't you signaling me while your supervisor said, 'No'?"

"Oh, no! I'm epileptic! I can't control them—but I will do everything I can to help you."

"You will?"

"Sure," he said and then quoted Bonaparte. *Four hostile newspapers are more to be feared than a thousand bayonets.* He smiled broadly, obviously pleased with the reference. I thanked him lavishly.

Hours passed—long, excruciating hours. I called Nick at Leyritz's house and instructed him to relay the license plates of all vehicles arriving there. I then ran those plates, fruitlessly, through Research. I scoured courthouse computers for more Leyritz lawsuits. I drank too much coffee. Then 3:50 P.M. arrived, and I hustled back to the criminal division for the receipt of more bad news. They had not gotten to the stalking charge. I hurried to circuit civil and found George. He said, "You know, your competitors were here . . . yeah . . . the *New York Post* came a few hours after you. They wanted his divorce, too, but they only asked for the first one. I told them it was purged, just like I told you." I nodded gravely and George winked: "I didn't tell them there was a second divorce—and they never asked. Over there, it's all yours." He pointed toward a table laden with boxes. They were there, all right. Probably eight boxes, in all, bursting with files. It was 4:25. I had, perhaps, thirty minutes before the courthouse closed. Finally, the news gods had smiled on me.

After I had dumped my notes to Rich Schapiro in New York and after he had relayed those notes to Rob and Stu and after he had resumed the line and told me, "They like it," I exhaled for what felt like the first time in three days. Leyritz's second divorce from Karrie (née) Cochrane had gone on for years, filled many boxes, and told as lurid a tale as a tabloid reporter could have hoped for. The files contained a bitter back-and-forth of postmatrimonial volleys—and an accounting of Leyritz's finances. Credit card bills, personal expenditures . . . the *News* now knew how much he had blown on booze, and the figure was large enough to pin a story on. The *News* also knew that, despite an eleven-year career during which he earned $10 million–plus, Leyritz was a deadbeat dad and heavily in debt.

Now, with Rich's having filed the story, I drove the ten miles from the Broward County Courthouse to the Unity Church of Hollywood, Florida, where Fredia Veitch was to be mourned. Nick was taking a cab there from Leyritz's house. When I arrived, Nick was already in the parking lot with Sam and Bill. Our stringer, Angela Mosconi, was inside covertly recording the eulogy. Bill and Nick shot mourners as they arrived; then switching to long lenses, shot through the open church doors so as to capture the funeral, inside. Night had fallen and they were using flashes, and the light from those flashes lit up the façade of the triangle-shaped nondenominational church. I watched this from my car until Sam approached, cheerfully, and asked, "How's everything?"

"Fine."

"Yeah? Life treating you well?"

"What do you mean?"

"You know: Life, the pursuit of happiness."

I told him, "Everything's fine," and abstained from all of the things I would like to have said but would have regretted the saying of after the catharsis of the moment.

Then, we rejoined Nick and Bill, and I listened as Nick regretfully announced, "I haven't gotten the mom." And then, no longer capable of resisting, feeling the venom for the *Post* that had been accumulating, I said to Nick, although loudly enough so that Bill and Sam could hear, "Don't worry. The funeral won't even lead. We've got something *much* better." Then I grinned and resisted looking at Sam, although I could feel his glare through the ensuing silence. Nick, knowing what had been gotten, turned, winked, and smiled.

After that, Fredia Veitch's mother exited the church on the arm of a fey, trim, plastic-faced Latin-looking man who asked us in a falsetto for "some space, please."

Nick, feeling her absence among his photos and likely fearing Mike Lipack, ignored this and shot her—with his flash—energetically while standing no more than three feet away, backpedaling as he shot and she limped toward her car. Bill, having already made her, shot more casually and from a distance. Sam and I bookended her and asked questions.

"I already spoke," she said, but I continued, nevertheless: "Three million people will read this paper tomorrow. Your daughter was killed by a drunk driver. If you could touch just one person with your words, powerful as they could be . . . I mean you're in a position to do so much good."

But the bereaved mother was unaffected by these ravings and repeated: "I already spoke."

The remainder of the night, Nick and I visited Fort Lauderdale–area bars, although now precisely and informed by the information from the divorce file. These were the places at which Leyritz had had drinks. I also called many bars and nightclubs, including Elaine's in New York City. Elaine Kaufman, the owner, gave me nice words about Leyritz and refused to speak ill of him despite my prompting her to do so. It was the first of many times I would speak to her, but the only time that was professional.

January 3, 2008

The following morning, I raced to the lobby computer, although with none of the dread of the preceding days, but instead with that emotion so much like what I once felt on Christmas morning. The news was good. The *Post* led with the funeral—and the *News* had used it only as a supporting anecdote to the information discovered in the divorce file. "JIM LEYRITZ WASTED MILLIONS ON BOOZE, RECORDS SHOW." The *Post* wooded with the Iowa caucus: "DEAD HEAT HAS HILL SWEATING . . . D-DAY IN IOWA." The *News* did the same—"THEY'RE OFF!"—but added news of Isaiah Thomas's vow to win the NBA championship—"SAY WHAT? . . . BUT THEY LOSE YET AGAIN, 107–97"—and, finally, David Letterman's having grown a beard: "HAIR'S DAVE! SEE PAGES 4–5."

Nick and I found only Farrington at Leyritz's house. Sam had returned to New York. The stakeout now felt anticlimactic. Or until Jim Leyritz threw us a bone. It was after 1 o'clock when Leyritz's father, Don, pulled out of the garage in the teal sedan and Farrington hopped from the Pontiac, raced to the car's passenger side, and shot through its windows. Farrington screamed, "He's in the backseat! He's lying down!"

I sprinted to our car, as did Nick, as did Bill to his own vehicle, and then we all flew after Leyritz in a chase that proceeded out of the development, then to the left, along the main road with the muck-covered creek to our right, then to a traffic light near an overpass, then onto a main highway, and then, incredibly, improbably, although beautifully, into a church parking lot. Bill and Nick exited, Bill neither shutting off his car nor closing its driver's-side door but leaving it idling and in park, while both he and Nick frantically shot Jim Leyritz as he entered the church. I watched. There was nothing to do. But I knew I had a great get even before the door had shut behind him. "LEYRITZ FINDS THE LORD! HAUNTED BY GHOST OF FREDIA ANN VEITCH! EX-SLUGGER BEGS GOD FOR ABSOLUTION!" It didn't matter if it was true. It was nothing a single word—a well-placed "likely" or "perhaps"—couldn't fix during the writing.

(Now, I should note here that it turned out to be very likely *not* true. The next day, Karrie Leyritz informed us that both her and Jim's kids went to a school associated with the church, and Jim probably had been dropping off a tuition check. The January 4 *Daily News* carried a story headlined, "LEYRITZ VISITS FLORIDA CHURCH," and this magic trick for a lede: "A day after the woman he killed in an alleged drunken-driving wreck was memorialized, disgraced ex-Yankee Jim Leyritz sought solace from the Lord." The *News* did not clarify until later in the story: "It was unclear whether Leyritz asked for forgiveness in the church.")

From there, the chase continued, Don and his son pulling out of the church parking lot and getting on 595, then consciously avoiding us as we needled through traffic, then exceeding 90 miles an hour, then 95, then 100, and my knuckles bloodless upon the wheel, as Farrington pursued recklessly, as well, both of us knowing that if we lost Leyritz and the other was successful, it could mean terrible defeat. Then into downtown Fort Lauderdale, and Don thankfully slowed and relinquished any design of losing us. He parked in a garage, beneath a tower—and neither I, nor Bill, who arrived shortly thereafter, was permitted to follow. So, we both parked, streetside, entered the building to inspect the tenant roster, and quickly learned that David Bogenschutz was on it.

Farrington and Nick garrisoned the garage's exit, and I entered the lobby and took an elevator to Bogenschutz's floor. The elevator door opened, and I exited and pretended to inspect office numbers. Then—and mindful of the hallway's surveillance cameras—I reluctantly entered the lawyer's office and sat in a waiting room next to an artificial fern. The camouflage worked for, perhaps, ten minutes, until a receptionist marked my presence and asked after its cause. I said I wished to speak with Mr. Bogenschutz, and she asked if I had an appointment. I told her, "I thought he accepted walk-ins."

She frowned and said I'd have to wait outside. I left a card—and requested that he call me.

Outside, Nick and Farrington said they were returning to New York, both having gained permission only after agreeing to mutually depart. *If you leave, we'll leave. Let's shake hands.* But I didn't ask the desk if I could, too. I had one more thing to do. I had argued to do it that morning, but Gittrich had objected, saying, "As long as the *Post* stakes out Leyritz, you must, too." But now I could. I had intended to do it since reading the divorce file. As I had told Gittrich, "Now I have the leverage I need to make her talk."

January 4, 2008

Karrie Leyritz lived in a small townhouse development in Davie, where all of the units had the same algae-stained, pale-yellow-colored stucco. No one answered the door, and so I reconnoitered to a glass one, off a patio— and found three young boys playing video games in the living room. They were good-looking kids and about the ages of Leyritz's two children, who they turned out to be. The third was a friend from the neighborhood.

When I had read about them in the file, they had seemed an abstraction, and their pain, as documented by the court, hadn't seemed real. I had not, for instance, thought about the cost, as noted in a motion, to send one boy to a psychiatrist to cope with a certain disorder. I had not considered how Jim had warned both of his children that if they told their mother he'd disparaged her during a visit, he would go to jail. But now, seeing them in person, I felt myself moved by their presence and recalled all I had read.

The younger said his mother would return in fifteen minutes, but his brother corrected him: "More like 6, tonight."

I said I would wait, and the third boy—the one from the neighborhood— said to the brothers, "You don't have to lie"; and then to me, "She'll be home in fifteen."

Shortly after, Karrie Leyritz returned from the grocer, and I asked, as she ferried brown bags brimming with provisions from car to doorstep, "Why didn't you hammer him? I read the divorce file. All of it," and Karrie, who had been so good-humored upon seeing me, grew dour-faced and pale and stopped the ferrying of groceries in mid-step. She set down very carefully the two bags she'd been carrying and asked in equal fashion, "You can read them?"

"Yes," I said.

"Then you know everything?"

"I do."

"What is it you want?"

"I want to know about the time he cracked you in the mouth."

I had said it carelessly—and without forethought. But after I had said it—and heard the words spoken—it felt to me as if I had hit her, again. I was shocked at myself.

"I can't," she replied.

"Karrie," I replied. "Look at how he's treated you. Here's your chance to make it right, to clean it up, to level the score. And I can get you paid."

And she said, "I love my kids. I love them more than anything and I can't bear them seeing that in the paper, seeing their mother attacking their father. You know they love him."

"Come on, Karrie! How would they ever see the *Daily News*?"

"Are you kidding me?" she asked. "Their friends read it to them on the Internet. They know everything."

"Jesus," I said, then tacked: "Do you have any photos of Jim partying?"

She snorted. "Do I ever. A boxful . . . upstairs."

"Would you let me see them?"

"You don't understand," she said. "Jim is vindictive. Vicious," but then relenting, offering a crevice through which I could worm: "You know he doesn't pay me a dime?"

"I know," I said. "It's in the file. Listen, Karrie, think of your kids. That's what this is about. If you can make money—nothing cheap, nice money— from those photos, then you should do it. For them."

While she considered this, I asked, again, if I could see the photos—"just to see them, nothing more." She agreed and shortly met me on the patio, although away from the glass door, through which the children could have watched us. She carried a cardboard box. It was filled haphazardly with photos that she rummaged through urgently, if not neurotically, in the way one would sort playing cards. Those she put aside showed Leyritz intoxicated: bug-eyed and face taut, arm draped around friends—some fellow Yankees. In others, his eyes drooped. Catatonic. Blitzed.

I told her we were interested—and she said she had to contact her attorney. She was pursuing full custody and didn't want the sale of photographs to queer her chances.

And I said, "Karrie, just be aware, they're going to run with the divorce file—all of it," even though no such intention had been articulated—and, moreover, the desk believed the material about her kids unsuitable for publication. But, having seen the horror on her face, I continued, regardless, "Yeah . . . the worst of it. They don't know you, Karrie. They haven't met you, like I have. You're just a name to them. I'll fight to make them stop. But I need something to offer to them, instead. Something . . . like the photos."

She mulled this, then told me to come back around 7:30, after she had returned from work. I left and advised Gittrich, who asked me if the photos were good.

"They're top-notch," I said.

Gittrich replied he would dispatch a photographer from New York, despite our agreement with the *Post*. The photos, after all, weren't technically covered by its scope. And the shooter could make it just in time for 7:30 if he was able to catch the next flight.

The *Post* wooded, again, that day with the Iowa caucus, although this time with the result: "BEATEN . . . HILL FINISHES 3RD TO OBAMA AND EDWARDS." The accompanying graphic showed the three Democratic candidates' heads superimposed on marathon runners. The one with Obama's head was portrayed crossing a finish line labeled, "IOWA." In place of each runner's marathon number the *Post* had put the percentage of the vote they had won. The *News*, meanwhile, opted for the more obvious, although no less effectual, motif: "BAM! IT'S HISTORICAL VICTORY FOR BARACK AS HE POUNDS DEM RIVALS IN IOWA. FULL ELECTION COVERAGE SEE PAGES 4–7."

When I returned that evening and offered Karrie Leyritz the $700 in cash I had withdrawn from an ATM, she at first refused and said she did not want money in return for the photos. But, continuing along stated lines, I replied that the proceeds weren't for her but for her kids, and she should take them to Walmart the following day and buy school supplies. The *News*, I was certain, would have appreciated getting the photos for free, but I had wanted to square matters with myself, even though I did not square matters, was—in fact—a very long way from squaring them, not that I would become aware of this lack of squaring until months after the fact.

Once she accepted the money, we returned to the patio. The photos we'd cherry-picked from the box were still arranged across a lawn table in that way the cops do on "Law & Order" when a witness comes to identity a "perp." Jeremy Bales, a *News* shooter, had, indeed, made it in time from New York; and he now snapped photos of the photos for publication in the *News*. Afterward, I called Gittrich and said, "It's done," and then, "I'm not doing your dirty work anymore." I had said this last part with disgust, but when Gittrich had asked, "What?" I replied, "Nothing. Just joking." You see, I had wanted to say something but wasn't so brave as to actually make it a point.

I returned to New York the following day, Saturday the 5th, although the story did not run until Sunday. It occupied part of the wood. "DAMN YANKEE," read the headline over one of Karrie Leyritz's photos—and I thought that the story had, at least partially, evened the score with the *Post*. Almost, I thought. But not all the way.

13

⠿

"If Spitzer Really Wore Socks in Bed, May Mean Fear of Intimacy: Sex Experts"

Daily News headline, March 23, 2008

March 10, 2008

SLOW NEWS DAYS were tailor-made for chasing big, un-gotten gets—principals from old stories who had never talked but were worth prolonged pursuit. For months, the most attractive of these was Alcides Moreno, an Ecuadorian immigrant and Manhattan window washer who had survived a 47-story (500-foot) plunge on December 7, 2007, after the scaffolding on which he and his brother, Edgar, had been working collapsed. Edgar died. Alcides spent 18 days in a coma and then, as if Gittrich had scripted it, awoke on Christmas Day and spoke his first words since the accident. *"It's a Christmas Miracle!"*

I'd worked the story on Day One, gotten to the Upper East Side scene before the *Post*, and found witnesses to describe the horror. The *News* notched a nice first-day win, although in some minds an asterisk was attached to it. Years later, *Post* runner Kevin Fasick accused me, although not bitterly so, of lying about the lack of on-scene witnesses after his tardy arrival. "It was freezing cold that day," he told me. "You said all the witnesses were gone and there was nothing to get. Then you said, 'Come, wait in my car and stay warm. I got the heat on.' I did and it wasn't until the next day I found out you were lying. Not about the warm car. The witnesses."

I hadn't run on the Moreno household in Linden, New Jersey, since Christmas Eve—or one day before the miracle first words (*What did I do?*). Since then, I'd been phoning, weekly, in hopes of obtaining the real prize: a first-hand account of Alcides's fall and recovery. The last time I'd called, his wife, Rosie, had told me the national media were circling. That likely meant "Good Morning America" and the "Today" show. On March 11, I convinced the desk to make a final attempt before the morning programs got him.

The house was in the shadow of the Linden Cogeneration Station, just off the New Jersey Turnpike. This was the apocalypse Springsteen had imagined on Nebraska. I knocked on the door; a cousin told me Rosie was at the West Orange rehab hospital where Alcides was learning to walk again. I asked if he was up and around. His first steps since the fall would be worth column inches. But the cousin, who barely spoke English, pantomimed the motion of a person using a walker. I called the desk, relayed the info, and asked Rob Moore to sit on the house until Rosie returned.

"I might need you," he replied. "[New York Governor Eliot] Spitzer is involved in some sort of prostitution ring. It looks like he's going to resign."

"Are you shitting me?"

"No. It's just a rumor. But there's a presser at noon."

"What a shame. He could've done so much."

"Yeah, he sure flamed out quickly."

Five minutes later, the phone rang: "Hold for Rob Moore."

Another moment and Rob assumed the line, then ticked off particulars: "Mark Brener, male, sixty-two years old. 307 Falcongate Drive in Monmouth Junction, New Jersey."

"10-4."

"He is apparently the ringleader of the prostitution ring in which our fine governor is allegedly involved. He lives, we think, with a woman named Suwal, who ran the day-to-day operations."

"Call you on arrival."

I scrawled a note to Rosario Moreno and left it with the cousin: "Dear Rosie, Stopped by to see how Alcides was doing. God Bless," along with this postscript: "Thrilled to hear he is walking," and then, finally, my phone number. I made the forty-minute drive along US 1 to Monmouth Junction. Mark Brener lived in a newish cul-de-sac of connected, two-story townhomes with single-car garages. I parked and awaited my photographer, Neil DeCrescenzo, who primarily worked Brooklyn and was about forty-five minutes out.

I braced neighbors, beginning with a teenage boy and girl.

"Do you know the people in 307?"

"Don't know 'em," the boy said, then paused and awaited an explanation.

"They were running a prostitution ring," I replied. "The one the governor used. You haven't heard?"

"Not a thing."

From there, I grabbed another neighbor backing a RAV4 out of her driveway.

"Don't know," she replied, "but it wouldn't surprise me. The police were there a few times."

She pulled out, and I continued. Next I got a teenager who screamed upstairs, "Dad!"

"Tell them to go away!" came the reply, but then the teen yelled, "They're looking for you," which brought a short, graying Indian man to the door. I explained the situation.

"They're running a prostitution ring . . . . Yes, the people in 307."

"Are you sure?" he asked. "307 is a young family. Koreans. They have small children."

"Well, the woman *is* named Suwal."*

"I don't know anything about them."

Another neighbor retrieving her mail said much the same. One more told me she'd just moved to the area. I called the local police and asked for the watch commander. But, at this moment, two children ran from 307's front door to a minivan in the driveway.

"Let me call you back," I told the cop.

A grown woman followed the children. I asked, "Suwal? Is your name Suwal?"

The woman looked perplexed. I didn't think she spoke English.

"How 'bout Mark Brener? Does Mark Brener live here?"

"Who?"

"Mark Brener."

"No. No Mark Brener here."

The neighbor from the mailbox watched this exchange with a curious expression, and when the Korean woman with her kids had pulled away in the minivan, she told me the reason.

"The Breners moved away six years ago," she said. "There's been two families since them."

I laughed. The neighbor realized why I was laughing, and she started laughing, too.

"They're not running a prostitution ring, are they, these people?" she asked.

---

* Her name actually was Cecil Suwal.

"No, not these folks," I replied. "But I certainly have told everyone they do, haven't I? Better tell your neighbors I was wrong."

She wagged her finger—then shot me a thumb's up. I called the desk and told Rob it was a bad address. He said, "I know. Just found out. Oren is heading to the right one now."

"OK, anything else?"

"Not in Jersey."

I looked at my watch. It was 3:40.

"You want me to call it a day?"

"Might as well."

"How 'bout in New York? Anything in the city?"

"They're all old addresses."

"OK," I said, disappointed to not have a larger piece of the story. But that turned out to be a temporary paucity. Before the week was out, I'd have Spitzer in spades—he and all the other shady characters, two-bit grifters, big-money donors, and one Jersey girl—part-and-parcel of the tale. Them and the *Post*, too. Always, the *Post*.

March 11, 2008

New York City awoke to a lurid tabloid tale to which the *News* and the *Post* had allocated eight pages each. Between both of them, they reported that Spitzer, a married father of three, had been caught by his private bankers' making a series of suspicious transactions from a commercial account. The bankers advised the IRS, which in turn informed the FBI's public-integrity unit. Anticipating official corruption, the Feds initiated an investigation. What they found instead was a John wiring thousands of dollars to multiple front companies controlled by a boutique escort service out of New Jersey called Emperor's Club VIP. The Feds then wiretapped the sex ring and captured conversations, painfully granular in detail, in which Spitzer arranged a roughly two-hour "date" with an Emperor's Club VIP girl for February 13 at the Mayflower Hotel in Washington, D.C., for $4,300. In legal papers, the FBI identified him as "Client No. 9" and the girl as "Kristen." For Spitzer, the story almost certainly meant curtains on his career. For the *News* and the *Post*, it meant the starter's gun on a sprint to find and unmask Kristen.

That morning, Rob ordered me to the midtown Manhattan home of Spitzer's parents, or as he'd gleefully said, "Let's go after mommy and daddy!" I, at once, called the photo desk and asked them to text me images of Bernard and Anne Spitzer. I'd need to know whom to approach if I were going to infiltrate, or more likely stake out, the building. Promptly, they sent me a photo, and just as quickly I tried to embellish the reflected parties with frowns. The photo showed them both smiling. I didn't think they would be on that day.

After a rush-hour slog into the city, I deposited my car in News Corp.'s Sixth Avenue NYP zone, then found 730 Fifth Avenue. It was as illustrious an address as any in Manhattan, just north of St. Patrick's Cathedral and just south of Central Park. But it wasn't Bernard and Anne Spitzer's residence but the midtown offices of Playboy International. I informed Rob, who chuckled and said, "That's pretty funny. Kill it. You want to go Greenwich or Rye?"

I said, "Greenwich" without thinking, naming the mostly stinking rich Connecticut exurb north of the city, home to hedge funders and old-money estates. Rob continued: "George Fox, Spitzer donor, Democratic bigwig and the man whose name our governor used to check into the Mayflower Hotel in D.C. Ask him how he feels about being used as a dodge for Spitzer sex."

Greenwich, Connecticut, was half-composed of gated estates with long, confident lawns abutted by driveways so serpentine you could get winded walking to the front doors. The other half was workmanlike—insofar as you didn't need to have $50 million to buy a home there. George Fox's mansion was in the former area of town.

The *Post*'s Gary Miller and Lorena Mongelli were curbside. Lorena said Fox's son had given her a "no comment" earlier that morning. My photo—staff shooter Howard Simmons—arrived, and we all settled into stakeout mode. It took two hours for the son to return. I added my card to the one Lorena had already given him. He wore a short-sleeve polo golf shirt, khaki chinos, and a St. Louis Cardinals ball cap. He politely told us his father was not home. Lorena called it in and told me—vaguely—she was headed elsewhere. I asked where. She said she couldn't tell me. She seemed embarrassed about it.

"My desk says Fox put out a statement," she added in consolation.

I informed Rob. He told me to hang in while he verified the press release. It took him fifteen minutes to call back and dispatch me eighty miles north, east, and deeper into Connecticut. *News* reporter Carrie Melago, formerly of the *New Haven Register*, had learned from an ex-colleague that the *Post* had been staking out a home in Waterbury for the past two days.

"They think it's Kristen," Rob said.

"No kidding. Anything to verify?"

"Nope. That's your job."

Meanwhile, *News* reporter Jonathan Lemire and shooter Andrew Theodorakis hopped a flight to Jacksonville, Florida. Greg "Cowboy" Smith, who worked on the *News'* investigative team (I-Team), had discovered a link from the Emperor's Club website to another belonging to a call girl named Kristen Lee Thomas. The library tracked down three Kristen Lee Thomases in the country, with one residing in Jacksonville. She topped our list. But the *News* didn't wait for Lemire and Theo to arrive. Fearful the *Post* was pursuing the same person, the desk hired a stringer to door-knock Kristen Lee Thomas's home. The stringer did and got Kristen's sister, who laughed off the notion of her sibling as Spitzer's foil. What's more, the sister, obligingly, put Kristen on the phone: "I've never been to New York," she insisted, "and I'm 5'5", 175 pounds." That did it. Our Kristen, Spitzer's Kristen, was 5'5" and 105 pounds, according to legal papers. "I wish I was that weight," Kristen Lee Thomas said.

Hours later, Lemire and Theo door-knocked the home again. This time they got Kristen's father, who didn't see nearly the same humor in their motivation for coming as the sister had before.

While all this was happening, I drove the eighty miles to Waterbury like the town was on fire. (It was that type of story.) And it was a good thing, too, because it turned out I was eating Lorena and Gary's dust the whole way there, not that I knew as much until arrival, upon which I found a *Post* freelance shooter staked out in front of the address Carrie Melago had given Rob, courtesy of the *Register*. I asked the shooter about his reporter, and he motioned to a home up the street. I door-knocked that home, and two college-age men answered. Lorena and Gary stood behind them in the kitchen.

"You know, I had a vision while driving here that you were right behind me," said Lorena, who was hovering with Gary over a laptop on the kitchen table opened to a young woman's Facebook page. The account's owner was named Kristen Mulcahy.

"This her?" I asked.

"Well, it's Kristen," one of the boys replied. "I don't know if she's a prostitute."

"Can you send me a link?"

"Sure, but it won't do you any good."

"Why?"

"Because in order to access it, you have to be one of her Facebook friends," he said.

From the screen, I could tell the man had already downloaded photographs from the account. I asked if he had sent them to the *Post*. The second one—who wore a hoodie—said, "Yes."

I asked him to send them to me, too.

"I don't know."

"How much are they paying you?"

"We're still negotiating."

"Whatever it is, we'll pay more."

Hoodie Boy whistled.

"Well, listen," I said. "How 'bout you send them to my editor so he can have a look?"

He began the transfer. As he did, I walked outside with Lorena. She looked as unhappy as someone who'd just been in a minor accident and was surveying the damage to their rear fender. She obviously did not appreciate the idea of participating in a bidding war over the photos.

"What do you want to do here?" I asked.

Lorena replied ruefully. "I hate this."

At this moment, Mike Lipack called about the photos appearing in his in-box. I briefed him on their provenance and the presence of the *Post*. He replied in a growl that conjured memories of Connery's Irish cop, Malone, in *The Untouchables*.

"Listen, kid, if they offer $1,000, you offer two. If they offer two, you offer four. You get my drift?"

"I got it," I said. *If they pull a notebook, you pull a camera. If they get a studio, you get a posed shot. That's the* Daily News *way, and that's how you beat the* Post!*

Lorena, meanwhile, sighed at having overheard one side of this conversation. She asked, "How are we going to handle this?"

I said, "We're going to the mattresses, Lorena."

Gary Miller, nearby, replied, "Oh, boy! It's Kerry Burke and the daycare center all over again."

"Yeah, but this time the *News* is winning!" I replied.

"Listen," Lorena added, "why don't we just both have them? You already have them and so do we."

That sounded reasonable, so I called back Lipack, who said through bites of his sandwich, "Yeah, kid?"

"Mike, the *Post* already has the photos," I said. "They're going to bid, too. We can either both have them for free, or something small, or we can go to $10,000 or more."

He thought this over, then said, "Yeah, even if they lose, the *Post* will use them. Those rotten fucks. Work it out."

---

* The actual quote is "They pull a knife, you pull a gun. He sends one of yours to the hospital, you send one of his to the morgue. That's the Chicago way! And that's how you get Capone."

Relieved, I told Lorena. I didn't mind a bidding war. I sort of minded getting into one with her. Also, we weren't even sure it was the right "Kristen" in the photos.

After that, we pumped the boys about Kristen Mulcahy and gave her Facebook profile the copper plumbing treatment. When done, there wasn't an iota of info not in my notes. Then we walked to her ex-boyfriend's house, which Hoodie Boy said was up the street. There, Michael Dorso answered the door. He said the Kristen he knew was the softball coach for the local high school team and had been dating the football coach for three years.

"This girl lives with her mom, right?" Lorena asked.

"Yup," Dorso said.

"Let me ask you . . . are you surprised by these developments?" This was a TV reporter.

"You mean that she's a hooker and brought down the governor? Of course I am. This is a good girl who went to a Catholic grammar school."

"Then she's definitely a whore," the TV cameraman replied.

By the time we made it to Kristen's house, located in the same sprawl of single-family homes, the media horde had swelled. The AP, the *New Haven Register* (I didn't know what had taken *them* so long!), two local TV crews. Others. It was to this mob Kristen's mother opened her front door and declared, "You're all on a wild goose chase!"

"How old is Kristen?"

"*My* Kristen is twenty-one," she added, careful to set her daughter apart from Spitzer's girl.

"What color is her hair?"

"She has brown hair."

"Can you describe her measurements?"

"She is a beautiful girl but she weighs more than 105 pounds. She used to be thin but that was about a year ago. I guess she takes after her mom. Who put you on to me? There has to be a different Kristen. I doubt very much it's my Kristen."

"When was your daughter last in New York City?" I asked.

"I think the last time was for a Yankee game a year ago. You know, we just told her the reason for all the excitement. She was very upset, to say the least. She said, 'Mom why would they think that about me? I haven't been to New York except for a year ago.'"

Lorena asked where Kristen had been on February 13, the night Spitzer met with "Kristen."

"She was in town," said the mother. "I remember because it was the day before Valentine's Day."

Someone asked about the last time she had spent a night outside the house.

Mrs. Mulcahy replied it had been a year ago, when her daughter visited relatives in Charlotte.

"That's it?" I asked.

"Well, she might have spent a night at her boyfriend's during the blizzard."

"What blizzard?"

"The one in January or February."

"The one in January or February," a TV reporter repeated, like Jack Webb after finding a clue.

Mercifully, a cop approached at this point and asked if everything was okay. The mother said it was, but then complained that someone had knocked on her door at 11:30 the night before. That would have been the *Post*, but it didn't seem worth saying.

"My husband told me to call 911 and another officer came and checked their credentials, but what nerve! Can you imagine knocking after 10 o'clock? What could possibly be so important that you would knock at that hour? Is all of this really that necessary?"

No one answered the question; the press conference was over, and she wouldn't have understood had we explained. At that point, I wasn't sure I understood, myself.

It was dark—perhaps 6:30—when Mrs. Mulcahy concluded her media remarks. But the *News* and the *Post* weren't done with her daughter—or Waterbury. Not by a long shot. Both desks, while now swayed against the possibility of Kristen Mulcahy's being Spitzer's "Kristen," felt that additional reporting was in order. But this mandate was not conveyed with specifics, and the lack thereof allowed more than enough room for *Post* runner John Doyle, who had relieved Lorena, to suggest a canvass of local strip clubs.

"If she *is* Kristen, girl probably stripped before hooking," he rationalized. "You gotta start somewhere."

And so, on the strength of this unassailable logic, both teams sought and received permission from their respective desks for an enforced pub crawl of Waterbury's exotic dancing establishments. *The* Post *says they're going. You want me to follow? The* News *says they're going. You want me to follow? Of course we do, what do you think?*

We—meaning Doyle, Gary Miller, and my late-arriving photographer, Alfred Giancarli—began at a dive bar called Mr. Happy's, flashing Kristen Mulcahy's Facebook photos to dancers in return for the flashing of things altogether different. (Expensable lap dances were also conducted under the dubious logic that the champagne room provided a more "intimate" setting for the solicitation of information.) It was a fool's errand. But we also knew we would eventually get all those dollar bills reimbursed! After Mr. Happy's, we proceeded to Peek A Boo's Café, then bedded down at a trucker motel that made a point of declaring on a roadside billboard that it had HBO.

March 12–13, 2008

That Wednesday, both tabloids wooded with the Spitzer scandal. "HOOKED! SEX ADDICT GOV SPENT $80,000 ON CALL GIRLS . . . REPORTS, ANALYSIS: PAGES 2, 3, 4, 5, 6, 7, 8, 9." "HOOKER HAPPY . . . SEX SHAME OF ELIOT SPITZER." The Waterbury teams did the only thing they could: hit more strip clubs, and if we had already exhausted Waterbury's supply, we re-solved to return to Mr. Happy's and Peek A Boo's to brace the A.M. shifts. At Peek A Boo's, Doyle had "fallen in love" with a dancer named Ruby and was thus keenly interested to re-interview her. But Waterbury's jiggle joints didn't open until noon, and so we compromised with an Irish pub. And I felt as if stranded on an outpost while events of great consequence occurred elsewhere.

At lunch, Gary and I played chess over coffee while John and Alfred drank Guinness. Maybe it was the collegiality—or the Guinness, or even the halo effect of Ruby's charms—but Doyle told Gary, very frankly, about a cache of photos the *Post* had obtained from a modeling agency. The photos, he said, portrayed the real "Kristen." I pretended to concentrate on the chessmen, waited five minutes, then excused myself to go to the restroom. Only I didn't go. I called Stu Marques, the *News'* city editor, and informed him. Stu, distracted, said, "Uh-huh, sure." It would prove a costly error.

When I returned, everyone was watching TV. Spitzer, onscreen and looking good for the circumstances, read what turned out to be a fairly rousing official farewell, if such a thing could exist in that sort of moment. *I go forward with the belief, as others have said, that as human beings our greatest glory consists not in never falling but in rising every time we fall.* (It all had a whiff of MacArthur's fleeing the Philippines to it.) His wife, Silda, meanwhile, stood next to him, looking much like a bottle of well-shaken Coca-Cola with the top still fastened on.

After that, our sense of a Waterbury exile only grew, and we voiced tacit protest with an over-the-top lunch at the most expensive eatery in town.

Our desks either couldn't be bothered to move us amid the ensuing frenzy of activity or were unwilling to do so on the one-in-a-million chance Kristen Mulcahy was, indeed, Spitzer's "Kristen." But what we didn't know—what, in fact, no one outside of the *New York Times'* newsroom knew—was that the jig was up and remarkably had been for almost forty-eight hours.

On Monday afternoon—just as I was chasing Mark Brener's ex-neighbors in Jersey—a 5′5″, 105-pound Jersey Shore girl named Ashley Youmans* made a brief appearance in Manhattan federal court. She was twenty-two years old and had been subpoenaed to testify about the four people charged with operating the Emperor's Club VIP. Superficially, the proceedings were procedural. The court appointed Ashley a lawyer—a Don D. Buchwald out of Westchester—and asked her to swear she'd accurately filled out an affidavit listing her financial assets. It was almost certainly for this reason that neither the *Post* nor the *News*, nor any other outlet aside from the *Times*, was present. But the *Times*, by quirk or savvy, *was* represented and thus able to cobble the pieces together. Over the ensuing forty-eight hours, the paper confirmed Youmans's bona fides as Spitzer's "Kristen." According to the *Times* article published online late Wednesday and in print on Thursday, the paper had conducted phone interviews with Ms. Youmans, known by the *nom-de-stage* Ashley Alexandra Dupre, Tuesday night from her ninth-floor apartment in Manhattan's Flatiron district. "I just don't want to be thought of as a monster," she'd told the paper.

The *Times* had obtained corroboration that Ashley Dupre was, indeed, Spitzer's "Kristen" through "a person with knowledge of the Emperor's Club operation." Buchwald filled in the rest. And while neither I, nor the public, ever got the full story about why the *Times* was present at Monday's hearing, Stu Marques did not soon forgive the Manhattan federal court reporter who'd missed it. In fact, Stu soon banished him, a respected journalist and nine-year *News* vet, to the outer borough outpost of Queens criminal court as unspoken punishment for this imagined crime.

Meanwhile, the *Times*—likely concerned that another outlet, probably the *Post*, was inching toward "Kristen's" identity—made what in 2008 still seemed a remarkable decision: it published its monster online.†

---

* Ashley Youmans changed her last name to Dupre after running away from her Jersey Shore home to New York City. As one runner noted in a nod to the 1984 rock song "Runaway," "Somewhere Bon Jovi is laughing his ass off."

† The *Post* also used the Internet to break a Spitzer scoop on Wednesday, albeit a far lesser one. The tabloid reported at 8:38 a.m. that the governor was going to resign, about three hours before the actual speech.

"THE YOUNG WOMAN IN QUESTION, 22 AND WORRIED ABOUT THE RENT."* The paper did so in time for Wednesday's 6 o'clock news, although not so early that the TV stations could do their own reporting and replicate the get. The *News* and the *Post* were more fortunate. Both papers still had five-or-so hours to first edition and two more to sports final to wage war in the field and on the phone. The first battle of Manassas, by comparison, took only slightly longer.

The goal was simple—find something, anything, to advance the *Times* story by reaching people who both knew Ashley Alexandra Dupre and were willing to speak about her past. To this end, the *News'* Edgar Sandoval rushed to a home in Jackson Township, near the Jersey Shore, where Ashley had lived from 2000 to 2003 and where her grandfather and brother still resided. Joe Gould ran on her mother's home in nearby Wall Township. The *Post* dispatched teams to the same addresses. Neighbors were called. Aunts, uncles, cousins, ex-roommates, teenage acquaintances, and ex–high school classmates with no more a tenuous connection than hallway gossip.

And yet, five hours to first deadline and seven to sports final proved an eternity—more than enough to paint a portrait of Ashley's youthful promiscuity for the eager masses. "She was one of those girls," Allison Scisco, a twenty-three-year-old former Wall High School classmate of Dupre's, told the *News*. "You hear things, and it's the way she carried herself." In fact, it almost seemed the following morning as if the *News* and the *Post* hadn't been trounced by the *Times*. "GOV'S GIRL . . . MEET THE 22-YEAR-OLD JERSEY GIRL RUNAWAY WHO EARNED $4G FOR SEX WITH ELIOT SPITZER." "HOOKER TALKS AS SPITZ QUITS, FULL COVERAGE ON PAGES 2–10." Corresponding photos pulled from Ashley's social media pages showed her on the *News'* wood looking over her shoulder with regionally appropriate blow-dried hair and a come-hither stare; and on the *Post's*, bikini-clad and lounging on the prow of a boat.

That morning, Thursday, the *News* and the *Post* redeployed chessmen. The object was now to cover the story's many facets—challenging when the real-life drama claimed so large a cast. There was the mother's house in Wall Township; Silda and Eliot Spitzer's midtown apartment; Ashley's abode in the Flatiron district; her stepfather Michael DiPietro's oral surgery office in Brick; the Spitzers' Columbia County estate; the grandfather/

---

* If you look this story up online, it notes its publication date as March 13. I can't account for that. Trust that the *Times* initially broke the story on Wednesday, the 12th, during the late afternoon/early evening hours.

brother's house in Jackson—and none of that counted the copious phone and leg work demanded to tackle the story's less obvious angles.

From New York, the *News'* dispatched reporter Larry McShane to meet Jason Itzler, the self-styled "King of All Pimps," at a Union Square coffee shop. There, Itzler described how he had hired Dupre to her first hooker's job upon her arrival in New York. "This was probably the sexiest, hottest girl I had," Itzler told McShane. "She's no joke." Even Richard Huff—the *News's* entertainment writer—got in on the action, penning a next-day account describing the millions Ashley now stood to earn from hypothetical *Penthouse* and *Hustler* cover shoots, tabloid TV interviews, and downloads of her pop song, "Move Ya Body," incidentally uploaded to the Internet on Wednesday and now available at $0.98 a pop.

My share of the chessboard was Ashley's family home in Jackson Township, where her brother, Kyle, had given Edgar and the *Post* words the night before. By Thursday morning, it was decorated with a handwritten sign, taped to the front door, reading, "NO TRESSPASSING. NO COMMENT." Whatever I would contribute to Friday's story, it seemed, would have to come by phone. I started with Wall High School, which Ashley had attended for two years before dropping out.

"Officially, the school has no comment," the receptionist told me.

"How 'bout unofficially?"

She laughed.

"I'd like to help you," she said. "But there's really nothing I can do."

After that, I left voicemails for the school's principal and its gymnastic coach, for whom Ashley had competed and from whom the *Asbury Park Press* had gotten words Wednesday night. Then, I called my old nearby high school and left messages for its principal and a favored teacher who now handled alumni affairs. Maybe one of the school's students had dated Ashley or her friends—or had an older brother who had done so. That scuttlebutt would move fast through a high school's hallways. It was a long shot, but not *that* long. After that, I called Michael DiPietro's oral surgery office and tried to make an appointment.

"Is this Dr. DiPietro's office?"

"It's one of his offices," a woman replied. "He has three."

"Is he here today?"

"Yes."

"Can I make an appointment?"

"Sure, what's the problem?"

"I need a root canal."

"This is an oral surgery office. We don't do root canals."

She'd said it like root canals were a downmarket procedure. Sort of a sneer. I said, "Oh," rang off, and swore. Then I googled "oral surgery," clicked links, and read. Quickly, I learned that if I wanted an audience with Ashley's dad, I'd need to have a tooth pulled. So, I called Rob and informed him of my plan; then phoned Joe Gould, who was in a standoff at the mother's Wall home with the *Post*'s Erin Calabrese. I asked Joe to call DiPietro's office and request an appointment in my name.

"Why not just call yourself?"

I told Joe I already had and had requested the wrong procedure, although I had not given a name. I told him if I called back so soon, the receptionist might recognize my voice and wonder why I suddenly needed a tooth pulled rather than a root canal.

"That's ridiculous!" Joe cried. "What are you going to do? Jump out of the chair and say, '*Ah-ha!* I'm a reporter and what do you have to say about your daughter?'"

"Well, I hadn't really planned on the '*Ah-ha*' part."

Joe agreed to make the call. After that, I settled into my car and awaited Edgar—whom Rob Moore had dispatched to relieve me at the Jackson scene so I could attempt the dentist ploy. While I waited, chaos enveloped the street—a circus of SAT vans and restless reporters with Dunkin' Donuts breath: the *Post*, the AP, the *National Enquirer*, the *Asbury Park Press*, and all the big-city TV affiliates, everyone laying siege to the two-story colonial while the neighbors watched aghast.

Meanwhile, Joe and Erin detected movement at the Wall home. Joe told me after he and I had spoken about the dental appointment that Ashley's mother, Carolyn Capalbo, had exited the house with bags slung over her shoulder. She'd gotten into a car and roared out of her driveway and down the block in an obvious attempt to elude the two runners. Erin and Joe, who'd been staked out in the same car, gave chase, but Ashley's mother gamely ducked into a neighbor's driveway after rounding a corner, then waited until Joe and Erin passed her by. She then presumably doubled back. Joe said that ensuing circuits of the subdivision proved fruitless—and both he and Erin were forced to return to an empty house.

Meanwhile, Rob Moore ordered me to skip DiPietro in order to monitor the growing media horde in Jackson. With the *Post*'s arrival on-scene, he said, it was too dangerous to allow the home to go unguarded. Adam Nichols, a city desk reporter, would be dispatched, instead, from Manhattan to attempt the dental chair coup.

We rang off and then, as if on cue, Kyle Youmans exited the Jackson home and ran what could only be described as a gantlet of media. *Did you know she was working as a hooker? Are you proud of your sister? Is your Mom? What's next for Ashley? Have you spoken to her?* Kyle ignored them all and marched blank-faced to the curb in order to retrieve—gasp!—that day's *New York Post*! The *Post* freelance shooter snapped away, although the photo ended up not running.

"This is pointless," someone muttered, and at that juncture I was inclined to agree.

Meanwhile, Joe and Erin, stymied by Carolyn Capalbo's well-executed jailbreak, paid a visit to the Atlantic Club, an all-things-fitness spot that a neighbor had blabbed was Mama Dupre's preferred workout digs. It made sense given Carolyn's svelte frame—so sculpted that *New York* magazine would later call her a "TOTAL MILF."

Once there, the two frustrated tabloid runners cased the parking lot, searching for the car whose driver had so effectually eluded them only ninety minutes earlier. But their efforts, like everyone's, proved fruitless. It was no soap there, no soap in Jackson, none at DiPietro's oral surgery office. Not anywhere. It was all-quiet on the Jersey Shore—so quiet, in fact, that some scoop-starved network ordered a complete, catered Italian lunch—meatballs, spaghetti, grilled vegetables, and iceberg lettuce—and had it deposited on the front porch of the Jackson Township home as a carb-heavy bribe to curry favor for a sit-down. But it wouldn't stay quiet. In fact, the *Post* was probably right then and there cooking up what would prove to be a big one. And while its tabloid feast—like the Italian one left outside the Youmans' door—could also come via home delivery, the *Post*'s meal satisfied a hunger for sleaze and sex rather than any hankering for spaghetti and meatballs.

March 14–16, 2008

The next morning arrived like a bad hangover . . . if you were a runner for the *News*. If you ran for the *Post*, daybreak brought the biggest win since Russel Timoshenko. While the whole media world—CNN and Fox News, in particular—ran an endless loop of Ashley's Myspace photos, the *Post* blew everyone out of the water. The tabloid devoted the whole of its wood to a rollicking, five-page exclusive photo spread of the Jersey Shore call girl in various states of undress. "BAD GIRL . . . PHOTO EXCLUSIVE OF SPITZER'S 'KRISTEN' . . . MORE PHOTOS, STORY: PAGES 4, 5, 6, 7." The front-page photo that kicked off the extravaganza was perhaps the most tantalizing of all. It portrayed a naked Ashley with bedroom eyes, blow-dried hair, and both breasts cupped beneath her hands. As reporter Murray

Weiss noted in one of the six accompanying stories the *Post* published along with the photos, Dupre, "in early 2007 had a photographer friend shoot glamour photos of her to use in her portfolio" as she pursued a music career. The photos—totaling four topless shots (breasts, likewise cupped) and two in barely anything—prompted an instant sensation, a rebuke from Ashley's lawyer, and a $1 million e-mailed offer from *Hustler's* Larry Flynt for what he described as "the whole enchilada." "It will be something that will be very tastefully done," Flynt explained. "*Hustler* readers don't like to compromise." The *News*, meanwhile, countered with a whimper: "KRISTEN'S STORY . . . FROM WELL-TO-DO JERSEY 'WILD CHILD,' TO THE CITY'S FAST LANE TO THE INFAMOUS NIGHT OF SEX WITH THE GOV. SEE PAGES 2–8."

It all was enough to raise the question of how the *News'* sworn enemy had obtained the images—and such a striking coup. I had my ideas, beginning with our disregard for the conversation between John Doyle and Gary Miller in the Waterbury pub two days earlier. From my morning perch outside Carolyn Capalbo's still-empty Wall Township home, I now phoned Doyle and asked him to confirm my suspicions. Doyle, candid in victory, did so and then elaborated, "We've been working on it for days . . . days."

"So, why did you guys wait?"

"We weren't sure it was Kristen. When the *Times* published, we knew."

The second clue—as if another was needed—came from the photo credit the *Post* squeezed onto its wood in print so fine as to compare favorably with that of a pharmaceutical warning. It read, "Wesley Mann of Contact Press Images" in an obvious reference to the "photographer friend" Murray Weiss had referenced in his story. I asked Roca, who also staked out Carolyn's Wall home that morning, about Wesley Mann, and the articulation of his name elicited a cackle from the seasoned shooter.

"Listen, Jacko-bazzi," Roca replied, "this turns my stomach. I've been working at the *News* a long time and every time a story has to do with strippers, prostitutes, the club scene, Wall Street, or celebrities, the *Post* hands us our ass. It's the way they task their enterprise reporters. They work on this shit day and night, so when something like this comes down, they're plugged in to the straight dope while we're left holdin' the bag!" Plugged in or not, though, the *Post* had had to pay. A newsroom source later gossiped that the tabloid had shelled out close to six figures for the spread—and that, amazingly, the *News* had gotten a last-second chance to match, or exceed, that offer, and had passed.

But the *Post* wasn't done bludgeoning its rival: As the *News* conducted a post-mortem, Lorena Mongelli stalked the Outer Banks of North Carolina in search of Ashley's biological father, William Youmans. She found him, of course, later that day, working as a stonemason and more than willing discuss his daughter's tumultuous past, along with a dramatic call she'd made to him exactly one week earlier on March 7, the same day the feds busted Brener and Suwal for running Emperor's Club VIP. "She was crying, she was really upset," Youmans told Lorena. "I was worried for her." The *News*, briefly, had a chance to counter that scoop, which would run the following day, Saturday, under the headline "'WHORE'IBLE ORDEAL: DAD." But the opportunity was lost amid the bustling crowds of midtown's Port Authority bus terminal.

While I languished in front of the Wall Township home with Roca and the *Post*'s Ron Romano,* Joe Gould manned my old perch in Jackson. Around 11 o'clock, Ashley's grandfather roared out of the driveway in a Corvette. Joe and the *Post* gave chase but lost him. Joe quickly returned to the house and arrived before the *Post*—but not before Grandpa, who candidly and inexplicably told him he had just dropped off Ashley's brother, Kyle, at the New Jersey Transit bus station in nearby Lakewood. Kyle, he confessed, had avoided their detection by slumping in the Corvette as they pulled out of the driveway—and he now planned to bus into Manhattan to meet his sister. It was an important clue, because Ashley had been in the wind since the *Times* exclusive, frustrating attempts at the follow-up interview or photo the whole media world so wanted. In fact, residents of her Manhattan building, the Chelsea Landmark, had grown so disgusted with the reporter horde staked out outside their address that the building's management had publicly released a statement declaring that Ashley was no longer home. The *Daily News* humorously riffed on this development with a witty headline: "SPITZER CALL GIRL, LIKE ELVIS, HAS 'LEFT THE

---

* Ron was a perma-lance shooter for the *Post* with a colorful backstory. His father, Joe, had worked as a city tabloid shooter, although for the *News*, during the 1940s and '50s. Ron followed his father, but not before a career as an Evel Knievel–like stunt man who performed under the stage name Ron Starr. It was because of this exotic past, Ron repeatedly told anyone who'd listen that the NYPD suspected him of being the notorious "Ninja Burglar," who allegedly committed some 160 audacious home break-ins over a 10-year period beginning in July 2007. In all, the black-clad thief made away with some $4 million—often by robbing occupied homes and exhibiting astounding dexterity in the commission of the crimes. As Ron told me that day in Wall Township, "The cops have seen me perform as Ron Starr—and they know I'm one of only three people on all of Staten Island who could have pulled off these heists. That's why I'm under constant suspicion." Alas, the real Ninja Burglar was finally unmasked in April 2016 as 47-year-old convicted rapist Robert Costanzo after a botched break-in in Connecticut. Finally, Ron Romano can sleep easy.

BUILDING.'" Now, Joe had gotten a lead on Ashley's location and had only to catch Kyle and pursue him to his sister.

On the desk's order, Joe raced to Lakewood, and while he didn't find Kyle, he did obtain a bus schedule indicating that only a single bus had departed Lakewood for New York during the interval when the grandfather had left the Jackson home—and when he'd returned. The *News* now knew on what bus Kyle was traveling to Manhattan.

As Joe raced up Route 9 in a futile attempt to overtake the bus, *News* runner Christina Boyle and shooter Sam Costanza raced to Manhattan's Port Authority, the sprawling transit depot off 42nd Street that would be Kyle's final stop. Christina, armed with an old photo of Kyle, staked out the gate at which the bus was due to arrive. Then she and Sam waited. Soon, Kyle exited and the *News* team followed. But rather than maintain the tail to Kyle's meeting with Ashley, Costanza took a photo! The brother, seeing them, took evasive action—and Christina and Sam lost him amid the Port Authority crowds. With him went the *News'* last chance to counter the *Post*'s onslaught.

Over the next two days, the *Post* ran Lorena's exclusive with William Youmans and another obtained by Matt Nestel in Palm Beach, Florida, with Ashley's ex-fiancé, Jason Jarocki. The former lovebirds, Jason said, had planned a Catholic wedding just a year before. "'GOOD GIRL' PLANNED CATHOLIC NUPS." The story painted Jarocki as "confused" over "what [had] happened to the 'wholesome' young woman he thought he knew." On the 16th, the *Post*—and Lorena—added a sprawling feature about Silda Wall Spitzer that exclusively quoted her relatives. "SECRET STRIFE OF HURT WIFE." A lesser, yet still humorous, analysis piece quoted experts as saying Ashley stood to make $2 million to $5 million from her notoriety, including $1 million from a porno offer. In reporting this fact, the *Post* deftly equated that amount to the cost of servicing "Spitzer 581 to 1,162 times." Another *Post* scoop reported that Ashley had hobnobbed with Hamptons habitués in the run-up to the Spitzer scandal. The *News*, meanwhile, countered with Ashley's cocaine use and an in-depth feature on the secretive world of high-end hookers. It also wrote about Eliot and Silda's planned retreat to their country estate, although the *Post* trumped even this story with a contrived, yet no less hilarious, take on Eliot walking his dog around Central Park prior to leaving: "HORN DOG TAKES PET FOR A WALK," roared the screamer abreast of a photo of man/beast.

As on Friday, I spent Saturday and Sunday marooned at the mother's Wall Township home. But after Friday, the *Post* didn't bother. With the imminent conclusion of the news cycle, the battle over Ashley and Eliot wound down, or at least in the field. Then on Saturday, a 200-foot, six-ton crane collapsed at a building site off 51st Street and Second Avenue, killing seven people and injuring twenty-four more—and just like that, the Spitzer story was knocked from the front pages for the first time in a week. "CRANE HORROR . . . BUILDINGS CRUSHED, 4 KILLED IN TRAGIC MIDTOWN COLLAPSE . . . FULL STORY: PAGES 2–5." The Spitzer/Dupre stories continued to get ink, but as for both tabloids' running corps—we mostly re-deployed to the new tragedy.

Then there was this ominous portent occupying the lower third of the *Post*'s Saturday wood: "BAD NEWS BEAR: FED BAILS OUT WALL ST. GIANT; SCARED MARKETS PLUNGE . . . SEE PAGES 4–5." I don't remember reading the story. But it—or, rather the events heralded therein—would come to mean so much more to me, the *News*, the *Post*, and every journalist working in America than Spitzer, Dupre, or pretty much anything in the months and years to come. I just didn't know it at the time. No one did.

14

"Ma Goes to Bat for Derek Jeter"

Daily News headline, November 17, 2007

A BIT OF WALL STREET LORE, I think, is applicable to the *News–Post* drama, or at least concerning the life and work of its runners. A trader, the story went, had lost some $20,000 on a single trade, but then made the far more unforgivable error of equating this amount to the cost of repairing his family's roof. His director knew at once that his subordinate was finished, not because of the loss itself but because of the tangible way in which he had articulated it. The trader, the director knew, had ceded the abstraction necessary to gamble astounding sums of money, and fear and paralysis could not be far behind.

In tabloid terms, there is a parallel: A runner could consistently knock on doors and ask grieving fathers for "good words" about their murdered daughters so long as that runner viewed the father objectively, in terms of his mission, the news value of his words, and the importance of obtaining them *vis-à-vis* what the *Post*—or the *News*—might obtain from the same or another source. But the moment a runner's focus shifted to the human being before him, his grief, as well as the inconceivable unnaturalness of asking a stranger to explain his innermost pain at that moment, of all moments, the runner would be professionally diminished, if not just as washed up as the Wall Street trader.

One good example of this phenomenon concerned a staff shooter for the *News* named Mike Albans, who had worked competently—even exceptionally—over many years. Then all at once, or rather "gradually then suddenly," he got disgusted. He's a good example because the moment he got cynical is so dramatically apparent—and his reaction to his disgust so colorful and swift. As the story went, Albans accompanied a runner to New York Yankee Derek Jeter's parents' home in northern New Jersey on November 16, 2007. New York state officials had accused Jeter the day before of evading state income taxes by claiming full-time residency in Florida. Florida did not impose state income tax, and, although Jeter had a home in the Sunshine State, New York analysts had concluded he'd spent the majority of his time in New York and thus had dodged state taxes. The runner was to ask Mr. or Mrs. Jeter if they felt that Derek was, indeed, a tax cheat, and Albans was to shoot them as they answered.

On the story's first day, the runner awaited Jeter's parents with shooter Andrew "Theo" Theodorakis, who had no qualms about the assignment, although neither Mr. nor Mrs. Jeter showed. On the second day, when Albans was assigned, the mother returned with groceries; and as she carried these groceries inside her home, the runner energetically questioned her about the tax problem. The mother, named Dorothy, responded by asking the reporter, "Do you have children? You know how hard it is to watch on the news that your son is a tax cheat?" and then, "My boy does everything right—*everything*! . . . It kills me. You're going to give me a heart attack!"

At this point, Dorothy Jeter, already diminished on her front porch, put down the groceries, clutched her chest, and sobbed; and it was only after she did so and the runner had gleefully documented her words and reactions in his notebook that he noted, with considerable dismay, that Albans had not photographed the spectacle. He questioned him at this point, and harshly so; and the shooter merely shrugged. When the runner said something to the effect of "You'd better shoot her," Albans replied, "You're scum." Albans then reluctantly made the shot, which occupied the *News'* next-day wood. A short time later, Albans resigned from the *News* and moved, I'd heard, to Montana or some similar rustic and remote place— "off the grid"—into a log cabin–like home, if not an actual log cabin.

As a rule, yet still generally speaking, for there are always exceptions— and one notable one—a runner typically worked no more than three years on the street, although likely less, without suffering some measure of disillusionment or, worse, disgust. It is a very natural phenomenon that comes from every day knocking on the doors of tragedy, knowing that if you didn't, the *Post* would and an editor might question you the following day about your failure to have done so. It is thus the gaining of this ability to honestly tell an editor you had accomplished the door-knock without going to the trouble of lying that motivated so much of a runner's actions after they had acquired a certain amount of disgust. *Let's just get it over with.* Such disillusionment, understandably, also develops in someone who earns their living by occasionally accosting mothers and widows outside the churches, synagogues, and mosques in which their sons and husbands have just been eulogized—and insisting on a quote. After some time on the street, I began traveling with a black *yarmulke* in my glove compartment to aid in the attainment of such quotes at Jewish funerals.

Once a runner went from objectively viewing door-knocks to humanizing those who answered them, this shift, and its consequences, could prove irrevocable. I have thus known runners, formerly ferocious and indomitable on the street and willing to knock on any door, develop a complex about knocking on any one at all—and even the most emotionally mundane. Other times, the disillusioned runner persisted on the street without running too hard, or not nearly as hard or as fearlessly as he had before. In one such case, a *Post* runner told me he saved his good running only for big stories and glided on day-to-day affairs. He had been running quite a long while when he told me this.

I once relieved a runner at a Staten Island scene who looked as if he had not bathed or changed his clothes—and certainly not shaved—for some time, and in the case of the shaving, probably longer than a week. I heard not long afterward that he'd confessed his disgust to his colleagues. I have known other runners to not perform door-knocks assigned to them unless forced to do so by the presence of a competitor, or after gaining some indication that the person behind the door would receive them sympathetically. They might, therefore, pass the whole of a shift in front of an occupied home, parked at the curb, napping in their car, aside from those moments when forced to inform the desk that no one was home or that the occupant, with whom they have had no prior interaction, was unwilling to speak. Again, I emphasize that such behavior was derived rarely, if ever, from a calculated intent to goldbrick but rather from an emotional inability to any longer confront a grieving widow or parent and request words representative of their pain.

Another coping method I have unfortunately seen runners deploy is to become contemptuous—even ruthless and cold-blooded—toward the people upon whose doors they knocked. By objectifying them beyond even their news value, the runner was able to isolate, and cordon off, the pain associated with doing something so unnatural as asking a grieving widow for a quote. But this method, effective as it might have been, had obvious liabilities and implications for a runner's humanity, hard as it is to view one person with contempt and others with empathy during nonworking hours. But as I said, this method had the benefit of allowing runners to persist on the street and in their drawing of checks.

Most times, a runner would graduate, after a tour on the street, to the desk or cop shack or become some hybrid of writer, runner, and maker of calls from the office. In this way, running and street work became a sort of apprenticeship for bigger—or at least better-titled—positions. Only a few people made a career solely out of running.* And, of these, I know of only one who never suffered any disillusionment but remained wholly committed to the holiness of the get. That would be Kerry Burke. Kerry never wavered in his faith, or at least not publicly, that what he was doing was important to the readers and the city he felt he served. My experience, however, was different.

On my third weekend running for the *News*, I phoned the city desk at 8:15 A.M., fifteen minutes after the appointed time. But I'd already learned that Sunday morning assignment editor John Oswald regarded the official 8 A.M. start of my shift as something of an abstraction. He typically wouldn't answer until 8:30, if not later. When I finally did reach him, he spoke groggily and ruffled the DCPI sheets, the NYPD bulletins faxed to city media outlets about overnight criminal activity. As Oswald searched for a crime worthy of chasing, he growled lowly, like Orson Welles muttering in his sleep: victims' names, actors, locations, approximate times, charges.

"My God!" he hooted. "I haven't seen so many bodies in the morning since Vietnam! The whole city's a killing floor!" Now, I should say here that only years later did I learn that John Oswald had not, in fact, served in Vietnam. But because of this statement, I believed for a very long time that he had and, perhaps, had even learned to write on the GI Bill and/or been mildly afflicted with posttraumatic stress disorder that could've justified his occasional irritability.

After this outburst, Oswald continued to read the sheets. Finally, he stopped and said, "Yes. Oh, yes, here's one. I like this one very much. Thirty-three-year-old victim, Ricardo Salinas, killed approximately 2100 hours— that's 9 P.M.—within the confines of the 121st Precinct, or . . . lemme see . . . Van Pelt Avenue on Staten Island. Okay? Okay? Call me when you have the whole story. Except if you see the *Post*. Then call me at once."

---

* I am excluding photographers. Plenty of shooters persisted on the street for years without exhibiting cynicism or disillusionment, perhaps (and I am only guessing) because of the greater distance afforded by shooting with the camera. More personal interactions are demanded of a runner in order to obtain words.

I arrived around 9:30 and found that Van Pelt Avenue evinced none of the drama of the prior night. It was cool and clear, and the birds were chirping, although I couldn't see them, and there wasn't a tree to guess them inside for a quarter-mile in any direction. It looked like a lot of Staten Island nabes—covered over in concrete and landscaped with two-family homes separated by alleys so narrow neighbors could shake hands through open windows. The homes were boxes with low-pitched roofs, one big bay window each over a ground-floor garage and steps from the sidewalk to the front door. It would be very easy in a neighborhood like that to shove your key into the wrong door after a night of blue-collar drinking and realize your mistake only after somebody started hollering. It was a neighborhood for cops, firefighters, taxi hacks, sanitation workers, corrections officers, teachers, and union tradesmen—people who read the *News*. Maybe that was why I didn't see the *Post*.

I questioned neighbors and soon discovered that Salinas had been a father, Mexican immigrant, and IHOP cook who'd been beaten to death by three white teenagers who had shouted, "Spic!" while they trounced him, then called his wife, Fabiola, to taunt her about his death. After that, I phoned Oswald, believing I had obtained a very nice scoop. His reply, however, wasn't what I had expected. "Did you get the widow?" he demanded. "Is she in mourning? I want every tear, every howl, every prayer for posterity."

Meekly, I replied that, no, I had not obtained "the widow," although I would now attempt to obtain her. Ten minutes later, I called Oswald back and informed him that Ricardo's widow, Fabiola, had told me an interview would be impossible at that moment.

"I . . . want . . . the . . . widow!" Oswald yelled, sounding much like the Queen of Hearts calling for Alice's head. "You tell that widow to bow down to the power of the press! You tell her the *Daily News* wants words!"

Years later, I recounted this anecdote to Oswald, and he reacted with an embarrassed grin. "Did I say that?" he asked. "I didn't say that? Well, maybe I did." Years after that, after he had been purged from the *News*, he said the perspective gained from his layoff allowed him to finally feel crummy about having issued ultimatums about widows. But on Sunday, March 16, 2008, my final day in front of Ashley Dupre's mother's house in Wall, Oswald was still in his pre-layoff form. He ordered me to go after ex–New Jersey Governor Jim McGreevey's former driver, Teddy Pedersen. Pedersen, according to stories posted to the *Newark Star Ledger*'s website at 5:22 P.M. and the *Post*'s at 9:33 P.M., told both papers he was fed up watching McGreevey's soon-to-be ex, Dina, go on TV to hypocritically decry Eliot Spitzer's cheating in the context of Jim's infidelities. Dina, he explained, was not a victim. She knew Jim was gay and had married him anyway, and he knew this because the three of them—Jim, Dina, and Teddy—had had *ménàges à trois* as early as 1999, a year before Jim and Dina wed. They even had a pet name for their romps: "Friday Night Specials," although it was unclear from the *Post* and *Star Ledger* if this moniker derived from the eatery where the trysts began—T.G.I. Friday's—or the day of the week on which they were conducted.

Oswald called me at 9:37 P.M., minutes after the *Post* published. I had been home for all of ninety minutes—the first time I could say as much since leaving the prior Wednesday. First, he gave me an address for Pedersen in Somerset—an hour's drive away. No one was home. Then he gave me one in Metuchen—another forty-minute drive. By the time I arrived at 11:37 P.M., knocked, and called the desk to say that no one was answering, Oswald sounded hysterical, or more hysterical than usual. He gave me another address—this one back toward Somerset in a town called Belle Mead and no longer for Pedersen but someone he, or research, believed was his relative. "But John!" I protested. "You can't want me to knock on someone's door at 1 A.M.!"

"Tell them tough noogies! If they had answered the phone, we wouldn't have had to knock. And if it's mommy or daddy, tell them to tell us where Pedersen is so we can stop harassing their relatives."

I didn't protest but just said OK and returned home, the first time I disobeyed a *News* editor's order. It wouldn't be the last. Also around this time, a young Manhattanite named Margaux Powers was murdered by an ex-boyfriend named Jonathan Smith. Smith slashed her throat, left her body in her Chelsea apartment, and then threw himself off a high-rise in the financial district. Powers was an Ivy Leaguer and from a wealthy Long Island family—and so the murder held the city and its warring tabloids in thrall. For three consecutive shifts, I remained in a parked vehicle in front of Margaux's family home in the affluent Long Island exurb of Glen Cove. It was a ranch house on a narrow street that concluded in a cul-de-sac. There were only, perhaps, eight homes on the street, and its limited width left little room for the media horde—the *Post*, *Newsday*, TV vans—to park. The home was set back by a decent lawn, although not so deep that the family would not be constantly aware of our presence as they grieved inside the house.

For three days, my editor repeatedly ordered me to knock on the home's door at what amounted to four-hour intervals, despite Margaux's father, Michael, first having preempted such aggression with a statement, then later with ever-more-emotional pleas to give his family space. And yet, the editor continued to push. *"Give 'em another shot. Maybe they've softened."* At one point, he conceded that the *Post* had scored, elsewhere, or at least the *News* believed it had, and something—anything—was needed to counter that get. In this way, he ordered me again to the door.

But the editor had not seen the father, nor spoken with him, on prior door-knocks. He had, of course, been advised of Michael Powers's reaction, but, in fairness, I suppose such a verbally conveyed brief is never as powerfully felt, or understood, as by the one who experienced it. *"Give 'em another shot. Maybe they've softened."* But I knew there would be no softening. And maybe in the past, I would have knocked again . . . and again . . . and again. I'm almost certain I would have. I would have employed all the rationalizations every runner used. The *Post* might get them. This would be a huge get, and the getting of the get would result in much recognition and glory. But somewhere, the weight of those rationalizations, while still robust, grew too light to tip the scales toward action. And so I conscientiously objected as I had on March 16. I told the editor I'd carry out his order, only to report back another no comment, all the while having remained, unstirring, in my car.

Through late March and April, the *News* and *Post* chased the embers of Spitzer/Dupre. On March 22, the *News* intercepted Andreia Schwartz aboard American Airlines Flight 951 as she was deported from New York to São Paulo. The former Emperor's Club VIP worker and midtown madam had been quizzed by cops in connection with Spitzer—and the New York media were desperate to learn what she'd told them. "I didn't really know [Ashley Dupre] that well," she told a *News* runner at 30,000-plus feet. "I knew her from parties and St. Tropez . . . . I feel very sorry for her." *News* headline: "BRAZILIAN MADAM FEELS PAIN FOR 'KRISTEN' IN SPITZER SCANDAL." One day later, the *Post* tracked Schwartz to her mother's home in the Brazilian coastal city of Vitoria, where she dished on Spitzer's fetish for live sex shows. "I found it strange that he has a beautiful wife but he likes to watch couples," she said. The *Post*'s next-day screamer: "SPITZER WAS A 'PEEP' DATE."

Then on March 26, another Manhattan madam connected to Spitzer was busted. As the *News* wrote, "Kristin Davis, 32, owned Wicked Models, which promised johns dates with Ivy League–educated, multilingual cover girls for as much as $1,600 an hour." On the same day, Manhattan District Attorney Robert Morgenthau warned both the *News* and the *Post* that the ex-governor was not among Davis's clients. And, yet, the *Post* devoted the whole of its March 27 wood to Spitzer and Kristin. "BUSTED (AGAIN!) SPITZER LINKED TO 2ND CALL GIRL RING . . . EXCLUSIVE." The story—which ran under the interior headline "AND THERE HE HO'S AGAIN"—called Spitzer a "regular patron" of Davis's.

That day, the 27th, Jose Martinez received an e-mail at 4:55 A.M. with the enigmatic subject line "Kristin Davis." He opened it—and read. "I have her black book from the past year: names, phone numbers, likes, dislikes and preferences of each john, money paid. 90 pages approx. 1500 names and numbers!" Giddy over potentially linking Spitzer to Kristin, Jose traded calls and more e-mails with the source, who turned out to be Davis's former booker. "I don't remember where he was calling from," Jose said. "It was one of those pervy South East Asian cities where tourists go for underage sex. I kept asking about Spitzer's name and he'd say, 'I don't know,' 'I'm not into names,' or 'It could be under an alias.' But he definitely suggested that the potential was there. In the end, we thought, 'We'll take our chances.'"

Shortly before 1 P.M., Jose e-mailed the source: "We'll send you a contract that promises exclusivity to the New York *Daily News* and allows us to take a look and verify things under a confidentiality agreement. So if for some reason we cannot verify or decide not to use the information we can pay you a kill fee. I just need to connect with you again."

At 1:03 P.M., the source replied, "Sure send over the agreement. Under promise and over deliver is my motto. You will get more than I quoted." The *News* then exchanged a $5,000 Internet transfer for the "black book," conveyed over Google Docs. Spitzer was not among its 2,000-plus names, but there were plenty of "lawyers, doctors, venture capitalists, out-of-town businessmen and even a professional poker player" among its pages. Together, the *News* team cold-called johns. "Not me, man, no way. I've never paid for it in my life, and I'm a good-looking guy," said Dominick, while another pleaded innocent: "If you knew my wife then you would understand why I wouldn't want to make a habit of going to call girls." On the 28th, the *News* published the book's "secrets," including the booker's annotations about Kristin's johns: who haggled, who liked conversation, who refused to pull down his pants, who objected to his "Hawaiian dream girl" not being blond, who left when overcome with guilt. And, of course, the *News* "shot down" the *Post*'s report linking Spitzer to Davis. Then, on the 29th, the *News* identified New York Rangers' forward Sean Avery as listed among the book's names. "SEAN AVERY IN HOOKER'S BLACK BOOK."

Predictably, the *Post* didn't endure the barrage quietly. On the 31st the tabloid published a rebuttal under the headline "RANGER A STRANGER, MADAM SAYS . . . ICE TALE MELTING," quoting Davis, through her lawyer, as saying Avery was not among her clients and the *News* had gotten it all wrong. Meanwhile, the ensuing sentence noted, "Avery was flying to New York last night to consult with [his attorney] about a possible lawsuit against the *Daily News*."

And so it went—on and on—through April, until the 28th, when the Audit Bureau of Circulation released its circulation report for the six months ending March 31, 2008. In New York, the data revealed an outright tabloid dogfight. The *News* notched a mere 649-paper margin[1] of victory over the *Post*, slim yet still enough for it to trumpet the triumph: "NY DAILY NEWS NO. 1: THANK YOU!" The *Post*, unsurprisingly, remained mum. Year-over-year, the *News* had shed 2.09 percent of weekday circulation, and the *Post* 3.07 percent.[*]

Then another story, this one incidentally also involving a perfidious politician, wiped the slate clean and moved the tabloid battleground to Washington, D.C. The story started small but mushroomed as the *News* and the *Post* untangled a web of deceit woven over many years—and yet one that, ultimately, proved gossamer once New York City's dueling tabloids set their runners to unraveling it. And this story, when the final word was written and the wood digitally cast, turned out to be even more sordid than Spitzer's.

---

[*] The figures, while a decline from the October 1, 2006–March 31, 2007, period, were larger than those both tabloids reported for the six-month period concluding September 30, 2007. This was likely a result of the perennial seasonal decline the *News* and the *Post* experienced most, if not every, year during the April 1–September 30 period. Fewer people bought the paper in the summer when commuter sales dropped because of vacations.

15

⠿

"What to Tell Kids When Daddy Has Two Families"

Daily News headline, May 8, 2008

ON THURSDAY, MAY 1, a four-term congressman from New York state's 13th District* was pulled over by Alexandria, Virginia, police at 12:05 A.M. after running a red light in the Washington, D.C., suburb, then jailed for driving while intoxicated. Vito John Fossella Jr. was forty-three, an Ivy League graduate, and a father of three with eighteen years of marriage to his record. He was affectionately known by his constituents as "Don Vito," although as New York City's lone Capitol Hill Republican, he faced a challenging reelection that November. Now, that reelection was further complicated and events set in motion that, behind the scenes, would constitute one of the *News* and *Post's* greatest battles.

Within hours of Vito's release from Alexandria Sheriff's Department custody, the *News* and the *Post* were on the move, although the former in far more force than the latter. It was never really known on the *News* side why the *Post* dragged its heels on Vito's arrest. One source said the *Post's* political editor was preoccupied with the Indiana and North Carolina Democratic primaries on May 6 and determined something to the effect of "We'll come back to it after the weekend . . . if it's still news." Some believed the *Post's* Manhattan bias and neglect of the city's outer boroughs, and particularly Staten Island, was in play. Still others blamed the *Post's* Republican prejudice for its inaction. But regardless of the reason, the tabloid would soon come to regret the decision.

---

* The 13th Congressional district comprises Staten Island and parts of Brooklyn.

While the *Post* covered the story by phone, the *News* allocated resources. Reporters door-knocked Fossella's family home in the Great Kills section of Staten Island and his parents' house a few miles away. The D.C. Bureau worked its sources on Capitol Hill, and by Friday, reporter Rich Schapiro and photographer Andrew Theodorakis were on the ground in Virginia. A day later, I joined them there.

Rich and "Theo's" early presence in the Capitol area proved particularly decisive. On Friday—just as Fossella acknowledged his "error" and vowed during a 1 P.M. presser at a Staten Island Hilton not to resign—Rich obtained court documents providing one all-important detail of his arrest thirty-six hours earlier: the name of the woman—Laura Fay—into whose custody he'd been released.

Smartly, Rich and Theo quickly motored to Fay's home, three miles from the arrest location* in a development called Cameron Station. They staked it out. About 4:30 P.M., a silver Ford Escape Hybrid SUV with Virginia plates exited the garage onto a cul-de-sac called Grimm Drive. Then—in a quirky, fateful moment that gave the *News* a commanding lead over the *Post* for days—a blonde woman exited the SUV and manually closed her automatic garage door. This inexplicable act allowed Theo a crucial opportunity to shoot photos and Rich to ask her about her having retrieved Vito from the drunk tank at 7:39 A.M. the day before.

"Oh, I'm sorry," the woman replied. "I don't accept solicitations."

"No," Rich protested. "I'm a reporter from New York."

"I'm sorry, but I have to go."

The woman, clad in hot-pink track shorts and a black tank top (an important detail in the days to come), reentered the vehicle and drove away. It was the last time anyone from the *News*, *Post*, or any media outlet would see her for sixteen days.

May 3, 2008

Saturday's papers evinced disparate priorities. The *Post* allotted Vito eleven inches on page 7 and hit the high notes—minus the name "Laura Fay." "'VINO' VITO WAS BADLY BLOTTO" roared its headline. The *News* ran twice that copy and devoted the bottom three-quarters of its wood to the story, using the same play on words as the *Post*: "VINO FOSSELLA! S.I. CONGRESSMAN BEGS FORGIVENESS FOR DRUNKEN DRIVING AT TWICE THE LEGAL LIMIT." Fossella's mug shot accompanied a *News* tease to

---

* Seminary Road and Library Lane.

pages 4 and 5, although aside from having named Fay, it didn't manage any overt victories over the *Post*. Instead, both papers included a rough accounting of Vito's movements, as known to that point, on Wednesday: Irish Prime Minister Bertie Ahern's address to Congress in the morning; White House reception for the Super Bowl–winning Giants at 3 P.M., evening reception for twenty-four supporters; then, finally, a fateful drive to meet a "friend" at an unknown location ending in arrest.

Only the *Times* and the *Staten Island Advance* reported a tantalizing morsel—and one that both papers cited to the police report: Vito told his arresting officer, Jamie Gernatt, that he was rushing home to take his daughter to the hospital, even though his actual daughter, four-year-old Rowan, was later found to be safely at home on Staten Island. Fossella was publicly known to have two sons and one daughter with his wife, Mary Pat.

On Saturday, the *News* staked out seemingly every home on Staten Island where someone named Fossella was listed on the deed. The *Post*, preoccupied with a national story about then-candidate Barack Obama's spiritual advisor Jeremiah Wright's having "stolen" a parishioner's wife, didn't deploy a single asset in the field. In fact, the *Post* wouldn't publish another Fossella story for an astounding three days, until Tuesday, May 6, by which time the *News* had an almost insurmountable—key word being "almost"—lead and Col Allan was reportedly having a conniption at his weekend editor's news judgment.

I arrived Saturday afternoon on Grimm Drive to a suburban tableau— three-story connected townhomes with just a whiff of the Charleston southern Gothic: arched front doors, half-moon windows, ornate shutters, and extravagant landscaping around brick-paved sidewalks. I came armed with the photo obtained on Friday by Rich and Theo. The *News* hadn't published it—uncertain whether the blonde was, in fact, Laura Fay. My job was to gain the confirmation needed to publish. Door-knocks were made. Weekend gardening hobbyists interrupted, soccer moms accosted— and questioned. And yet only one neighbor talked, and she couldn't be 100 percent certain the woman whose image I produced on my cell phone was, indeed, Fay. A leafy branch obscured the subject's face and prohibited definitive identification. But the neighbor did offer this as consolation: Laura was a divorcée, and her ex-husband also lived at Cameron Station. Moreover, Fay, she added, lived alone with a daughter around three years of age. My source didn't give a name—and I didn't press for it. Fay remained an enigma—a ghost who'd collected a boozy congressman from the cops. Intriguing, but the story was still the DWI.

That afternoon, Tom DeFrank—the *News'* D.C. bureau chief—asked Susan Del Percio, Fossella's "crisis management pro," about Laura Fay. He pointedly asked how Vito knew her—and whether they had had an affair. "They're old friends," Del Percio replied—not really a denial—before elaborating on the circumstances giving rise to that "friendship." Fay and Fossella, she said, had met five years earlier when Fay had worked as a congressional liaison officer for the Air Force. An obscure Wales government document posted online added texture, listing Vito and Laura as guests at a dinner held in honor of then–House Speaker Dennis Hastert on July 27, 2003. As the *Advance*, which also unearthed that document, noted in its Sunday paper, "the event took place during the week that Fossella took a trip to England, Denmark, the Netherlands and Spain with Hastert and seven other House members to discuss the Iraq War with U.S. allies."

Key points and potential headline fodder emerged: Why did Fossella call Fay in the wee hours of Thursday morning when his chief of staff, Thomas Quaadman, also lived in Alexandria? Why did Fay live so close to the arrest location? Was she the "friend" whom Vito said at his Friday press conference he was going to meet? Why did Vito tell Officer Gernatt he was rushing to see his daughter when his daughter, Rowan, was home—and in bed? And why hire a crisis pro in the first place? Gittrich called me around 5 P.M. on Grimm Drive and relayed the results of DeFrank's interview, sneeringly referring to Del Percio as "some GOP operative." "We need to find Vito," he said. "He's nowhere on Staten Island. Head to his Alexandria home and ask residents if they've ever seen him with a woman. Show 'em the Fay photo."

I complied, but the neighbors there proved as recalcitrant as those on Grimm Drive. Also, Vito's home looked as desolate as Fay's. Then it was back to Cameron Station and an address the library unearthed for one Guy Shoaf—the ex-husband referenced by my Grimm Drive source. A quick door-knock evoked a pregnant middle-aged woman clothed in summer wear and a scowl. She may have been approached earlier, or she may have anticipated a reporter's arrival. Regardless, she preempted my pitch with a strident "No comment." After a day of failure, I'd had enough: "Look, I'm not here looking for scandal for scandal's sake. This man is an elected official, and don't you think his constituents deserve to know if he's fathered a love child?"

It was the first time I—or anyone with whom I'd discussed the story—had said it. It just slipped out, as if my subconscious had been puzzling over the problem, and the angst elicited by another angry face had teased the conclusion from the muddle of my mind. I didn't even know if it was true. But the remark's shock value had the intended effect. The woman took my card and agreed to give it to Mr. Shoaf. It was as close to a victory as I'd managed all day. After that, I swung by Fay's house for a runner's nightcap. Nothing had changed, or at least I judged as much after staring at the house for ten minutes. I was calculating whether the curtains had moved, some minute shift in their arrangement, anything to indicate inhabitance in the interim since my last departure. It was a mental errand I would repeat over and over again in the days and weeks to come and always with the same results. Everything was just as I had left it.

May 4, 2008

The following day, Sunday, the *News* did everything but report that Laura and Vito were lovers. In a pair of stories teased on the wood—under Big Brown's Kentucky Derby victory and abreast Roger Clemens's still-unfolding extramarital affair with Mindy McCready—the *News* rolled out its prior day's reporting on Fossella and the retired Air Force lieutenant colonel. The narrative was shifting, you could tell, from one of a congressman busted for DWI to one about a politician who had a mystery gal pal in the D.C. suburbs: "THE DWI CONGRESSMAN AND LT. COL. LAURA . . . PAGE 2," read the *News'* suggestive tease. The *Post*, meanwhile, remained devoid of Vito stories.

Things moved fast that morning: *Daily News* editor-in-chief Martin Dunn demanded a "full court press," as morning assignment editor Marie McGovern told me. Edgar Sandoval hopped a flight to Phoenix to brace Laura Fay's brother. Joe Gould continued his vigil at Fossella's home on Staten Island. When he knocked around 10 A.M., a man later described as wearing electrician's clothing answered and said, "This is private property. You should know better than to ring doorbells early on Sunday morning." Calls were made to Guy Shoaf's mother in Florida, who said: "Let me guess what you want to talk to me about," before hanging up. The *Post* was still in the wind when I returned to Grimm Drive. The Fay photo had, again, gone unpublished for fear of a mistaken ID, although the *News* was no longer willing to tolerate neighbors' uncertainty. Martin demanded an up-or-down answer.

I started with a guy a few doors down who had refused to examine the image on Saturday—but hadn't told me, outright, to fuck off—a polite reply that left room for a second approach. "If I look at the photo will you park someplace else?" he asked. I was parked in front of his townhouse.

I said I would "go to Ohio" if he helped. He gave the photo a look. "It's tough," he said. "That branch in front of her face isn't helping you. But I've seen Laura in that outfit. She's a runner and I could swear I've seen those shorts."

"Take another look," I said, suddenly Lennie Briscoe from "Law & Order"; the source was a frightened witness at a line-up, trying hard to make the ID. "I can't be sure," he said. "Best guess, it's her."

From there, I returned to the compliant neighbor/source from Saturday and gave my Briscoe routine an encore: "Take your time," I said soothingly. "Look closely. There's no rush." She grimaced. She strained. She held the photo up close to her eyes and studied it with care.

"It's probably her," she said.

"Would you run it?"

"What did he tell you?"

"Your neighbor? He said it was her shorts. He recognized them, said it made sense she would wear that because Laura's a runner. He also thought the face was the same."

"I'd run it."

"Good enough."

I called it in to the desk, collected plaudits . . . and miscellaneous field scuttlebutt. Mary Pat, Fossella's wife, had returned to the family's Great Kills home with an overnight bag slung over one shoulder and two of her three kids in tow. Joe Gould approached. Mary Pat hustled her kids up the front steps. One tripped. Mary Pat blamed Joe. "You should be ashamed of yourself!" she cried. "I don't know how you sleep at night." Joe's reply: "I didn't create this situation." The *News* would write in Monday's story that Mary Pat "berated reporters." Meanwhile, the *News'* local freelance shooter, Elisa, and I settled in for stakeout sun. Twice, we saw a silver SUV with plates beginning with "K" around Grimm Drive. Twice, we didn't mark the vehicle early or fast enough to see the driver or effectively pursue. Then came a tan Honda Civic with Maryland plates. It was almost 5 P.M. This time, there was no mistaking its driver.

"Who are you with?" I asked.

"Your direct competition," answered the man. Ron was middle-aged, burly, and a *Post* stringer. My ambition for an early civilized dinner evaporated with his arrival. Meanwhile, Austin Fenner arrived outside Fossella's Staten Island home. The *Post* was finally in the game, perhaps prompting Mary Pat to tie up the family St. Bernard outside the front door. The irony of a canine courier known for bringing brandy to the distressed guarding a boozehound's family escaped the notice of neither the *News* nor the *Post*.

At 9:30 P.M., Ron spoke to his desk, then told me, "They said, 'If you'll say *kumbaya*, we'll say *kumbaya*.'" I said, "*Kumbaya*." A handshake made it official, but I still followed his tail lights out of Cameron Station, then double-backed briefly to the house. Out-of-town jobs of consequence and foreign freelancers made me nervous.

May 5, 2008

On Monday, the *News* finally showed its hand, publishing the first photo of Laura Fay—not an enormous scoop for news value but magnified by the *Post*'s not having had it. "This is the first look at the mystery woman whom Rep. Vito Fossella (R-S.I.) called for help after he was charged with drunken driving in Virginia," read the story's lede. The *News* also added a Michael Daly column full of moral outrage. The *Post* continued its two-day string of lama-like silence. Heavy advantage to the *News*.

I arrived on Grimm Drive to find Ron from the *Post*, angry neighbors, and no Laura Fay. The house was the same as the night before, the same as on Saturday when I'd first arrived. If someone was coming in the night, I couldn't tell. Sunday night, before leaving, I'd meditated on the curtains for fifteen minutes, then placed a tiny wedge of paper at foot level, between the storm door and its frame. Now, I found the paper in the same place as I'd left it and the curtains the same position as when I'd departed.

Vito, meanwhile, looked like a fighter tiring in the late rounds. The *News* obtained Guy Shoaf and Laura Fay's divorce documents from an Arlington County court. The marriage was inked in 1995 in Honolulu, dissolved when Guy filed on December 26, 2003, five months after Lieutenant Colonel Laura accompanied Rep. Vito on the Air Force junket to Europe that July. More compelling: The docs stated the couple had no children when they'd stopped living together. Conclusions: If Laura Fay's child—the one referenced by Grimm Drive neighbors—was not Guy Shoaf's, whose was it? Or did she give birth to Guy Shoaf's child *after* they stopped cohabitating? The *News* dug into Guy Shoaf's Accurint, calling all listed family members and known associates. Tuesday's story would quote "a source familiar with the proceedings" as describing the Fay/Shoaf divorce as a "bad breakup."

Meanwhile, the *News* dispatched a runner to Florida to pressure Shoaf's mother. A concurrent search for the Fay kid's birth certificate in Virginia was stymied by local privacy laws. Later that day, I would indirectly be made part of the Shoaf-mother gambit.

Other developments: A D.C. blogger filled in the missing portion of Vito's Wednesday night with an online post stating he had seen Vito and a pal drinking at a local pub called Logan's Tavern, the friend so drunk he "belly-flopped" onto a table. The desk ordered me to Logan's. I told them the *Post* was on-scene at Grimm Drive. The desk, instead, deployed Richard Sisk from the D.C. bureau. Sisk was welcomed at Logan's and given the straight dope. Vito and a friend named "Brian" had acted very poorly.

Back in New York: Vito's crisis flack held a presser. A *Staten Island Advance* reporter went for the jugular: "Is Congressman Fossella the father of Laura Fay's child?" Susan Del Percio replied, "That question is inappropriate and demeaning." The *Advance* responded, "But you didn't really answer the question." Susan Del Percio stood firm: "That's my answer." It wasn't a denial. During the day, the *Post* replaced Ron on Grimm Drive with staffers and quasi-staffers from New York: Lorena Mongelli and perma-lance shooter James Messerschmidt. I was joined by Anthony DelMundo.

Meanwhile, the *News* executed a 5:30 P.M. door-knock of Guy Shoaf's mother in Florida. She answered and cried, "They're here! Oh my God! They're here!" and slammed the door. The desk was pleased. The elderly woman's response indicated potential for a wedge play on Guy Shoaf. *Come across and we'll leave your ma alone.* We proceeded around 7:30. Anthony and I approached Shoaf's home. We found him tending a meager lawn. He wore shorts and a weary expression. He greeted my introduction curtly and as if rehearsed: "I'm not talking." Anthony shot him from our car.

"How 'bout off the record?"

He sighed.

"Is Laura's kid yours?"

"No. I don't know who the father is."

"Okay. Is Ms. Fay having an affair with Mr. Fossella?"

"I honestly don't know. I broke up with my wife five years ago. I've remarried and have a pregnant wife. I want to move on. I don't have anything to do with [Fay] anymore."

"But you live a mile away?"

"Coincidence. You know, it hurts me to hear about this stuff, but all I know is what I'm reading online. I'm sorry. I just don't have anything for you."

"Guy, why did you leave your wife?"

"I'm not discussing it."

"What happened in Britain in 2003?"

"I can't tell you. I won't tell you."

"Our electorate deserves to know who this man is."

He shook his head.

"This is a civic matter."

"I don't care."

"Guy, this man stole your wife! Don't you want some measure of . . ."

"I don't want anything but for you to leave!"

I got back into the car. Guy Shoaf followed and spoke through the driver's-side window: "My father is in intensive care. I'd hate to think you sent a reporter all the way from New York, but my mother is shook up and has a lot going on. Can't you lay off?"

Plans coming to fruition. Oswald's plans. Gittrich's plans. I replied, "We'll see," and phoned the desk. Oswald greeted Guy Shoaf's earnest entreaty with ruthlessness.

"Tell him we'll leave 'ma' alone if he goes on the record. *'The kid's not mine.'* That's all I want."

I relayed Oswald's response and raised the possibility of a prolonged stakeout of his mother in Florida. Guy Shoaf looked like he'd been hit with a shovel.

"No," he replied. "I don't want to have my name connected to this."

"That's impossible, Guy. They've got the divorce filing. Just put that one quote on the record and we'll pull our reporter from Florida. It'll be easier for everyone, especially your mom."

Guy shook his head: "I don't want to be associated with it. I'm moving on."

"Are you sure? One quote: 'The kid's not mine.' That'll get it done."

"I can't."

"O-kay," I said, and Guy Shoaf walked away and went into his home. He looked dazed. He'd left the mower on his lawn. Silently, I wondered if Oswald would actually follow through on his threat of a prolonged stakeout of the man's mother out of spite. Meanwhile, the *Post*—and Fay's home— looked just as I'd left them. Everyone knocked off around 10 P.M. I'd been in Alexandria for three days. It felt like three weeks.

May 6, 2008

On Tuesday, the *News* wooded with a massive headline: "VITO'S WILD NIGHT. FOSSELLA AND PAL BOUNCED FROM BAR HOURS AFTER POL'S ARREST. SHOCKING DETAILS PAGES 4–5." The headline ran abreast of a photo of a scantily clad Gisele Bündchen beaming at the Met Gala: "STARRY NIGHT."*

The *Post*, too, finally scored, publishing a fifteen-inch mini-profile of Fay's life as contextualized by Vito's career. It quoted unnamed relatives and provided substance to the silhouette of her mysterious persona. Key quotes and details to emerge from the piece: Fay's marriage to Guy Shoaf was her second; it ended when Shoaf, an Air Force urologist, "ditched her for another woman." Fay's child was born two years later. Fay retired from the Air Force in 2006 because she found it "too challenging to be both a mother and a colonel." That information was sourced to "long, frank talks with family."

One relative also told the *Post*, "Fay was always 'vague' about who fathered the child."

The story ran under Lorena's byline and did not include taglines, a frightening development because Lorena was my Grimm Drive counterpart. If she'd gotten Fay's relatives from our shared position, it called into question my effort of the prior day. I am asked as much by morning assignment editor Marie McGovern, who tactfully couched the question in terms of whether Fay's relatives are Alexandria-based. I assured her Lorena was only momentarily out of my sight after her arrival from New York around 2 P.M. on Grimm Drive—then again for twenty minutes when I door-knocked Guy Shoaf in the evening. (Lorena later told me her byline was incidental to quotes obtained via phone from New York. Jeane MacIntosh was the mover, she explained, an ominous development. It was Jeane "Mac" who had brought me so much Leyritz and Miss New Jersey pain.)

The *Post* story—and the quoted "Fay family source"—was also alarming to the *News* beyond its news value on that particular day. The *News'* runners had crisscrossed the country for almost a week, unsuccessfully hunting a Fay relative who would talk—so much so that some on its side now grumbled the *Post's* source was a fiction dreamed up by Col Allan to stanch the *Post's* bleeding. It was a ridiculous presumption founded on the *News'* failure, despite the astounding resources the paper had allocated. Also, both tabloids employed the same Accurints, containing the same relatives/associates, etc. Thus the logical leap underpinning the theoretical conspiracy: *"Why have they found one, and we can't?"*

---

* A great headline, although technically inaccurate. The Van Gogh portrait of that name was displayed then—as it is now—at Manhattan's other big art museum, the Museum of Modern Art.

Decisive action was demanded—more reporters to door-knock more Fay family addresses around the country. On that day, *News* runners performed door-knocks in five states. One would unsuccessfully door-knock Fay's sister in Washington state. Another flew to Spencer, Iowa (pop. 11,500), for a futile, second attempt at locating Fay's brother after Edgar's original attempt in Phoenix. Christina Boyle and photographer Julia Xanthos flew to St. Cloud in central Minnesota to door-knock Fay's parents. No one answered. Finally, Oren Yaniv traveled to Colorado Springs, where the *News* believed Fay's first ex-husband—a Dale Zeller—resided. But an early-evening door-knock proved fruitless, there, as well; and, moreover, Zeller's home seemed devoid of recent habitation. A Realtor's sign decorated its front lawn. Oren left a voicemail for the listed agent and resolved to ask for Zeller's forwarding address if the Realtor called him back.

On Capitol Hill, Vito emerged for the first time since Friday's presser. Wearing a charcoal suit and a sheepish expression, he entered the House chamber with hands jammed in his pockets for a morning hearing. Over the next forty-five minutes, he received handshakes and hugs from a half-dozen GOP colleagues. Richard Sisk spied the affair.

Meanwhile, behind the scenes, the *News* dug for dirt—and fresh Vito photos.

Andrew "Theo" Theodorakis staked out Vito's legislative office at the Rayburn Building, south of the U.S. Capitol, and ambushed him in a hallway after Vito returned from Capitol Hill. "Don" Vito donned a stupid "how ya doin'" grin. Theo went click, click, click . . . *paparazzi* style. Everyone wondered about the Rayburn Building's porous security.

Meanwhile, Rich Schapiro, back in D.C., staked out the high-rise building in which sources had told the *News* Vito rented a condo from his uncle, Frank Fossella, an ex–New York City Councilman known around Staten Island as "Uncle Frank." The *News* believed the condo might be the Fay–Fossella love nest. Rich braced incoming/outgoing lobbyists and bureaucrats. No one had seen—or admitted to seeing—the young couple.

On Grimm Drive, Lorena Mongelli was coolly detached. James Messerschmidt was going bananas. Shit was seriously rolling downhill or, in his case, down I-95. Col Allan had now seen the *News'* photo of Laura Fay multiple times. The *News* kept running it, day after day, knowing the *Post* didn't have it and playing the exclusive angle for all it was worth.

"I am so fucked," Messerschmidt kept repeating.

Otherwise, the *Post* moved stealthily and out of sight. The tabloid fog of war was thick—and those with the *News*, already edgy, felt serious heebee-jeebies. We knew the *Post* was on it; we just didn't know where or what its runners were doing.

May 7, 2008

Wednesday provided insight into the *Post*'s movements, although the larger picture remained shrouded behind unnamed Fay family sources. The *Post* story ran under the headline "OMERTA ON VITO 'BABY TALK,'" and Jeane Mac's byline. It quoted the anonymous Fay relative as describing a frantic series of phone calls from Fay to her family, "urging them not to talk to the media about the identity of her baby's daddy." Additional sources—these political—described Vito as making his own "hush-hush" calls to Republican Party bigwigs to "gauge their support amid the swirling scandal."

The *Post*'s story engendered obvious logical leaps . . . and more speculative grumbling: The *Post* was breaking the cardinal rule. The source was bogus. The comments were just vague and generalized enough, yet still sufficiently incisive, as to constitute a scoop. Cooler, more cogent minds at the *News* believed otherwise—and they were the ones truly nervous about what this unnamed source could mean in the days to come.

The *News* responded, in its story, with innuendo and chains of logic. Vito told his arresting officer he was going to Grimm Drive to pick up his sick daughter. Ergo, Fay's child must be his. It was a logical thesis, although a cheap approach by conventional news standards. Still, in lieu of substantive reporting providing a smoking gun, it was all the *News* had.

On the 6th, a man visiting Fay's Grimm Drive home told Lorena and me that Fay was in Coral Gables, Florida. He said he was there to water her plants. The *News* ran his quote on the 7th, adding intrigue to an already compelling "Fay in the wind" narrative. Over prior days, the Pentagon had revealed that Fay was an intelligence officer by trade. The fact/detail provided tremendous "we're chasing a spook" fodder among stir-crazy runners marooned on Grimm Drive. Many fake mustache/wig jokes were thrown about.

"Are you Laura Fay? I'm not Laura Fay, but how can I be sure you're not?"

Messerschmidt, alone, did not enjoy the humor. On Wednesday, the 7th, he got into his car, muttering. Lorena asked him where he was going. "I don't know," he replied. "I just have to do something." Later, he confessed to driving aimlessly around Cameron Station, as if a Laura Fay photo would somehow materialize on the side of the road.

It was unfair. The seeds of Messerschmidt's distress—Rich and Theo's photo—had been sown long before his arrival in Virginia. The *News*, once again and mercilessly, ran the only Laura Fay photo in circulation. Col "Pot" Allan, I was told, was gearing up to give unspecified scapegoats the "drawn blinds" treatment back in New York.*

Both the *News* and the *Post* wooded that day with Hillary Clinton's North Carolina primary defeat. The *News'* headline read: "HIL NEEDS A MIRACLE." "CLINTON CRUSHED IN N.C., LIMPS TO INDIANA . . . VOWS TO FIGHT JUBILANT OBAMA TO BITTER END." The *Post* was all tabloid bombast: "TOAST!" The *News* devoted a half-wood to Uma Thrurman's stalker's conviction. "CREEP STOLE HER FREEDOM, NOW IT'S HIS TURN TO SUFFER . . . JURORS' DAMNING VERDICT." Vito was knocked to inside pages.

Publicly, the story was building to a crescendo. It just *felt* that way— even on Grimm Drive. Just before 2:30 P.M., the *News* posted a story to its website reporting that Vito was "preparing to make an announcement— perhaps as early as today—about his drunken driving arrest in Virginia last week." A classic *Daily News* expository second-graph then quoted a Republican source as elaborating, "I think we can all surmise what it's going to be about." No presser occurred. The *Post* later reported that Vito had had an eleventh-hour change of heart. And, yet, behind the scenes, the *News* and the *Post* relentlessly drove Vito to that same, ultimately inevitable, climax.

Vito spent Wednesday projecting calm at his eldest son's Catholic confirmation at Church of St. Clare on Staten Island. *News* and *Post* runners attempted to crash the ceremony, but "security" stationed at the church doors ensured Vito sanctuary. Both papers regrouped and, ultimately, reached their man.

Rich Schapiro and Theo staked out Ronald Reagan Airport in anticipation of Vito's return flight to D.C. Someone was finking Vito's connections. The *News* knew exactly at which terminal to hide and wait. Theo blasted Vito . . . again. Rich gave him the TMZ treatment. Vito was all grim silence before hurrying to his office in the Rayburn Building. There, Kevin Fasick of the *Post* lay in wait. He got the same response.

Back in Great Kills, Mary Pat played driveway basketball with all three Fossella kids. The tabloid "Joes"—Gould for the *News*, Mollica for the *Post*—requested comment between points. The "no comment" from a fed-up Mary Pat was as awkward as her jump shot.

---

* Numerous reporters have described the peculiar manner in which the *Post* handled failure. They said they would be called into an editor's office to find the blinds drawn and the room shaded aside from slats of light. They would be questioned about their competence—and the failing moves they had made that prompted the meeting. Often, screaming occurred.

Meanwhile, the *News* went back at Fay's relatives and, again, got nothing. In Colorado Springs, Oren finally reached the Realtor named on the sign in front of Dale Zeller's old house. The Realtor then reached out to Zeller, Fay's first ex, on Oren's behalf. Zeller declined comment. He was only one Fay source/relative/associate to do so among many.

Atypically, the story was advanced by newsroom phone work and tabloid verve, rather than running. Larry McShane wrote around three Fossella photos that were all snapped on different dates circa 2003–2004. "LET'S PLAY 'IS VITO FOSSELLA WEARING HIS WEDDING RING TODAY,'" blared the eventual headline. Larry's lede: "Now you see it, now you don't."

More *Daily News* innuendo came courtesy of 2003 Euro junket sources: "When the congressional delegation made stops in Britain, Denmark, the Netherlands and Spain, Shoaf and Fossella often disappeared together," three sources on the trip said. "She wasn't around as much as I expected her to be," another source added. "He wasn't around much, either."

The *Post*, meanwhile, let Mary Pat's pals do the talking for her. A "source close to the family" told the tabloid the scorned wife "was blindsided by allegations he may have fathered a love child, and is unlikely to stay at his side if it turns out to be true."

On Grimm Drive, time ticked slowly. Five days in front of an empty townhouse is a lot of time. Sometimes, I swore I could see the curtains move if I stared at them long—and hard—enough.

May 8, 2008

On Thursday, the chickens came home to roost, for Vito, the *News*, for the *Post*—for everyone connected to the story. It was D-Day, or Denouement Day, on Capitol Hill.

That morning, Vito appeared on the House floor for procedure and penance. Rich Schapiro and a *Post* runner staked him out. A teary-eyed Vito huddled with the House chaplain and shared unheard words. Rich fielded a fortuitous phone call from an unknown source who had been following his bylined work and asked the city desk, on a whim, for his cell phone number. The source was transferred by the desk to Rich's cell. The source said, "I think I have something you might want." Rich heard out the offer. It was *important*. Rich told the *Post* runner, "Peace out!" and jetted from the Capitol Rotunda.

Meanwhile, noon arrived like white water gushing through a busted dam. Vito held the anticipated presser and admitted what everyone in the world had known for four days. "*The kid is mine.*" "I have had a relationship with Laura Fay, with whom I have a three-year-old daughter."

The next day, the *Post* drew the obvious comparison—and noted, a single, essential distinction: "Fossella—sounding an awful lot like the disgraced Eliot Spitzer—apologized 'to the people I love' for the 'enormous pain' [he] caused by [his] 'personal failings and imperfections.' Unlike Client 9, however, Fossella refused to resign."

The *Post* also played the Catholic guilt card, reporting on Friday that Vito had been moved to action by his son's confirmation ceremony on Wednesday at St. Clare's.

"His whole family was there," a friend told the tabloid. "Seeing what it was doing [to them], it just really hit home."

Following the presser, both the *News* and the *Post* leveraged their websites in ways the public had seldom, if ever, seen, posting stories in real time, building on the *Times'* use of the platform for Ashley Dupre. The *Post* ran a piece at 3:02 P.M. on Vito's admission. The *News* ran three stories: at 9:03 P.M., 10:06 P.M., and 10:08 P.M. Exclusive details were held in abeyance. But things were changing, if you had time to note as much.

On Grimm Drive, Gittrich called with a weighty request: "A rumor is circulating. The *Post* purchased a photo of the Fay kid for $5,000," he told me. "See if you can get it out of whomever you're with out there."

It was a big ask, a favor for which I would owe. It also put Lorena and Messerschmidt in a tough spot. I'm not sure I would have given the straight dope if our roles were reversed. In retrospect, both were honest. In retrospect, Lorena possibly hedged and played it the only way she could. Messerschmidt swore he didn't know. He swore the *News* and the *Post* had both been infiltrated by turncoats covertly working for the other side.

"How the fuck do you guys hear about these things?" he cried. "There are rats everywhere! I know it!"

Lorena told me the *Post* had been working the day before to purchase a photo of Fay, but not the child.

"I know that was in the works," she said. "But I don't know anything about the kid."

I called Gittrich and relayed the dirt.

"Oh, it's Fay," he said, obviously relieved. "Okay, thanks."

When Lorena had spoken, she had been looking at the townhouse—and not at me.

May 9, 2008

On Friday, Vito's dishonor, coupled with Laura Fay's Christmas card list, begat improbable, stinging defeat for the *News*. "OH, BABY!" roared the

Post headline in 140-point type over a photo of Laura Fay nuzzling her love child. "FIRST PHOTO . . . Here's the first peek at the adorable baby who has left the political career of Rep. Vito Fossella on life support . . . Laura Fay pictured here on a Christmas card." The child, who finally had a name (Natalie), looked happy. She had no inkling of the maelstrom that was her birthright.

I checked my cell phone. A text from Lorena, time-stamped at 11:33 P.M., noted that she had been "mistaken," about the *Post* photo. She wrote, "It *was* the Fay kid they were after."

In total, the *Post* published three stories and two opinion pieces. One of the former was headlined, "'POP' GOES THE WEASEL VITO," and quoted "several sources with Staten Island ties" as saying Vito had long had a "wandering eye in Washington." One source outright called him "a horn-dog for years." A second story cast Laura Fay as a wanton Jezebel. It stated that her first husband, Dale Zeller, whom she'd married in 1984, discovered her cheating from a love letter to a boyfriend. Dale, a by-then-retired Air Force lieutenant colonel, didn't press adultery charges via courtmartial. Laura, transferred to Hawaii, met Guy Shoaf—and they both cheated on each other, according to the story. Enter Vito as fly in her web. "HIS MISTRESS HAS HISTORY AS FAY LAY."

The quotes and information were all, once again, quoted to "sources." But if it wasn't crystal clear already, Jeane Mac soon cleared up the mystery. She later told me she had reached Zeller by phone "on her very first day on the story," which was probably Monday—and slowly squeezed him for source-level quotes—*and*, ultimately, talked him into selling her the Natalie Christmas card photo. Zeller was, at that point, living in California. The *News* had sent Oren to Colorado Springs, one home removed from Zeller's current address. Itinerant Zeller's Accurint read like a garage band tour of the west coast: California City, California; Seattle, Washington; Visalia, California; Porterville, California; Central Point, Oregon. By the time Oren had reached Zeller via the Realtor represented on the sign staked into his old front lawn, Dale was ensconced in Jeane's back pocket "and didn't want to talk to anyone else," as Oren later said. Zeller was the *Post* source who had so vexed the *News* and motivated some in its newsroom to conjure a bogeyman. In the final accounting, the *Post*'s victory was attributable to Accurint vagaries and the *News*' choice of the wrong state—and address—to send Oren.

The *News*' wood countered with the photo Rich had obtained the day before from his guardian angel source—the one who had reached him by cell phone inside the Capitol. The photo publicly showed Vito and Laura together for the first time, side-by-side at a bar in Malta during an earlier European congressional junket that had transpired in 2002. "VITO'S GIRL . . . FIRST PICTURE WITH SECRET LOVER WHO HAD HIS DAUGHTER . . . FOSSELLA 'FESSES UP'—PAGES 2–4." It wasn't Natalie. Not even close. But the photo cauterized a potentially catastrophic wound—and maybe even saved Stu Marques's job, by his own admission. Stu would call Rich later that day and confess that the *Post* wood might have spelled curtains for him, if he had not gotten the image.

Back on Grimm Drive, the *Post* proposed throwing in the towel. *If you go home, we'll go home.* I relayed "the deal." Morning assignment editor Marie McGovern yelled her reply: "*No deal!* Martin is on a slow burn this morning over this photo. We *need* to counter."

Marie espoused deductions and plans of attack. The *Post* image looked professional, she said. Rich and Theo would hit every photography studio near Fay's Grimm Drive home, beginning with those closest and then expanding outward in concentric circles. The search's boundaries, she said, were a fifteen-hour day or the Maryland state line, whichever came first.

Shortly afterward, Gittrich called for an update. I asked, "How are you today?" and braced for the response. He said, "I was pissed off this morning, now I'm just aggravated."

It was only the second time I had ever detected a fissure in his impenetrable *sangfroid*. The other had been Sean Bell, Day One. *Just gimme a fucking money quote!* The memory seemed like something he'd said a decade ago.

The photo hadn't come from Alexandria, I noted. It was a craven thing to say—but if there ever was a day to cover your ass, that seemed to be it. Gittrich replied, "I know . . . California."

I asked how he knew; he said, "Don't worry about it."

Later that day, Nancy Dillon—my O.J. *confrère* and the *News'* L.A. bureau chief—door-knocked Dale Zeller and convinced him to give the *News* the Laura/Natalie photo. Tangentially, Christina Boyle got Fay's aunt in Ely, Minnesota. Oren got Dale Zeller's daughter in Aurora, Colorado. She called Fay "a wonderful stepmother" and "still my friend." After a week of silence, Fay's family suddenly was talkative.

But it all felt like too little, too late. The *Post* wood felt like the end, the zinger to conclude a long debate, the field goal with no time on the clock, the final trick to make the opening bid. And yet . . . the *News* would neither countenance the *Post*'s victory nor concede defeat. The tabloid, losing circulation, adopted radical measures. Gittrich ordered Joe Gould to shadow Mary Pat. On Saturday, he chased her to the First Communion party of her and Vito's goddaughter. (Vito was absent and believed to be no longer living at home.) Joe then tailed her to her son's Little League game. On Sunday, May 11, Mother's Day, both Gould and Mollica chased Mary Pat to her son's soccer game.

"They're at a soccer game?!" Oswald howled. "I want every detail! I want to know when she cheers! When she hugs the kid! I want to know if she gives him a juice box! Get it all!"

Gould called me after the game. He spoke as one who had grown cynical and disillusioned. He told me, "[Oswald's] insane and although we tried to hide so [Mary Pat] wouldn't see us, she eventually did. And when she did see us, she was flabbergasted! She couldn't believe we were there watching her watch her son's soccer game!"

Mary Pat, predictably, declined comment: "MOM'S THE WORD FOR VITO FOSSELLA'S WIFE."

One day later, Gould experienced a second incident that shook him. *News* runner John Lauinger staked out Fossella's family home in Great Kills. A neighbor, whom the *News* suspected as acting on Mary Pat's orders, informed him where Vito was crashing—perhaps out of spite, perhaps just to get him off the block. The neighbor said Vito was sleeping in his sister's attic—her home also on Staten Island. Gould and *News* shooter Aaron Showalter headed there. An NYPD precinct commander arrived soon after they did and pointed out illegal deficiencies with Showalter's car and credentials. *Your taillight's broken. Your registration is two months expired.* Ticky-tacky harassment.

"I'm not going to give you a hard time about it . . . but *someone* might," he said, ominously.

The cop left . . . but was replaced by something worse. An SUV pulled up; the driver warned Gould and Showalter that if they set foot on the sister's property, "I'll rip out your eyes."

The SUV then pulled away from their cars, motored up the street and reversed course. It then barreled directly toward Showalter's car, increasing speed, as if to collide with it. The car screeched to a halt before impact. The driver stared balefully—then drove off. The next-day headline: "VITO FOSSELLA CAMPS OUT OVER GARAGE."

Meanwhile, the *News'* Adam Lisberg had remarkably flown to Malta—the island nation located in the Mediterranean Sea, off the coast of Sicily, on which Fossella and Fay's love had bloomed during the 2002 congressional tour. The story ran on Mother's Day—and shocked once it did, not just because of the costs involved but, more notably, because a reading of the story proved it could just as easily have been reported from Staten

Island, or even Grimm Drive. Lisberg's quixotic trek was just that—the essence of what it meant to "get the dateline," or travel to a place for no other reason than wowing readers with exotic geography and having gone to the place in question. Basically, the *News* spent thousands so that Adam could get this quote from a British tourist in Malta's capital: "I don't think it's the kind of place you would come to for romance. It's more for history." Everything else about the 2002 junket came from sources reached inside the States.

On Monday morning, the *Post*'s Perry Chiaramonte relieved Lorena on Grimm Drive. Jeremy Bales had already relieved DelMundo. That evening, Gittrich called for an update. I informed him that a neighbor said he often saw Vito and Laura walking a cocker spaniel together.

"A cocker spaniel?" Gittrich asked. "Is that code?"

"No," I replied.

"What's up with the *Post*?"

"Their reporter is being relieved by a runner from New York."

Gittrich laughed: "Wish I can say the same for you, my friend."

It was May 12, the twelfth day of the Fossella story and my tenth on stakeout on Grimm Drive.

On the 13th, the *News* recalled all the runners it had dispatched across the country to door-knock Fay's family members. In fact, the only runners to remain at post were those stationed on Grimm Drive—me—and those in New York.

Cynicism ran very high in Alexandria—and an order issued for reasons that now escape me to "go back at" Guy Shoaf was met in just those spirits. I remember Perry and me fulfilling the edict, although despite ourselves and after considerable handwringing. We approached the door like two pre-adolescents effecting a ring-and-run. We knocked, counted to five— "1 . . . 2 . . . 3 . . . 4 . . . 5"—then booked back to our cars.

Afterward, Perry got thoughtful: "Do you remember why you got into journalism?"

"To write," I replied. "To go to an event, cover it, come back, and try to describe it as best I could."

Perry got wistful.

"Writing," he said, and the way he had said it sounded like when someone invokes the name of a city in which something immensely personal and important has transpired. *New York. Paris.* Or maybe the name of a friend, or lover, one hasn't seen in a while.

"This is absurd," he finally added, his voice now hardening. "We're only down here to one-up each other. We're in a war no one else cares about."

On Wednesday, May 14, I was finally recalled to New York, although the stakeout survived me. Joe Gould assumed my position on Grimm Drive. On May 18, Laura Fay returned home. Cop cruisers idled just beyond her driveway. She slipped the SUV into the garage and the door clack-clack-clacked behind it. "BACK TO LOVE NEST FOR CHEATIN' CHICK AND BABY." Five days later, on the 23rd, Fay led Joe and Debbie Egan-Chin—and *Post* runner Matthew Nestel and his shooter—on a furious, winding, half-hour chase through Alexandria that paused, if only briefly, at a local strip mall. Cops waited there and placed the tabloid teams on ice while Fay "bolted back onto the road." At this point, I'll let the *Post*'s next-day account describe what happened:

> Fay then made her way to a Lexus dealership near a police precinct house, where she cooled her engine until a female cop in a patrol car came to escort her to the highway. She eventually pulled off at an exit and headed for a nondescript, two-story brick home. Fossella was waiting in the messy yard, his own black Jeep Laredo SUV parked nearby . . . Talking on the phone, Fossella, in a black T-shirt and pants, made his way to Fay, tossed an overstuffed duffel bag into her SUV and got in the front passenger seat. The lovebirds started to head out of town when Fay, realizing they were being tailed, pulled a sharp U-turn. Fossella quickly ducked down in his seat—as Fay tore through town at top speed, blew through red lights and hit the interstate. She wove in and out of lanes and pushed past 85 mph before disappearing into the busy holiday traffic.

During the chase and before Laura Fay met up with Vito Fossella—a chase I was told exceeded 100 miles per hour despite the more conservative figure quoted in the *Post*—Joe and Debbie lost Fay. The *Post* didn't. Nestel and his shooter were present to witness the lovebirds meet. The *Post* scored an exclusive: "ILLICIT LOVERS GO INCOG-VITO." The absence of any Fay/Fossella story on the 15th in the *News* seemed *huge*.

The stakeout continued. Twelve days later, on May 27, Joe and Debbie tailed Fay from Grimm Drive to a park, where they watched and photographed her "walking briskly." Later in the day, the website Politico reported Fossella's having been observed jogging with a "very leggy blond" on Capitol Hill. The *News*' headline on the 28th: "LAURA FAY SPOTTED IN PARK THEN JOGGING WITH VITO FOSSELLA IN D.C.?" The *Post*, luxurious in its prior victory, did not publish a matching story.

On June 15, Father's Day, Gould spied Fay and Natalie strolling their Alexandria nabe. To that point, he'd been on Grimm Drive stakeout for more than a month. Meanwhile, Vito spent the day in Staten Island with his three kids by Mary Pat. When runner Matthew Lysiak requested comment, he got angry. "IT'S DAD DAY, BUT VITO'S NOT WITH VA. GAL PAL & LOVE CHILD."

Five months later, Vito did not seek reelection. Six months after that— on April 17, 2009—he commenced his fulfillment of a four-day prison sentenced handed down for the DWI. The *News* was on hand for his arrival. Its next-day story noted that Fossella would be treated no differently from any other inmate—and would subsist over the period of his penalty on a prison-issued diet like "chicken dogs and boiled succotash."

16

⁂

"Temple of Doom ... Madoff Fleeced Fifth Avenue Synagogue"

New York Post headline, December 21, 2008

AS IS TYPICAL OF WARS, tabloid or otherwise, this one concluded in principle long before the actual declared cessation of hostilities. And, as was typical of Gittrich, he foresaw what was coming before anyone else—and acted accordingly. On May 20 at 6:04 P.M., Gawker published a short— really a journalism gossip item—headlined "DAILY NEWS LOSES 'TABLOID WARS' STAR?" that asked, rather than reported, if Greg Gittrich had resigned from the *News*. "He was the anointed next-in-line to managing editor Stu Marques, supposedly," the story read. "But now . . . ? Is it true?" It was. Ten days later, the *Post* answered Gawker's question with an item in its media column. "Insiders at NBC tell Media Ink that [Greg] is going to be the news editor of the digital operations of NBC Local Media Group, a new job," wrote Keith J. Kelly, who predictably framed the editor's departure in the context of a "morale-challenged *Daily News*." "If you're young and talented and you see someone throwing a life buoy into the water, you better swim to it as fast as you can," Kelly quoted a "former news hand" as saying.

But while Kelly's analysis fit the *Post*'s preferred narrative, it missed the mark. There was no widespread discontent at the *News* in mid-2008. And Gittrich was, as the story noted, the heir apparent to the city desk throne of one of America's most formidable journalistic institutions. NBC.com was, at that point, a repository for wire copy and error-riddled rewrites. More likely, the "Great Gittrich," alone among everyone, spied the catastrophe on the horizon and boldly made his move. And it wasn't a morale-challenged newsroom he fled, but a hurricane swirling just off the industry's coast.

The *News–Post* war proceeded that summer—without Gittrich—in typically tabloid fashion. Obama won the Democratic Party's nomination for president; Clinton, "kicking and screaming," as the *Post* put it, ended her doomed run. A man dubbed "The French Spider-Man" climbed the *New York Times'* new fifty-two-story midtown tower. Then a guy from Brooklyn repeated the feat just seven hours later.* Christie Brinkley and Alex Rodriguez both had public divorces play out over the same two weeks. "D-ROD. WIFE DIVORCING ALEX—BLAMES MADONNA." "V FOR VENGEANCE . . . SLAM-DUNK VICTORY FOR CHRISTIE." Door-knocks in the Hamptons. Door-knocks in Miami. Door-knocks in Paris. *News* and *Post* runners waged war on two continents.

Then some real news broke—the kind they'll teach about one day in history class. On September 7, the U.S. government assumed control of Fannie Mae and Freddie Mac. Seven days later, Bank of America purchased Merrill Lynch. A day later, Lehman Brothers filed for bankruptcy. "WALL ST. CRISIS" . . . "MOVE YOUR A$$! DEMS DAWDLE ON BAILOUT AS FEAR HITS STOX" . . . "FRAUD ST." *News* and *Post* runners staked out Goldman Sachs. They prowled the World Financial Center for quotes. They waylaid suddenly ex–Lehman Brothers employees as they carried "boxes filled with personal possessions and painful memories"† from the midtown bank. Outside AIG, worried workers issued anonymously rendered throwaway quotes in the form of gallows humor. Hungry runners, assembled at the front door like vultures near a dying buffalo, feasted on the pain.

Then, on October 8, the New York Federal Reserve bailed out AIG, again. Four days later, Wells Fargo acquired Wachovia. By December 11, the U.S. government declared the American economy in recession. It was a train wreck in slow motion. And the consequences for journalists would prove durable and reach far beyond our 401(k)s.

---

* The morning Alain Robert climbed the *New York Times* building, Sal dispatched me to the scene with orders to collect quotes and color, and, as he put it, "make sure no one does it again." I thought he was crazy—an impression only emphasized as the day marched wearily on. Another climb? Impossible! Then, at 3:30-ish, I began my campaign for an early departure; a half-hour later I achieved my desired result. Even Sal could no longer refute the obvious—the stakeout was a futility. I was in the Lincoln Tunnel when I first heard it on 1010 WINS—a second man, Renaldo Clarke, had commenced his own ascent, completed at 6:38 P.M. "THE NEW YORK CLIMBS," both the *News* and the *Post* proclaimed on their next-day woods.

† *News* rewrite man Corky Siemaszko.

Over the course of 2008, daily newspapers shed an eye-popping 5,900 full-time newsroom positions,[1] or 11.3 percent. The next year, they bled another 11.1.[2] These staffing losses, predictably, coincided with financial ones. In 2008, total newspaper ad revenue plunged nearly 17 percent, before free-falling another 27 percent in 2009.[3] Still, the *News* and the *Post* gave no ground. That December, we staked out Bernie Madoff's midtown apartment nearly 'round the clock after news emerged that the money man had bamboozled clients of billions—including $2 billion from Fifth Avenue Synagogue members, alone. On the 15th, shooters Joe Marino for the *News* and Marcus Santos for the *Post* were outside Madoff's swanky East 64th Street pad along with me and a *Post* runner. Marcus got the shot, the first of the fraudster since the scandal broke. Whether by skill or fortunate positioning, he obtained it while Joe had not, after a vehicle carrying Madoff came roaring out of a private drive. But while Marcus made the image, he did not possess knowledge of Marino's failure because Joe astutely concealed this fact from him for the remainder of the day. This presented Marcus—or rather his editors—with a dilemma, because the *Post* very badly wanted to market his shot as an exclusive. But was it? It would look very silly to trumpet the photo as such only to have the *News* wood portray much the same image the following day. So Marcus resorted to skullduggery. He called me that night, after we had departed the scene, and asked if Joe had made Madoff. He did not tell me his true reason for asking, but only said, quite uncomfortably, that he wanted to know because, if Joe had not made the shot, he wished to instruct him on how to properly photograph a subject in a moving vehicle. "It's a very difficult thing," Marcus said quite earnestly. "If he doesn't know how to do it, he really should." I told him that I did not know if Joe had made the shot or whether he wanted to be so instructed, but that he should call him and find out. And although Marcus is an aficionado of skydiving and assuredly courageous—not to mention a decent person—I do not know if he mustered the incredible *cojones* necessary to phone Marino with this absurd inquiry.

It should also be noted here that Marcus Santos has been accused generally—and for quite some time—of killing Paul Newman, or at least having played a role in the actor's death. It was around this time of Madoff's scandal that Newman was dying of cancer and Marcus was staked outside his Manhattan building in order to get a shot. Marcus waited and, upon seeing Newman, requested permission to photograph him, informing him that he, too, had been stricken with cancer and had survived. (This was true.) This last part about the cancer did not have the intended effect upon

Newman, who promptly told Marcus, *"Fuck you!* Go fuck yourself." After that, Marcus felt quite justified in snapping Newman in a very no-holds-barred way. The photo would prove to be the final one taken of Newman alive, at least according to Marcus, who does not enjoy having it pointed out that Newman likely became so disgusted with the world after this unfortunate interaction that he finally decided enough was enough.

At first—and to *News* and *Post* runners—it felt as if little had changed. We ran like crazy on Plaxico Burress's gun fiasco—the one that robbed the New York Giants of a shot at a Super Bowl repeat. We laid siege to the Trump International Hotel amid reports that Tiger Woods had holed up, there, amid his sex crisis. But then the situation did change. First, *News* editors cut overtime, or began to monitor it—and even occasionally question the slips after you turned them in. *I'm not saying you didn't work the hours. I'm just asking you . . . can you give me a break here?* Then came the edict that runners could no longer work seven days per week as a matter of course, then the notice that they could no longer work more than their given five unless circumstances demanded it. Then came a reduction in the number of freelance runners; and, finally, an air—initially imperceptible but palpably felt over time—that we weren't quite willing to go to the same lengths to beat the *Post* as we once had. And, of course, there were the numbers.

Over the two years from September 30, 2008, to September 30, 2010, the *Daily News* shed 19.0 percent of its daily print circulation, or about 120,000 copies.[4,5] And the *Post* logged an even steeper drop of 19.8 percent, or almost 124,000 copies. This trend would only continue. From September 30, 2010, to September 30, 2012, the *Daily News* ceded another 128,415 copies, the *Post* 156,766.[6] Fast-forward to September 2016, and the *News'* weekday print circulation had tumbled to a mere 207,680 and the *Post's* to 230,634.[7] As one *News* editor bemoaned, "Why do we even bother? By the time the bodegas return the unsold copies, there might be 100 people who bought the paper!"

Predictably, all those sloughed customers prompted buyouts and layoffs. On October 14, 2011, Stu Marques was canned.[8] A month earlier, Michael Daly followed Gittrich to the digital arena—and *Newsweek Daily Beast*.[9] On November 4, the *News* pink-slipped fifteen-plus staffers, including Kappy and Roca.[10] In March 2013, Oswald negotiated a "quiet exit."[11] Two months later, the *News* axed twenty more.[12] That same month the *Post* announced a 10 percent staff reduction.[13]

I got fired during the November 2011 layoffs. But I had long since begged off the street. I had grown cynical and disillusioned—fed up with the traffic, the stakeouts, the door-knocks. Especially the door-knocks.

I didn't want to ask one more grieving mother what it was like to have just lost their child. I grew almost constitutionally unable to ask, suddenly hypersensitive to the glare of a mourning widow, to the awkward stares from funeral-goers as they spied me stealing jotted notes from a eulogy amid the pews. I was the Wall Street trader who suddenly saw his loss in terms of a needed roof. And it felt raw—and Joel Cairo must have sensed my rawness, because at some point he grew fond of taunting me with the observation: "Jaccarino's lost his edge!" He was right, of course. I had.

When I was a child, my parents would take me into New York City from our home in New Jersey for plays, and ball games, sometimes just to stroll around. I used to look up, during those trips, at the orange-lit tenement windows and wonder what extraordinary lives these people must live, here in the big city. It became a mystery I obsessively wanted to solve. Well, now I had. Now, I knew what dwelled behind those windows, those doors—the good *and* the bad—and I didn't want to see any more. I'd gotten to write for the only paper for which I'd ever had a mind to write. And in accomplishing my goal, I'd ceded an essential part of the romance and mystery that had motivated me to fulfill the ambition in the first place.

After the street, I spent a sleepy, coddled eighteen months in the Bronx bureau followed by a capstone six months on the *News'* vaunted rewrite desk. It wasn't running. Not even close. At my farewell party—or, really, the group one arranged for all of us who'd been laid off in that round—Marino grinned me out the door. We said the sort of things people say to each other in such a spot, but then he concluded with something humorous. "Go home, Rambo," he said. "The war's over. Go home." It worked on so many levels.

I am now a casual and distant spectator of the *News–Post* conflict. I follow it as one does a local sports team, or the comings-and-going of an ex, which is to say I gather updates when paths cross with old friends and colleagues and I read about the latest misfortune to befall both papers on social media.

In July 2014, the *News* sacked seventeen more staffers, including shooters Andrew Theodorakis and David Handschuh, a twenty-seven-year veteran who'd shattered his right leg and been buried alive while covering 9/11.[14] Then on September 16, 2015, the *News* "disemboweled" what was left with a layoff the *Times* described as coming with "the swiftness of a Soviet-era purge."[15] Dozens of reporters fired. Cheap, Internet-first talent replaced grizzled, scoop-savvy vets; the newcomers didn't so much report stories as rewrite those first published elsewhere. As one "veteran" told the *Times*, "When I first got to the *News*, it was all about reporting and writing, but now it's about self-promotion. I can't remember the last time someone on the staff sent a note saying, 'Hey, good piece.' What they say now is, 'Hey, we broke the March record for page views!'"

Along these lines, many felt the *News* had ceded something more than simply staff—but something ineffable and important. This was, after all, the *Daily News*, the paper that once proclaimed itself in radio ads "the most New York you can get." It still gives me goosebumps to recall hearing them on WFAN as a child, because they were true. "That's Mike Lupica. He writes for *us*! The *Daily News*. The most New York you can get." Somehow, the paper and the city shared a soul, or a part of one. But, by this point, the *News* was emphasizing the digital product over its print ancestor. And the website was certainly not the *Daily News* any longtime reader would recognize. It was, after a rebranding, *Daily News America*. And how appropriate because the site showed little allegiance to New York City. Its web-first staffers hunted "rewrites" out of Des Moines with the same zeal runners once had gets in Dyker Heights. It was like when Springsteen moved to L.A. Only Bruce found his way home. The *Daily News* never did.

By 2015, the *News* was said to be losing $29.1 million a year and the *Post* anywhere from $25 million to $110 million, depending on the source. That February, Mort Zuckerman conducted a shameful public auction of the *News* that ended without a single bid. (Cablevision chief James Dolan had contemplated offering a buck but never got around to it.) By that point in February 2015, the once-ferocious *News–Post* war was so diminished that ex–*News* columnist Lloyd Grove quoted one "battle-scarred veteran" as describing it as "two bald guys fighting over a comb." It's "become a pitiable spectacle," Grove wrote.

That September, the *Times* published a piece headlined "THE DAILY NEWS LAYOFFS AND DIGITAL SHIFT MAY SIGNAL THE TABLOID ERA'S END." In it, Michael Daly was quoted as saying, "The *Daily News* has always been a New York paper for New York people. It's been part of the city's life in a way no other paper has been—or at least it was [until] now." Added *Times*man Alan Feuer:

> At the very least the job cuts meant that the recent attrition at newspapers across the country had finally arrived in force in the nation's media capital. But it also suggested something deeper—about the city and the industry. Mortimer B. Zuckerman, the owner of the *News*, known for its crusades against municipal misconduct, was dismissing ace reporters while bolstering his global online platform.

William D. Holiber, the chief executive, had also created a satellite operation, in New Jersey, with a mission in part to aggregate content from across the web and repackage it for the *News'* own site. While both men promised that the *Daily News* would not give up its city-centric mandate, the shift toward a digital edition, which would read the same in Brooklyn and Bahrain, was the end of something. The *News*, after all, is the ultimate local paper, and the real-life model for Clark Kent's *Daily Planet*. If focusing on the Internet was not the end of the tabloid itself, then perhaps it was the end of the city's tabloid era.

But if the *News'* shift to a nationally focused digital platform was one way to diagnose its sickness, staffers, both current *and* ex, had a more intimate touchstone to draw upon in reaching the same conclusion. In 2014, sources told the website Capital New York that the *News* and *Post* had actually considered merging! One scenario had News Corp. purchasing the *News* and another the *Post*, employing the *News'* printing presses in Jersey City.[16] For those of us who had run—and fought—the war, it was unthinkable.

In 2017, Tronc, the newly rebranded Tribune Publishing Co.,[*] indeed, bought the *News* for $1, plus the assumption of $30 million in pension liabilities.[17] *New York Times* reporters Sydney Ember and Andrew Ross Sorkin wrote the following in their September 4,, 2017, account: "The *News* once boasted A-list columnists including Liz Smith, Jimmy Breslin and Pete Hamill, but it has been worn down by a grinding tabloid war with the Rupert Murdoch–controlled *New York Post*. And like the rest of the newspaper industry, the *News* has been battered and bruised by the internet age, when the equivalent of pithy headlines—a staple of the *News*—come a mile a minute on Twitter."[18]

In July 2018, Tronc fired another forty-five journalists from the *News*, half of its remaining editorial staff. The entire photo department was eliminated, Todd Maisel and Anthony DelMundo included. New York's "Picture Newspaper" now had no staff photographers. Most of its sports desk was scrapped as well. "Everyone was crying," one newsroom survivor told Digiday.com. "It feels like the paper died."

Today, few runners remain on the street—and the *News–Post* competition is muted, if present at all. Both papers might field one, perhaps two, runners per shift, instead of the armies that had once battled during the

---

[*] The company has since returned to its historical name, Tribune Publishing.

war. As one shooter told me, "No one runs. And when we do, there's no urgency. Nobody cares. If you get the shot, great. If you don't, that's fine, too."

At this writing, one runner, though, is still running as hard as ever, sneaking into buildings, pleading for "good words" for the dead, racing to scenes, getting the get. Kerry Burke is still out there, undefeated and undiminished, fighting the good fight even though more often than not, no one from the *Post* is any longer running against him.

A BRIEF GLOSSARY OF TABLOID TERMS OF ART
NOT OTHERWISE DEFINED IN THE TEXT

B-roll (n) Supplemental video in a television news report used to buttress the main shot. For instance, video of cops loitering at a crime scene, doing little or nothing, or squad cars idling with their party lights flashing, would constitute B-roll. Likewise, a TV news report concerning the exhibition of a new Leonardo at, say, the Metropolitan Museum of Art might include B-roll of art enthusiasts milling about the museum's famous Great Hall.

bulk (or junk) circulation (n) Circulation that is not paid for but usually given away as a promotion—sometimes in order to inflate the circulation figures used to sell advertising.

color (n) Details peripheral to those considered indispensable to a well-reported story. For instance, whether a victim is shot at 1:14 A.M. at 23rd Street and Sixth Avenue on September 15 could be deemed essential to any serviceable account. But those details concerning the victim's mode of dress, whether the resulting pool of blood was diffuse or concentrated, and whether the murder elicited shocked howls or eerie silence from bystanders could appropriately be classified as color.

desk (n) Shorthand for city desk, sports desk, photo desk, or whichever may be the controlling authority of a runner or shooter in the field, as in, "I gotta call my desk," or "My desk says to give the stakeout another hour." Notably, the term served as the basis for a joke recounted during season 5 of "The Wire," in which a fictional newspaper editor tells the story of a reporter forced to repeatedly ask a mayor follow-up questions by order of "his desk" until, finally, the fed-up politician put his ear to his own desk, a piece of furniture, and said, "My desk tells your desk to go fuck itself."

effort (v)   Tabloid term of art utilized to describe one's pursuit of a story, interview, relevant phone number, photograph, or any component part of a newspaper story. A runner might therefore tell his editor, "I'm efforting witnesses at the scene" or "I'm outside Rikers efforting a jailhouse interview" or even "I'm staked out at the victim's house efforting a studio photograph."

kicker (n)   The final line of a newspaper story, and ideally one that is appropriately dramatic, humorous, or revealing so as to conclude the preceding account. It follows that a kicker quote is a quote that serves as a story's final line.

lede (n)   The first paragraph of a news story.

point-and-shoot (n)   A small, nonprofessional camera that can be easily hidden in one's pocket.

popped (v)   Jargon for photographing a subject—and especially one whose cooperation has not been obtained. A tabloid shooter might therefore say, "I popped the perp coming out of the precinct."

made (v)   Conveys much the same meaning as "popped," as in "I made the widow at the funeral home."

money quote (n)   Typically a reporter's best quote, obtained by either phone or in the field, and that usually, although not definitively, occupied the third paragraph of a news story, according to conventional tabloid style.

sit-down (n)   A face-to-face interview usually, although not necessarily, conducted while sitting down.

skybox chip (n)   The small box along the top of a newspaper's front page wherein a secondary story's headline—and perhaps a photo—is represented above those concerning the main, featured story.

stand up (v)   To corroborate a previously published account, or a detail contained therein. For instance, if the *Post* published a story reporting that the means by which a victim was brutally murdered involved a hacksaw, then the *Daily News* might seek to *stand up* that aspect of the *Post*'s story by obtaining such information from the police, witnesses, or others so that it could then publish the same detail in its own pages without the indignity of referencing its rival.

wood (v)   The act of putting a particular story on a tabloid's front page, as in "The *News* wooded yesterday with Miss New Jersey." By the same token, a story deemed "woodable" was sufficiently dramatic and newsworthy that it could reasonably occupy the front page.

words (n)   Runner's slang for a quote, as in "The widow gave me good words for the dead."

NOTES

Prologue: "Shell Shock for News Nuts"

1. Dan Mangan, "Shell Shock for News Nuts." *New York Post*. March 24, 2005. Accessed January 13, 2018. https://nypost.com/2005/03/24/shell-shock-for-news-nuts/.

1. "Serb Thug to New York . . . Kiss My Ash"

1. Paul Hiebert, "A Q&A with a '*Daily News*' Crime Reporter." *The Awl*. January 20, 2012. Accessed January 13, 2018. https://www.theawl.com/2012/01/a-qa-with-a-daily-news-crime -reporter/.

2. Ibid.

3. Corey Kilgannon, "Beer by the Barrel, Stories by the Scoop." *New York Times*. December 29, 2005. Accessed January 13, 2018. http://www.nytimes.com/2005/12/29/nyregion/beer-by -the-barrel-stories-by-the-scoop.html.

4. Hiebert, "Q&A."

2. "All Play, No Pay for Page Fix"

1. Choire Sicha, "A Look Back: Ten Years of Branding Mort Zuckerman as a Boring Monster." *The Awl*. February 15, 2010. Accessed January 13, 2018. https://www.theawl.com /2010/02/a-look-back-ten-years-of-branding-mort-zuckerman-as-a-boring-monster/.

2. Lars-Erik Nelson, "Murdoch's Not Paying Any Taxes on Pols He Buys." New York *Daily News*. October 21, 1996. Accessed January 13, 2018. http://www.nydailynews.com/archives /opinions/murdoch-not-paying-taxes-pols-buys-article-1.736649.

3. Ken Auletta, "The Fixer." *The New Yorker*. February 12, 2007. Accessed February 4, 2018. https://www.newyorker.com/magazine/2007/02/12/the-fixer.

4. John Roca.

5. Ben McGrath, "Tab War." *The New Yorker*. April 11, 2005. Accessed February 4, 2018. https://www.newyorker.com/magazine/2005/04/11/tab-war.

6. "Top 50 Newspapers by Circulation." May 10, 2006. Retrieved January 16, 2018. http://adage.com/datacenter/datapopup.php?article_id=109126.

7. Company-Histories.com. (n.d.). Retrieved January 16, 2018. http://www.company-histories.com/New-York-Daily-News-Company-History.html.

8. Deirdre Carmody, "Seeking to Build Circulation." *New York Times*. December 26, 1976. Accessed January 17, 2018. http://www.nytimes.com/1976/12/26/archives/seeking-to-build-circulation.html.

9. David Gelman, Betsy Carter, Ann Ray Martin, Nancy Stadtman, Tony Clifton, Nicholas Proffitt, and Ronald Kaye, "Press Lord Captures Gotham." *Newsweek*. January 17, 1977, 48.

10. Jonathan Friendly, "*Daily News* Says It Will End Its Tonight Edition on Aug. 28." *New York Times*. August 14, 1981. Accessed January 17, 2018. http://www.nytimes.com/1981/08/15/nyregion/daily-news-says-it-will-end-its-tonight-edition-on-aug-28.html.

11. Deirdre Carmody, "Dorothy Schiff Agrees to Sell *Post* to Murdoch, Australian Publisher." *New York Times*. November 20, 1976. Accessed January 21, 2018. http://query.nytimes.com/mem/archive/pdf?res=9801E4D71F38E73ABC4851DFB767838D669EDE.

12. John Cassidy, "The Hell-raiser." *The New Yorker*. September 11, 2000. Accessed January 21, 2018. https://www.newyorker.com/magazine/2000/09/11/the-hell-raiser.

13. Steve Cuozzo, "How Page Six revitalized the celebrity gossip column." *New York Post*. December 4, 2017. Accessed January 21, 2018. https://nypost.com/2017/12/04/how-page-six-revived-the-celebrity-gossip-column/.

14. Jeffrey R. Toobin, "The Day the *News* Died." *The Harvard Crimson* (Cambridge). January 8, 1982. Accessed January 21, 2018. http://www.thecrimson.com/article/1982/1/8/the-day-the-news-died-pbtbhe/.

15. "New York press; Rupert the ruthless." *The Economist*. October 7, 1978, 52.

16. "Murdoch Believed to Back New York Strike Paper." *Washington Post*. August 20, 1978, Final ed., first sec.

17. "3 New Papers Start Up in News-Starved New York." *Washington Post*. August 22, 1978, Final ed., first sec.

18. Lee Lescaze, "N.Y. Strike Paper Runs into Its Own Labor Difficulties." *Washington Post*. September 7, 1978, Final ed., first sec.

19. Lee Lescaze, "*N.Y. Post* Is Back; to Publish Earlier and on Sundays." *Washington Post*. October 6, 1978, Final ed., first sec.

20. Helen Dewar, "Murdoch Set to Launch 10-Cent Morning Tabloid." *Washington Post*. October 20, 1978, Final ed., first sec.

21. Lee Lescaze, "N.Y. *Daily News* Studies Starting a P.M. Edition." *Washington Post*. June 6, 1980, Final ed., Business & Finance sec.

22. Jerry Schwartz, "New Yorkers Are Confronted with a Newspaper War." Associated Press. June 20, 1980, AM Cycle ed., Domestic News sec.

23. John F. Berry, "Wingo! Zingo! The Games Papers Play." *Washington Post*. September 19, 1981. Accessed January 28, 2018. https://www.washingtonpost.com/archive/business/1981/09/19/wingo-zingo-the-games-papers-play/eba3ae04-8bfc-45ab-9708-b03144a1ec60/?utm_term=.5df1f9fd02b2.

24. Lee Lescaze, "N.Y. *Daily News* Studies Starting a P.M. Edition."

25. Ibid.

26. Lee Lescaze, "New York Newspapers in a New Survival Contest." *Washington Post*. May 11, 1980, Final ed., first sec.

27. "*Daily News* Asks Union Support for Afternoon Edition." Associated Press. June 20, 1980, BC Cycle ed., Domestic News sec.

28. "Murdoch Details Plan for Move by the *Post* into the Morning Field." *New York Times*. June 27, 1980, Late City Final ed., sec. B.

29. Schwartz, "New Yorkers Are Confronted with a Newspaper War."

30. James L. Rowe Jr. and John Kennedy, "Drivers' Strike Halts *N.Y. Post* Morning Edition." *Washington Post*. July 22, 1980. Accessed January 17, 2018. https://www.washingtonpost.com /archive/politics/1980/07/22/drivers-strike-halts-ny-post-morning-edition/e3e9dce0-1ed5-42d7 -9d38-6769308db217/?utm_term=.2b736f86f798.

31. "Daily News Publishes Last Tonight Edition." *New York Times*. August 28, 1981. Accessed January 17, 2018. http://www.nytimes.com/1981/08/29/nyregion/daily-news-publishes -last-tonight-edition.html.

32. Ibid.

33. "Three Big Manhattan Dailies Show Circulation Gains." The Associated Press. November 16, 1982, AM Cycle ed., Domestic News sec.

34. Friendly, "*Daily News* Says It Will End Its Tonight Edition on Aug. 28."

35. Alex S. Jones, "Murdoch's *Post*: Futile Battle or Missed Opportunity?" *New York Times*. March 7, 1988, Late City Final ed., sec. B.

36. Alex S. Jones, "Optimism at New York's Tabloids." *New York Times*. May 5, 1988, Late City Final ed., sec. D.

37. Felicity Barringer and Jayson Blair, "*Daily News* Opens a New Front in the Tabloid War; Free Paper Raises Stakes in Battle with *Post*." *New York Times*. September 11, 2000, Late–Final ed., Business sec.

38. Ibid.

39. Jayson Blair, "The *Post* to Halve Its Newsstand Price." *New York Times*. September 1, 2000, Late–Final ed., sec. B.

40. Ibid.

41. Lloyd Grove, "Rupe's Attack Dog Gets September 10, 2007. *New York*. Accessed January 24, 2018. http://nymag.com/nymag/features/37257/.

42. Keith J. Kelly, "*News* Reels—Snooze's Circulation Hits an All-time Low." *New York Post*. November 8, 2005. Accessed January 28, 2018. https://nypost.com/2005/11/08/news-reels -snoozes-circulation-hits-an-all-time-low/.

43. Jesse Oxfeld, "Because Where Other Cities Are Losing Their Papers, New York Still Has a Tabloid War." *New York*. October 24, 2007. Accessed February 4, 2018. http://nymag.com /news/articles/reasonstoloveny/2006/25617/.

44. Grove.

45. "The *New York Post*: Profitless Paper in Relentless Pursuit." *Bloomberg Businessweek*. February 21, 2005. Accessed January 28, 2018. https://www.bloomberg.com/news/articles/2005 -02-20/the-new-york-post-profitless-paper-in-relentless-pursuit.

46. Ibid., 126; originally: Newspaper Association of America, "NAA Releases ABC FAS-FAX Analysis." November 7, 2005.

47. *State of the News Media 2007*. Report. March 19, 2007. Accessed January 14, 2018. http://assets.pewresearch.org/wp-content/uploads/sites/13/2017/05/24141602/State-of-the -News-Media-Report-2007-FINAL.pdf. pg. 119.

48. Katharine Q. Seelye, "Newspaper Circulation Falls Sharply." *New York Times*, October 31, 2006, Final ed., sec. C. February 20, 2018. http://www.nytimes.com/2006/10/31/business/newspaper-circulation-falls-sharply.html.

49. *State of the News Media 2008*. Report. March 19, 2008. Accessed January 15, 2018. http://assets.pewresearch.org/wp-content/uploads/sites/13/2017/05/24141607/State-of-the-News-Media-Report-2008-FINAL.pdf. pg. 14.

50. Maria Aspan, "2 Free New York Newspapers Are Doing Battle on Web Sites as Well as in Subways." *New York Times*, March 21, 2007, Late–Final ed., sec. C. http://www.nytimes.com/2007/05/21/business/media/21metro.html.

51. Seelye, "Newspaper Circulation Falls Sharply."

52. Ibid.

53. *State of the News Media 2006*. Page 637.

54. Barringer and Blair.

3. "Ford to City: Drop Dead"

1. Paul Hiebert, "A Q&A with a '*Daily News*' Crime Reporter." *The Awl*. January 20, 2012. Accessed January 13, 2018. https://www.theawl.com/2012/01/a-qa-with-a-daily-news-crime-reporter/.

2. Howard Kurtz, "Bravo Dishes the Dirt on the *Daily News*." *Washington Post*. July 17, 2006.

3. "Follow that Reporter." WNYC. July 21, 2006. Accessed February 2, 2018. https://www.wnyc.org/story/128661-follow-that-reporter?tab=transcript.

4. Oxfeld.

5. Erica Fahr Campbell, "The First Photograph of an Execution by Electric Chair." *Time*. April 10, 2014. Accessed February 2, 2018. http://time.com/3808808/first-photo-electric-chair-execution/.

4. "Cops Shoot Groom Dead"

1. Georgett Roberts, "Groom Dies in NYPD Barrage; * 50 Shots Fired at Qns. Partiers * Kin Demand Answers from Cops." *New York Post*. November 26, 2006. Accessed February 5, 2018. https://nypost.com/2006/11/26/groom-dies-in-nypd-barrage-50-shots-fired-at-qns-partiers-kin-demand-answers-from-cops/.

5. "N.J. Miss in a Fix Over Her Pics!"

1. Cynthia R. Fagan, "*Post* Beats *News* Again." *New York Post*, April 30, 2007. Accessed February 5, 2018. https://nypost.com/2007/04/30/post-beats-news-again/.

2. Lloyd Grove, "Rupe's Attack Dog Gets September 10, 2007. *New York*. Accessed January 24, 2018. http://nymag.com/nymag/features/37257/.

3. Matthew Flamm, "*NY Post* a Paper Tiger after Pricing Misstep." *Crain's New York Business*. May 20, 2007. Accessed January 24, 2018. http://www.crainsnewyork.com/article/20070520/FREE/70520023/ny-post-a-paper-tiger-after-pricing-misstep.

4. Ibid.

5. Grove.

6. Jo Piazza, "Queen is Way out of Line." New York *Daily News*. December 16, 2006.

6. "2 Cops Shot During Traffic Stop"

1. Paul Hiebert, "A Q&A with a '*Daily News*' Crime Reporter." *The Awl*. January 20, 2012. Accessed January 13, 2018. https://www.theawl.com/2012/01/a-qa-with-a-daily-news-crime-reporter/.

2. Ibid.

7. "Tracked Down and Busted in Pa. Woods"

1. Colin Moynihan, "Once Behind Bars, Now Behind the Lens, with His Freedom at Risk." *New York Times*. October 9, 2007, New York ed. Accessed February 5, 2018. http://www.nytimes.com/2007/10/09/nyregion/09photog.html.

11. "Preppie Killer Robert Chambers Acts Like a 'Dumb' Doper"

1. Matthew Flamm, "*Daily News* circulation beats *NY Post*." Crainsnewyork.com. November 5, 2007. Accessed February 6, 2018. http://www.crainsnewyork.com/article/20071105/FREE/71105012/daily-news-circulation-beats-ny-post.

2. Ibid.

3. Louis Hau, "Newspaper Circulation Falls Again." *Forbes*. November 5, 2007. Accessed February 6, 2018. https://www.forbes.com/2007/11/05/newspapers-circulation-tribune-biz-cx_lh_1105circulation.html#711d29b11f9f.

4. *State of the News Media Report 2008*. March 19, 2008. Accessed February 6, 2018. http://assets.pewresearch.org/wp-content/uploads/sites/13/2017/05/24141607/State-of-the-News-Media-Report-2008-FINAL.pdf. pg. 131

5. Ibid., 1.

14. "Ma Goes to Bat for Derek Jeter"

1. Tim Arango, "The *Daily News* and the *Post* Talk Business." Nytimes.com. July 16, 2008. Accessed February 8, 2018. www.nytimes.com/2008/07/16/business/media/16paper.html.

16. "Temple of Doom . . . Madoff Fleeced Fifth Avenue Synagogue"

1. "2009 census." ASNE 2009 Census. April 16, 2009. Accessed February 14, 2018. http://asne.org/diversity-survey-2009.

2. "2010 census." ASNE 2010 Census. April 11, 2010. Accessed February 14, 2018. http://asne.org/diversity-survey-2010.

3. "Newspaper Industry Estimated Advertising and Circulation Revenue." Journalism.org, Pew Research Center. June 1, 2017. www.journalism.org/chart/newspaper-industry-estimated-advertising-and-circulation-revenue/. Original data comes from the Newspaper Association of America, now News Media Alliance.

4. Jane Kim, "Table for Two?" *Columbia Journalism Review*. March 8, 2009. Accessed February 12, 2018. http://archives.cjr.org/behind_the_news/table_for_two.php.

5. Matthew Flamm, "NY Daily Newspapers Show Circulation Declines." *Crain's New York Business*. October 25, 2010. Accessed February 12, 2018. http://www.crainsnewyork.com/article/20101025/free/101029921/ny-daily-newspapers-show-circulation-declines.

6. "Circulation Numbers for the 25 Largest Newspapers." Associated Press, October 30, 2012.

7. Keith Kelly, "*News* Bleeds as *Post* Prospers." *New York Post*. November 17, 2016, p. 34.

8. Kat Stoeffel, "Managing Editor Stuart Marques Out at *Daily News*." *Observer*. October 17, 2011. Accessed February 14, 2018. http://observer.com/2011/10/managing-editor -stuart-marques-out-at-daily-news/.

9. Keith J. Kelly, "It's Foodie Ferment as Last Can't at 'Everyday.'" *New York Post*. October 19, 2011. October 19, 2011. Accessed February 14, 2018. https://nypost.com/2011/10/19/its -foodie-ferment-as-last-cant-at-everyday/.

10. Foster Kamer, "*NY Daily News* Layoffs Massacre Continues: Two More Shown the Door, Bringing Total Count to 16." *Observer*. November 8, 2011. Accessed February 14, 2018. http:// observer.com/2011/11/ny-daily-news-layoffs-massacre-continues-two-more-shown-the-door -bringing-total-count-to-16/.

11. Joe Pompeo, "Another Top Editor Is Out at the '*Daily News*': Features Chief John Oswald." POLITICO Media. March 19, 2013. Accessed February 14, 2018. https://www.politico .com/media/story/2013/03/another-top-editor-is-out-at-the-daily-news-features-chief-john -oswald-001015.

12. Joe Pompeo, "'*Daily News*' Chief Colin Myler Tells Staff Layoffs Were 'Inevitable,' Announces New Digital Initiative in Boroughs." POLITICO Media. May 9, 2013. Accessed February 14, 2018. https://www.politico.com/media/story/2013/05/daily-news-chief-colin-myler -tells-staff-layoffs-were-inevitable-announces-new-digital-initiative-in-boroughs-001085.

13. Joe Pompeo, "'*New York Post*' Offers Buyouts; Seeks 10-Percent Staff Reduction in Attempt to Avoid Layoffs." POLITICO Media. May 9, 2013. Accessed February 14, 2018. https://www.politico.com/media/story/2013/05/new-york-post-offers-buyouts-seeks-10-percent -staff-reduction-in-attempt-to-avoid-layoffs-001082.

14. Joe Pompeo, "Tears at the *Daily News* as Veterans Get Pink Slips." POLITICO Media. July 21, 2014. Accessed February 14, 2018. https://www.politico.com/media/story/2014/07/tears -at-the-daily-news-as-veterans-get-pink-slips-002552.

15. Alan Feuer, "The *Daily News* Layoffs and Digital Shift May Signal the Tabloid Era's End." *New York Times*. September 28, 2015, New York ed., Region sec. September 27, 2015. Accessed February 14, 2018.

16. Joe Pompeo, "A New York Tabloid Detente That Wasn't." POLITICO Media. October 23, 2014. Accessed February 14, 2018. https://www.politico.com/media/story/2014/10/a-new -york-tabloid-detente-that-wasnt-003014.

17. Jennifer Saba, "Breakingviews—Mort Zuckerman to Newspaper Industry: Drop Dead." Reuters. September 5, 2017. Accessed February 14, 2018. https://www.reuters.com/article/us -daily-news-m-a-breakingviews/breakingviews-mort-zuckerman-to-newspaper-industry-drop -dead-idUSKCN1BG2O8.

18. Embers and Sorkin.

INDEX

Mike Jaccarino is a New York City–based journalist whose work has appeared in the New York *Daily News*, *FoxNews.com*, *The Press of Atlantic City*, *The Jersey Journal* of Jersey City, N.J., *The Asbury Park Press*, and *The Week* magazine.

Mark Naison and Bob Gumbs, *Before the Fires: An Oral History of African American Life in the Bronx from the 1930s to the 1960s*

Robert Weldon Whalen, *Murder, Inc., and the Moral Life: Gangsters and Gangbusters in La Guardia's New York*

Joanne Witty and Henrik Krogius, *Brooklyn Bridge Park: A Dying Waterfront Transformed*

Sharon Egretta Sutton, *When Ivory Towers Were Black: A Story about Race in America's Cities and Universities*

Pamela Hanlon, *A Wordly Affair: New York, the United Nations, and the Story Behind Their Unlikely Bond*

Britt Haas, *Fighting Authoritarianism: American Youth Activism in the 1930s*

David J. Goodwin, *Left Bank of the Hudson: Jersey City and the Artists of 111 1st Street*. Foreword by DW Gibson

Nandini Bagchee, *Counter Institution: Activist Estates of the Lower East Side*

Carol Lamberg, *Neighborhood Success Stories: Creating and Sustaining Affordable Housing in New York*

Susan Celia Greenfield (ed.), *Sacred Shelter: Thirteen Journeys of Homelessness and Healing*

Elizabeth Macaulay Lewis and Matthew M. McGowan (eds.), *Classical New York: Discovering Greece and Rome in Gotham*

Susan Opotow and Zachary Baron Shemtob (eds.), *New York after 9/11*

Andrew Feffer, *Bad Faith: Teachers, Liberalism, and the Origins of McCarthyism*

Colin Davey with Thomas A. Lesser, *The American Museum of Natural History and How It Got That Way*. Foreword by Kermit Roosevelt III

Wendy Jean Katz, *Humbug! The Politics of Art Criticism in New York City's Penny Press*

Lolita Buckner Inniss, *The Princeton Fugitive Slave: The Trials of James Collins Johnson*

For a complete list, visit www.fordhampress.com/empire-state-editions.